Hollywood Martyr **Joan**
CRAWFORD

Hollywood Martyr **Joan**
CRAWFORD

David Bret

DA CAPO PRESS
A MEMBER OF THE PERSEUS BOOKS GROUP
NEW YORK

Cataloging-in-Publication data for this book is available
from the Library of Congress.

HC: ISBN-13: 978-0-7867-1868-9; ISBN-10: 0-7867-1868-4
PB: ISBN-13: 978-0-306-81624-6; ISBN-10: 0-306-81624-5

First published in the United Kingdom in 2006 by Robson Books
First Carroll & Graf edition 2007
First Da Capo Press paperback edition 2008

Published by Da Capo Press
A Member of the Perseus Books Group
www.dacapopress.com

Da Capo Press books are available at special discounts for bulk purchases
in the U.S. by corporations, institutions, and other organizations. For more
information, please contact the Special Markets Department at the Perseus
Books Group, 2300 Chestnut Street, Suite 200, Philadelphia, PA, 19103,
or call (800) 255-1514, or e-mail special.markets@perseusbooks.com.

10 9 8 7 6 5 4 3 2 1

This book is dedicated to Fritzi (1993–2005) and to Melanie Letts and
to *Les Enfants de Novembre*

N'oublie pas . . .
La vie sans amis c'est comme un jardin sans fleurs

Contents

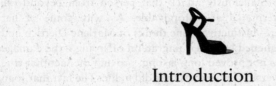

Introduction

She was one of four genuinely great movie actresses of the twentieth century – the others were Garbo, Hepburn and Bette Davis. Like them she was totally uncompromising, on and off the screen. Hers was the classic Hollywood rags-to-riches story: the tramp who became a lady; the girl from the wrong side of the tracks who unashamedly slept her way to the top.

Joan Crawford was not the first to use sex as a stepping stone towards immortality; nor will she be the last. Yet despite being a product of the now-defunct all-powerful studio system, she kept her dignity intact. The fans, and to a certain extent the media, never found out what was happening behind that big red curtain of megastardom. Each time Crawford stepped into the public arena, she looked every inch the legend she became in her own lifetime, and behaved accordingly – something that does not happen today, with the emphasis so often placed on grungy appearances and tabloid-exploited moral turpitude.

Aspects of Joan Crawford's extraordinary, complex psyche were incorporated into many of her films, within which the actress and character became as one, but such was the naivety of America during the Depression, few made the connection. The same may be said for Crawford, gay icon par excellence. Few people realised, at the time these events were unfolding, of her fondness for gay and bisexual men – on account of their fear of being exposed by the media. Three of her husbands slotted into this category, as did many of her lovers, including Clark Gable.

After her death in 1977, Joan Crawford's reputation was sullied in one fell – or foul – swoop with the publication of *Mommie Dearest*, her adopted daughter Christina's frequently scathing account of what it had allegedly been like to be a Hollywood child raised by a megalomaniac. How many, if any, of her mother's reported acts of cruelty are authentic is not known, but with any lack of real evidence they are thought to have been exaggerated. Walking in the shadow of an international monument – proven to be more talented, beautiful and charismatic than oneself will ever be – can never be easy. Being taken in by such a person and offered a lifestyle beyond one's wildest dreams, then to maliciously attack that person from beyond the grave, can only be interpreted as unforgivable. As with some of her contemporaries, however – instinctively one thinks of Marlene Dietrich and Bette Davis, similarly maligned by bitter, ungrateful offspring – the damage inflicted by Christina has not proved long-lasting, proving the fact that true legends survive every adversity, in death as they did in life. The fact that Joan was accused of beating her children with wire coat-hangers even extended her fan base during the early Eighties, with some American gay magazines giving away such items as part of their subscription packages!

It was another renowned 'fag-hag', Tallulah Bankhead, who with the greatest respect awarded Joan Crawford her so-called 'under-the-counter' nickname, 'The Lady With the Fuck-Me Shoes' – owing to the call-girl ankle-straps she wore in her early films. Joan loved the moniker, and more than once found herself 'bleeped' in television and radio interviews for repeating it.

This is her remarkable story.

CHAPTER ONE

Billie Cassin and the Casting Couch

'Bette Davis used to tell everyone that Joan Crawford only got into movies by way of the casting couch – until Joan hit her back with, "Well, my dear, it sure beat the cold, hard floor!"'

Marlene Dietrich

She was born Lucille Fay LeSueur, most likely on 23 March 1904 (though she always maintained it was 1908, when birth certificates became state mandatory, and also the year of arch-rival Bette Davis's birth) in San Antonio, Texas – and not in humble circumstances, as has been often stated. Although her French-Canadian father, Thomas, deserted his family shortly after her birth, her Irish-Scandinavian mother, Anna Bell (Johnson) coped rather well looking after her two children – Daisy, her first-born, had died in infancy and Hal Hayes was born 1902 – until a certain Henry 'Billy' Cassin came along.

Cassin was a jack of all trades. Where there was a dollar to be made he would be there, whether bail-bonding or acting as a disreputable notary public. His chief source of income came from two small theatres in Lawton, Oklahoma: the grandly named Ramsey Opera House, where the ballerina Anna Pavlova and the notorious chanteuse Eva Tanguay had once appeared, and Cassin's Air Drome, an open-air establishment that engaged the more regularly performing (and cheaper) vaudeville acts and put on minstrel shows.

Lucille loathed her first name, and by 1912 was calling herself Billie – the female equivalent of her stepfather's nickname. She was also very much the tomboy, preferring the company of the neighbourhood's roughneck boys to the more genteel girls, always getting into scrapes, and leaning more on Billy Cassin than her feisty, wayward mother – usually because he allowed her to have her own way and, against Anna's wishes, not only turned a blind eye to her truancy but encouraged her to mingle with the rough-and-ready grease-paint crowd. By the age of eight, Billie knew next to nothing about schooling, but she was already a fairly accomplished hoofer – half-ballet, half-tap.

During the summer of 1913, this relatively idyllic world came crashing about Billie's ears when Cassin was accused of misappropriating bail money and forced to flee town, with his family, and seek refuge with the Johnsons, Anna's parents in Phoenix, Arizona. They stayed here but a few weeks before relocating to Kansas City, Missouri, where Cassin claimed he had connections – quite likely this was untrue. While waiting for the money to come through from the sale of the small bungalow he had owned in Lawton, Cassin rented them a single room at the New Midland Hotel, a hostel for down-and-outs in the city's red-light district. When the Lawton property was eventually sold, it brought in less than Cassin had been expecting, and certainly not enough to buy the house Anna had set her heart on. Then he learned that the owners of the New Midland were moving on and, hoping this would provide him with enough revenue to set up another theatrical venture, Cassin took over the lease.

In Kansas City, Billie was enrolled at the Scarritt Elementary School – and, because of her sore lack of education, was forced into a class with children up to three years younger than herself. Needless to say there were problems with Billie here, allegedly to do with bullying and more truancy, and within a few months Cassin moved her to the St Agnes Academy, a reputable Catholic school, though he was the only one in his family of this faith. And to curb the truancy, this time Billie was enrolled as a boarder.

Life at St Agnes was no bed of roses for a girl with an innate rebellious streak. Unlike most of the other pupils, Billie was not on a scholarship, and in common with the other 'charity cases', after class she was made to help with the chores: cleaning the toilets, scrubbing floors, washing dishes. Even so, she welcomed this as an escape from her studies. In the latrines or in the kitchen she was occasionally given the opportunity to practise her steps and daydream of her greatest ambition – to become a professional dancer like Anna Pavlova and star at the New York Winter Garden. Or perhaps, in a rather less glamorous capacity, become a taxi dancer, like one of the good-time girls who sometimes worked with the ragtime musicians in the foyer of the New Midland Hotel.

Yet no sooner had Billie settled in at St Agnes than she learned that her family had been walked out on once more. Henry Cassin, his reputation in tatters and all hope of re-founding his show-business emporium dashed after news of the bail-bonding scandal finally caught up with him, had left without even saying goodbye to his wife. Two weeks later, evicted from the New Midland, Anna and the children moved into a tawdry apartment at the rear of a wash house, where she took poorly paid work as a skivvy.

Billie appears to have been told at this time that Cassin was not her real father. Later she would write in her memoirs (*A Portrait of Joan*), 'I wish he'd taken me with him. My mother was a nagging bitch and my brother was a lazy good-for-nothing. I cried when I found out Daddy Cassin wasn't coming back, and that's when Hal told me Henry wasn't my real father.' Hal's sadistic streak did not end with his taunting Billie about her stepfather. 'He used to lock me in a dark closet,' she would tell reporter Frazier Hunt many years later, in *Photoplay* magazine, February 1934. 'That's why it always frightens me now to be hemmed in – whether by walls or by a crowd.'

In 1918, Billie Cassin made her debut performance in front of an audience, in St Agnes's annual week-long production of *The Maypole Dance*, at the Orpheum Theater. Dressed as a snowdrop, she played the part of January in a tableau entitled *Months of the Year* – quite an achievement, for a month or so previously she had trodden on a broken bottle, severed a tendon in her right foot and was told by doctors that she might end up with a permanent limp. (Ironically, her character January was professed in the playbill to be 'pure as the driven snow'; the would-be thespian was already anything but.) Billie's success in the revue resulted in her being shunned even more than usual by the other girls at St Agnes and she began playing truant again, usually to hang around Budd Park, a suitable distance from the academy, where she hoped she would not be recognised and word of her exploits be reported back to the nuns. One day she happened upon the boys from the Northeast High School football team, engaged in a practice session, and at once decided to make a play for at least one of these oversexed youths, despite her own physical shortcomings. The fact that Billie was plump and ungainly with huge buck teeth, and that it was widely known that she had crabs due to her hatred of bathing, did nothing to deter would-be suitors in search of what appears to have been an easy lay.

The good sisters, in fact, knew exactly what Billie was getting up to, but refrained from expelling her because they considered her mother *such* a bad influence – since Henry Cassin's departure, Anna had shacked up with one man after another, and at times even resorted to prostitution, allegedly to make ends meet – that they thought to send the girl home would send her completely off the rails. By the late summer, however, some indiscretion (thought to be pilfering) led to Billie being summoned to the Mother Superior's office. An altercation ensued. Never backwards at coming forwards, or answering back, Billie settled for the lesser of the two evils: she walked out of St Agnes and moved back in with Anna and her latest 'meal ticket', as Joan Crawford scathingly referred to them – a delivery man named Harry Hough.

Mere days later, Anna LeSueur received word that Billy Cassin had died. She promptly announced to her young daughter that she and Harry

Hough would now be getting married, presumably assuming that in doing so she was assuaging the youngster's grief. In fact, some sources claim that neither Thomas LeSueur nor Henry Cassin had actually been married to Anna, and it seems unlikely now that any ceremony took place – rather, the announcement was probably made so that if Anna moved into Hough's house on upmarket Genessee Street as his *wife*, she might avoid being regarded as the neighbourhood tart.

Whereas Daddy Cassin had genuinely loved Billie and had always treated her with the utmost kindness, Harry Hough appears to have been a creep with a penchant for very young girls – certainly according to Joan Crawford, who several times told reporters that he had tried to seduce or even rape her. She, meanwhile, had become even more of a handful since leaving St Agnes. Anna, now promoted to running the wash house, made her daughter work for her keep, always assigning her the worst jobs, so much so that Billie rebelled, as she had at the academy, seeking solace in the 'friends' she had made during her trips to Budd Park.

Hough was so appalled that any 'daughter' of his could resort to prostitution – though apparently he was not put out by the fact that the woman everyone thought was his wife was still doing the same thing, or that he himself was finding it increasingly more difficult to keep his hands off Billie – that he arranged for her to attend a private school as a student-teacher, an establishment that seems to have leapt straight out of the pages of *Nicholas Nickleby*.

The Rockingham Academy was run by a Mrs Stuttle, a Wackford Squeers-like harridan who made life hell for anyone possessed of the misfortune to cross her threshold. It was in fact more of a correction house than a school – almost all of its alumni were from rich broken homes, with parents who could afford the dubious privilege of seeing their problematic offspring being knocked, literally, back into shape. Billie was enrolled here in March 1919 under the name Lucille LeSueur (having just learned that this and not Cassin was her real surname); at around the same time, her brother Hal augmented the roster at Manual Training High, a technical college where young men learned a trade. If there had been animosity between the siblings before, it now became open warfare. In later years, when Joan Crawford had achieved worldwide fame, and Hal LeSueur virtually nothing, she would still resent the fact that he had not had to suffer the indignities of a reformatory. What she had not known was that seventeen-year-old Hal had been just as unstable and addicted to sex as herself – ethereally handsome, he was to sleep with dozens of women before coming of age, and would later develop a narcissistic complex that would lead to a severe drink problem.

As had happened at St Agnes, Billie was expected to help with the chores after class – but while the nuns had merely caned the girl for her misdemeanours, Mrs Stuttle would apparently drag her by the hair into her study, beat her with a broom handle, then lay into her with the toe of her boot. Billie stuck this out only until hearing that her mother had left Harry Hough and moved back into the wash-house apartment – then she decided, once she had spent a week listening to Anna's incessant carping, that maybe she would be best back at Rockingham. There was, however, to be one condition: unless the horrid Mrs Stuttle kept her fists and feet to herself, *she* would get more than she bargained for, courtesy of one of Billie's Budd Park cronies. Rockingham would remain Billie's home for three more years.

Billie's return to Rockingham coincided with Prohibition, following the 1919 Volstead Act, though the restrictions on Kansas City – the self-professed 'Sin Capital' – were not quite so stringent as in New York. It was a heady, hazardous period that Billie was intent on making the most of. Not that Mrs Stuttle was aware of this. So far as she was led to believe (though maybe she was obliged to turn a blind eye on account of Billie's protector), the young man who pulled up at the front door Saturday evening in his fancy automobile (and never the same man twice) was from a respectable family that might be coerced into handing over a suitable donation towards the establishment's upkeep. One such was Ray Thayer Sterling, a student from Northeast High who, Joan always maintained, was interested only in a platonic relationship; but so far as the others were concerned, more often than not the car was borrowed, and the couple invariably headed for a speakeasy where they drank the night away and danced the Black Bottom – or headed to Budd Park for a little *al fresco* sex.

Billie 'graduated' from the Rockingham Academy in March 1923 – the month she turned eighteen; Mrs Stuttle awarded her a fake certificate. She began working at once, behind the counter in Kline's department store, where she earned $12 a week – not one cent of which was handed over to her mother. Anna had moved into a bigger apartment on Armour Boulevard, in a slightly better part of town, courtesy of the latest man in her life, and Billie felt that Anna would get by without her contributing to the budget – after all, she needed every penny for having fun. 'I worked all day, danced all night,' she later said, 'That's all that I lived for in those days.'

Yet out of the dozens of men Billie got to know at this time, Ray Thayer Sterling – a man she never bedded, though not through lack of trying – is the only one she remembered with fondness in her autobiography, *A Portrait of Joan*:

> After three years at Rockingham . . . I didn't want to go home, but my
> salvation was a swell guy, Ray Sterling. He was my first beau and *I* was in

love, but I wasn't good enough for him. He never said so, and tried very
hard to make a lady out of me. Ray changed my life like Daddy Cassin by
encouraging me . . . I leaned on Ray Sterling. I was never intimate with him.
I wouldn't have gotten to Hollywood if he'd wanted me, but he didn't.

Not one to let the grass grow under her feet, in September Billie used her
phoney diploma to get herself into Stephens College, an all-female establishment in Columbia, Missouri. Again it was as a working student, though this
time the tasks were not so menial and there was no psychotic principal. Billie
was employed in the canteen, and by all accounts was happier there than she
had been in years. This was the age of the flapper – a radical young thing,
much like the turn-of-the-century Parisian demimondaines. Flappers lived
life to the full, insulted their peers, drank spirits and smoked, and used 'in
words' such as 'divine', 'darling' and 'crazy'. Many shocked their parents
and guardians by shedding inhibitions along with their corsets. Like their
early French counterparts they behaved 'atrociously' by accepting costly gifts
from paramours and patrons of both sexes with whom they had usually
spent the night, though few actually turned tricks for hard cash.

Some flappers, such as Billie, 'double-booked' – attending a dance with
one partner, then feigning illness and leaving on the arm of another. She was
a regular at weekend parties and midweek dances at the nearby University of
Missouri, and loved to dance to the Orville Knapp Orchestra, resident at the
College Inn. Off and on she was still being escorted by Ray Thayer Sterling,
the wealthy sap who was still more interested in her sparkling company than
in getting physical with the darling of the Phi Delta Theta fraternity. Why she
opted to drop out, midterm and only days before her first exams, is not
known; she seems to have been a very popular student – though not a
particularly able one, being more interested in collecting dance trophies
(more than twenty in four months!) than in studying. Similarly, one finds it
incomprehensible that she wanted to go running back to the mother she
professed to dislike so much.

Billie was in for a shock when she arrived back in Kansas City. Anna
LeSueur had ousted her latest lover and reconciled with Harry Hough, who
had moved back in with her. Again he made advances on Billie, but she was
having none of it. After a violent quarrel she fled into the night, and ended
up being taken in by two friends, Lucille and Nellie Cook, a sisters act she
had met on the dance circuit in one of the more reputable clubs.

The Cook sisters were decent, well-raised young women who lived with
their mother, a prim, religious woman who chaperoned them everywhere
and obviously had no idea what her house guest was really like. To all three,
Billie Cassin was a nice, hard-working girl (she had found herself a job at

another department store, Emory Bird & Thayers). What they did not know was that she had also renewed contact with her Budd Park cronies, who took turns to escort her almost nightly to clubs and speakeasies. Her speciality was table-top dancing, mainly the Black Bottom and the recently introduced Charleston. According to some contemporary reports, Billie always 'sussed out' the atmosphere and politics of the establishment to see how far she could go – showing as much thigh as she could get away with and, if the rules were really lax, leaving off her panties. Like her contemporary Tallulah Bankhead, whom she would soon meet and who was about to shock London society with *her* antics, she was already developing into something of a magnet for gay men; she believed that they made for better dancing partners, because they were able to let themselves go with a woman without fear of reprimand from jealous wives and girlfriends. Indeed, Billie's favourite 'lavender' beau, Ray Thayer Sterling, was almost certainly gay.

Billie continued picking up trophies for her more legitimate dancing, and on a 'good behaviour' evening at the Ivanhoe Club, with the Cook sisters and their mother, she was spotted by the notorious Chicago-based singer-producer, Katherine Emerine, then working in conjunction with the impresario Nils Granlund in search of chorus girls – and potential bed mates – for the travelling revue she was putting together. In those days it was not unusual for chorus members and bit-parts to be engaged locally for the length of time the company was in town, then dispensed with when the tour moved on. Emerine was one of those agents who travelled ahead of the main company to set up the bills. With her predilection for the casting couch, it was figured that she was also quite possibly Billie's first lesbian fling.

Billie ditched her job with the department store, and as Lucille Cassin made her vaudeville debut in Springfield, Missouri, in February 1924. Her contract appears to have stipulated that she supply her own costumes, and as she was almost always broke, she 'compromised' by stealing the outfits that Mrs Cook had made for her daughters to wear on a forthcoming Temperance Society tour – figuring that if need be, the outfits could be shortened. The engagement, of which nothing is known save that she was billed as one of Emerine's Sixteen Vocal Chorines, was for two weeks.

Exactly how Billie raised the money for a one-way ticket to Chicago depends upon which version of the story one wishes to believe. Years later, she claimed that in order to get away from her mother's lover (Harry Hough) and her hard-drinking, moody brother, she put in all the hours she could at the department store. But according to other, more reliable sources – in particular, gossip-column hacks Louella Parsons and Hedda Hopper, who made it their business to know everything about everyone in Hollywood – she sold herself to the highest bidder.

Jane Ellen Wayne met the star many times, and in her first book, *Crawford's Men*, quotes an Ohio journalist, Robert Slatzer, who claimed to have seen one of Billie's porno-flicks at a stag party. She also reports an incident at a press conference when, aware of this fact, Crawford marched up to him and snarled, 'Keep yer fuckin' mouth shut!' Wayne's book refers to Billie's mysterious benefactor only as 'E S', and describes this period in her life as 'a blur of steamy sex, booze, torrid dancing, drugs and laughter'. 'E S' is almost certainly the man who, in return for her favours, apparently arranged for Billie to pose firstly for 'What the Butler Saw' stills shown in penny-arcade machines, then pornographic films. Another journalist, Helen Laurenson, writing for *Viva* magazine in August 1978, mentions one such flick, *The Plumber*, co-starring Harry Green, a now-forgotten silent comedy actor. Others have quoted such titles as *She Shows Him How*, *Coming Home*, *Velvet Lips* and *The Casting Couch*. The latter certainly existed, as will be seen, and its theme might almost be said to mirror what would soon become Billie's own philosophy for achieving recognition – that of the starlet who is so desperate to break into the movies, she administers a blow-job to the surprised producer before whipping off her clothes and hopping onto the couch in his office. Stills from this film and others, including a turn as a topless Mata Hari and a topless lesbian romp entitled *Bosom Buddies*, appeared in the original edition of Kenneth Anger's unputdownable *Hollywood Babylon*.

In any event, Billie arrived in Chicago and headed straight for Katherine Emerine's office. Emerine was on the road with a revue, and the receptionist told Billie that she would have to make an appointment and come back another day. This was out of the question: she had been so confident of being engaged by her old flame that it had never crossed her mind that she might end up returning to Kansas, and she had no money for a hotel. Barging into manager Ernest Young's office, she shouldered her way to the front of the long queue of hopefuls and, in a fit of crocodile tears, blurted out that she was so broke that if he did not find her a job, she would end up sleeping rough and hitching a ride back to Missouri. Young fell for the ruse, invited her back to his home and fed her; after a perfunctory 'audition' he offered her an eight-week contract. Reverting to the name Lucille LeSueur, she was ostensibly paid for what until now she had been doing for fun – dancing the shimmy and the Black Bottom on nightclub tables for the delight of mostly middle-aged men. It is widely reputed that while here she fell pregnant, and underwent a botched backstreet abortion (the first of many) arranged by a fellow chorus girl who had recently found herself in the same predicament.

The fact that some of these lechers pushed banknotes into Lucille's garter and asked her to go home with them – or, if they were married, to accompany them for a quick tumble in the back of their car – did not bother her unduly. Very much the same happened again after she had served her 'apprenticeship' and Ernest Young booked her for the plush Oriole Terrace, one of the biggest nightclubs in Detroit, where she augmented the chorus – dancer-prostitutes, every last one, in an establishment where soliciting wealthy clients was encouraged by the management: if the girl gave the gentleman a good time, then he would hopefully return to the club and bring his business associates with him. And if there were trouble with the vice squad, the manager would always be close at hand to bail the girl out.

In Detroit, there *was* trouble when Lucille was arrested with a man in a hotel room and dragged off to the city jail. Her fingerprints and mug shots were taken, and she was forced to spend the night behind bars. Many years later, Joan Crawford's police file would conveniently vanish from the Detroit vaults after she had convened a meeting with J Edgar Hoover of the FBI – and threatened to expose him as a cross-dresser unless he agreed to remove the evidence that *she* had once been a hooker.

Lucille LeSueur might not have progressed much further up the show-business ladder beyond a succession of chorus engagements and turning tricks, had it not been for a chance meeting with one of the most powerful impresarios in America, the legendary Jake Shubert, in the Oriole Terrace cabaret room. Shubert was in town because it was the closing night of his big revue, Tot Seymour and Sigmund Romberg's *Innocent Eyes*. The star of the show was the awesome Mistinguett (1875–1956), an institution in her native France. (Almost fifty at the time, she was in the middle of her first American tour – and behind the scenes she was every bit as controversial as the girl she was about to meet.) Dubbed *Innocent Arse* because La Miss's English was sketchy, the revue had successfully played Atlantic City, Washington, Philadelphia and Chicago; after Detroit it was scheduled to return to Washington before finishing off at the pantheon of American entertainment, New York's Winter Garden Theater. Mistinguett and her partner-lover, Earl Leslie, were with Shubert. Also present were Shubert's equally eminent impresario brother, Lee, and Dédé, the great star's infamous masturbating marmoset.

Joan Crawford always maintained that she had not known who Shubert was and that, waitressing between spots in her own show, she had accidentally spilled a drink down him – enabling him to look up and be captivated by her big blue eyes and terrified smile, and subsequently engage her for the chorus of *Innocent Eyes*, which was scheduled to open on 21 May 1924. This was only partially true, and Mistinguett (who nicknamed Joan 'The Perspiring One', *suer* being the French verb for 'to sweat') herself repeated what had really happened to her much later partner (and this writer's godfather), Roger Normand:

We were sitting there, quietly minding our own business, when this frumpy thing strode up to the table. Aware that Shubert was in the room, she had changed places with the waiter, and now she audaciously tipped the glass she'd been carrying into his lap. Shubert was amused, especially when she crouched and began dabbing his crotch with her napkin. Then she smiled a pretty smile and asked him straight out if he would like to audition her. She told him, 'I give good head – and they also say I'm a capable dancer.' Shubert gave her his card, and when she'd gone I whispered in his ear, 'That one has the makings of a good bitch. She'll go a long way in life, but she'll eat you whole, cock first, and spit out the pips!'

The next afternoon, Lucille turned up at Jake Shubert's office, backstage at the Opera House, and – after reputedly finishing what she had started on her knees at the Oriole Terrace cabaret room – she was promptly engaged. That same evening, leaving the establishment one chorus girl short, she hit the road for Philadelphia with Mistinguett's troupe.

Lucille LeSueur is not mentioned in the archives of Philadelphia's Sam S Shubert Theater – indeed, some (albeit unreliable) sources have postulated that she missed most of her performances because she was being treated for venereal disease. She was certainly in the line-up when the show opened in New York and she stayed until it closed on 28 June 1924. Her best friend at the time was a 21-year-old chorus boy named Lew Offield – as with Ray Thayer Sterling, it was a platonic relationship (Offield was gay). A few years later he would hit Hollywood as Jack Oakie, and like Sterling would be remembered with particular fondness by Crawford because sex had never got in the way. 'Knowing Jack taught me that girls and fellows can be friends,' she wrote in *A Portrait of Joan*. 'That there is a wealth of sharing for two people who have a relationship uncluttered with coquetry. This is something every girl should learn.'

There is considerable speculation (primarily in Patricia Fox-Sheinwold's *Gone But Not Forgotten*) that Lucille married for the first time during her stint with the Winter Garden. The man's name was Jimmy Welton, a saxophonist with the resident orchestra, who is said to have fallen under her spell while helping her make the rounds of music publishers in search of suitable material. (She figured that if Mistinguett could get away with performing showstopper tunes with one of the worst voices in vaudeville, then there was a good chance of the name Lucille LeSueur going up in red lights above a Broadway theatre.) It is true that La Miss had not voice, beauty nor any particular dancing ability – but, like her American counterpart Fanny Brice, she was possessed of limitless charisma and, unlike Lucille, would not have compromised her inordinately high theatrical standards by resorting to the casting couch. In any case, no songs were forthcoming, but Lucille fell for the handsome musician, and is thought to have become Mrs Welton during the final week of *Innocent Eyes* – and to have filed for divorce less than two months later, when it all turned sour.

Meanwhile, during the late autumn, Lucille joined the chorus of *The Passing Show of 1924*. After each evening performance she table-danced at several New York speakeasies, including the one on West 56th Street owned by Harry Richman, who had written some of the songs for the new revue. She briefly occupied Richman's bed, and it was he who arranged her first screen test, courtesy of Nils Granlund.

Harry Rapf, one of the three most powerful men at MGM at the time, checked Lucille out on behalf of the mogul everyone called The Messiah (though never to his face) – Metro's demi-god patron, Louis B Mayer. Within days, Lucille and several other chorus girls were screen-tested. The results were perused by the great man and his equally belligerent associate, Marcus Loew, who ordered Rapf to hire the girl who pleased *him* the most. Douglas Fairbanks Jr the first *proved* Mr Crawford, claimed in his memoir *The Salad Days* that Lucille had dated Rapf – indeed, if there was any time for her to jump onto the casting couch, it would have been now. Whatever, she must have assumed she had failed the second test he arranged, for when *The Passing Show of 1924* closed in the middle of December, she returned to Kansas City.

Again, not unexpectedly, Lucille walked into a volatile situation. Later she claimed that her mother had found out about her porno-flicks, and that Anna's very first words were: 'You're dirt, Lucille.' Her mother had a new (unnamed) lover, no less odious than his predecessor. Hal had recently married, but for some reason was still living at home, and Ray Thayer Sterling had left Kansas City for good. Matters were not helped when Lucille discovered she was pregnant again – most likely with Jimmy Welton's baby. She was recovering from her second botched abortion when, on Christmas Eve, a telegram arrived from Metro. Louis B Mayer had offered her a contract.

CHAPTER TWO

Cranberry: Darling of Homosexuals

'Her loyalty to those who have stood by her and gloried her in her blossoming is like some fine marble statue.'
Katherine Albert, journalist-friend

Lucille LeSueur's contract with Metro was for five years, providing she got through an initial six-month probationary period. She was offered $75 a week – a good salary for a former table-top dancer and chorus girl. She was instructed to collect her expenses from Metro's Kansas City office – $400, most of which she spent on clothes, rather than waste what she said was good money on a sleeper. However, she had no idea that while there was snow on the ground in Kansas, Los Angeles was caught in a heat wave. Subsequently, she arrived at her destination on 3 January 1925, exhausted through sitting upright for three days and still wearing winter clothes.

She was met at the railway station by Larry Barbier, whom Louis B Mayer had assigned as her publicist, and driven to the nearby Washington Hotel. (Barbier was assistant to Pete Smith, who later handled Greta Garbo and produced-narrated the famous *Pete Smith Specialities* documentaries.) Her first part had already been lined up: the minor role of Bobby in Monta Bell's *Pretty Ladies*, starring Zasu Pitts and Norma Shearer. Based on an idea by reporter-scriptwriter Adela Rogers St Johns, who later became a friend, this was a paltry reworking of the Florenz Ziegfeld story and the tale of the birth of his famous Follies. It was notable only for its then innovative use of colour in the vaudeville sequences that linked the unravelling of the love-triangle between Pitts, Tom Moore and Lilyan Tashman. Lucille got to dress up as an eighteenth-century courtesan for a scene with Pitts, immediately after which she was screen-tested again and asked to improvise a series of emotions. Crying, she later confessed, was the easiest thing to do in front of a camera – all she had to think of was her mother, her brother and the horrendous existence she had just escaped from. Extremely nervous, she was encouraged by a sympathetic young technician named Tommy Shagrue, whose reward would come later when he would be asked to work on just about every major Crawford film.

Pretty Ladies was shot back-to-back with *The Only Thing*, a costume drama by British novelist Eleanor Glyn (a specialist in mildly erotic fiction for women). It was set in an imaginary European province and starred Conrad Nagel and Eleanor Boardman. Lucille was billed as 'Young Lady Catherine', and during shooting had a fling with Mario Caracciolo (later Carillo), a hunky Italian in his mid-thirties who was also Valentino's lover and personal fitness adviser. The reviews were appalling. Regina Cannon of the *New York Evening Graphic* denounced it as: 'A nightmare which must have been inspired by a midnight reading of *Dante's Inferno*.' Next came a walk-on in *The Ziegfeld Follies*, important only in that William Haines visited the set one afternoon and began chatting to her – inaugurating an extremely close friendship that would last five decades, a platonic bonding that Crawford declared was much more important than anything she had ever shared with her husbands.

Born 'with the century' in Staunton, Virginia, on 1 January 1900, Haines was almost as popular a silent star as Rudolph Valentino, though today his work is sadly almost forgotten. Over six foot tall, muscular, with boyish looks and a charisma that simply leaps off the screen, he was generally typecast as the cocky, wisecracking, usually financially strapped guy-next-door who always ended up with the rich girl in the last reel. Some movie experts have labelled him an early Jack Lemmon.

After military service and graduation from drama school, Haines had hit the big time in 1922 after winning Samuel Goldwyn's *New Faces* contest. Like all the important men thus far in Joan's life, he was gay. Unlike Ray Sterling, he had never been *in* the closet, but he was making so much money for the studio that they were willing to turn a blind eye towards his sexuality so long as he remained discreet. A few days after meeting Lucille, he took her home to meet his lover, Jimmy Shields, almost as ethereal-looking as himself. Lucille was surprised to learn that in an even more prejudiced, homophobic Hollywood than today, the couple were just as accepted among the acting fraternity as any other – joining them at the dinner table at their sumptuous self-designed Beverly Hills mansion were Marion Davies and her press-magnate lover William Randolph Hearst, and 'lavender' husband-and-wife actors Edmund Lowe and Lilyan Tashman.

It was William Haines who accompanied Lucille on her nightly excursions to the top dance clubs in town. Loew's State Theater, a respectable establishment frequented by Hollywood glitterati, engaged her for a while as their twice-weekly star Charleston dancer, and the pair regularly visited the jazz clubs of Harlem. Lucille still had her room at the Washington Hotel, but more often than not she spent the night at Haines's place, though rarely alone in her room. Life away from the studio was spent doing what she enjoyed the most – entering and winning dance contests, and revelling in her role as the prize parcel passed from one influential man to the next. Courtesy of Haines she met Carey Wilson, a go-getting publicist, and it was he who suggested that she try for commercials; slimmed down, made up and dressed fashionably, she photographed well and was nominated Miss MGM of 1925. The accompanying paragraph, however, suggested that she had not been entirely honest when submitting her CV: it was alleged that she had knocked four years off her age by stating her date of birth as 23 March 1908, and added three inches to her height by declaring herself 5 foot 4 inches.

In *Lady of the Night* (1925) Lucille was asked to double for Norma Shearer and loudly voiced her disapproval – but heads rose every time she walked into a room, and pictures of her soon began appearing in movie magazines. Not one of her peers, though, liked her name – even Louis B Mayer thought it sounded too much like 'sewer', and that with her unbridled lifestyle this would only court publicity of the very worst kind. In April of that year, the readers of *Movie World* were invited to write in with their suggestions for an alternative moniker. The winner was a woman who came up with Joan Arden, but no sooner had this been announced than the real Joan Arden, a bit-part actress, came forward and threatened Louis B Mayer with legal action. Metro therefore opted for the runner-up's suggestion – Joan Crawford – a name she initially loathed, claiming that it sounded too much like 'crawfish' – until William Haines convinced her that it was not that bad. In her memoirs she would recall how her friend had joked, 'They might have called you Cranberry and served you with the turkey at Thanksgiving!' The jibe was appreciated, and for the rest of his life Haines would affectionately call her 'Cranberry'.

During the summer of 1925, Joan Crawford was at the bottom of Metro's very glittering ladder, the uppermost rungs of which included such luminaries as John Gilbert, Ramon Novarro, William Haines, Erich von Stroheim and the recently signed Greta Garbo. With the exception of von Stroheim, Crawford would work with them all. Soon, Louis B Mayer would engage Buster Keaton and Marion Davies. King Vidor, Fred Niblo and Rex Ingram were among his top directors, and Mayer had also just brought in Universal's 'Boy Wonder', Irving Thalberg, who happened to be Norma Shearer's lover. Way ahead of Bette Davis, Shearer became Joan's first arch-rival, quite simply because she resented the fact that Shearer was given the best parts solely due to her closeness to Thalberg. The latter was the archetypal mother's boy and was already suffering from extremely delicate health – and therefore allowed too much of his own way – on account of a congenital heart defect. Not only did Joan wound Shearer's usually ineffable pride by telling her, during their first meeting, that she had never heard of her, but she also persistently derided her.

Another big Metro star Joan could not stand was ten-year-old Jackie Coogan, who a decade hence would hit the headlines with an acrimonious court battle with his parents, whom he accused of stealing $4 million of his earnings during his years as a floppy-haired wunderkind with enormous appeal. Coogan had made his debut aged eighteen months, in *Skinner's Baby* (1916), and now he was signed to play the lead in his own father's production of Willard Mack's *Old Clothes*. The story tells of junk-shop partners Timothy Kelly and Max Ginsburg (Coogan and Max Davidson respectively) who run into financial difficulties when a stock investment goes wrong. To make ends meet they take in a lodger, Mary Riley (Joan) who becomes surrogate mother to the younger boy. With his connections, Timothy gets Mary a secretarial position with a handsome stockbroker. The pair fall in love, initially face condemnation from his snooty relatives who feel he is dating beneath him, but marry in the last reel when Timmy and Max's shares escalate and put them back in the black. It was Joan's biggest and most important part to date. Even so, she hated playing second fiddle to someone she had always looked upon as a 'spoiled brat', though she could not have been displeased when holy-terror columnist Louella Parsons wrote in the *New York Journal-American*, albeit inaccurately, 'That [destitute] girl, Joan Crawford, is a discovery of Jack Coogan Sr. She is very attractive, and shows promise.'

Working alongside William Haines was a dream come true for Joan, and in August 1924 shooting had begun on *Sally, Irene and Mary*, a 'flapper' story starring Haines, Constance Bennett and Sally O'Neil. The scenario was controversial for its day: three showgirls from vastly differing backgrounds set out to ensnare husbands by flaunting their equally differing charms. Sally (Bennett) is the bitchy one who becomes a kept woman; timid Mary (O'Neil) ends up with a young plumber (Haines); but there is no happy ending for Irene (Joan). She is the reckless one who falls into a loveless liaison with a playboy heel (Douglas Gilmore). When he forces himself upon her, telling her that he is only interested in getting physical, she flees his apartment, meets up with another lover and the two elect to elope – only to die when their car crashes into a speeding train when they try to overshoot a level crossing.

The film, released in 1925, was directed by Edmund Goulding, a gay pal of William Haines who would go on to much bigger things with Joan

Crawford, whose gay-friendliness in the days of the acutely homophobic studio system would greatly impress him. Regina Cannon of the *New York Evening Graphic*, no Crawford fan, called this one 'pretty cheap and tawdry', but the review Joan clipped and pasted into her scrapbook came from *Photoplay*'s James R Quirk, who wrote, 'This is one of the nicest pictures of backstage chorus girl life it has been our lot to see', and singled Joan out as the best of the three actresses in it. This brought an outburst from Constance Bennett, a tetchy, standoffish woman who never even spoke to Joan or Sally O'Neil away from the set. Incensed that Joan had stolen her thunder, she barged into Louis B Mayer's office and told him that she would never work with 'the Crawford upstart' again.

Joan's next two films were not so well received. *The Boob*, with Gertrude Olmstead and Charles Murray and in which Joan played an unconvincing Prohibition agent, was dismissed by the *Baltimore Sun* as: 'A piece of junk.' *Tramp, Tramp, Tramp*, with gormless comic Harry Langdon entering a cross-country hiking contest and getting into all manner of scrapes to impress his girlfriend (Joan) and win her hand, was *so* bad that some critics refused to review it.

Much better was *Paris*, Joan's second film with Edmund Goulding, her most artistic vehicle to date and based on an earlier French film with Mistinguett. The action begins in a *café-concert* where The Girl (Joan) doubles as resident slut and *meneuse de chalopée* (or apache-dancer), performing a difficult and potentially dangerous routine introduced by the great French chanteuse, Damia (1889–1978), whom Joan would later emulate. When The Girl is chatted up by a visiting American millionaire (Charles Ray), her jealous boyfriend, The Cat (yet another sinister performance from Douglas Gilmore), stabs him. Unsure which man to have, The Girl nurses the American back to health while hiding The Cat from the *flics*. She then persuades him to hand himself in and get off with a lighter sentence, while the American unsuccessfully woos her, though she does agree to live with him on a platonic basis. Things turn ugly, however, when The Cat gets out of jail. Assuming The Girl has been cheating on him, he attempts to strangle her. The American saves her life and is in the process of throttling The Cat when The Girl screams out that she has *only* loved The Cat all along, and in keeping with the *chalopée* story the lovers slope off, leaving the American bereft and about to drown his sorrows – or maybe himself.

The *réaliste* element of *Paris* was beyond the comprehension of the American critics, who could not understand why Joan's character appeared unkempt, crude and without make-up. Leading the detractors was *Variety* which, responding to 'picture mob rumours' that Joan was rapidly heading towards the very top of the MGM ladder, observed, 'Undoubtedly a "looker" (when profiled she can double for Norma Shearer in a close-up), Miss Crawford will nevertheless have to show more talent than in this instance to make *that* billing entirely unanimous.' Others disliked the ending, believing that Joan should have been seen strolling off on the arm of the handsome Charles Ray, but Edmund Goulding had insisted upon sticking with tradition, and this mini masterpiece is all the better for it.

Shooting *Paris* had been a tense experience, however, with everyone ignoring Joan once the cameras had stopped rolling. Her only ally had been a young freelance reporter named Katherine Albert, formerly an MGM publicist. Some years later, Albert would allow *Photoplay* to publish a copy of the Christmas card that Joan had sent her while making the film. On the back of it she had scribbled, 'Everybody is so happy. I feel as if I'm no part of it. What makes me unhappy? Why can't I enter into the fun they're all having?'

Louis B Mayer was not just aware of the press's bias towards Norma Shearer – his studio was actually paying some journalists to praise her unduly because of her relationship with Irving Thalberg. Similarly, he recognised Joan's enormous potential, and raised her salary to $100 a week. She celebrated the unexpected windfall by moving out of the grubby Washington Hotel into a small, rented, unfurnished bungalow. William Haines who, as will be seen, was an acknowledged expert with such things, offered to help her decorate and refurbish the place, but Joan was adamant: this was her first real home, she said, and she wanted to do the work herself. This way, she figured, she would save money and be able to send a little more to Kansas – incredibly, despite all the misery she had caused her, Joan was now paying her mother a weekly allowance. With a wealth of cheap fabrics, gaudy colours and second-hand furniture bought from junk shops, she created a domicile that Haines told her looked more like a whorehouse than a film star's retreat.

The next man in Joan's life, and one of the first visitors *chez* Crawford, was Paul Bern (born Paul Levy). Known as 'Little Father Confessor' on account of his puny build and the fact that he loved nothing more than listening to other people's problems – though not always helping them to solve them, or face up to his own – German-born Bern was Irving Thalberg's right-hand man, a talented scriptwriter and producer who had worked with the likes of Josef von Sternberg and Ernst Lubitsch. Sophisticated, intellectual but unattractive, Bern's powerful position had permitted him to date some of the biggest names in Hollywood – female and male – though after his death it would be revealed somewhat ungallantly that on account of grossly under-developed genitals he had been incapable of consummating any relationship, and that his many (almost always much younger) 'conquests' had merely regarded him as a kindly surrogate father figure. The most recent of these had been 29-year-old Barbara LaMarr, six-times married, who had just died of a drugs overdose – 'Hollywoodised' for the press as 'too rigorous dieting'. In the year or so that she had been at Culver City, Joan had slimmed down considerably – from 145 to 120 pounds – and the wily Bern was confident that she would take over where the luckless LaMarr, referred to in one newspaper headline as 'The Girl Who Was Too Beautiful', had left off. Joan's friend Katherine Albert would write in *Photoplay*'s August 1931 issue:

> If you were at all discerning, you could look into those great eyes and know that Joan wanted something more out of life than she was getting in a Charleston contest. Paul Bern knew that Joan was miserable and he began the awakening of her mind. Paul taught her the things she had not known existed . . . the beauty of words on paper, the feeling for musical harmony, the appreciation of form and colour on canvas . . . that one simply cannot exist in a room cluttered with wildly painted Coney Island dolls.

It was Bern who escorted Joan to the classiest nightspots in town and who guided her through *The Taxi Dancer*. As von Sternberg would later do with Dietrich, he taught her about lighting, how to get the best out of the very bad camera angle, and how *not* to let the likes of Constance Bennett upstage her. Her co-star in the film was the prissy Owen Moore, billed above her in the credits, though it was Joan's film and the first noticeable 'Crawford martyr' role that she would later uniquely perfect. She played Joslyn Poe, a taxi dancer from Virginia who, despite her obvious talents, is unable to find work upon her arrival in New York in search of fame and fortune. She is rescued from despair by Lee Rogers (Moore), the man in the next apartment who has listened to her crying herself to sleep every night. Lee, a cardsharp, fixes her up with a job at the local palais, where she immediately falls in with bad company – Kitty (Gertrude Astor), a chorus girl, who teaches her how to solicit wealthy patrons. She hooks onto a greasy millionaire (Marc McDermott), and uses him to get what she wants, but cannot resist the charms of unbalanced ballroom dancer-crook Jim Kelvin (Douglas Gilmore, more or less reviving his *Paris* role). Matters are further complicated when Jim gets into a fight with a mobster and kills him. At first Joslyn hides him from the police, but eventually she realises that it is Lee she truly loves, and the film ends with them returning as a couple to Virginia, though we are not sure whether or not they have married. *The Taxi Dancer* also contains the first Crawford ultra-camp moment when, during the final scene, the subtitle fills the screen. '*He* is convinced of Joslyn's purity when she *refuses* a cocktail before dinner!' Paul Bern's presence was also much appreciated on the set of *Winners of the Wilderness*, but only until she became interested in Tim McCoy (1891–1978), an all-round action hero if ever there was one.

Thirty-six when he worked with Joan, though he looked a good ten years younger, McCoy had served as an artillery major in World War I, after which he had become Adjutant General of Wyoming. In 1922 he had been hired by Paramount as technical adviser on *The Covered Wagon* – and the acting bug had struck. Though he would only appear in around a dozen films (including 1956's *Around the World in Eighty Days*), most of them are memorable. The plug for *Winners of the Wilderness* was: 'He's The Real McCoy! Big Tim is The Fastest Draw The Wild West Has Ever Known!' – to which Joan added, tongue in cheek, 'The fastest draw, sure, and the weapon's got staying power and sure as hell don't fire blanks!'

In the film, set at the time of the Franco-Indian War of 1756–63, Joan was the oddly named Renée Contrecoeur, the general's daughter who falls in love with the dashing Colonel O'Hara (McCoy), who is fighting on the side of the Red Indians. It was directed by W S Van Dyke – the infamous 'One-Take Woody' who had assisted D W Griffith on *Intolerance*, and who saved Louis B Mayer money by shooting this one back-to-back on the same location with McCoy's *War Paint* – though Joan was unaware that her handsome stud was also servicing Pauline Starke, his leading lady in this film.

No sooner had Joan finished shooting the film with Tim McCoy – and brought the curtain down on their relationship – than she began working on *The Understanding Heart*, the third 'Crawford hides a criminal' movie, under the not-so-very-able direction of Jack Conway, who appears to be making up the story as he goes along. Her co-stars were Carmel Myers and 'flapper-queen' Francis X Bushman Jr, a strapping young actor of andro-gynous beauty whose father had two years previously portrayed Messala in Ramon Novarro's *Ben-Hur*. Joan played Monica Dale, an unlikely forest rangers fire-scout, who also has to cope with a wayward sister (Myers) whose lover, Bob (Rockcliffe Fellowes), kills another suitor in self-defence and is sent to jail. When he escapes, Monica conceals him in her observatory, resulting in complications when he falls in love with her – she is amorously involved with ranger Tony Garland (Bushman Jr). From this point, the storyline borders on the ridiculous when a forest fire suddenly threatens to engulf the observatory but is extinguished by an unexpected downpour as encircling planes begin dropping parachutes and the authorities arrive on the scene to announce that the murder charge has been quashed and Bob is a free man. Then the titles explain that Bob has discovered his 'understanding' heart and given up on his pursuit of Monica, whom we assume will live happily ever after with her ranger lover.

If most of the critics dismissed *The Understanding Heart*, they were very enthusiastic about *The Unknown*. 'When Lon Chaney is in a picture,' remarked the *New York Evening World*, 'one can rest assured that the picture is worth seeing. When Joan Crawford and Norman Kerry are also present to help Mr Chaney put it over, its value is that much enhanced.'

The so-called 'Man of a Thousand Faces' was certainly Joan's most offbeat co-star, and the film was superbly directed by the acknowledged master of horror, Tod Browning. The part had come about by way of a recommendation from William Haines after Mary Philbin, the heroine of Chaney's phenomenally successful *Phantom of the Opera* (1925), had refused to work with him again, claiming he had pestered her with unwelcome advances. The previous year, Haines and Chaney had bonded – there is no other way of defining the unlikeliest pairing thus far in the American cinema – in *Tell It to the Marines* (1926), released around the time Joan was working with Chaney. This had a not-so-subtle gay subplot: as Kenneth Anger observed in *Hollywood Babylon*, 'Sergeant Lon Chaney and New Recruit Haines have what can only be described as an odd love-hate sado-masochistic love-affair.' Equally ironic was the fact that, between lovers herself, Joan was accompanying Haines on his nightly jaunts to the bars around downtown Los Angeles's Pershing Square, a notorious gay pick-up area where, mingling freely with the rent-boys and rough-trade, there were scores of on-leave sailors from which he could make his choice. Neither was Joan joking when she told Haines, 'Save any leftovers for me!'

The Unknown, set in Madrid, revolves around the character of Alonzo (Chaney), a knife thrower with Zanzi's Circus. Strapping his arms to his sides, he bills himself 'The Armless Wonder' and throws knives with his feet at Zanzi's pretty daughter, Estralita (Joan), who just happens to have a phobia about hands and hates to be touched. Alonzo also has a double-thumb, central to the plot when during a fight with Zanzi (Nick de Ruiz), Alonzo's arms break free and he kills him. Estralita is the only witness, but all she sees is the double-thumb – and as Alonzo is known to be armless, he is not questioned by the police. Alonzo then develops a crush on Estralita and, this being a typical Chaney film, upon learning of her phobia he has his arms amputated for real so that she will not reject him! Disaster beckons, however, when during Alonzo's hospitalisation Estralita falls for Malabar (Kerry), the circus strongman who cures her of her affliction and asks her to marry him. But Alonzo exacts his revenge. Malabar's speciality is holding back two teams of horses that are pulling in opposite directions – actually, they are on a treadmill and only appear to be doing so. Alonzo rigs the contraption, but the ruse goes wrong when he slips and is trampled to death under the horses' hooves. Dizzy stuff!

Later Joan would accredit Chaney – in every sense a pre-Method actor, renowned for going to inordinate lengths to perfect a role – with turning her into the consummate actress she became. Writing in *A Portrait of Joan* she observed:

If I had to name one person who taught me not only how to act and how to concentrate, but also how to master a role that was practically impossible, it was Lon Chaney. On the set nothing distracted him. He *became* that armless man. Lon Chaney didn't exist . . . the man was a perfectionist.

By now, Langdon W Post, the critic from *New Evening World*, was singling Joan out as 'One of the screen's acknowledged artists' – resulting in her immediate summons to Louis B Mayer's office, apparently the very first time she and The Messiah had met. Mayer told her that her salary had been upped to $250 a week, and that she had now joined the privileged few permitted to call him 'Papa'.

Mayer, whose informants were everywhere, was well aware of the stories circulating around town concerning Joan's wild dancing and even more frenzied libido. He also tried to ignore the rumours that had winged their way from Kansas – started by Anna LeSueur, whose weekly allowance had nevertheless been raised by her daughter – regarding the trail of broken hearts and abortions Joan had left in her wake. So far, however, none of these extracurricular activities, real or invented, had affected her work or the studio's standing, and Mayer was pleased to read in the press about her 'near-maternal' attachment to Mike Cudahy, the neurotic nineteen-year-old heir to the Chicago meat-packaging emporium.

Cudahy had appeared on the scene at just the right moment, when Joan was mourning the death of her friend, Jerry Chrysler. Tall and powerfully built, yet effeminate and regarded as 'one of the girls', Chrysler had partnered Joan at the Cocoanut Grove tea dances and they had walked off with first prize every time they had entered a competition. Then the young man, the same age as Joan, had inexplicably contracted pneumonia and died within a week, leaving her devastated. Cudahy, one of Chrysler's pals and already an alcoholic, had helped her choose the wreath and escorted her to the funeral. He had also paid to have her teeth fixed, and Joan now returned the favour by helping him with his drink problem.

The movie tabloids reported how this 'God-fearing girl' who called in at St Augustine's Church *every* morning on her way to the studio (true) and never balked when it came to 'helping out' her fellow men (which, of course, depended upon how one interpreted the term) had been seen driving her new beau to an Alcoholics Anonymous meeting in her studio-supplied car (not true, for she had bought this herself to celebrate her pay rise). The reason for Cudahy's drinking appears to have stemmed from confusion over his sexuality, and the pressure his mother was putting on him to take over as head of the family business, when all he wanted to do was party with friends and squander the $1,500 a month he was getting from his father's estate until

he came of age and inherited his fortune. 'Mike was the answer to that
mother-love yearning within me,' Joan wrote in her 1962 memoirs. 'I was
determined to do for Mike what Ray Sterling had done for me. I wouldn't let
him drink when he was with me. I wanted Mike to be perfect, to be the one
man I had always envisioned in all my dreams.'

In her syndicated column, William Randolph Hearst's ace reporter
Adela Rogers St Johns described Joan and Cudahy as *the* perfect Hollywood
couple – albeit that it was common knowledge in their circle that Cudahy
was gay – and few were surprised when they announced their engagement.
What they had not reckoned on, however, was the staunch opposition that
would come from Cudahy's mother – he was, after all, still legally a minor.
She publicly declared that she had no intention of bringing shame on the
family name by having her son wed a woman who was effectively little more
than a prostitute, no matter how many times she attended mass.

Joan returned to Paul Bern, and in the meantime was announced as
one of the thirteen up-and-coming actresses named that year's most
promising by the Western Association of Motion Picture Advertisers.
Aged nineteen to 22, they were collectively known as The Wampas
Babies, and copied New York's infamous Algonquin Round Table by
convening regular lunch meetings at the Montmartre, one of the plushest
restaurants in town.

Years later, the notorious *Confidential* magazine would refer to these
young women as 'Tinsel Town's Baritone Babes' – the group included Dolores
Del Rio, Janet Gaynor, Fay Wray, Mary Astor and Dolores Costello, several
of whom subsequently endured 'lavender' marriages to spare their sexuality
from becoming public knowledge. Very soon, these gatherings were extended
beyond the press federation nominees: hoping to be seen hobnobbing with
Hollywood's newest and most exciting pack, gatecrashers began bribing the
Montmartre's waiters to secure them places at tables adjacent to the one
occupied by these Loquacious Bright Young Things, and catfights were par
for the course. A thirteen-year-old starlet named Gretchen Young who
boasted that she had appeared with Valentino in *The Sheik* (1921), though
she had not worked since, was allowed into one meeting, given the task of
hanging up everyone's coats, then promptly shown the door when she would
not stop talking. The following year she would become Loretta Young, but
henceforth Joan never called her anything except 'Gretch The Wretch'.

Another actress starting to make big strides in Hollywood was eighteen-
year-old Jane Peters, a friend of William Haines – though Joan did not know
this. When she attempted to usurp Joan's place as head-of-the-table and to
add insult to injury had arranged to be photographed for *Picturegoer*, Joan
strode into the room and bawled for her to move. Peters waited until the

session was over before loudly pronouncing, 'Madam, I find your manner most offensive. Now will you please go and fuck yourself?' A few weeks later, Jane Peters changed her name to Carole Lombard. Devotees of the same sense of vulgar humour, she and Joan became and would remain friends.

Another hanger-on was the slightly older Betty Compson, who had just starred with Lon Chaney in *The Big City* and so impressed Louis B Mayer that she was now given equal billing with Joan in *Twelve Miles Out*, a then topical tale of thug-rivalry during Prohibition – though in this one, everyone is eclipsed by John Gilbert as Jerry Fay, the motorcycle stuntman who thirsts for revenge when bootlegger Red McCue (Ernest Torrence) absconds with his girlfriend. The two men's mutual loathing sees them at each other's throats across Europe, South America and Asia as both compete in illegal money-making rackets, with Jerry always emerging victor, particularly if a woman is involved. Matters come to a head when the pair return to America. Jerry sets up a rum-running operation on the coast, and commandeers the house belonging to Jane (Joan) to store his liquor. Here, a love-hate relationship develops between them, though she is affianced to the foppish John Burton (Richard Earle). The moralists had their say, however, and in a hasty script rewrite Jane was prevented from living in sin with her love: the film ends when *both* thugs die in the final shoot-out and Jane returns to her former sedentary life with Burton – though Jerry is allowed the luxury of expiring in her arms.

Today, one finds it hard to comprehend John Gilbert's massive appeal during the early days of the cinema. Born John Pringle in Logan, Utah, in 1895, he had taken over from (but would never eclipse) the recently deceased Valentino as the screen's great lover. He was, however, nowhere near as handsome as Rudy, his acting style was extremely camp, and when not engaged in a hot, amorous clinch, he lacked charisma. He also frequently appeared more feminine than his siren co-stars, the most famous of all, of course, being Greta Garbo. Their *Flesh and the Devil* would prove *the* film of 1927 and a follow-up was already on the cards. At the time of his first film coupling with Joan, Gilbert had divorced actress Leatrice Joy and was said to be half out of his mind with worry, trying to get Garbo to the altar.

Gilbert is alleged *not* to have wanted to work with Joan, aware of her reputation as a man-eater and his own inability to resist a pretty face. Why his wish was ignored – as Hollywood's number-one leading man, he was being paid in excess of $10,000 a week, whereas Joan was on a mere fraction of this amount, even less than Betty Compson – was not obvious at the time, though on reflection not difficult to work out. The truth is, Louis B Mayer ordered the pairing because he could not stand Gilbert and was intent on destroying him. Gilbert already had a drink problem brought about by Garbo's marriage deliberations, yet Mayer despised him not for this, but because Garbo had announced that *if* she became Mrs Gilbert, she would also become a naturalised American.

Garbo was the only Hollywood star in those days (aside from Tallulah Bankhead, never less than a law unto herself) who steadfastly refused to kow-tow to the pesky studio system. Flaunting convention, she sunbathed in the nude, went out with whom she liked, and frequently failed to turn up on the lot if she felt she could not give of her best that day. Mayer had so far kept her under reasonable control by threatening to deport her back to Sweden. She was, however, by far the biggest draw in the *world*, earning millions for Metro, and Mayer knew that if she became legally American, she would cause him even more grief. Between them, he and Paul Bern were hoping that Gilbert and Joan would find each other irresistible and that someone would 'catch them at it' and relay the news to Garbo, who would abandon all hope of ever marrying him.

Matters between Mayer and Gilbert came to a head on 8 September 1926 at the wedding of King Vidor and Eleanor Boardman – intended as a double ceremony with Gilbert and Garbo. It did not involve Joan, though she witnessed the event along with the other guests, including Irving Thalberg and fiancée Norma Shearer, Marion Davies, Sam Goldwyn, and the whole of the Hollywood press. Garbo, however, infamously failed to show, and in front of the distinguished gathering, Mayer marched up to a distraught Gilbert and bellowed, 'What's the matter with you, Jack? What do you have to *marry* her for? Why don't you just fuck her and forget it?' In a fit of not-unexpected rage, the actor bunched his fist and socked Mayer under the jaw, sending him sprawling and breaking his spectacles. Astonishingly, the incident did not get John Gilbert fired, but it certainly set in motion his lengthy, agonising downfall – whereas Garbo's career would only move from strength to strength.

In the spring of 1927 Joan and William Haines travelled to New York, where *Spring Fever* and *West Point* were shot simultaneously. The former was a homely tale based on Vincent Lawrence's big hit Broadway production. Haines played Jack Kelly, a humble shipping clerk who so impresses his boss with his golfing skills that he enrols him at his club, hoping to pick up a few tips to beat his business rivals, and introduces him to everyone as his nephew. Success goes to Jack's head, however: wearing loud clothes, he boasts that he is heir to a fortune, and latches onto socialite Allie Monte (Joan). When Jack proposes, she pretends to be poor and the marriage takes place, only to turn sour when she learns the truth and walks out on him. But this is a Billy Haines film, and happy endings are obligatory. Deciding that a change of employment is necessary now that he has tasted the good life, Jack becomes a professional golfer, wins $10,000 in a tournament at which Allie turns up as cheerleader, and the pair are reunited. Despite her fondness for

Haines and the film's success, Joan hated it. 'Spring Fever was a waste of everybody's time and money,' she would tell fan-chronicler Ray Newquist (of whom more later). 'God, golf is dull on film!'

In West Point, Haines again played the cocky upstart – Bruce Wayne, the rich, spoiled cadet who looks down his nose at the other recruits, who put up with him this time on account of his prowess on the soccer pitch. Bruce falls for hotelier's daughter Betty Channing (Joan), who initially finds him pretentious and wants nothing to do with him. He, however, feels that he is a law unto himself and when he gets benched by his coach, he exacts his revenge by giving a scathing interview to the press. This results in his being dropped from the team, but he is reinstated when a friend (William Bakewell) intervenes on the eve of the Army-Navy final. During the match, Bruce is badly injured but with typical Haines aplomb he battles it out to the finish and scores the winning goals – impressing Betty, who now wants to be his girl.

In New York, both Haines and Joan played away from home, so to speak – he cheating on long-term lover Jimmy Shields with West Point's William Bakewell, she hitting the clubs with third-lead Neil Neely, an affair that could have had very serious implications had it been made public knowledge at the time. Neely appears to have been as promiscuous as Joan, and when his wife found a love letter in his jacket pocket, she decided to sue Joan as co-respondent in the divorce – a ruse that backfired when Neely told his lawyers that if Joan had to be called to the witness stand, so would two dozen others!

Joan's next film saw her plunging to the depths of the downright abject – a silent musical! Following The Student Prince and The Merry Widow, MGM elected to transfer Otto Harbach and Oscar Hammerstein's Rose Marie to the big screen, with Joan vamping things up in the title role. Playing her soldier lover, Jim Kenyon, was James Murray, the flagrantly neurotic star of King Vidor's 1927 monster smash, The Crowd. Already alcoholic and a nightmare to work with on account of violent mood-swings and dreadful time-keeping, Murray would soon fall by the wayside after this one. Within a few years he would be ousted from Hollywood and sleeping rough, and in 1936 the authorities would list him as 'just another bum' when his body was fished out of New York's Hudson River.

Rose Marie had made laughing stocks out of its stars long before completion of shooting, and prompted Joan into bawling out Irving Thalberg – something even the fearless Garbo would have thought twice about before doing. Cornering the sickly executive on the set of Norma Shearer's latest picture she levelled, 'Mr Thalberg, why the fuck does she always get the best parts? Aren't there any more actresses in Hollywood than her?' Thalberg is reported to have very nearly collapsed through shock, and gone straight to

Louis B Mayer to demand her dismissal. The Messiah, however, knew that Joan was right. She had been contracted to star opposite Ramon Novarro in *Across to Singapore*, which was still being scripted. Therefore, in the interim period, and to pacify Thalberg, Joan was 'taught a lesson in humility' by being put into another western with old flame Tim McCoy.

The Law of the Range tells of two brothers, separated from their mother as children and unaware that they are related, who end up on opposite sides of the law. Jim Lockhart (McCoy) is the ranger charged with bringing sadistic bandit The Solitaire Kid (Rex Lease) to justice. Betty Dallas (Joan) is Jim's girlfriend, but even so does not fight off The Kid's advances when he holds up the stagecoach she is travelling in. She eventually makes the connection between the two men – both have identical tattoos – but before the inevitable shoot-out all have to battle their way through a ferocious prairie fire. Not unexpectedly it is the baddie who dies – in the arms of his long-lost mother – while the lovers tearfully look on. The film enabled Joan to briefly resurrect her affair with the hunky cowboy star, and unlike *Rose Marie* it attracted favourable reviews.

Meanwhile, Joan was presented with a major problem when, out of the blue, her brother Hal turned up on her doorstep – not for a visit, which would have been unwelcome enough, but to announce that he had come to Hollywood for good. Hal had walked out on his wife; according to Joan he had told her sarcastically, 'If *you* can make it here with your reputation, anybody can!' Cynics have suggested that Joan should have sent him packing and thus saved herself a great deal of future trouble and expense. What has to be taken into consideration, however, was Joan's status in Hollywood by then. Now elevated to equal billing – the press were making a great deal of the pairing with Ramon Novarro – she had to be *seen* to be behaving responsibly, even towards unworthy relatives, and Louis B Mayer was a man who rigorously supported family values, no matter what that family was like.

This was the age of the Hays Office Motion Picture Code – a powerful censorship law that not only outlawed such 'immoral' activities as on-screen open-mouthed kissing, the display of navels and hirsute chests, drinking and substance abuse, violence and sexual innuendo – but also dictated how actors and studio personnel should conduct themselves *away* from the set, *including* the way they treated their relatives. Kenneth Anger would later denounce former Postmaster General Will Hays, a man who knew absolutely nothing about the film world, as 'a prim-faced, bat-eared, mealy-mouthed political chiseller', and others such as Joan, Tallulah Bankhead and Mae West would be even less polite when telling him to his face what they thought of his so-called ideals. In conjunction with the Catholic Church and the Bank of America, Hays had set up his Code in 1922 to clean up Hollywood, and he had personally compiled a 'Doom Book' that contained the names of 117 stars – Joan's being near the top of the list – whom he considered were guilty of 'moral turpitude'. There is little doubt that Hal LeSueur knew this, and blackmailed Joan into not just taking him in, but their mother as well. Within the week, 'the washerwoman and the drunk', as Joan called them, had taken over her tiny bungalow. More than this, Hal had borrowed her Ford roadster without asking permission and wrapped it around a lamppost – and Anna had run up a huge bill, buying clothes and jewellery and charging them to Joan's account. On one occasion she was caught shoplifting and gave her daughter's name to the store-detective who arrested her.

Joan figured that the only way she would rid herself of her bloodsucking relatives would be by putting some space between them. So as to give the Hays Office spies the impression that she cared, she spoke to Paul Bern and he found Hal ad-hoc work as an extra/bit-part player at the Culver City studio – not because he could act, but because Bern declared he made pretty scenery. Anna was put onto the Crawford payroll and paid an official allowance for doing precisely nothing. Joan next approached Louis B Mayer and asked him for a loan: she had seen a bungalow at 513 North Roxbury Drive, Beverly Hills, and the asking price was $18,000. For anyone else this would have been tempting fate. Joan had recently been arrested for failing to stop after knocking down a female pedestrian and, courtesy of Metro's head of publicity, Howard Strickland – who had persuaded the victim to drop the charges in return for a $1,000 pay-off – Joan had been let off with a caution. Mayer loaned her the money, but only on condition that she continue supporting her mother and upped Anna's allowance each time she received a pay-rise. Joan agreed. She moved out, and the LeSueurs were given the original bungalow, rent-free – so long as neither of them spoke to the press, or attempted to visit Joan at her new home. They were also promised legal action, should they run up any more bills in her name.

Her biggest problem sorted for the time being, Joan began working on *Across to Singapore* with Ramon Novarro, without any doubt the best-looking co-star of her silents period. The two had a great deal in common in the way they had climbed to the top. Born José-Ramon Samaniegos in Durango, Mexico, in 1899, he had arrived in Hollywood in 1913 after fleeing the Huerta Revolution. His first job had been washing dishes in a restaurant, and there had followed a variety of occupations: dancing the tango, working as a bit-part player in summer stock, dancing ballet in Anna Pavlova's chorus, working as an extra in Mary Pickford films. Very muscular, narcissistic and *extremely* handsome, José-Ramon had quickly amassed a coterie of lovers of both sexes – including Rudolph Valentino, whom he had met in 1920 while working as a bit-part on *The Four*

Horsemen of the Apocalypse. Within an hour of their brief scene they had become lovers, and Rudy had written in his journal, 'Samaniegos was ferocious – we made love like tigers until dawn.' The film had been directed by Rex Ingram, who astonishingly did not meet José-Ramon until shooting was completed. Mistinguett, who knew Novarro well at this time and whose dancer-lover Frédéric Rey left her for the actor, told Roger Normand:

> When Ingram met him after the film, he was posing nude for art students in Los Angeles, and didn't take too much persuading to *bounce* onto the casting couch. Ramon told Frédé how Ingram had taken a lingering look at his beautifully hirsute buttocks and commented how much they reminded him of his favourite haunt, the Novarro Valley. That's how he got his name – because his arse looked like a tourist attraction!

Joan was desperate to have an affair with the man who was unafraid of boasting that Valentino had been the greatest love of his life. Novarro, however, had given up having sex with women since Rudy's death, though he did offer a compromise, as Novarro's later lover, French dancer Pierre Bernay explained to me in 1999:

> Valentino commissioned a sculpture, an exact replica of his manhood. I don't know how many copies he had made, but he gave one to Novarro – a ten-inch Art Deco dildo embellished with his signature, the same one he was later choked to death with. Sometimes he carried it around with him. He would show it to friends he trusted so that they could see what it must have been like, getting the real thing from Valentino. So far as I know, though, Joan Crawford and Vladimir Horowitz [the famous pianist] are the only ones who actually asked to borrow and *use* it.

Across to Singapore had previously been filmed in 1923 (as *All the Brothers Were Valiant*, the title under which it would reappear in 1953 with Robert Taylor). Its storyline here is virtually incomprehensible in parts and it remains important only as a curio for connoisseurs of beautiful men – as the hero, Joel Shore, Novarro *shines*, and next to him even Joan looks positively plain as his demure childhood sweetheart, Priscilla Crowninshield. Joel, however, has a rival – his elder brother, Mark (Ernest Torrence) – who before setting sail for Singapore with him on their clipper ship arrogantly gets the local priest to announce their forthcoming marriage. During the voyage, Mark regrets what he has done and spends much of the time drinking below deck. With him thus indisposed, when the ship reaches its destination and first-mate Finch (James Mason) orchestrates a mutiny, only Joel has to be overpowered. Leaving Mark ashore, Finch claps Joel in chains – rewarding Novarro's legion of closeted gay fans with lots of delicious bare-torso shots and much obligatory flexing of sweaty muscles – and the ship returns to England, where Finch evades court martial by declaring that he took command of the vessel because Joel left his brother to die. Joel breaks free, and eager to put matters right sails back to Singapore, taking Priscilla with him. He finds Mark drunk and dishevelled in an opium den, and manages to get him back to the ship and sobered up before there is another mutiny, during which Mark dies the hero trying to save his brother's life.

Across to Singapore, for which Joan was little more than superfluous decoration, would be largely overshadowed by Novarro's other film of 1928, *Forbidden Hours*, and the following year's *The Flying Fleet*. Director William Nigh had wanted her to team up with the Mexican star again for her next project, *Four Walls*, but when Novarro refused to work with 'that nymphomaniac lady', Nigh persuaded Louis B Mayer to let him have John Gilbert – mindless of the fact that Gilbert was in Mayer's bad books again for dismissing *Twelve Miles Out* as 'garbage' and refusing to attend the premiere.

Four Walls was superbly photographed by James Wong Howe, Cecil B DeMille's assistant cameraman, who would bow out as late as 1975 with Barbra Streisand's *Funny Lady*. Gilbert plays East Side mobster Benny Horowitz; Joan is Frieda, his moll. When Benny is sent to jail for killing a rival, his crony, Monk (Louis Natheaux), takes over the gang – and Frieda – relinquishing his hold a few years later when Benny is released, a changed man who now wants nothing to do with either. While inside he has fallen for Bertha (Carmel Myers), a young reformist. When Bertha refuses Benny's marriage proposal, thinking he is still carrying a torch for Frieda, he goes to a party at Monk's place to drown his sorrows and sees Frieda flirting with Monk. Later the pair announce their engagement, but all ends badly, enabling the former lovers to be reunited, when Benny's old gang are attacked by a rival mob and he resumes command. During the ensuing scuffle Benny and Frieda flee across the rooftops, pursued by a thwarted Monk, who accidentally falls to his death.

If John Gilbert monopolised his first film with Joan, he failed to do so with this one. Joan's sluttish on-screen behaviour attracted the comment from *Photoplay*: 'For getting down to earth with the practical sort of love-making that folks like, our hat is off to John Gilbert and Joan Crawford. John certainly takes that girl in hand – and boy, how she loves to be taken!' The piece angered the Hays Office – and Garbo, who was by now living with Gilbert. It was, of course, inordinately good for business though, and the other critics were unanimous in their opinions that this was Joan's film. Leading the plaudits was the *New York Evening World*'s usually waspish George Garland:

It isn't often that a supporting player manages to steal a picture right from under the nose of John Gilbert, but that's what happens in *Four Walls*. Miss Crawford simply walks off with it. The picture will go a long way toward lifting Miss Crawford to a point nearer the top in Hollywood circles . . .

CHAPTER THREE

Cinderella and the Prince

'Though theirs was a love-match, it was also Joan Crawford's desperate attempt to better herself.'

Adela Rogers St Johns, journalist-friend

Exactly when Joan became involved with Douglas Fairbanks Jr is not clear. Paul Bern credited himself with introducing them on 27 October 1927, three weeks after the premiere of *Spring Fever*, a meeting he claimed took place backstage at Los Angeles's Vine Street Playhouse after a performance of the play *Young Woodley*, in which Douglas was cast as the lead. Joan herself maintained she had first met the suave, sophisticated young man earlier, in July, but dismissed him as 'pompous'. Douglas adds to the legend by claiming he did not meet Joan at the theatre, but received a congratulatory telegram in the middle of the night ('Your performance was the greatest since Lionel Barrymore in *The Jest*') along with an invitation to have tea with her the next day. He concludes that he kept the appointment, taking her red roses, while she gave him something 'equally beautiful' in return – a signed studio photograph of herself! Joan said that this occasion had led to her falling hopelessly in love with him: several evenings in succession she had sneaked back into the Vine Street Playhouse and watched him from the wings, and in next to no time they had been playing tennis and golf, addressing each other as 'Dodo' and 'Billie', enjoying cosy soirées at the best restaurants in town – and with Joan always picking up the tab. She concludes (in *A Portrait of Joan*) that Douglas proposed marriage two months after they met, and that he bought a *wedding* band which she began wearing at once after he explained that the engagement ring would come later. Whichever version of the story one cares to believe, their engagement would not be officially announced until 8 October 1928.

That this son of Hollywood 'royalty' was an arch snob goes without saying. Therefore one may only wonder whatever it was that he saw in a girl who, though undeniably beautiful and talented, was regarded in the silver-spoon circles he moved in as little more than a hooker. Douglas Fairbanks Jr had been born in New York on 9 December 1909, the son of swashbuckler-par-excellence Douglas Fairbanks (born Douglas Elton Ulman) and Anna Beth Sully, who had divorced in 1918 soon after Fairbanks Sr had hit the Hollywood big-time. Initially, young Douglas had shown no interest in following in his famous father's footsteps, with Fairbanks Sr arrogantly declaring that one legend in the family was sufficient – while at the same time mocking him as 'foppish' on account of the boy's preference for art over the more manly game of baseball.

By the time Fairbanks Sr married 'America's Sweetheart' Mary Pickford in 1920, Douglas and his mother had relocated to Paris, where she proceeded to squander her divorce settlement. In 1922, as part of a publicity campaign to cash in on the Fairbanks name, young Douglas had been called to Hollywood to appear in *Stephen Steps Out*, with Noah Beery. Wholly inexperienced, he had been paid $1,000 a week – more than the rest of the cast added together – but the film had flopped and he had rushed back to Europe with his tail between his legs. His father, declaring him a smudge against the family name, had promptly cut him out of his will. One year later, strapped for cash, Douglas had come home for good, joined a repertory group and begun accepting walk-ons in films – earning himself Fairbanks Sr's enmity because, by 1927, some of the critics not receiving pay-offs from the studio moguls to praise him unduly were saying that he was getting past his heyday, and that maybe the time was ripe for him to hand the reins over to his son. Douglas Fairbanks Jr would eventually succeed as a movie star, but he would never eclipse his father.

Meanwhile, Joan was elevated a few rungs up that all-important Hollywood ladder, courtesy of her portrayal of Dangerous Diana in Harry Beaumont's *Our Dancing Daughters* – pretty innocuous stuff today, though it caused a tremendous furore among the moralists upon its release in October 1928, with the title proclaiming on behalf of Joan's character: 'It's so good just to be *alive*.' She was also championed by F Scott Fitzgerald as 'doubtless the best example of the flapper', though the Hays Office were far from pleased when Fitzgerald publicly declared that flappers were at their best, sexually, between the ages of fifteen and 25. Her co-stars were two important actors of the day, Johnny Mack Brown and Nils Asther. Brown (1904–75), a big hunk who as an all-American half-back had scored the winning touchdown for the University of Alabama in the 1926 Rose Bowl Final, was new to movies but had got off to a good start opposite Garbo in

The Divine Woman and *A Woman of Affairs* (both 1928). Asther (1897–1981) was another Garbo leading man (in *Wild Orchids*); he was a handsome Dane, raised in Sweden and given his big break by his lover and Garbo's mentor, Mauritz Stiller. Joan made a play for both actors, though they were much more interested in each other than they were in her.

The first film to feature Joan Crawford's name *above* the credits opens with a close-up of her shapely legs, dancing lasciviously as she steps into her underwear in front of a mirror. Next we see her doing a frenetic Charleston, whipping off her skirt and dancing in the skimpies she has just pulled on. Diana and her friend Anne (Anita Page) are socialites interested only in partying and picking up wealthy young men, though in Diana's case her recklessness is only pretence so that she can be part of the clique. Both girls are in love with Ben Black (Brown), but while he only wants Diana, he is put off by her flighty ways – whereas Anne's feigned innocence whenever Ben is around is more to his liking. The pair marry, but no sooner is the ring on Anne's finger than she returns to her former sluttish ways and Ben, now aware that Diana also has been putting on an act, realises that he should have wed *her*. When Anne turns up at a flapper party, drunk and clinging to her lover's arm, and accuses Diana of having an affair with Ben, fate decides Ben and Diana's future together: Anne falls to her death down a flight of stairs.

It mattered little that the storyline was trite. With a controversial new, short hairstyle more favoured by chic lesbians than typical flappers, Joan Crawford more than epitomised the jazz baby. She *sizzled*! On the night of the star-studded premiere she received her first standing ovation, so impressing Irving Thalberg (by then married to Norma Shearer) that he invited Joan to join him for supper. In not-so-very-polite terms, she refused.

Rumours circulated that the part of Dangerous Diana had been written especially for Clara Bow – and that to show she had just as much 'It' as the girl with the bee-stung lips, Joan had marched into (uncredited) producer Hunt Stromberg's office, stripped naked, and asked if Clara's 'goods' were as appealing as the ones he was ogling right now. Stromberg is said to have been impressed, but not tempted, adding that in any case he had left the job of casting to Harry Beaumont. Without even bothering to dress, Joan had reportedly walked into Beaumont's office – and half an hour later had been given the part.

Clara Bow enthusiast Bland Johaneson, writing for the *New York Mirror*, had sharpened his quill in anticipation of denouncing Joan for messing up the film – but now reluctantly admitted that he had watched her doing the greatest work of her career to date. 'She gives Clara a lively run around for first honours as a modern flap,' he observed, adding, 'Joan has beauty, charm and more refinement than the trim-legged Bow . . . and she can dance a *mean* varsity drag!' Although no one knew it at the time, Johaneson's observation sounded the death knell for Clara Bow's popularity.

Meanwhile, Joan had to cope with the phenomenally wealthy Douglas Fairbanks Sr and Mary Pickford's public denouncement of her relationship with Douglas Jr – telling all and sundry that Joan was not good enough for him, and that neither of them would ever be welcome at Pickfair, their lavish mansion nicknamed 'The Buckingham Palace of Hollywood'. Pickford had already witnessed first-hand the damage flappers and loose women could do to a man. In 1920 her actor brother, Jack, had married twenty-year-old Ziegfeld girl Olive Thomas. The pair had planned a honeymoon in Paris, but she had set off without him – and had later been found dead in her hotel room after swallowing poison. A subsequent police investigation had revealed that Olive had got on the wrong side of an underground drugs cartel which had been supplying her with heroin for husband Jack's addiction.

Joan's future in-laws were not impressed to learn that she had begun taking elocution lessons, either – though, on Louis B Mayer's advice, more to help her cope with the proposed talking pictures than to please a bunch of snobs. She was also dancing less in the clubs these days, much preferring the tea dances and elite social gatherings that made up her fiancé's calendar. The Fairbanks were particularly aggrieved to read romanticised press stories about the 'teenage sweethearts' – Hollywood still did not know Joan's real age – which likened them to a modern-day Romeo and Juliet, and whose authors were entirely on their side. The couple, they declared, were just as maligned as Shakespeare's tragic lovers, for Joan had concealed few facts about *her* pre-movie years: the way she had been shunted from pillar to post, and the abuse she had suffered at the hands of a cruel stepfather. And privileged or not, the press nurtured an enormous sympathy for the young man who – like the mother he was personally supporting while Fairbanks Sr and Pickford were earning in excess of $20,000 a week between them – had been conveniently cast aside for the second Mrs Fairbanks.

Joan regarded Mary Pickford as a huge joke, as did many of her peers. When Pickford mocked Joan's birth-name, placing emphasis on the sound 'sewer' and declaring that this was where she belonged, Joan politely reminded reporters that 'Lady Pickford' had entered the world as the humble Gladys Smith. Vastly overrated by the late Twenties, though she had once been feted as America's leading screen actress, Pickford was still playing little-girl roles at 36, which Joan thought ludicrous. And the more Pickford refused to allow Joan to visit Pickfair – her stepson, too, she declared, until he saw sense and sent 'the Kansas City hooker' back to the gutter – the more Joan loathed her.

Meanwhile, Joan was rushed through *Dream of Love*, again with Nils Asther. It was a take on the classic play-turned-opera *Adrienne Lecouvreur*, which detractors soon pointed out was almost a reflection of real life: a poor girl (aka Billie Cassin) falls in love with a prince (aka Douglas Fairbanks Jr) and hopefully they live happily ever after – rather than ending up poisoned by a love rival, as happened with the real Lecouvreur.

The film opens with Mauritz de Saxe (Asther), heir to a Middle European country that has been seized by a dictator, whiling away his time by having affairs with the dictator's wife and a comtesse (Aileen Pringle and Carmel Myers) – the former plotting to assassinate her husband and Mauritz's father, so that she and Mauritz can marry and rule together. Mauritz makes this impossible when he falls for Adrienne, a gypsy girl from a travelling circus. Effectively the pair have a one-night stand, but she takes offence when he pays her afterwards, and it is many years before they meet again – by which time Adrienne is a famous actress, Mauritz's father is dead, and Mauritz himself is in the middle of staging a coup to reclaim his throne. This proves successful, and the film ends with him crowned and Adrienne by his side – which is not what happened in history.

Following the runaway success of *Our Dancing Daughters*, *Dream of Love* received a lukewarm reception from the critics (even with former Valentino director Fred Niblo at the helm), and even from Crawford fans – who much preferred to see their idol kicking up her heels and having riotous fun. Much better was *The Duke Steps Out*, with best pal William Haines, whose fans had already heard him speak, as he was the first MGM star to be allowed to take what Irving Thalberg regarded as a career-suicidal risk – in *Alias Jimmy Valentine*. Joan had accompanied him to his sound test. Very nervous, he had mumbled his lines and Louis B Mayer, aware of Haines's sexuality but unaware of his reputation for 'giving the best head in Hollywood', had called him 'lip-lazy' – to which Haines had smugly retorted, causing an uproar on the set, 'I've never had any complaints so far!'

Now the fans got to hear Haines again (though not Joan) as millionaire's son Duke, a semi-professional boxer who encounters student Susie (Joan) in a roadside diner and rescues her from a bunch of thugs. Duke flattens them, and to get closer to Susie enrols at her college, where he soon gets on everyone's nerves, flaunting his wealth and boasting of his fighting skills. No one takes him seriously, and when he loses a fraternity bout, being out of training, he becomes a laughing stock and Susie wants nothing more to do with him. Determined to woo her back he trains in earnest, wins the San Francisco Championship and all ends well.

The film was a big hit. 'Miss Crawford is as gorgeous as ever, and offers a vivid performance,' enthused the *Los Angeles Daily News*. Louis B Mayer, ever worried about his golden boy being outed by the press, hit the roof when he read the thinly disguised attack on Haines's sexuality in *Photoplay*, purporting to be an accolade: 'Another cream puff for the antics of the Metro-Goldwyn playboy Billy Haines.' What Joan's fans really wanted, of course, was to see her playing opposite Douglas Fairbanks Jr and work out for themselves if the chemistry between them was as 'electric' as the movie magazines were saying.

At this stage in her career, Joan did not have an actual fan club, though she was receiving around five hundred letters a week – which she insisted upon answering personally, as opposed to letting them be handled by a studio publicist or secretary (a task that the Pickfair residents regarded as abnormal). Most of the time she sent out signed photographs, but the letters she considered to be sincere sometimes received lengthy responses: many of these fans became friends who Joan trusted and leaned upon for support, far more than any colleagues – or even her husbands. Armed with a clutch of their pleas, Joan approached Louis B Mayer and begged him to find her and Douglas a suitable Garbo-Gilbert-style vehicle.

Mayer's response was that Joan's request presented him with two problems. Firstly, Douglas was contracted to Warners-First National. Secondly, Mayer did not consider him sufficiently important, despite his pedigree and high-profile engagement to one of Metro's biggest stars, to take on a joint-lead. After a great deal of wrangling, however, a compromise was reached. Douglas was hired as a loan-out for third lead, and Mayer brought in Rod La Rocque. The film was *Our Modern Maidens*, and it would be Joan's last silent movie.

After Ramon Novarro, Rod La Rocque (Roderique La Rocque de la Rour, 1896–1969) was Joan's most glamorous (and narcissistic) leading man. Six-foot-three and tipping the scales at 180 pounds, he was incredibly butch; Joan later said that his deep drawl very much reminded her of Rock Hudson, and had given her goose bumps. La Rocque had scored a massive success in *The Ten Commandments* (1923), and an even bigger one in *The Coming of Amos* (1927), later regarded as an inappropriate title for an actor who was sexually interested only in other men. His other 'screamer' titles included *What's Wrong With the Women?* (1922), *Let Us Be Gay* (1930), *The Gay Bandit* (US title *Beau Bandit*, also 1930) and *Hi, Gaucho!* (1935). Despite telling the press that she would always be fiercely loyal to her fiancé, and despite Rod's recent 'twilight-tandem' marriage to vamp Vilma Banky which would happily endure another forty years, Joan made a tremendous effort to seduce 'Big Rod', as he was nicknamed, but she failed to find out for herself if the rumours about his being phenomenally endowed were true. In 1941, tired of the threats of press exposure, La Rocque would turn his back on Hollywood and go into radio and real estate.

Our Modern Maidens was promoted as a sequel to *Our Dancing Daughters*, which it is not: all that it has in common with its more popular predecessor is its theme of Jazz Age flappers and a 'saucy' storyline which Irving Thalberg – like some of the other studio heads, opposed to sound – hoped would lure picturegoers away from the talkies. Joan played Billie Brown, the fun-loving daughter of a motorcar tycoon, who plans to marry childhood sweetheart Gil Jordan (Fairbanks Jr) as soon as his diplomatic promotion comes through. To expedite matters she enlists the help of senior diplomatic Glenn Abbot (La Rocque), and the pair fall in love – while Gil gets drunk and seduces Billie's best friend, Kentucky (Anita Page) and gets her pregnant. Morals, of course, win the day in every film sanctioned by the overtly righteous Louis B Mayer. Glenn is dispatched to a diplomatic post in South America, and though Gil and Billie's wedding goes ahead, she finds out about the child just as they are about to leave on their honeymoon, vows to apply for an annulment, and leaves for the tropics to catch up with her lover. As the film ends we get the impression that *she* is about to propose to him, while Gil and his floozy *appear* to be destined for the altar. In fact, the scriptwriter (*Our Dancing Daughters*'s Josephine Lovett) did add a final scene in which the Crawford-Fairbanks characters *stay* married. Mayer scrapped this, however, preferring to keep the audiences guessing. It was all political, of course. Joan's intended was on loan from *another* studio, therefore it was deemed inappropriate that Douglas Fairbanks Jr should stay 'wed' to a star from Metro, while Rod La Rocque was one of their own!

Hot on the heels of *Our Modern Maidens* came *Hollywood Revue of 1929*, thrown together in a matter of weeks – a corny, plotless mishmash that nevertheless included some of the biggest stars on the recently amalgamated Metro-Goldwyn-Mayer and loan-out roster: Marie Dressler hilariously crooning 'I'm the Queen', Conrad Nagel painfully ripping apart 'You Were Meant For Me', Buster Keaton dancing 'Salome', cameos from William Haines, Laurel and Hardy, Marion Davies, Lionel Barrymore – and the ubiquitous Norma Shearer, who in a ludicrous pairing (she was 29, he 34) played Juliet opposite John Gilbert's Romeo. In one of the film's better moments, Joan is introduced (while standing next to the MC – and at one point, someone clearly shouts from off-camera for her to smile) as, 'The personification of youth, beauty, joy and happiness.' Then, after a clumsy curtsy, she climbs atop the piano and emulates Helen Morgan with a better-than-average rendition of 'I've Got a Feeling For You'. And in the crude Technicolor finale, wearing a yellow mackintosh, she joins Cliff Edwards and the rest of the cast on the stage to help murder 'Singin' in the Rain'.

'If this film doesn't catch on, I am Calvin Coolidge's electric horse,' enthused the *New York News*'s Mark Hellinger. Even so, how such a turkey came to be Oscar-nominated is anybody's guess, though with such a glittering array of talent it is hard to imagine it *not* being a success. Harry

Rapf, however, had refused to include Douglas Fairbanks Jr in the line-up; his father and stepmother, the self-styled King and Queen of Hollywood, had made it very clear that otherwise Douglas and Joan would *never* be welcome at Pickfair. Neither did they approve of Louis B Mayer loaning Joan the $40,000 to buy a ten-room house at 426 North Bristol Avenue, Brentwood Park, and they made quite a splash about it in the press, giving the impression that Joan was the one wearing the trousers in the relationship, while 'poor innocent Doug' was little more than the kept man – 'Crawford's gigolo', according to *Variety*. The final insult to the Fairbanks came when the young couple was also asked to place hand- and footprints in the famous cement outside Grauman's Chinese Theatre – and when word reached Pickfair that Douglas's mother Beth and her actor-fiancé, Jack Whiting, were being involved in their wedding preparations, though like everyone else in the know, they were sworn to secrecy regarding the date and location.

Louis B Mayer had wanted his 'daughter' to be married in a glitzy blaze of Hollywood publicity, as had happened with the Vidors and the Thalbergs, and he was bitterly disappointed to learn, after the ceremony had taken place – on 3 June 1929 at St Malachy's, the actors' Roman Catholic church in New York City – that he had not been invited because Joan had been terrified of his letting the news slip to the Fairbanks and her mother and brother, who she said were the *last* people she wanted to share the happiest day of her life.

There had been a slight hitch at the City Hall when the couple had applied for the licence. Joan had conveniently 'lost' her birth certificate, she told the registrar, though she did have a document in her handbag – a letter from Anna LeSueur – proving that she had been born in 1908, making her *just* 21. Douglas, however, was eighteen months away from *his* 21st birthday, and therefore still legally a minor at the time. To solve this problem, his own mother lied under oath that he had been born in December 1907, and not 1909.

The first Louis B Mayer heard about the wedding was when he received telegrams from the Algonquin Hotel, where the couple were honeymooning. Joan's ended, by way of an apology, 'I HAVE WORKED HARD IN THE PAST – WATCH ME NOW!' The one from Douglas to his studio was more to the point: 'NOW THAT HAVE WIFE TO SUPPORT NEED RAISE IN SALARY.' The 'official' photographs were actually nothing of the kind, having been posed for several days before the wedding at a nearby studio. Douglas looks effeminate in an ill-fitting, light-coloured jacket and creased trousers, while Joan looks slightly perturbed but lovely all the same in a flounced, spotted dress. They declined to give interviews, other than to show off their gifts to one another: the platinum and diamond wristwatch Joan had bought him; the gold lighter and cigarette case he had given her. Then a late-night telephone call from Louis B Mayer persuaded them otherwise and the next morning they gave their first 'exclusive' – not at the Algonquin, but at the more appropriate (from Mayer's point of view) St Moritz Hotel.

'I hate to be interviewed about marriage,' Douglas told *Silver Screen*'s Dora Albert, as though speaking from a lifetime of experience, 'And writers write such mushy, oogly-woogly stuff about Joan and me.' There was certainly no 'oogly-woogly' stuff in this interview – and absolutely no input from Joan, who according to Albert paced up and down the room all the time she was there, looking every inch the screen goddess in her expensive blue serge dress and a pair of floppy mules. And when Albert somewhat grandly asked the groom, 'Are there any rules by which you are going to try to steer the fail craft of marriage through all the shoals that beset it?', the response was a coy, 'If two personalities click, other things can be adjusted if you have intelligence enough. I don't think that married people ought to be conscious of the fact that they are married. They ought to live in sin, so to speak.' When the journalist reminded Douglas that such a statement might well be misinterpreted, he added quickly:

> I *mean* that after marriage it is a very good thing to attempt to keep up the same relationship that existed *before* marriage – to keep right on *courting* your wife. In marriage you ought to live with the constant knowledge before you that if you do not work at marriage, you may lose the one you love . . . the minute you think your marriage is sure, that minute your marriage becomes *insecure*. To keep a marriage from going on the rocks, it is necessary first of all to be honest with yourself, next to preserve the essence of comradeship.

The fact that an apology-of-sorts had been printed immediately after the 'live-in-sin' faux-pas cut no ice with the moralists, who would never regard Joan Crawford as anything but a scarlet woman, and many saw the underaged Douglas Fairbanks Jr as yet one more hapless victim caught up in her spider's web. Others, of course, thought him something of an arrogant fool, particularly the MGM executives who denounced his futile attempt at buffing up his image and yet-to-be-proved star status outside of the Pickfair social gatherings. So far as Louis B Mayer was concerned, the younger Fairbanks would never be more than a B-list actor – and not always a very good one at that. His last few films had been unremarkable to say the least, and it was obvious to everyone at MGM that he *was* only riding on Joan's name, just as he had ridden on his father's – whereas Joan had worked her way up from nothing and now seemed destined for even dizzier heights. During the summer of 1993, when he was in London to promote a volume of memoirs for our mutual publisher, Douglas told me:

Marrying Joan was a big, big mistake. Don't get me wrong, she was a *very* sweet girl, but she was also uncultured and uneducated, except in life, which I certainly was not. I was a naïve young man and she was power-crazy, but I was too besotted with her to notice. Looking back, I can see the marriage was doomed from the start – far too many outside influences. And all the way through it we were both seeing other people. That can't have helped, can it?

Upon her return to Hollywood, Joan called her friend Alma Whitaker of *Photoplay* and told her, 'I want you to come over, dear, and take a look around what I think is the perfect setting for a perpetual honeymoon!' Whitaker, who used these exact words to introduce her lengthy feature, spent a whole afternoon at Brentwood Park, along with her photographer – who snapped Joan in every room, each time wearing a different outfit. She described to her readers how one approached the house via rustic stepping-stones set in velvety lawns, then entered a Spanish patio to summon attention by tapping with a brass knocker fashioned like male and female kissing heads. Once through this hallowed portal, Whitaker added, one crossed the terracotta-tiled hallway and entered the Fairbanks's haven.

Joan was not as superstitious as most of her Hollywood colleagues. Almost every room in the house was done out in 'unlucky' bright green, with gold embellishments. On a low table in the living room was Joan's current reading material: Emil Ludwig's *Life of Napoleon* and Wells's *Outline of History*. The dining room was 'pure Spanish', as was the sun porch, which contained Joan's toy collection. 'Modern, diabolically clever, or irresistibly funny,' Whitaker enthused. 'A life-size hen that cackles and lays an egg! A life-size baby pig that walks and grunts! Rag dogs, rag dolls, gorgeous lady dolls, clowns that sing – and, at the end of the porch, a little table about two-feet high, with four chairs and four funny dolls seated in them – with the table laid for dinner.'

The journalist was surprised to observe that the newlyweds had separate bedrooms: Joan's regally furnished with a canopy bed, antique chairs and dozens of pillows with cases she had embroidered herself; Douglas's 'reeking of lordly comfort', its walls hung with his etchings.

Next, Whitaker was escorted around the gardens with their exotic shrubs and dryad fountains, and introduced to the Fairbanks's collection of pets: the pair of love-birds twittering in the breakfast-room window, a pug called Coquette (after the character in the Mary Pickford film, though Joan had wanted to call the dog Mary because she thought it looked like her mother-in-law), a bulldog called Patrician and a mongrel named Four-Spot. There was Boots, the black Persian cat, which had just had two kittens and, lastly, Douglas's marmoset, which slept in the pantry. The tour was rounded off with an inspection of the bathrooms, kitchen and the innumerable closets where Joan kept her clothes, all immaculately arranged. 'I don't know *how* to be lazy,' she told her guest, 'I never had a servant *before* I went into pictures, so I know how to do everything myself. I *always* have to find something to do.'

In August 1929, a few days after Alma Whitaker's visit – it had been of paramount importance to gain press approval first, and relay this to the fans before throwing the doors open to Hollywood's elite because, from Joan's point of view, the fans were the ones who really mattered – Joan and Douglas held a housewarming party at Brentwood Park and baptised the property El JoDo, the new bride declaring that if her unfriendly in-laws could combine *their* names for their fairytale palace, then so could she. The party ended promptly at 10 p.m., with Joan politely informing her guests that she had to be up at 6.30 the next morning to begin shooting her first talkie, *Untamed*. Her co-star in the film was Robert Montgomery, who is said to have 'serviced' the hostess in one of the upstairs rooms while the party had been in full swing. Montgomery (1904–81) was a rough-edged ex-railway mechanic from New York's Greenwich Village who through Hollywood tuition quickly developed into a suave, sophisticated, but grossly underrated leading man. *Untamed* was only this third venture, and for a little while he would be a regular Crawford co-star – and occasional partner in the bedroom.

Untamed tells the Tarzanesque tale of Bingo, the estranged daughter of an oil tycoon who for some reason has been raised in the Amazonian jungle, hence the title. When her father dies, Bingo is located by her unscrupulous prospector guardians (Holmes Herbert and Ernest Torrence) and brought back to New York, where she is introduced to culture and prepared to take command of the family business. During the sea voyage she falls in love with dashing engineer Andy (Montgomery). Later he proposes marriage, which naturally displeases her guardians, who are after her money for themselves. Similarly, Bingo's hellcat ways – brawling, knocking down any man who opposes her – are tolerated because of her wealth. Andy, though, does not wish to be thought of as a gold-digger, so he sets his sights on another girl. This pushes Bingo too far. She shoots him, fortunately only wounding him in the arm; they make up and marry – and the guardians, no longer jealous, accept that Andy is not going to abscond with Bingo and offer him a job with the company.

Joan Crawford was one of the few big names in Hollywood to successfully make the transition from silents to sound, an era that resulted in even more casualties than through Will Hays's 'Doom Book' and the later McCarthy witch-hunt. In April 1973 she would tell her publicist friend John Springer, 'Everyone panicked at Metro, and I mean everybody – executives, actors, actresses. Starlets didn't know enough, and I was a starlet so I wasn't afraid.' The tropical setting that had rounded off *Our Modern Maidens* was re-created for Joan to croon 'Chant of the Jungle' in *Untamed* – in deep, guttural tones that one critic said made her sound like she had gargled with bleach, and which even Joan herself disapproved of at first. 'I said, "That's not me, that's a man!"' she told Springer. Louis B Mayer, however, was of the same opinion as the *Brooklyn Eagle*, which enthused, '*She* is an actress for whom the microphone should hold *no* fear.'

Jerry Vermilye observed in *The Films of the Twenties* (1985), arguably the finest study of the period to date, that 'It was as if the movie moguls had been mass-ordered to clean their houses of proven silent-screen talent, except for that collection of Broadway-trained actors whose film careers burgeoned as the Twenties waned, and start casting from a clean slate.' The stage recruits included Maurice Chevalier, Fredric March, Barbara Stanwyck, Jeanette MacDonald and the Marx Brothers. Joan's fellow survivors included Myrna Loy, Ronald Colman, Norma Shearer, Dietrich and Garbo, and among those to fall by the wayside were Douglas Fairbanks Sr and (after winning an Oscar for 1929's *Coquette*) Mary Pickford, Lillian Gish, Bebe Daniels, Harold Lloyd and Richard Barthelmess. Most of these were hammy performers whose extraneous gesticulations, in lieu of vocal expression, had got them through mostly melodramatic pot-boilers. Charles Farrell and John Gilbert, good actors who should have gone on for many years, sounded effeminate – but only, it is now known, because studio bosses like Louis B Mayer with axes to grind ordered technicians to tamper with their sound tests. Clara Bow's voice, on the other hand, with its dreadful Bronx nasal twang, did not have to be sabotaged. Lon Chaney *would* have made the transition, had he sadly not died in the middle of it.

Joan had never had to study a script before, and once said that she had never been 'the brightest button in the box'. In January 1968, in a television interview with David Frost, she confessed with an honesty that can only be admired, 'Pictures have given me all the education I ever had, since I never went beyond the Fifth Grade – no formal education whatsoever. And I used to have to read the scripts and look up the words in a dictionary, how to pronounce them and what they meant, before I could learn the lines.'

Untamed premiered on 30 November 1929, in the immediate wake of the Wall Street Crash, which resulted in mass unemployment, soup kitchens, endless queues for basic necessities – and an unprecedented boom at box offices across America, where fans always seemed to find those extra few cents to go to the movies. MGM's profits in the 1929–30 season rocketed to $15 million, a record that would not be beaten until after World War II. *Untamed* did well, though not so well as the *Hollywood Revue* had, and some critics believed that Louis B Mayer had been wrong to show favouritism towards Norma Shearer by offering her and not Joan MGM's first talkie, *The Trial of Mary Dugan* (1929). This was a courtroom drama – an excuse for some studios, with the crude sound techniques of the time, to allow actors to be heard better by shouting rather than speaking their lines properly. The film had proved a big success, and Irving Thalberg now announced a follow-up, *Within the Law* (filmed in 1917 with Alice Joyce, and more successfully in 1923 with Norma Talmadge), in which Shearer would portray, out of character, a woman imprisoned for a crime she did not commit. 'Maybe they should leave Titless in the clink and throw away the key,' Joan told William Haines; 'While ever *she's* around, I'm never going to get good parts!'

The gods must have been listening, for shortly after the film was announced, Norma Shearer discovered that she was pregnant, and the part was offered to Joan. In the meantime, while the script was re-adapted to suit her, she was obliged to press on with the so-so schedule she had been assigned to prior to the film with Robert Montgomery.

Montana Moon again saw her working with Johnny Mack Brown, and there was a sizeable part for fake Valentino heartthrob actor Ricardo Cortez (1899–1977), whom Joan was also aggrieved to learn 'licked the other side of the stamp'. She played yet another wealthy heiress: Joan Prescott, whose father owns the biggest ranch in Montana. Wholly selfish and interested only in the high life, Joan is on her way home from having a wild time in New York when she impulsively gets off the train, intending to catch the train back there for more fun, when a chance encounter with hunky Texan cowboy Larry (Brown) soon makes her change her mind. They fall in love, announce their engagement, and even Joan's grumpy father is happy for them, hoping that the quietly persuasive Larry will tame the wild child.

Naturally, there are complications. At the wedding reception, Joan causes a scandal by doing the tango with local lothario Jeff (Cortez), and when the pair virtually devour each other after the music stops, Larry gives Jeff a thrashing. Joan, deeply ashamed, feels that the only way out of the sticky situation she has created will be for her to go back to New York. She is halfway there when the train is held up by bandits. Their leader captures her and carries her off – it is Larry, in disguise. He has forgiven her and is taking her home!

The critics were cruel for their attacks on a better-than-average film, at a time when producers were still trying to cope with getting as much out of the new sound techniques as possible: in this instance, having Joan burst into song – with the technicians upping the volume – when audiences were least expecting her to. The *New York Times* denounced it as: 'An interminable, amateurish talking picture with spasmodic snatches of melody,' adding perhaps a little too sarcastically, 'Taking it all in, the most pleasing features of this production are Miss Crawford's camel hair coat and her jodhpur riding outfit.'

Much better received was *Our Blushing Brides*, Joan's second pairing with Robert Montgomery, who looks more handsome than ever in what is effectively a shopgirls' reworking of *Sally, Irene and Mary* (one of Joan's 1925 films). Jenny, Frankie and Connie (Joan, Dorothy Sebastian, Anita Page) work in a department store and share an apartment in the dreariest part of town, dreaming most of the time of how the other half live. Of the trio, only Jenny is level-headed enough to know that dreams do not always come true, therefore when the store-owner's son Tony (Montgomery) tries to latch on to her, she sends him packing. Connie has a frivolous affair with Tony's brother, and when he ditches her for someone of his own class, she kills herself. Frankie marries a mobster, gets into trouble with the law, and Jenny gets her off the hook so that she can go back to her mother's place and start over – leaving Jenny, the sole survivor so to speak, to confess to Tony how much she really loves him. And, of course, they marry.

The story was simplicity itself and proved a winner for MGM, for Joan's fans were led to believe that what they had just watched on the screen could just as easily happen to one of them. Indeed, the film set a trend and rapidly made her the heroine of shopgirls everywhere. Hundreds of them wrote to her, and Joan infuriated Douglas by filing the letters and replying to every last one. 'My fans are more important to me than anything in the world, and I mean *everything*,' she told *Photoplay* in January 1930, an admission not appreciated by Douglas Fairbanks Sr and Mary Pickford, who were persistently being asked by reporters *why* Hollywood's hottest young couple had not yet been invited to party at the palace.

The invitation finally came in the March, shortly before *Montana Moon* went on release – not because of media pressure, but because *real* royals Lord and Lady Mountbatten were on an official visit to Hollywood and wanted to meet as many of the major stars as was possible under one roof – the roof in question being that of Pickfair, of course. Garbo was the first to be summoned, by royal courier, and had the Mountbattens known anything about Garbo, it should have been that she did not like to be commanded. 'I don't care if the King of England himself wants to see me,' she is recorded as saying. 'The lady does not want to see *them*!' Joan, too, was all for turning the invitation down, and wanted to ask the Mountbattens to a more intimate supper party at El JoDo. Eventually she submitted to pressure from Douglas, went out and spent $300 on a gown, and for a whole week before the engagement submitted to lessons in 'Pickfair etiquette' from her husband – though the fact that she succumbed to the fickle whims of people who until now had looked upon her with disdain, who were only showing interest in her now to save face, only reveals Douglas's weakness as a husband.

Even so, Joan managed to get one over on her in-laws. Face to face with a glaring Pickford and an unsmiling Fairbanks Sr, she noticed that her shoe-strap had come unfastened (doubtless a pre-arranged 'accident') and, while all eyes were on her, she hitched up her dress so that Douglas Jr could effectively pay homage by going down on one knee to tend to the loose strap. The event was covered by a reporter from *Hollywood Tatler*, who had been briefed over what he might or might nor write about the bash. In the end he pleased himself, though chose to remain anonymous when enthusing, 'What a triumph for Joan! She did it without pretence, by being herself – by proving she wasn't the wild, reckless creature the gossips had painted her.'

Mary Pickford would soon have her say. Having learned from her studio that she *was* too old to be playing little girls, she was desperate not to be thought of as past her best, and the next time Joan visited Pickfair – for there was no question of the press ever learning that the visit honouring the Mountbattens was supposed to have been a one-off – Pickford collared Joan and growled, 'Make *me* a grandmother and I'll kill you!' Henceforth, Joan would be on her guard when hobnobbing with her in-laws. Though she got along with Douglas Fairbanks Sr, thanks to his seeing the funny side about the loose shoe-strap and his own realisation that she really was a nice girl, Mary Pickford would be scathingly addressed as 'ma'am' to her face – and on account of her fondness for dressing in white and wearing tiaras at official engagements, behind her back Joan lampooned her as 'The Virgin Mary'.

Of course, there was no pleasing everyone, and for each reporter who applauded Joan for 'winning over the establishment', there were many who had regarded her as 'one of the guys' before her marriage and now attacked her for becoming 'ritzy' and 'high hat'. Katherine Albert, one of the few journalists she trusted implicitly, penned a defence on behalf of *Photoplay*, but it would take another year (until August 1931) for this to appear in print, for fear of offending the Fairbanks and probably putting herself out of a job. 'Joan was always in a mess,' Albert wrote, citing her affairs with Mike Cudahy, one Jimmy Hall, the boys on the set, the boys she met at parties, and her 'escapades' with close friend Shirley Dorman, of which nothing is known. She concluded:

> Shortly after her wedding, the gossip began, 'Now that she's a member of the Fairbanks family her old friends aren't good enough for her.' Today, Joan Crawford Fairbanks is no more Lucille LeSueur than Will Rogers is Mahatma Gandhi. But Hollywood is intolerant of changes – particularly changes for the better. Joan has become a woman of importance with poise and a clear-thinking mind . . . It is natural that since she is so changed, so much the real

woman, she should find no more time for the superficial friends . . . that her
new acquaintances must be those who can give her something in return for
all her fineness . . . that she should change the harsh middle Western twang
of her voice into a soft cultured one . . . that she should throw out of her life
all the cheapness and tawdriness with which it abounded and take the quiet
culture with which she surrounds herself.

Within the Law, the film that had been commissioned for Norma
Shearer, began shooting in July 1930 under its new title, *Paid* (though the
original title was used for its British release after the censor there deemed that
the word *paid* suggested prostitution). Joan's co-stars were Robert
Armstrong, best remembered for *King Kong* (1933), and Marie Prevost, the
former Mack Sennett Bathing Beauty who would prove a delayed casualty of
the talkies explosion – her Bronx twang came across as even more ear-
splitting than Clara Bow's, and the critics showed her no mercy. Prevost was
already drinking heavily while working on *Paid* and started to pile on the
pounds; a series of crash diets would only make matters worse and result in
near-starvation. When she was found dead in 1937, aged 38, her corpse part-
devoured by her pet Chihuahua, the US coroner's department recorded the
death as the worst case of malnutrition it had ever seen.

Joan proved what an accomplished actress she could be with *Paid*,
directed by Cecil B DeMille alumnus Sam Wood (who later directed the Marx
Brothers), though the plot is contrived and heavy-going at times. Comparing
her with Garbo, Norma Shearer and the handful of true *grandes dames* in
Hollywood at that time, *Variety* concluded, 'Histrionically, she impresses us
and is now about ready to stand up to any sort of dramatic assignment.' She
played shopgirl Mary Turner who, having been imprisoned for a crime she did
not commit, plots her revenge on those who put her there: Gilder (Purnell Pratt)
and District Attorney Demarest (Hale Hamilton). Central to her machinations
are Agnes and Polly (Prevost and Polly Moran respectively), and the three form
a flimsily disguised lesbian clique that continues after they are released. They
decide to set up a swindling operation, aided by Agnes's friend Joe Garson
(Armstrong), which will nevertheless stay 'within the law'. Basically this
involves fleecing wealthy pensioners by getting them to write love letters to the
three young women, then having these fall into the wrong hands so that they
can demand 'heart-balm' compensation. Mary then takes her greed for money
one step further by seducing Gilder's son, Bob (Kent Douglass), and marries
him, after which point the storyline totters on the absurd. The police, eager to
capture Joe Garson, spread the rumour that the *Mona Lisa* has been stolen from
the Louvre and hidden in Bob and Mary's house. Naturally, Joe turns up to filch
the painting, and the police capture him, leaving the newlyweds to live happily
ever after – which they appear to have been doing anyhow.

The film caused concern for Joan's husband, for whereas she was going from strength to strength, the films he was being offered amounted to little more than dross. Douglas's problem seems to have been that, like Norma Shearer, rather than push for better roles he was content to sit back and allow his 'royal position' to work for him – save that being the son of the now-fading elder Fairbanks did not offer the same privileges as being Thalberg's wife. Fairbanks Sr and Mary Pickford's only pairing, *The Taming of the Shrew* released to coincide with press reports that *their* marriage was on the rocks (it would soldier on until 1936), had proved little more than a high-camp exercise in overt gestures and high-pitched, over-delivered lines, and it had bombed at the box office. And because he was nowhere near as successful as she was, Douglas tried his utmost to persuade Joan to stay at home so that *he* could be breadwinner – knocking one more nail into the coffin of their already crumbling marriage. Back in June 1929 he had told *Silver Screen*'s Dora Albert, 'Some couples are happier when the woman devotes all her time to the home. Love, kindness and comradeship can all begin at home.' More problems arose when, attempting to turn the house into a mini-Pickfair, Douglas insisted upon inviting influential, to-be-seen-with friends who Joan could not stand: Constance Bennett, Norma Shearer, Fredric March and his standoffish wife, Florence Eldridge. Joan was so appalled that she removed the kissing-couple knocker from her front door, and changed its name from JoDo to Cielito Lindo – Little Heaven – though once the guests were gone it was anything but inside the place.

Photoplay's Marquis Busby, a forty-something journalist who had bedded more than his share of Hollywood actresses 'in the line of duty', gave Joan's fans hope that her marriage was in no way floundering when he referred to her as 'about the most devoted wife in the State of California'. Five months earlier, the magazine's readers had been invited to write in, nominating which actress *they* would like to see Busby going out on a date with. Heading the list had been Norma Shearer and Gloria Swanson, both of whom had dismissed the idea as preposterous. Tallulah Bankhead had turned Busby down, claiming to have 'been there' already. Joan, the next reserve, had not balked at entertaining the handsome hack at her home – one evening in mid-July when Douglas had been on late call at the studio. 'Her favourite subject is Douglas,' Busby observed ruefully. 'Another man has about as much chance as an Orangeman at a St Patrick's picnic.'

Whether Joan succumbed to Busby's not-inconsiderable charm is not known – they were certainly possessed of the same carnal temperament; neither can we be sure whether the journalist was merely ribbing when he wrote, 'I *did* wait until I heard that Doug was working nights at First National. What's the use of having a date with a married lady if there are husbands about, cluttering things up?' That the conversation seems to have centred around Douglas Fairbanks Jr all evening may, of course, have been Joan's Machiavellian way of trying to hoodwink her fans and other journalists into believing that her marriage *was* rock solid. Similarly, Marquis Busby's boastful, cocky tone might have been a front to cover his tracks if he *had* seduced Joan – based on the premise that fans, colleagues *and* Douglas Fairbanks Jr were suitably naïve enough to believe that the whole idea of a 'humble journalist' hoping to get Joan Crawford into bed could *only* have been wishful thinking.

By the time Busby's 'A Warning to Lotharios' reached the printed page in October 1930, however, it had been brought to Douglas's attention that Joan was amorously involved with the second male lead in *Paid* – Kent Douglass (1907–66), a big blond Canadian in his first film role. Two years later he would revert to his real name, Douglass Montgomery, and not long afterwards score his biggest success with *The Cat and the Canary* (1939). Joan's other Douglas, however, had no reason to reproach her: he was seeing one of the female bit-parts from his most recent film, *Loose Ankles* (1930).

CHAPTER FOUR

Gable

'He represented Man at his most primeval – virile, rough-and-ready with the instincts and passion of a wild beast, absolutely no airs and graces. Gable had more balls than any man I've ever known!'

Joan Crawford

Shortly after finishing *Paid*, Joan began working on *Great Day*, which Louis B Mayer boasted would prove *the* musical revelation of 1931. Directed by Harry Pollard, its co-stars were Johnny Mack Brown and Cliff Edwards, who later provided the voice for Jiminy Cricket in Walt Disney's *Pinocchio* (1940). The score was by Vincent Youmans, with lyrics by Billy Rose and Edward Eliscu. Joan's big production number was Rose's 'More Than You Know', written for his wife Fanny Brice and later revived by Barbra Streisand in *Funny Lady*. Exactly why Mayer pulled the plug after just ten days' shooting is not known. Much of the film had been canned, $300,000 of the $700,000 budget had been used, and there were no reported problems. Mayer was cagey when issuing a press statement, declaring that he had watched the rushes but decided 'they didn't feel right'. Joan said at the time that producer Irving Thalberg had given orders for the project to be aborted because *he* had wanted Norma Shearer to be in it, but by 1983 Joan had changed her story. Putting on a very good Deep South accent she would tell publicist John Springer,

> I went to Louis B Mayer and I said, 'Ah can't kick this stuff around and talk Southern. And ah'm *never* gonna be an ingénue. Ah never was, and ah jess can't talk that kinda dialogue. It stinks! Ah've shot ten days and nobody's told me what the hell ah'm doing!'

The truth probably lies somewhere in between. At the end of 1930 on account of there being a glut of films in this genre, MGM had embarked on a brief 'musicals purge', which cost the studio several million dollars. The major casualties, besides *Great Day*, were *The March of Time*, abandoned near completion because critics who saw the rushes declared it too *bad* to ever be reviewed – and two Marion Davies extravaganzas, *The 5 O'Clock Girl* and *Rosalie*, which would benefit from a costly remake in 1937. It may well be that Joan, having learned that Davies had been requested to be released from *her* films because of their predicted failure, had made the same plea to Louis B Mayer, who just happened to agree with her. Sections of *Great Day* were incorporated into Harry Pollard's *The Prodigal*, released the following year with several of the original actors and with Esther Ralston in the revised Crawford part. It bombed at the box office.

The year 1931 introduced two major career-affecting forces into Joan's life: Gilbert Adrian and Clark Gable. Adrian (Adrian Adolph Greenberg, 1903–59) had been MGM's chief costume designer since 1927. Prior to this he had worked with, among others, Rudolph Valentino on *Cobra* and the abandoned *Hooded Falcon* (both 1925). Outspoken and flagrantly gay, Adrian had risked incurring Joan's wrath by telling her that her hips were on the large side, but that he could counterbalance this by 'widening' her already broad shoulders – two generations before *Dynasty* and *Dallas*, he perfected the 'coat-hanger' look that over the years would become more and more exaggerated, bringing the acid comment from soon-to-be rival Bette Davis, 'These days, Crawford's starting to look more and more like fucking Johnny Weissmuller!'

Adrian, who worked with Garbo in her first talkie, *Anna Christie* (1930), would also draw attention to Joan's large, languid eyes by designing spectacular headgear. In later years he would enter into a 'twilight-tandem' marriage with actress Janet Gaynor, bringing the caustic remark from Joan (who for some reason could not stand her), 'Adrian may be Miss Gaynor's husband, but Mary Martin's always going to be her wife!'

It is an undisputed fact that Clark Gable – like Joan, the uneducated, inarticulate scion of a broken home – was the great love of her life. Born William Clark Gable in Cadiz, Ohio, in February 1901, he was not even good-looking in the Hollywood sense: of Dutch descent, he was gangling, six foot one and loutish, with jug ears, oversized hands that looked like studio props Lon Chaney would don for schlock-horror roles, acute halitosis and decaying teeth. The archetypal drifter, Billie (as he was known at this time) had dropped out of high school and worked as handyman, roustabout, lumberjack and cattle-herder before deciding upon a career on the legitimate stage. In Portland, Ohio, he had met a drama coach named Josephine Dillon, fourteen years his senior, and in a reversal of the casting-couch method had offered his stud-services in exchange for acting and voice lessons. The couple had married in December 1924 and, getting him to drop the 'Billie' in favour of the more artistic-sounding 'Clark', Dillon had put him into summer stock and secured him a bit-part in *Forbidden Paradise* (1924): he appears in an extended locker-room scene with twenty nearly naked men – very homo-erotic for its day – and reveals a pleasantly muscular body, but is uglier than everyone else on display. There were also 'blink-and-miss' walk-ons in never-theless important films of 1925 – including *The Merry Widow* and *Ben-Hur*. Then, disillusioned with movie-making, and favouring the company of set labourers and technicians to that of actors – a trait he would retain until the end of his life – Gable had returned to the stage, and in New York had met and fallen for wealthy, thrice-married Houston socialite, Ria Langham, *seventeen* years his senior.

Dumping Josephine Dillon, who later tried to claim that their marriage had never been consummated, Gable had moved back to Los Angeles with Ria Langham, where he had scored a moderate success on the stage playing a death-row killer in *The Last Mile*. At around this time he had had a fling with actress Pauline Frederick, almost twice his age and who (according to Lyn Tornabene in *Long Live the King*, 1976) had spoiled him rotten with silk shirts and underwear, and paid to have his teeth fixed. Ironically, his reluctance to face a camera again had diminished when, during the run of the play, he had been approached by a talent scout and tempted to play a thug in the *Fighting Blood* picture-serials. Shortly after this, he had signed a $650-a-week short-term contract with MGM, and having proved his worth with a few more bit-parts, Louis B Mayer assigned him his first important character role in *Dance, Fools, Dance*.

The title was supposed to allude to Joan's flapper image, but has nothing to do with the storyline, being set in Chicago in the wake of the 1929 St Valentine's Day Massacre. It is possibly the most unintentionally high-camp of all Joan's films, largely on account of two of its stars – Lester Vail and William Haines's ex-lover William Bakewell – being 'remnants' of the pre-talkies era and for the better part of their time on screen, thinking they are *still* in a silent movie, with their over-the-top gestures and hammy acting. Even Gable looks ridiculous, wearing suits that are too small, the too-short sleeves making his hands appear shovel-like. Added to this, the fake upper-class accents are dreadful, especially every time somebody pronounces the word 'you'. Only the dancing saves the situation, particularly Joan's and Vail's step-by-step emulation of the Argentinian tango danced by Rudolph Valentino and Beatrice Dominguez in *The Four Horsemen of the Apocalypse* (1921).

Bonnie and Roddy Jordan (Joan and Bakewell) lead privileged lives, courtesy of their wealthy father (one William Holden – though not the star of *Sunset Boulevard*), having dropped out of school to devote their time to hedonistic pursuits, such as the party aboard their yacht, the *Bonnie*, which is in full swing when the film opens. Bonnie and her millionaire lover, Bob Townsend (Vail), are dancing, but she is bored with the music until he gets the band to up the tempo for the tango. Afterwards, they and the other bright young things cool off with a midnight dip in the ocean: with not enough costumes to go around, the lights dim and everyone strips to their underwear. 'You little minx – sometimes I'm sorry you're too old to spank,' admonishes Mr Jordan – a line that barely got past the Hays Office censor, though nothing like the trouble caused by 'Mr Vail's flagrant display of under-arm hair', or the ensuing scene in which Bonnie and Bob are in her stateroom the next morning, having obviously spent the night together – or the fact that he has waited until *after* the event before telling her he loves her, only to have her respond that she would rather have love on approval.

The young Jordans extend their outrageous behaviour in their home, acting more like lovers than siblings: Roddy is extremely effeminate, drinks heavily and comes down to breakfast in his pyjamas, while Bonnie smokes at the table and calls her father 'darling'. This idyllic life ends abruptly, however, when Mr Jordan's fortune is wiped out by the Wall Street Crash and he suffers a fatal heart attack. 'Nothing left but my reputation,' Bonnie laments, faced with the prospect of having to work for a living. Bob offers to marry her, but she is too proud to accept charity. Forced to leave the family mansion, she and Roddy share an apartment, and she gets a job with *The Star*, the city's biggest newspaper, as a cub reporter. Initially, Bonnie covers events such as a local poultry show while the other journalists are assigned to the important mobster stories, unaware that Roddy is working as a bootlegger and getaway driver for the most fearsome mobster of all, Jake Luva (Gable).

Roddy is a dithering weakling, but he is invaluable to Luva on account of his former society connections and his ability to poach clients from Luva's greatest rival, O'Lansky. One of these is Bob, who gives every impression that he is just as interested in her 'working goil' brother as he is Bonnie. 'You'll come here again, won't you, Bob?' Roddy pleads, 'I'm living alone here at the club and I'll be glad to see you *any* time!'

When O'Lansky and six of his gang are machine-gunned to death by the Luva mob, Roddy gets sick at the wheel – he had thought he was only going to be involved in a hijacking. When he blabs to *The Star*'s ace reporter, Bert Scranton (Cliff Edwards), believing that he is also one of Luva's men, Roddy is given the task of eliminating him – if Roddy fails, then he too will be killed. The murder takes place, and though the editor of *The Star* knows that Luva is behind the recent spate of deaths and offers a $25,000 reward for information, he needs proof in case no one comes forward. Bonnie therefore welcomes the opportunity to infiltrate the Luva gang, get to know him better – 'Use *any* weapon you've got,' the editor tells her – and nail him.

Bonnie charms the odious Luva into giving her a job dancing the shimmy at his club, where Roddy is also in hiding. She is now ex-gangster's moll Mary Smith, from Missouri, and finds Luva so repulsive that each time he tries to kiss her, she blows smoke into his face or shrinks from his touch. Bob sees them together, almost blows her cover, and only goes away when she says that she is in love with Luva – as the band plays 'Little White Lies'. Then she answers the phone in Luva's apartment, recognises Roddy's voice, and at once knows that he is the killer she is looking for. Roddy goes to pieces when she confronts him, from which point *Dance, Fools, Dance* takes on all the elements of a very bad Keystone Cops denouement.

Luva, having worked out who Mary Smith really is, plans to have her and Roddy executed, but in one of the most ham-fisted shoot-outs captured on celluloid, he and Roddy both die, the young man beautifully in Bonnie's arms as she plants a kiss on his mouth – with Joan at her best, tortured and torn apart, giving an indication of what was to come in Crawford films over the next thirty years. Bonnie could quite easily allow Luva to take the blame for Bert's murder, but instead chooses to play the martyr and grasses on Roddy, so impressing Bob that he asks her to marry him again – not to get her out of a fix, but because he loves her. And as she leaves the newspaper office, we are reminded of the later abdication scene from *Queen Christina* (believed by some to have been loosely modelled on this) as she brushes past the desks and her colleagues touch or call out to her as she passes them for the last time.

Apparently Gable and Crawford were terrified of working with each other – he thinking that she would ridicule him on account of his inexperience; she because, in the wake of the talkies boom, stage actors were generally regarded by the critics as superior to movie stars. Gable's story may well be believed, though with hindsight it is likely that when Joan made the statement, shortly after Gable's death in 1960, she was allowing her grief to play tricks on her memory – and that during the summer of 1930, when she began working on *Dance, Fools, Dance*, she knew little, if anything, about him. This certainly changed, though, once shooting was underway. 'I felt such a sensation, my knees buckled,' she wrote in her memoirs.

Exactly when Joan became sexually involved with Gable is not known, though it seems likely that they bumped into each other at the party following their film's March 1931 premiere. Ria Langham was fond of showing off her seemingly macho toy-boy, who thought nothing of excusing himself and heading for the shrubbery with whoever might have taken his

fancy, female or male. William Haines – who with Rod La Rocque, and later
Rock Hudson, disproved Hollywood's misconstrued notion that gay meant
effete – was bigger and more muscular than Gable, and equally butch. More
importantly, he did not feel the need to hide his sexuality under a cloak of
intense homophobia. There had been a time when Haines had regarded
Gable as his ideal 'bit of rough', in contrast with his long-term lover Jimmy
Shields, who knew nothing of Haines's 'extra-marital' affairs, conducted
when their careers separated them sometimes for weeks on end.

Haines told Joan (quoted in Jane Ellen Wayne's *Golden Girls of MGM*)
that he remembered Gable 'hanging around' (in other words, cruising for
sex) on the set of *The Pacemakers* in 1924 when working as an extra, and he
is further quoted as telling her how Gable would have done absolutely
anything to get money or employment, adding, 'Cranberry, I fucked him in
the men's room at the Beverly Wilshire Hotel. He was that desperate. He was
a nice guy, but not a fruitcake.' In the not too-distant-future, as will be seen,
this incident would have far-reaching, almost disastrous consequences.

Another conquest appears to have been Ben Maddox, an influential,
bisexual reporter with *Screenland*, who would later have flings with Tyrone
Power, Errol Flynn and Robert Taylor. Gable is believed to have 'loaned his
meaty charms' to Maddox in exchange for a high-profile interview and
public-relations exercise that resulted in Gable's salary being upped to
$2,000 a week, still much less than the likes of John Gilbert and some other
talkies casualties were getting, despite their declining status. Likening
Gable's appeal to the Valentino boom of yesteryear, Maddox observed:

> This he-man with dimples, this gangster who went heroic by human
> demand, this most desired of all current screen lovers – where does he
> go from here? Can it be true that fame is splitting up his second marriage?
> Nine out of ten great stars let Hollywood spoil their home life. Clark Gable
> won't, so here's the marriage we can depend on . . . Clark is married to
> a cultured, charming woman who has the knack of completely satisfying
> him in every way. Will *he* last? I think so. He isn't temperamental and high-
> strung like John Gilbert, not sheikish like Valentino. He has a depth and
> virility that the juveniles lack.

William Haines's fondness for relaying to Joan the most intimate details
of his sex life must at least have made her curious enough to find out for
herself if Gable really was the 'one hot suck' Haines had described. And
anyone who had 'socked' Norma Shearer, even if it had only been on the
screen (in *A Free Soul*, 1931) simply *had* to be admired! Gable was, of course,
the archetypal repressed bisexual, the hallmarks of which were clearly evident
in his early years. Firstly (as would be the case with the husbands of Judy

Garland, Edith Piaf and several others), he had married a much older woman, and would do so again; moreover, his relationship with Pauline Frederick had been similarly more filial than amorous. Throughout his life, like Cary Grant and Rock Hudson, he would overplay the machismo and conceal a feminine side that would have made him a great actor instead of an inordinately good one – the result of being raised by a bigoted father who had persistently drummed it into him that all actors were 'sissies'. And, of course, he became passionately involved with three of the twentieth century's acknowledged 'fag-hags' – Crawford, Carole Lombard and Marilyn Monroe.

Courtesy of William Haines, still one of the biggest names in the movies, Gable successfully tested for a small part in *The Secret Six* (1931), starring Wallace Beery, and a screen executives convention was so bowled over by the rushes that all of a sudden Clark Gable was the actor everyone wanted. Over the next few months he would appear in *Hell Divers* (1932) with Marie Prevost, and more importantly opposite Garbo in *Susan Lenox, Her Fall and Rise* (1931). But before these came another – many thought quite unnecessary – film with Joan.

Joan had already begun working on *Complete Surrender* with Johnny Mack Brown, her co-star from *Our Dancing Daughters*. Media visitors to the set predicted that with Brown's contribution, this would prove Joan's biggest success ever, and elevate Brown to major star status. His rich, resonant voice translated well to sound, and his screen presence could not have been more impressive. However, as usual, Louis B Mayer only saw the dollar signs flashing before his eyes, and shooting was near completion when he inexcusably fired Brown from the production, replaced him with Gable, gave instructions for the whole film to be shot again from scratch and changed the title to the more controversial *Laughing Sinners*.

Of their eight films together, *Laughing Sinners* is Joan and Gable's least effective collaboration. Mayer had originally hired Gable to portray the heavy, telling him to his face that he was no matinee idol in the looks department. Sidekick Irving Thalberg, however, did not agree. Whereas thousands of women – and more than a few men – across America had dreamed of swapping places with Agnes Ayres to be snatched, spirited away and ravaged by Valentino as the gorgeous savage in *The Sheik*, Thalberg held the opinion that there were just as many women who preferred their lovers caveman-rough-and-ready, inasmuch as there were a lot of men who liked their ladies brassy and sluttish like the up-and-coming Jean Harlow. The Boy Wonder was right (though not so long before, he had regarded Johnny Mack Brown as the new Valentino, and had been instrumental in his playing the lead in King Vidor's *Billy the Kid*, 1930), but he was making a huge mistake in casting the handsome but aggressive-mannered Gable in the role of a saintly

Salvation Army captain. It was a role that Brown would have played more convincingly, and without attracting fierce criticism from the Hays Office – though so did Joan, courtesy of the scene in which she is seen standing on a table banging her tambourine and wearing her infamous 'Fuck-Me' ankle-strap shoes, which remind onlookers of what she used to be.

Joan played Ivy Stevens, a small-town café chanteuse who, when dumped by her lover, Howard (Neil Hamilton), tries to jump off a bridge into the river. She is saved by Carl (Gable), who immediately sets out to transform this rough diamond into a worthy, God-fearing citizen. Under his Svengali-like influence she dons the Army uniform, preaches from street corners and is *almost* reformed when she bumps into Howard in a seedy boarding house. They are about to make love when Carl barges in, and – in very un-Salvation-Army-like style – gives Howard one under the chin, pronounces a few words from the Bible, forgives Ivy her sins, and returns the situation to how it was between them.

Today, one wonders what all the fuss was about and whether it was worth going way over budget to re-shoot Johnny Mack Brown's scenes with an actor who, certainly for this type of film, was artistically inferior. Brown's *Billy the Kid* went on general release at around the same time as *Laughing Sinners*. It was a smash hit at the box office, whereas the Crawford-Gable fiasco barely recovered its costs. As for Brown, henceforth there would be few good parts. Louis B Mayer's greed, just as his spite had brought about John Gilbert's decline, had seen to that.

Immediately after completing *Laughing Sinners*, Joan was offered the role of Marian Martin in *Possessed*, and asked for Gable as her co-star. The request was granted, but while the studio awaited a gap in Gable's unprecedented busy schedule, she replaced Clara Bow – denounced by Louis B Mayer as 'getting to be all washed-out at 25' – in *This Modern Age*. The 'It' girl would appear in just two more films before opting out of the Hollywood scene, and in August 1931 a studio-financed feature headed 'What Now, Clara?' would be published in *Photoplay* as a warning to others, like Bow, who had paid the supreme price for looking down their noses at the fans, 'When big stars go down the chute, there's just one answer – namely, they have ceased to lure enough kopeks into the little ticket window. And that is the answer to Clara Bow's swift slide down the well-greased toboggan.'

Joan's co-star in *This Modern Age* was Pauline Frederick, the woman who had reputedly taught Clark Gable the staying-power for which he was renowned. The screenplay was adapted from Mildred Cram's story *Girls Together* – something of a misnomer, because it was not 'just another bari-tone babes movie' as the wags had predicted. Joan played Valentine Winters, whose wealthy parents had divorced when she was a child, after which she had been cared for by her father. The decent life stops, however, so far as the Hays Office was concerned, once Valentine travels to Paris to be reunited with her mother, Diane (Frederick). Diane is the 'kept woman' of an aristocrat, André de Graignon (Albert Conti), and Valentine herself soon becomes involved with the philandering Tony (the foppish Monroe Owsley, unconvincingly playing against character). When she and her speed-freak lover crash his car in the middle of nowhere, they are aided by vacationing college jock Bob (Neil Hamilton). Pretty soon, Valentine loses interest in Tony and marriage with Bob is on the cards. His parents, however, are disapproving and there are histrionics all around when they learn, courtesy of the jealous Tony, that the bride-to-be's mother is living in sin with a man – until Diane elects to be virtuous at last (some might think a little late in the day) by ending her relationship with de Graignon.

Joan had tremendous admiration for Pauline Frederick (1883–1938), a five-times-wed Broadway legend (almost the American equivalent of the French actress Sarah Bernhardt) who was extremely fussy in her choice of film roles and these days working less on account of failing health. All of Frederick's husbands had been bisexual or gay – the most celebrated being the actor-playwright Willard Mack. Similarly, her discreet extramarital conquests were thuggish types such as Clark Gable, or strong-willed women like Joan, Lilyan Tashman and Jeanne Eagels. For several weeks, Frederick provided Joan with a shoulder to lean upon and a sympathetic ear. Joan was already regretting her marriage to Douglas Fairbanks Jr on account of extracurricular activities that in this instance meant long, boring nights at home, or seemingly interminable weekends at Pickfair, where she was persistently terrified of slipping up in front of her snobbish in-laws. She was also desperate to take her affair with Clark Gable 'to the limit' – in other words, go public and be damned, as Pauline Frederick had in *This Modern Age*. An unsigned reporter from *Photoplay*, visiting Brentwood Park in May 1931, saw through the charade. 'Her dream life had failed,' he observed, 'She was still fond of Dodo, still the loyal wife. But her heart was empty. And to Joan, an empty heart meant she must seek a new tenant.'

Her relationship with Gable progressed in leaps and bounds while they were shooting *Possessed*. Douglas Fairbanks Jr knew she was cheating on him with *someone* and for the first time began paying attention to her when she came home from the studio, putting into practice the 'after-marriage courting' he had spoken of in his honeymoon interview with Dora Albert. They were observed at the Cocoanut Grove by Adela Rogers St Johns, sitting at opposite ends of the room to Gable and his 'mother-wife', Ria Langham – but also 'necking behind the bandstand', though St Johns decided not to include this little snippet in her column.

Possessed is a corker of a film, the best Joan had made so far – largely because much of the scenario resembles her own story, and was readily accepted by fans who were non-judgemental because *she* had never been less than honest with them from the outset. It was also so 'torrid' in parts that it had the Hays Office in a spin, as had happened recently when Garbo had played an all-out whore (in 1931's *Susan Lenox: Her Fall and Rise*) opposite Gable. The film was directed by Clarence Brown, Garbo's favourite helmsman (seven productions in all), who had come to the fore in 1925 as the force behind Valentino's *The Eagle*, following this up with *Flesh and the Devil* (1927).

Marian Martin works in a cardboard-box factory in a hick town where nothing ever happens. She has a sweetheart of sorts, labourer Al Manning (Wallace Ford), but finds his attentions boring because they are so predictable: marriage, dreams of running his own business and of one day signing the big contract that will make him rich. Until then, he says, they will have to make do with what they have. Marian scoffs at this: 'Buying happiness on the instalments plan, and some day a fella comes and takes it all away.' She does not know *exactly* what she wants, only that she will never find it here. 'All I've got's my looks and my youth and whatever it is about me the fellas like,' she declares. 'Do you think I'm gonna trade that in for a chance that'll never come? I *do* like you, but it just isn't good enough.'

Marian leaves Al thinking, and on her way home is held up at the railway crossing when the train for New York pulls in. Through the carriage windows she observes how the other half live, and gets talking to drunken toff Wally (Skeets Gallagher), who offers her her first taste of champagne. When she tells him of her aspirations and where she works, he gives her his card, tells her to look him up if ever she is in New York, and cracks, 'Nothing like *you* ever came out of a paper box!'

Marian arrives home. Her mother (Clara Bandick) has invited Al for dinner and both are shocked to find her tipsy – and to see her laughing, apparently for the first time because until now she has had little to laugh at. When Al rebukes her, she points at the vegetables Mama is about to prepare and calls him 'turnip' – an appellation that went straight over the heads of Thirties cinema audiences, but which was Hollywood slang for a man with minute genitals. Marian argues that her life is hers to mess up as she chooses, and when we next see her she is standing outside Wally's plush Park Avenue apartment.

Wally is surprised to find Marian in a city where she has no connections and nowhere to stay, but neither does he feel obliged to take her in, or qualified to advise her what to do. 'The East River is full of girls who took advice from men like me,' he says. Then he changes his mind and asks her to sit in the light so that he can examine her features – not in front of the window but under a lamp, the kind of light *she* will end up working under (i.e. as a prostitute), suggesting that she might therefore be better off latching on to a rich man and allowing nature to take its course.

Marian leaves, and out in the corridor sees two of Wally's smartly dressed friends arriving. Eavesdropping, she learns that one of these is Mark Whitney (Gable), a wealthy society lawyer with political ambition. They meet, and it is love at first sight. He tells her that he is *very* rich, and she pulls no punches by responding, 'That's nice. You see, I wouldn't waste my time with you if you weren't!'

Three years pass. Marian is Mark's mistress, he is in politics, and for the benefit of the folks back home, and to avoid a political scandal, she has a new identity: Mrs Moreland, a respectable widow who Mark wants to wed but dares not because he has already had one ex-wife take him to the cleaners. Mistresses are dispensable, should they get in the way of one's career – as he tells a friend, 'Losing a sweetheart is a private misfortune. Losing a wife is a public scandal.'

In the ensuing scene the couple are about to leave for a dinner engagement, and Marian is putting on the jewellery Mark has bought her for their anniversaries – each one spent in a different European city. The last item to go on is the 'wedding ring' bought by the fictitious Moreland. Mark asks her if she has any regrets, and the reply reminds one of Crawford's afore-mentioned British television interview: 'I left school when I was only twelve – never learned how to spell *regret*.' He kisses her passionately, and her mink hits the floor as the bedroom beckons, making them late for their appointment. At the party she plays the piano and sings with belated sophistication, delivering a stunning three-language version of 'How Long Will This Last?' – no less potent and heartfelt than a Libby Holman or a Zarah Leander, causing one rough-diamond female guest to bark, 'What is this, Ellis Island?'

More of The Joan Crawford Story is woven into the plot when Marian realises how she has erred by letting her heart rule her head, for she has broken her own rule that a woman can get anywhere with a man so long as he never falls in love. Then Al turns up out of the blue, now a successful businessman on the verge of signing the big deal he spoke of the day Marian finished with him. She also learns that she is wealthy in her own right: the weekly allowance she has been sending her mother has been turned over to Al and shrewdly invested. Al is at Marian's apartment when Mark shows up – for Al's benefit demoted to a mere acquaintance, but from his point of view an important political ally to have on his side if he is hoping to land his contract. Mark agrees to help, but is distressed to learn that Al needs money only so that *he*

can marry Marian and keep her in the style she has become accustomed to.
Their relationship edges several steps closer to disaster when Marian overhears
a conversation between Mark and his friends. He is now standing for
Governor, and must choose between his lover and his public duties. 'What's a
woman, compared to a career?' one asks – while another levels, 'It's a sad thing
to see you give up a brilliant future for a woman like *that*!'

Mark is foolish and arrogant enough to believe that he can have both,
and asks Marian to marry him. Naturally she turns him down, declaring that
his pretty speeches have come too late – she has *never* loved him, and she is
going to marry Al. And much of what ensues refers directly to Joan's
floundering marriage to Douglas Fairbanks Jr due to class difference:

> MARK: I don't believe it. No woman could have pretended to love a man
> as you've loved me.
> MARIAN: Oh yes, she could, if that was the way she earned her living.
> Even if I do say it myself, I think I've made a pretty good job of it. Now that
> I've got my little pile tucked away I'm ready to sit back, take off my shoes
> and relax. It's been a strain [flicks cigarette ash on to the floor] being a lady!
> MARK: You can't mean what you're saying? It's unbelievable . . .
> MARIAN: Unbelievable? Because after three years of your priceless care
> and guidance I'm walking out on you? Because you taught me how to
> wear a Paris gown, how to eat ice-cream with a fork, how to talk to
> servants, how to order food and wine? . . . Well, all the schooling you've
> hammered into me, all the clothes and perfume you've put on me, all the
> jewellery you've hung on me didn't change me. Inside, I'm exactly what I
> was when you found me – a factory girl, smelling of sweat and glue.
> Common! That's what I am – common! And I like it! That's what I like
> about Al. He's my own kind. That's the level I belong to, and that's the
> level I'm going back to!

All across America, Joan's shopgirl fans applauded. Most had read the
tabloids and recognised the comparisons being made, and booed the cad
whose next response was to slap her and call her 'little tramp', for muttering
as she handed back the fake wedding ring, 'Might have given me two weeks'
notice – even my cook does that!'

In the first example of Crawford suffering in diamonds and splendour,
superbly gowned by Adrian and setting a valuable precedent, Marian holds
herself together until she gets outside Mark's apartment, then goes to pieces.
She seeks solace in Al, and on the rebound becomes engaged to him. He,
however, has grown too cocky and preoccupied with making money – with
Mark Whitney as Governor, he will build a highway from here to China.
Marian therefore feels that she has no option but to tell him the truth – that
she is not a widow, but a kept woman. He reacts by telling her he does not

want second-hand goods, a woman no better than a streetwalker – then takes it all back, realising that he must have her support to sweet-talk Mark into securing him his contract. Marian throws him out, and the scene shifts to the electoral campaign, where Mark's opponents plan on exposing the scandal to discredit him.

The theme of the meeting includes Mark's plans for prison reform, and he counteracts a heckler by pronouncing, 'I believe that no man's or woman's past should be held against them.' Marian is in the audience when it is showered with leaflets wanting to know, 'Who is Mrs Moreland?' Mark is rendered speechless, so it is left to her to defend them both: she tells the throng that she *was* his mistress, that it is over, and that he now belongs to them – that he has no right to be judged by a handful of hypocrites when his only crime was loving a woman. And for a second time she leaves in floods of tears, rushing out into the pouring rain, where Mark catches up with her. 'I don't care what they do to me back there,' he says, enveloping her in his arms and, for the first time in his life, getting his priorities right. 'If I win it'll be with you, and if I lose it'll be with you!' Magnificent stuff!

The love scenes in *Possessed* were 'hot' for their day, and the critics compared the on-screen chemistry between Crawford and Gable with that of Garbo and Gilbert in *Flesh and the Devil*. Some drew their own conclusion that, as with the latter pair (now reported to have split up for good), matters between Joan and Gable would be no different away from the set. They were not wrong, as Joan later observed in her memoirs:

> I knew that I was falling into a trap that I warned young girls about – not to fall in love with leading men or take romantic scenes seriously. Leave the set and forget about it because that marvellous feeling would pass. Boy, I had to eat those words, but they tasted very sweet.

Joan would be shockingly forthright (for 1968, and bleeped at the time) when speaking to David Frost, declaring that no sane woman would have been capable of resisting Gable. When asked by Frost what Gable's special attraction had been, she looked him in the eye and replied, not for the first time in an interview, 'Balls – he had them.'

While working on *Possessed*, the pair had conducted their affair discreetly in hotel rooms, but on occasion they had cast caution to the winds by sneaking into Gable's trailer, or the cottage Joan was renting on Malibu Beach. She, who had not been overly fastidious with personal hygiene (she arrived in Hollywood with crabs!), found herself driven crazy by her lover's obsession with cleanliness. Gable *never* took baths because, he declared, this would mean sitting in water he had contaminated. Instead, he showered several times every day, shaved not just his chest but his armpits and pubic region too, and drenched himself in costly cologne. Joan was to likewise develop a mania for insisting upon her surroundings being absolutely spot-less – even going to the extreme of scrubbing the bathrooms and toilets of hotels she stayed in, no matter how exclusive these might be.

It was at around this time that Douglas Fairbanks Jr threatened to have Joan followed by a private detective, anxious that if they did divorce, she would be seen as the guilty party though he too was cheating on her. Joan dared him to so much as try. In November 1931 she gave an interview for *Photoplay*, comparing herself with Marian Martin/Moreland when it came to getting exactly what she wanted out of life:

> I had to attract attention any way I could in the beginning, and continue doing so until I got better parts. Also I learned to know men pretty thoroughly, and very few of them kept my confidence. I reached out eagerly to believe and confide in all my various Hollywood acquaintances, with the usual results. Yes, I learned a lot about men. But if a woman knows nothing about men, how in heaven's name can she consider herself capable of judging for herself and choosing the *one* man she can trust implicitly, the man that could satisfy the many vagaries of a woman's heart and soul?

The interviewer, and the fans, knew that with this last statement Joan was *not* referring to her husband, and the rumours about her and Gable reached Louis B Mayer, who came down on the lovers like a ton of bricks. Joan was about to be offered the biggest role in her career in so far – as Flaemmchen in *Grand Hotel* – and she was told to choose between Gable and the film. When she plumped for Gable, the ultimatum was Gable or her *career*. Gable then told The Messiah that he would divorce his wife and marry Joan, to which Mayer replied that if he did continue seeing 'the washerwoman's tramp daughter', he would dispatch a memo to the other studios that would ensure neither of them *ever* worked again.

For the sake of MGM, Joan and Gable agreed to cool things. Of course this did not prevent them from seeing each other, and going to inordinate lengths to evade Mayer's spies and the press – indeed, successfully pulling the wool over everyone's eyes for another 28 years.

CHAPTER FIVE

The Stenographer and Sadie

'*Little Joan was called upon to match Garbo, Wallace Beery and the Barrymores and she came off smelling like a rose.*'

Joan Crawford (to Roy Newquist)

Viennese-born Vicki Baum (1888–1960) had published several novels and short stories, but it was *Grand Hotel* that made her a household name. Irving Thalberg had purchased the rights to *Menschen in Hotel* in 1930 for $13,500 and paid to have it translated and adapted into a play, which he had 'tested out' on Broadway before giving the go-ahead for the film. The budget was a staggering $700,000, though the takings during its first box-office season would more than quadruple this.

Like the later *Gone With the Wind* (1939), everyone wanted to be involved in the battle of over sized egos once photographs were released depicting Garbo as she would look in the guise of fading ballerina Grusinskaya. Marlene Dietrich, Tallulah Bankhead, Mae West and Marie Dressler offered their services for free just to play character parts. Douglas Fairbanks Jr and Clark Gable audaciously asked Louis B Mayer for the second lead: Baron von Gaigern. Neither would have been suitable, but fortunately this role had already been assigned to John Barrymore in what is generally regarded as the finest role of his career.

Barrymore (1882–1942), the youngest member of Hollywood's *true* acting royal family, was a tremendous presence revered by colleagues and critics alike as The Great Profile, and at the time was married to Joan's friend Dolores Costello. When Buster Keaton dropped out of the production, Barrymore's brother Lionel (1878–1954) was brought in to play doomed clerk Otto Klingelein. He had just worked with Garbo in *Mata*

Hari (1931), and later that year would win an Oscar for *A Free Soul*. Completing the distinguished line-up were Wallace Beery, a recent Oscar recipient for his portrayal of a has-been boxer in *The Champ* (1931); Lewis Stone, another Garbo stalwart, who would later play Judge Hardy in the famous *Andy Hardy* series; and Danish actor Jean Hersholt. Italian character actress Rafaela Ottiano played Grusinskaya's fussy, birdlike maid, the studio's second choice after Pauline Frederick, who was too ill to take on the commitment.

Irving Thalberg had gathered together the most scintillating cast ever seen in a Hollywood film, one that today would prove impossible to finance even if there were comparable talent around. 'A galaxy of stars that have just made the Milky Way sit up and keel over,' was how *Motion Picture Herald*'s de Casseres put it. Garbo and Barrymore were the world's greatest actress and actor when the film was made – and have yet to be surpassed, for quite honestly they could act every one of today's so-called superstars off the screen.

Garbo had been following Joan's career closely. Culturally, they were worlds apart, but she was suspicious that Joan might attempt to steal every scene, as had happened with Gable in *Possessed*. So far as director Edmund Goulding was concerned, they were *almost* equal, and this was reflected in their salaries: Garbo was being paid $68,000, Joan $60,000 (which was even more than John Barrymore). Because she detested *any* kind of competition, but most especially from other actresses, Garbo told Louis B Mayer that she would not be doing any scenes with Joan and risk having her steal the picture from under her nose – 'Otherwise, Mr Mayer, I go back to Sweden!' She also avoided bumping into Joan by imposing a self-curfew which meant that Joan was not allowed on the set until Garbo had left at 5 p.m. – though she frequently hung around in her dressing room for an hour or so after this. Joan was specifically instructed not to pass Garbo's 'cocoon', but to walk the long way round to the set. She would, however, not hear of this. 'I just wanted to say hello to Garbo and curtsy,' she later told John Springer. She therefore walked past Garbo's dressing-room each evening, and called out a greeting, but was always ignored. Then one evening – the first time she did not call out – Garbo emerged and caught up with her. Joan told Springer,

> I was on the top step, she was two steps below me and I didn't know what to do. I said, 'Excuse me, Miss Garbo!' And she took my face in her hands and she said, 'Oh, I am so *sorry* we have no scenes together.' And I looked at this beautiful face with the sun [coming through the window] in the West, and she was the most beautiful thing I have ever seen in my life.

What astonished Joan all the more was the fact that Garbo had confided in a friend just how beautiful she thought *Joan* was. Later, Joan would be unabashed enough to write in her memoirs, 'My knees went weak. She was breathtaking. If ever I thought of becoming a lesbian, that was it.' In fact, Joan had already had at least two same-sex affairs, with Katherine Emerine and Pauline Frederick, and there would be several more. Garbo, however, would not become a notch on the Crawford bedpost.

Beautifully photographed by William Daniels – almost Garbo's personal cameraman (he was with her for twelve films) – *Grand Hotel* (1932) represents a series of cleverly linked vignettes spanning a 48-hour period in the lives of a set of frequently odd-bod characters at an exclusive establishment in Weimar Berlin. There is the porter (Hersholt), who worries about his pregnant wife; Kringelein, who has worked his fingers to the bone and, having only a short time to live, has invested his life-savings so that he might die here in unabashed luxury; the textiles magnate Preyshing (Beery), Kringelein's odious boss who cares for no one but himself and the deal he hopes to clinch with an English company, which will save him from the receiver; Flaemmchen (Joan), a stenographer; and the Baron, a professional gambler who is at the hotel to thieve from the wealthy patrons to pay off his debts. There is Grusinskaya, the beautiful but highly strung Russian dancer whose performances are beginning to suffer because she is homesick and mourning her dead lover, the Grand Duke Sergei – a woeful error on the scriptwriter's part, for he had been assassinated 26 years before the story begins! And finally there is the surly, facially disfigured doctor (Stone), the hotel's long-term resident and a real Job's comforter who seems to glean little pleasure from life. 'Grand Hotel,' he drawls. 'People coming, people going. Nothing ever happens!'

In the opening scenes we see the Baron befriending Kringelein, almost a copy of Kafka's K, who has seen nothing but friendless, loveless misery in his whole life. The Baron's creed is basically to burn one's candle at both ends – which, of course, was John Barrymore's own personal philosophy. Flaemmchen's is to achieve success and material possessions by way of being an easy lay – again, an actress-character amalgamation. And Preyshing, the middle-aged lecher who is more interested in staring at his stenographer's legs and touching her up than he is in dictating notes, *is* Wallace Beery playing himself. Next we see Grusinskaya, with Garbo making the most unremarkable entrance of her career, yet still stealing the show as she awakens after a drug-induced slumber. She looks totally *unlike* a ballerina – far too tall, and clod-footed as she strides across the room like an elephant, but who cares when the magic is so potent? Tonight's performance is imminent, but she has no intention of dancing again to a half-empty hall and

glacial silence. Her maid and manager get her to change her mind by
fabricating a story that the show is a sell-out with a wealth of attending
crowned heads, and so she leaves for the theatre.

The Baron, meanwhile, has been flirting on the balcony with
Flaemmchen, who mistakenly assumes that he will be a wealthy catch. She
tells him she is a stenographer, but this man of the world knows what she
really is and poses the question, 'I don't suppose you'd take some dictation
from *me*, some time?' She says that she also has to work at her other
profession because she is so poor, adding, 'Did you ever see a stenographer
with a decent frock on – one she'd bought *herself*?' The Baron wants to take
her dancing that night, but cannot because he will be otherwise engaged –
stealing Grusinskaya's priceless pearls – so they decide upon the next day's
afternoon tea dance.

Flaemmchen returns to her duties, telling temporary employer Preyshing
of her aspirations – the movies, perhaps. She has already posed for 'art
studies' and just happens to have a copy of the magazine handy to show him.
She has also travelled around Europe, each trip tagging onto a different man,
and so does not mind that this one is vile, and old enough to be her father.

Cut to *Grand Hotel*'s most famous scene: Grusinskaya's room, to
which the tetchy star has returned, still wearing her tutu, having fled the
theatre after discovering that her entourage's claims that all the seats had
been sold were lies. She changes, pausing to kiss her shoes, while the Baron
watches from the shadows. Naturally she is startled when he reveals himself
– the last man she caught in her room was honour-bound to choose suicide
over shame, something she had been about to do when the Baron surprised
her. '*I want to be alone!*' she drones, Garbo's trademark line, which she
utters twice more before he talks her out of it, for like Kringelein she is
desperately starved of affection and wears her heart on her sleeve. The pair
fall in love, she nicknames him 'Flix', and he spends the night with her –
talking, we are led to believe.

The next morning, the Baron admits what he has done and returns the
stolen pearls. At first she wants him to leave. Then she realises that she has
always hated the pearls – they have only brought her bad luck – and decides
that he may have them. What she *really* wants is him, the man who has
unexpectedly made her life worth living again, the man who makes her want
to dance *and* sing! Tomorrow she is leaving for Vienna, and of course he
must go with her!

The Baron promises to meet Grusinskaya on the train, then leaves for
the tea dance, where he joins Flaemmchen and Kringelein. The two men take
it in turns to whirl around the floor with her, even though Kringelein has
never danced in public before – but the pleasant interlude is interrupted by

Preyshing. His business deal has fallen through and he needs his steno-grapher to take notes while he is duping another group of magnates into saving his skin. For the first time, Kringelein stands up to the man who has made his life so unhappy – for years he has worked as Preyshing's book-keeper, and knows he is a swindler. When the Baron saves him from attack, Kringelein offers him all his money, which he refuses, though he does agree to join in with a card game with several others, believing that he will *win* the money – after all, this is how he makes his living. The ruse backfires. Kringelein cleans everyone out, gets drunk and drops his wallet, which the Baron pockets – but then returns, having had a twinge of conscience.

Preyshing, meanwhile, has been rumbled by the men he has tried to cheat, and now must travel to England to renegotiate his original deal. Naturally he expects Flaemmchen to accompany him, and asks her to name her price – he has already fixed her up with the room annexed to his own. And he so admires her independence . . .

> PREYSHING: You know, you're so different than I expected . . . I thought you were more of a coquette, not so ladylike. Are you going to be nice to me – *very* nice to me?
> FLAEMMCHEN: Well, you're still a stranger to me, but *that* doesn't matter . . .

In the next scene, however, Preyshing finds the Baron stealing his wallet. A fight ensues and he bludgeons the thief to death with his telephone. Flaemmchen rushes to Kringelein for help, and the beastly boss who has treated his employee like dirt now wants to be furnished with an alibi – a lie, that Flaemmchen was in league with the Baron to rob him, and that he has killed him in self-defence. Instead, Klingelein calls the police. Meanwhile, elsewhere in the hotel, Grusinskaya senses that something is wrong – the flowers the Baron sent her suddenly remind her of funerals.

Grusinskaya leaves for the station, having been told that the Baron has left already and will be waiting for her. Preyshing is carted off to jail, while Flaemmchen has found an unexpected ally in Kringelein, who has promised to take care of her because, along with the Baron, she is the only person in the world to have shown him compassion. They cry tears of joy together and leave for Paris, where he may find a cure. Only the miserable doctor stays put, mumbling as before, 'Grand Hotel, always the same . . .'

Such was the media interest in *Grand Hotel* – shot quickly between New Year's Eve 1931 and mid-February 1932 on account of the cast's other commitments – that Irving Thalberg set the premiere for 12 April long before production wound up. Continuity man William A Drake's mania for photo-graphing Garbo from every conceivable angle had resulted in over 270,000 feet of film, when Thalberg had asked for a maximum 12,000 feet for the final print. This led to an invidious editing massacre which, upon Garbo's insistence, saw much Crawford footage ending up on the cutting-room floor ahead of the media preview that took place on 12 March, supervised by Thalberg, Edmund Goulding and Paul Bern. At this preview, members of the press and paying audience were requested to fill in 'suggestion' cards. The consensus of opinion was that there were too many lingering close-ups of Garbo and not enough of Joan. This led to the seven leading cast members being recalled on 29 March, when several retakes took place along with a publicity shoot, the only time Garbo – looking decidedly lost – posed for a photograph with Joan.

The opening night of *Grand Hotel*, at Grauman's Chinese Theatre, was *the* show-business event of the year. Twenty-five thousand fans lined both sides of Hollywood Boulevard to cheer the arrival of the stars and guests of honour: Marlene Dietrich on a rare public outing with her husband, the Gables, the Shearers, Louis B Mayer and the MGM executives, Harry Warner and his rival team from Warner Brothers, and Paul Bern, who had just announced his engagement to Jean Harlow. Only Garbo was conspicuous by her absence. 'She's frightened of large crowds,' Edmund Goulding told the press, 'But you may rest assured that she's here in spirit.' Later it was announced that Garbo *had* turned up, and a near-riot erupted as hundreds of reporters and photographers invaded the front of the stage, where she had suddenly 'materialised', looking rather larger than expected – it was Wallace Beery in an oversized gown and blonde wig!

Joan had gone straight from the set of *Grand Hotel* to that of *Letty Lynton* – the premieres were barely a week apart. The production again teamed her up with Robert Montgomery and Nils Asther. Clarence Brown directed, and Gilbert Adrian's gowns were far better than the 'shopgirl frock' he had designed for Flaemmchen. There was also tremendous support from two of Hollywood's most eminent senior citizens: May Robson and Louise Closser Hale, a delightful little lady who died shortly after the film's release. Both walked away with the real acting honours.

Letty Lynton (Joan) is a wealthy, spoiled New York socialite who travels to South America in search of love, but instead encounters the seemingly asexual Emile Renaul (Asther), who turns out to be something of a cad: when the climate starts to disagree with her and Letty announces that she will have to sail back to New York, Emile threatens to make public the 'scandalous' love letters she has written him. During the voyage, she meets the dashing, more stable Jerry Darrow (Montgomery), they fall in love, and by the time the ship reaches New York they are engaged. Things turn nasty, however, when they find Emile waiting on the quayside – he has flown to New York to renew his threat. Letty lets him believe that she is going along with him, meets him at his apartment, promptly poisons him and is arrested. Her future appears grim indeed until Jerry provides her with the alibi he has concocted with her mother (Robson), thereby effecting another happy ending!

Much better than *Letty Lynton* (though far worse received by both the critics and Joan's fans) was *Rain*, directed by Lewis Milestone, the man responsible for *All Quiet on the Western Front* (1930), probably the greatest anti-war film ever made. Joan was loaned out to Universal – on Milestone's not-so-flattering recommendation that *only* a woman with Joan's or Tallulah Bankhead's track record would be capable of portraying Sadie Thompson, Somerset Maugham's anti-heroine so aptly described by Tallulah as 'the theatre's very first all-out slut'.

Since 1923, after seeing Jeanne Eagels in the role on Broadway, Tallulah had more or less had an unwritten monopoly on the film adaptation. It had *almost* been filmed in England by Basil Dean – until Tallulah had met Maugham, been told by him that she could not act but only titillate, and responded by calling him a 'fucking old wasp' – after which the part had gone to Gloria Swanson. Since then Maugham had seen her on the screen and revised his opinion, but Tallulah was unable to accept the role now because after eight staggeringly successful years on the London stage she was back in Hollywood, the heroine of Paramount and about to begin shooting *The Devil and the Deep* with three co-stars Joan yearned to work with: Gary Cooper, Cary Grant and Charles Laughton.

So far as is known, until now Joan had met Tallulah just the once – shortly before working on *Grand Hotel* when, aware of their marital problems and hoping the break might bring them closer together, Louis B Mayer had financed a brief trip to New York for Joan and Douglas. The couple had apparently spent most of the time arguing, and a few days before the Christmas of 1931 had boarded a train that had boasted almost as sterling a cast as would *Grand Hotel*: Marlene Dietrich, Garbo and her scriptwriter friends Salka and Berthold Viertel, the actor Clifton Webb, and Tallulah and her entourage. Joan naturally had wanted to meet Garbo, but she had shut herself up in her compartment for the entire journey. Joan claimed she had bumped into Tallulah in the corridor, and after exchanging pleasantries had invited her to dine with her and Douglas in the restaurant car – insisting that this should be a strictly informal occasion. In her memoirs, Tallulah later observed, 'I turned up in slacks, only to find Joan rigged out as if she was going to the opera!' Joan later wrote, 'Tallulah was very sweet, but she frightened the *bejesus* out of me.' Douglas Fairbanks Jr put the record straight, confirming how Tallulah had walked up to their table and told Joan, 'I've *already* fucked with your husband, darling. Soon it'll be *your* turn!'

Although Joan and Tallulah never became very close friends, other than allies in their later mutual loathing of Bette Davis, they nurtured a tremendous admiration for one another and, despite the class differences between them (Tallulah was the daughter of Congressman William Bankhead, later Speaker of the House), they had much in common – not least a mutual ability to grab life with both hands and shake it dry.

When *Rain* was about to go into production, Tallulah called Joan and wished her luck – she would finally get to do the play, three years later on Broadway – and Joan reciprocated by finding her a place in Hollywood while she was shooting *The Devil and the Deep*. William Haines and Jimmy Shields were out of town long-term, and on Joan's recommendation rented Tallulah their mansion – at a song – for the summer. It was Tallulah who, after seeing Joan as the Salvation Army recruit, dancing atop the table in *Laughing Sinners*, had baptised her 'The Lady With the Fuck-Me Shoes'.

Joan detested working on the film. She had complained to Louis B Mayer about Wallace Beery's unpleasantness to her while shooting *Grand Hotel*, but nothing had prepared her for Walter Huston's reference to her as a 'real-life tramp' during their first cast meeting. On top of this, Lewis Milestone was a 'man's director' who disliked working with women, period – and she was treated with disdain by Joseph Schenck (the head of United Artists and nicknamed 'Joe Skunk' on account of the way *he* treated people) when she protested over the inordinate number of takes demanded for each scene by Huston and William Gargan, her love interest in the film. Both had been trained for the stage and acted in early Method style, later perfected by the likes of Marlon Brando. They infuriated Joan with the way they 'psyched' themselves up before facing the camera. Gargan told Joan that he had never seen any of her films, and never wanted to. Another character actor, Walter Catlett (quoted by Bob Thomas in *Joan Crawford*) is alleged to have told her, 'Listen, fishcake, when Jeanne Eagels died, *Rain* died with her.' Joan had asked for Gable to play opposite her, and after just a few scenes with Gargan asked once more – arguing that if Gable had 'gazumped' an actor once (Johnny Mack Brown in *Laughing Sinners*), then he could do so again. She further protested that, though only 26, Gargan looked much older, and was completely void of the animal magnetism his role demanded. The pleas fell on deaf ears: Louis B Mayer refused to release Gable, having already played safe by putting him in *Strange Interlude* (1932) with Norma Shearer, after which he would be doing *Red Dust* (1932) with Jean Harlow, the 'trollop' Joan had accused of taking Paul Bern away from her.

Joan's Sadie Thompson was her first unfettered all-out camp role and saw her looking more like a badly made-up drag queen than a member of the world's oldest profession. 'Pavement pounders don't quite trick themselves up as fantastically as all *that*,' observed *Variety*. Sadie is one of a group of offbeat passengers quarantined on the island of Pago Pago when the ship they are travelling on is threatened with a cholera epidemic. They hole up at the general store – a kind of low-grade South Seas *Grand Hotel*, where hormones have always run high and morals are virtually non-existent.

All this, however, is about to change with the arrival of religious reformers the Davidsons. 'They'll break your back to save your soul,' one character says of this bigoted, obnoxious pair. Their work is to be cut out for them by Sadie, who is (literally) revealed to us little by little. First we see her hands and wrists, cluttered with cheap rings and pawn-shop bangles; next her fishnet stockings and high heels; and finally a face bedaubed in so much garish paint that it makes the earlier Gloria Swanson caricature look positively beautiful. Sadie drinks her liquor from the bottle, curses, and dances to the 'devil's music' she plays on her phonograph, mindless of the Sabbath! Even so, she blends in well with the tawdry dockside scenario, and soon becomes the focus of attention for the horde of sex-starved marines also stationed on the island. Indeed, she may well have been willing to service the lot of them until she runs into the Bible-bashers – Davidson (Huston), whose only quest in life is to put Sadie back on the path towards righteousness, while his equally fanatical wife (Beulah Bondi) carps and preaches from a palpable distance.

Enter the handsome-ish but decidedly dull Sergeant Tim O'Hara (Gargan), who takes a shine to Sadie and believes that *he* can save her (for himself). The Davidsons have travelled the South Seas for many years, and tell O'Hara that their opinions of people have never been wrong. At first, Sadie fights them: if Davidson wants to claim another scalp, it will not be hers. She agrees to keep herself to herself, but for him this is not enough. She was aboard ship after evading San Francisco's vice squad, and he insists that once he has 'cured' her, she must complete her penance by returning there and serving time in the penitentiary. Davidson makes sure that this will happen by getting the Governor to issue a deportation order. Then he sets about cleansing her soul. She abuses him, calling him 'scum', 'snail-snatcher' and worse, but Davidson breaks her by endlessly reciting the Lord's Prayer until she submits and joins in.

O'Hara then comes to the rescue. He has arranged for her to travel to Sydney, where he will join her so that they can be married. Initially, Sadie resists. She has found religion, wears dowdy clothes and *wants* to accept her fate. Davidson, however, only ends up ruining his good intentions by succumbing to temptation, going berserk and raping the woman whose soul he has valiantly tried to save. Then he finally does everyone a favour by walking into the sea and cutting his throat – bringing the wry comment from Joan, 'If only Mr Huston might have done so in *real* life!' The film ends with

Sadie reverting to her doxy's mannerisms – though for those in the audience unfamiliar with Maugham's story, one instinctively feels that it will only be a matter of time before she is back where she started – trawling the quaysides.

The critics hated *Rain*, period. Leading the attack should have been *Film Weekly*'s W H Mooring (of whom more later), attending his very first Hollywood premiere. But his review was *so* scathing that the editor refused to run it until some very offensive personal remarks about Joan had been removed, and as the journalist would not comply, it never saw the light of day until parts of it were used for another Crawford feature in April 1939:

> The great actress's presence had been created and an air of hushed expectancy hung over the audience. They were saying that she had become a great actress, worthy to follow [Eleonora] Duse. I had never seen Duse, but after the show I was ready to bet that Joan Crawford's *Rain* was not going to wash away any records, either from the scroll of artistic triumphs or the money sheets at the box-office.

Joan's fans generally disapproved of the film: they had tolerated characters of easy virtue such as Marion Martin and Flaemmchen because, lurking beneath their harsh exteriors, beat hearts of almost pure gold. Sadie *was* a whore, with no redeeming qualities – pretty much like Dietrich's Lola-Lola in *The Blue Angel* (1930) – and upsetting her beloved camp-followers distressed Joan far more than some acid-tongued critic ever could. When they wrote to her telling her how *Rain* had been a big mistake, she made a public apology to *them*.

Rain had been shot on Catalina Island, where United Artists had provided a small bungalow for Joan and Douglas Fairbanks Jr to hopefully reconcile their differences – and to keep Clark Gable at bay. Douglas, however, chose not to be around. He had taken a great deal of flack from the residents at Pickfair for 'allowing' his wife to appear in such a film, declaring that it had been *too* true to type, and had gone off on a 'boys only' sailing expedition with Robert Montgomery, Laurence Olivier and an unnamed friend. Therefore, when Joan fell ill and a studio doctor told her that she was pregnant, he proved impossible to find – until the same doctor had arranged for her to have an abortion (allegedly, as suggested earlier, not her first). The child, of course, could just as well have been Gable's as Douglas's – or that of one of half-a-dozen men for that matter – but the fact that Douglas was not there to support her very definitely sounded the death knell for their marriage. When Douglas finally did reach Catalina Island, she refused to see him. For the benefit of the press, the 'official' story was that Joan had suffered a miscarriage following a fall on the slippery deck of a boat.

Joan's abortion, coupled with the fact that she headed straight for Clark Gable's arms immediately after *Rain* wound up, pushed Louis B

Mayer into taking whatever drastic action he could, without ending up out of pocket, to avoid a public scandal. He announced that he would *personally* finance a belated honeymoon for the couple in Europe. It was, of course, a publicity exercise paid for by MGM; one that would effectively kill two birds with one stone: it would enable Joan's British fans to see her in the flesh now that her films were doing well there, and it would place an ocean between her and Gable.

With seemingly few friends she could trust, and certainly a husband she felt she could no longer confide in – if indeed she had ever done such a thing – Joan never had any problem opening up to select fans and reporters. *Photoplay*'s Hale Horton, who spoke to her on the eve of the trip for the magazine's July 1932 issue, fitted into both categories. 'She is searching for happiness,' he observed, 'but deep down in her heart she will never find it.' What concerned Horton most of all, however, was Joan's *mental* state. Declaring that she no longer enjoyed parties, and that since making *Possessed* she had been unable to sleep at night, yet was terrified of staying awake because while awake she could not stop contemplating a future that she increasingly feared, she confessed,

Happiness to me means peace of mind, which of course is a *mental* state. And I know that unless I acquire it pretty soon I'll have a severe and protracted nervous breakdown. And yet, on the other hand, if I *should* find a certain peace of mind, it would mean that I had come to a point in my life where I no longer cared to develop. In other words, I would be standing still, simply existing – for to develop is to live, to stand still is to exist, and to go backwards is death. Obviously if I arrived at a point where I was standing still, it wouldn't be *long* until I went backwards. In the meantime some peculiar force keeps forever pulling me on and on, until I think I shall die unless I find rest . . .

What Louis B Mayer had to say about Joan's obvious suicidal tendencies is not known, though the reaction from her fans was near-hysterical, with hundreds of them writing in to *Photoplay*, begging her not to do anything rash. She was thousands of miles away when Horton's feature was published, of course, and unaware of the chaos she had left behind. Accompanied by Laurence Olivier and his actress wife Jill Esmond, the Fairbanks sailed on the German liner SS *Bremen* at the end of June, having been escorted to Brooklyn pier by a bevy of motorcycle 'gendarmes' organised by the Mayor of New York – at MGM's expense.

For Joan, the trip was but an extension of what had been happening at Pickfair for years – one bunch of snobs showing off to any number of others. Nothing is recorded of the crossing, save that Louis B Mayer had cabled ahead to ensure a welcoming committee at Southampton, headed by the actress Heather Angel and Noel Coward – of whom Joan observed, 'He was utterly repulsive, like an English Mary Pickford.'

The charade, which delighted Douglas but only irritated Joan – who had hoped to be free of her husband's snooty connections for a month or so – continued when they were driven to a reception at Noel Coward's Belgravia home, where the guests of honour were the Mountbattens and the Duke of Kent. Then, with Joan worn out from the long sea journey and still suffering the after-effects of the abortion, they were taken on to Drury Lane and compelled to sit through a performance of Coward's *Cavalcade*. Joan had been looking forward to relaxing in her suite at the Savoy Hotel, courtesy of MGM, but instead spent her first weekend in England at Coward's country home before being driven to spend several more days with the equally overbearing Ivor Novello. When Joan remarked to a journalist, 'I just *adore* Noel Coward,' though truthfully she could not abide him, a report appeared in an evening newspaper that she and the flagrantly homosexual star were having an affair! When she told another that she and her husband would soon be going to Paris to get a divorce, this too was believed. Even more ridiculous, Douglas's jest that he and Joan had secretly had twins which, so that parenthood would not hamper their careers, they had buried under the patio back home – also ended up in print.

When the Fairbanks checked in to the Savoy, however, there were so many rows that word quickly spread that they soon *would* be calling it a day – and the pair did little to help scotch these rumours when interviewed by *Film Weekly*'s Donovan Pedelty. Probably thinking that his comments would not be relayed back to Hollywood – as frequently happened in Europe, where the press were known for not being as easily shocked or judgemental as their American counterparts – Douglas admitted that he had taken a British musical-comedy star to a polo game because Joan had been otherwise engaged – *and* that he had taken bit-part player Hope Williams dancing at the Cocoanut Grove. Then, according to Pedelty, Joan and Douglas had become oblivious to his presence and engaged in friendly banter – which he had *tried* to ignore, but of course published verbatim:

JOAN: So what? What does it mean if we go out with other people? We spend every hour we can together. But even if we didn't, so what of it? No sensible woman keeps her husband on a leash. Let him go. Give him his head – and a blonde one to go with it, if he wants. Say, 'Go ahead, darling. Take her where you like and have a good time!' then he doesn't want to – because it's love, not rules and regulations, that holds a home together.
DOUGLAS: I never can see why those sentiments are left to women to

express. *You* do as you like, don't you, Joan? You always have. I want
you to be happy – and I trust you.
JOAN: I trust you too, Dodo!

Paris was only marginally better. After a Channel crossing hit by a
force-ten gale which resulted in Joan spending the whole time below
deck suffering terribly from seasickness, the couple were driven to Paris
where they stayed at the Plaza-Athenée on the avenue Montaigne – in the
honeymoon suite which, seven years earlier, had been famously occupied
by Rudolph Valentino and his 'husband', André Daven. Completing the
Valentino connection, so to speak, they had their portraits painted
by another of Rudy's lovers, the Spanish artist Frederico Beltran-Masses.

Joan later maintained that, aside from meeting British fans at a 3,000-
strong factory workers convention outside London, she hated every last
minute of her European vacation, and could hardly wait to get home. Yet no
sooner had she unpacked her trunks than, like the rest of Hollywood, she
was knocked sideways by the film capital's biggest scandal since the Fatty
Arbuckle shocker of 1921.

Paul Bern and Jean Harlow had met on the set of *The Secret Six* in the
summer of 1931, and despite the fact that he was twice her age, the two had
got along like a house on fire – much to Joan's annoyance, for though she
and Bern were never more than close friends, she felt that with a woman of
Harlow's reputation he would only end up making a fool of himself. Harlow
did not know the meaning of the word discretion: telling everyone that even
on the screen she never wore underwear, about her fondness for dying her
pubic hair platinum, and flashing it at anyone who might be interested.
While trying to relax in Noel Coward's living room, Joan had been appalled
to read the newspaper headlines of 3 July 1932 reporting the couple's
marriage the previous day at Bern's Hollywood home – yet in one sense she
had felt relief because *Red Dust* was about to go into production and Harlow
might not now be likely to make a play for Clark Gable, as she had while
shooting *The Secret Six*. Exactly two months later, Joan was sitting in her
own living room when she received a call informing her that her former
mentor was dead: his naked body, drenched in Harlow's favourite Mitsuko
perfume, had been found face-down on his bathroom floor, a gunshot
wound to the head and a .38 pistol still in his hand.

In her interview with *Photoplay*'s Hale Horton, published while she had
been overseas under the heading 'The Girl With the Haunted Face', Joan
had spoken of how Paul Bern (though without referring to him by name) had
given her a book, *In Tune With the Infinite*, to help her through her
depression, adding,

He possesses a great mind and a rare ability to listen. He lets me rave on about my troubles, troubles which to such a man as he must seem pitifully small . . . He never makes me feel that I'm acting in anything but a normal manner. It's not that I'm necessarily getting religion [from the book]. It's only that I'm gradually learning to *believe* in things, in life, in people, most especially in myself. He is making me realise that unless you believe in a thing you can never understand it, and as a result it frightens you. Furthermore he's teaching me to laugh at myself by explaining why it's foolish to take life so hard. Perhaps if I learn to believe in myself utterly and chuckle at myself when I'm doing something perfectly absurd, I shall lose my fear of the future. Perhaps I'm finding permanent relief. If so, I shall face life bravely.

Over the coming weeks, as the shocking facts emerged, Paul Bern's death was revealed to have been more than a simple matter of suicide. Unable to have sex on account of the severe genital abnormality he had hoped the sexually torrid Jean Harlow might have been able to cure (though he was physically attracted only to men), Bern had taken his frustration out on his bride and severely beaten her with a cane on their wedding night. Harlow had been examined by a studio doctor, and the whole episode might have become lost in the annals of Hollywood folklore, had it not been for Bern's attempts to please his wife on the evening of 4 September 1932. It emerged from the subsequent investigation that he had bought a huge ejaculating dildo, complete with testicles, strapped this on and walked into Harlow's bedroom. Whether he had attempted to use this on her is not known – only that she had shrieked with laughter and, after leaving a note apologising for the abject 'humiliation', Bern had shot himself. The butler had discovered his body, and in accordance with the unwritten laws of Hollywood, had immediately called Louis B Mayer, enabling the mogul to personally check out the scenario and pocket the suicide note (he subsequently handed it over to MGM publicist Howard Strickling) before contacting the police some three hours later. Mayer had continued the hypocrisy by having Harlow conveyed to her mother's house, where she had been briefed on how to behave when the police arrived to inform her of her tragic loss.

The matter did not end there. Three days later, the body of a bit-part actress named Dorothy Millette was recovered from the Sacramento River, and it emerged that she had been Paul Bern's common-law wife – that after she had suffered a mental breakdown, he had committed her to an asylum from which she had recently been discharged. Further evidence suggested that Millette had been blackmailing Bern and threatening to expose him as a bigamist, hence the 'humiliation' he had referred to in his suicide note. Unable to cope with her own shame, Dorothy Millette had drowned herself.

Joan was summoned to Louis B Mayer's office the day after Paul Bern's funeral, and learned that The Messiah was less interested in offering his condolences for the death of a dear friend than he was in demanding that Joan refrain from driving her car until she had been examined by a studio psychiatrist. Mayer had read the interview with Hale Horton, and was concerned that Joan was about to kill herself and cost the studio a fortune in lost revenue. He reminded her how others had taken their lives for one reason or another, but that none of these had *advertised* the fact in a national movie magazine. Speaking of her 'wild thoughts', Joan had told Horton,

> On occasion I feel that I must get into my car and speed through the night over some lonely road. Naturally, people are beginning to think I've gone a little cuckoo. I'm sorry, but I find a certain consolation in these wild night drives along the road by the ocean . . . watching white foam lash the rocks. I order my car to move faster and faster as though to rush away from the terror of the night as it hems me in . . .

Joan's gut reaction was to tell Mayer to mind his own business; instead, she assured him that she now had plenty to live for, though she did not let on *why* she suddenly had to get away for a while. Paul Bern had lied to Jean Harlow about being a wealthy man, leaving her a mountain of debts that her creditors now expected her to honour. Terrified that Harlow would sink her claws into Gable now that she was bereft of her anchor, Joan swooped on him like a sex-starved bird of prey and their affair became even more passionate than before.

Gable, however, was not Joan's only bed-mate as 1932 drew to a close and she rented another cottage in Malibu, the exact location of which she refused to divulge to the studio or her husband. Among the heavy traffic were tougher conquests – tougher in the sense that they were gay and out of the closet, but not too exclusively gay to turn down a night of passion with Crawford – including Francis Lederer, an ethereal-looking 26-year-old Czech actor recently arrived in Hollywood. Lederer would often accompany Joan, William Haines, Jimmy Shields and Carole Lombard to the gay bars of downtown Los Angeles, or put on 'hedonistic' plays in the small theatre Haines had designed for Joan at Brentwood Park. Another member of the gang was Ricardo Cortez, one of her co-stars from *Montana Moon*. It tickled Joan to read in one of the tabloids that he was 'Crawford's Latin lover' – his real name was Jacob Krantz, and like Paul Bern he was a Jew of German extraction. Since working with her he had scored a big success in *The Maltese Falcon* (1941), but subsequently had found himself at the centre of a scandal almost comparable with the Bern-Harlow tragedy when his 'twilight-tandem' bride, Alma Rubens – committed to a psychiatric institution for trying to knife a gas-station attendant – had died of heroin addiction. Since Rubens's death in January 1931, Cortez had flung himself indiscriminately into any number of affairs, the most all-consuming of these being with Loretta Young and director Edmund Goulding, but Joan was the one seen driving him to dinner engagements, and when she asked Louis B Mayer if Cortez could be in her next film he whole heartedly agreed. The (unnamed) production was, however, quickly aborted in the wake of a ferocious argument between Mayer and Tallulah Bankhead.

After Paul Bern's suicide, Mayer had taken Jean Harlow off *Red Dust* – the official version being that she had left the production out of respect for her husband and not on the recommendation of the Hays Office who, in confusing the actress with the part (though in this instance they were not too far out) deemed it most inappropriate that a recently bereaved widow should be playing a whore who took open-air barrel-baths – and authentically nude ones at that. Mayer had offered Tallulah the Harlow part, but she had turned it down, angrily informing him that she had principles, even if he did not. 'To damn the radiant Jean for the misfortune of others would be one of the shabbiest acts of all time,' she later wrote in her memoirs.

Mayer, who expected to be obeyed at all times even by his biggest stars, had nevertheless seen Tallulah's point, and offered her the part of the snobbish English playgirl Diana Boyce-Smith in *Today We Live*, a love-triangle set in rural England during World War I. When Tallulah rejected this and the staggering $10,000 salary that went with it – she was rehearsing for the New York production of *Forsaking All Others* – Mayer was so outraged that he spitefully threatened to turn her over to the Hays Office for contravening its moral turpitude clause. Tallulah, however, was clutching all the aces. When Mayer accused her of sleeping with half the major actors in Hollywood she did not deny it – but rather threatened to hand their names over to the press along with the names of the six top *actresses* with whom she said she had also been sexually intimate: these included Garbo, Barbara Stanwyck and Joan. Mayer backed off, retained Tallulah on salary, and informed Joan that instead of working with *fagelah* Ricardo Cortez, her next leading man would be Gary Cooper.

Today We Live should have been an important, if not groundbreaking film. It certainly had all the essential components of the recent *Farewell to Arms*; besides Paramount's Gary Cooper, there were able second leads in Robert Young and Franchot Tone, a fine script faithful to William Faulkner's original story, and sterling direction from Howard Hawks, fresh from his triumph with *Scarface* (1932).

Louis B Mayer knew of the risks he was taking, teaming a high-spirited force like Joan with Gary Cooper, who was then recovering from love affairs with two of American's most voracious man-eaters – 'Mexican Spitfire' actress Lupe Velez and Tallulah Bankhead, who called Joan and warned her to be wary of 'Big Coop's untamed two-hander trouser-snake'.

Joan's last-minute inclusion in *Today We Live* (1933) effectively only helped ruin it: not possessed of Tallulah's perfect King's English intonations, her accent comes over as truly dreadful. Diana Boyce-Smith is involved with naval officer Claude (Young), but cannot resist having a fling with visiting American fighter pilot Bogard (Cooper). When he is reported killed in action, she resumes her relationship with Claude almost as if nothing has happened. However, when Bogard shows up alive, Diana tries to keep both men interested, aided and abetted by her brother Ronnie (Tone), and a battle begins between the three men as to which is the better of the armed services – the Navy or the Air Force. The quartet take it in turn doing loops in Bogard's plane and braving the waves in Ronnie's speedboat. Needless to say in an MGM saga where morality must be seen to triumph, this derring-do goes woefully wrong when the real warfare begins. Claude is blinded in a skirmish, and so that Claude and Diana can be together, Bogard embarks on a suicide mission to sink an enemy ship – only to have Claude and Ronnie get there before him, the latter's boat armed with a single torpedo, and though their mission is a success, both are killed.

Joan surprised everyone by *not* making a play for Gary Cooper – whose other conquests had been as diverse as Valentino (as Frank Cooper he had appeared with Valentino in *The Eagle*, 1925) and Marlene Dietrich – but for the fourth lead, the more sensitive Franchot Tone.

CHAPTER SIX

'Mother Goddam' and the 'Jaw-Breaker'

'Trifling incidents that are not worth a moment's consideration wound Joan terribly. Maybe there's some psychological reason for it, emanating from the days when she had to struggle to become what she is now.'

Fred Astaire

Stanislas Pascal Franchot Tone, born 27 February 1905 in Niagara Falls, New York, was the younger son of the president of the Carborundum Company. Unlike Joan, and even the privileged Douglas Fairbanks Jr, he had been brought up with an entire set of silver spoons in his mouth – educated at a succession of private schools, and expelled from at least one of these on account of his left-wing views and unruly behaviour, though to look at him one would not imagine him to have an aggressive bone in his body. By way of the almighty dollar, he had ended up at Cornell University, where after a short time he had been elected president of the Dramatic Club. After graduation he had sailed for Europe and lived in Paris with a much older woman whom he had only ever referred to as Yvonne. The affair had ended, and after a brief spell at the University of Rennes he had returned to America, where an influential cousin had found him work with the Gary-McGary Players Stock Company in Buffalo – as stage-manager for the princely sum of $15 a week.

Franchot's big break had occurred in 1928 when, filling in for a sick actor friend, he had been spotted by Broadway director Ralph Murphy, who had secured him an audition with the New Playwrights Theatre in New York. This has led to a three-year contract. Small parts had followed, and because, like his future spouse, he had not been averse to hopping onto the casting couch – that of top producer Guthrie McClintic – he had been rewarded with a sizeable part in a stage version of *The Age of Innocence*, starring McClintic's wife, the legendary Katherine Cornell. Subsequently Franchot had, independent of his father's wealth, helped found the Group Theatre and trod the boards alongside Sylvia Sidney, Lenore Ulric and Jane Cowl. While working with the latter he had been approached by an MGM talent scout who had offered him a five-year contract, which he had rejected – declaring that he was doing well on the stage, that he had no way of knowing if he would make it in the movies, and that in any case, he did not want studio moguls bossing him around. He was also aware of the film-world hierarchy's loathing of homosexuals, who had always been better tolerated in the legitimate theatre. Therefore a compromise had been reached: Franchot would 'give Hollywood a go' for twelve months; any money he earned above living expenses would be ploughed back into his Group Theatre project; and if by the end of this time he was dissatisfied, he would return to the boards. His first part, in 1932, had been in *The Wiser Sex*.

When Joan first met Franchot Tone, his family was embroiled in a scandal. His political-activist mother, Gertrude Franchot Tone, was having an open relationship with the writer Dorothy Thompson and Franchot himself was living with another man. This was brought to the attention of Harry Warner, who had only just realised that *every* man within Joan's inner circle was either gay or bisexual. Warner gave orders for Douglas Fairbanks Jr's own sexuality to be investigated by his studio (how such an investigation was conducted was anybody's guess) and Joan was also cautioned after being observed on the dinner-dance circuit with Cesar Romero. ('The undisputed *queen* of homosexuals,' Marlene Dietrich told me. 'I don't think there was a gay actor in all Hollywood who hadn't been *there*.') Even Clark Gable's father had fanned the flames of discontent by telling a reporter that in his opinion, *all* actors were 'sissies', including his son! Franchot was a law unto himself but to stave off the rumours surrounding Douglas, Warner Brothers orchestrated an elaborate 'shock headline' to the effect that he was being sued for $50,000 by a wealthy Dane named Jorgen Dietz – the charge being that Douglas had 'alienated the affections' of Dietz's wife, Lucy, a studio dresser. The press made a meal of the affair, Douglas was reported as having been ticked off by Harry Warner, but emerged from the fiasco with the reputation of being 'just a regular guy', and the Dietzes were paid their $50,000 for assisting with the charade!

From the fans' point of view, of course, Douglas Fairbanks Jr was perceived only as the cad who had cheated on his lovely wife – *their* beloved Joan! It mattered little to them that she had never been faithful to any man, and that she had at least three 'lovers' in her coterie at the same time: Cortez, Romero and new kid on the block Franchot Tone – and in any case, in these pre-Kinsey Report days, only a minute proportion of the general public actually knew what homosexuality *was*. All of a sudden,

Douglas had become the villain of the play and Joan received dozens of letters, urging her to get shot of him. This she did in the most brutal manner. While he was filming at an overnight location, she packed his personal belongings and had them taken to the Beverly Wilshire Hotel. Then she changed all the locks at Brentwood Park, changed her telephone number, informed close friends that her 'lodger' was gone – and for good measure changed all the toilet seats!

Joan also stage-managed the public announcement of their separation and her husband's eviction, summoning *Modern Screen*'s Katherine Albert, one of the few journalists she trusted implicitly. Then as now, magazines had a two-month-plus closing date for features, and giving Douglas the impression that all was well between them she had seen him off at the door, kissing him fondly for the benefit of the few fans and photographers who often loitered outside the house – less than an hour before Albert's arrival.

Within days, Joan had filed for divorce, though *Modern Screen* did not hang on to the scoop. Just days before the magazine was scheduled to hit the stands, someone tipped off Louella Parsons, and she published the piece *before* Douglas even knew Joan was divorcing him. The proceedings were handled by Jerry Geisler, the celebrity lawyer who would later handle Busby Berkeley's drunk-driving manslaughter charge, and get Errol Flynn off the hook after he had been charged with statutory rape. A decree nisi was granted on 13 May 1933 on the grounds of irreconcilable differences. Geisler called his 'key witness' to the stand – MGM make-up artist Sybil Jones, who testified that Joan had frequently burst into tears when recalling the way Douglas had 'grilled' her about her movements. Joan herself blinked back crocodile tears while explaining to the judge how her husband had monitored her activities, how he had sulked for hours on end and made unflattering – in other words, homophobic – comments about some of her male friends.

In the autumn of 1933, Joan gave an interview for *Photoplay* – not to one of the magazine's regular reporters but to Frazier Hunt, a broadsheet journalist who imperiously announced in his piece, published February 1934, 'I've interviewed kings and presidents, generals and revolutionary leaders, bandits and bankers – but never before had I interviewed a motion picture star.' Joan was slightly hostile towards him at first: Hunt had told her during the telephone conversation that preceded their meeting of some of the big names he had been associated with, and she had heard of none of them. A chance remark, however, that Hunt was a close friend of the *New York Times*'s O O McIntyre melted the ice. Joan confessed that over the previous four years she had clipped every single entry of McIntyre's popular *New York Day By Day* column, and *personally* pasted them into her scrapbook. 'Until I get my coffee in the morning I'm a fit companion only for a sore-toothed tiger,' she added, 'but I have to read O O's kindly philosophies even before I *touch* my coffee!'

In fact, Joan could not stand McIntyre, having once run into him at Pickfair – it was Douglas who had clipped his snooty observations about New York society. She sucked up to Hunt – and who else would have got away with telling Joan Crawford he knew absolutely nothing about her films? – quite simply because he told her that he was also a friend of Irving Thalberg. And Joan, of course, wanted the whole world but most especially the Boy Wonder himself to know how much she admired him – even though she really could not stand him either:

> Men of great imagination and talent, such as Thalberg, are more and more approaching pictures as a very great art. I believe that Irving Thalberg alone will carry far ahead the torch that will light the trail to a whole new conception of the vast possibilities of the motion picture. I want to be part of this development . . . I'd like to do *The Merry Widow* with Maurice Chevalier, with Irving Thalberg to supervise it.

Thalberg is reputed to have said, upon reading this, 'Over my dead body!' – and in any case, Jeanette MacDonald had already been contracted to play opposite Chevalier in this film.

Eventually, the conversation got around to Joan's failed marriage and she confessed, unfairly to herself, that she was largely to blame for the split because of *her* lack of breeding and education. 'He'd use big words,' she said, 'and I'd embarrass him terribly when I'd stop him even when there were a lot of people around and ask him what so-and-so meant.' She was much closer to home when she hinted at the competition between them, at Douglas's inability to accept that a good pedigree mattered little to the masses who flocked to the cinemas – and that she had always been the more popular of the two *and* the breadwinner. 'He could never quite get over his two heroes – his distinguished father and Jack Barrymore,' she said. 'He thought he was himself, but for a long time he really was the shadow of those two great actors.'

The ending of Joan's marriage inadvertently sparked off a bitter feud with Bette Davis that would last another four decades. For years Bette had battled with her studio, Warner Brothers, to give her parts that would not make her look like 'some second-rate Crawford clothes-horse'. Earlier in the year she had somewhat grandly told *Screen Book*'s Miriam Gibson, 'My very youthful appearance is a hindrance rather than a help. When casting directors are looking for a girl to fill a serious role, they take one look at me and say No!' And now, at 25, Bette's wish had been granted. *Ex-Lady*, released in May 1933 and co-starring Gene Raymond, was the first Bette Davis film to feature her name above the title. It was also exactly the sort of

role that could have been tailor-made for Joan: a married woman who
flaunts convention by wearing her wedding ring only when not out painting
the town with the lovers – in other words, not very often. The publicity logo
read: 'Lots of Girls Could Love Like She Does – But How Many Would
Dare?' Another ploy ahead of the film's release was to promote it as too
shocking for anyone over the age of sixty – which, of course, only served to
stimulate interest. Bette herself was in New York when it went on release,
and Harry Warner had pulled the strings to ensure that a paid-for,
syndicated exclusive detailing his star's rise to the top appeared on just about
every front page in the country. Joan's divorce, however, had put paid to this.
The New York Times, instead of dedicating its headline to Bette, devoted
four pages to the divorce and relegated the Ex-Lady feature to a small
paragraph in the newspaper's reviews section. As a result of this, and other
papers following suit, few people even knew the film had been released, and
cinemas took it off the bill after its first week because of poor attendances.

Douglas Fairbanks Jr evaded much of the unwelcome press attention
by completing the film he had been working on, and leaving for England.
During the trip home he fell ill with pneumonia, said at the time to have
been aggravated by the strain Joan had put him through – untrue, for he had
been equally instrumental in their marriage collapse, and if Joan had played
a 'dirty trick' on him by going to the press behind his back, it was the least
he deserved for going along with the Dietz fiasco. For several weeks he lay
seriously ill in a New York hospital, and Joan offered to take turns with the
rest of the Fairbanks clan to sit with him – but she made it clear that from
now on they would never be more than just friends.

Joan flung herself into her work and her relationship with Franchot
Tone, still platonic during the autumn of 1933. Franchot, acknowledged as
one of the few actors in Hollywood capable of out-cursing Joan and Bette
Davis, was at this time involved with Ross Alexander, who had appeared
with him in The Wiser Sex. He is also reputed to have paid out a large
amount of hush-money to prevent the news from leaking out that he had a
small son, born to him by a well-known New York actress. Joan was hoping
to woo Franchot by persuading producer David O Selznick to give him a part
in Dancing Lady a lavish big-budget musical directed by Robert Z Leonard,
co-starring Clark Gable and featuring two brief appearances by Fred Astaire
in his first film role.

Astaire (1899–1987) – who was about to begin shooting Flying Down
to Rio, the film that put him on the map – had been working for years on the
theatre-dancehall circuit with his sister Adele. Joan had seen the pair many
times on the stage, and once or twice had them over to dinner. During the
New York run of The Gay Divorcée (1934), Astaire had asked Joan out and

apparently tried to seduce her – not usually a difficult process, though in this instance her rejection had been less than subtle: she had told him, point-blank, that while she regarded him as the finest dancer she had ever seen, he was too scraggy for lover material. Surprisingly they had stayed friends, and it was Joan who got Astaire the part in *Dancing Lady*. He was not, however, convinced that the public would approve of his somewhat equine features in close-up. 'Although you may be the biggest success imaginable on the stage,' he wrote in the December 1933 issue of *Film Weekly*, 'it does not necessarily mean that you're going to be a success on the screen. I said as much to Joan, and she was honest enough to agree with me.' Astaire was in London for the film's British premiere: he had not attended the American one, and at the last moment would chicken out again.

Initially, Selznick had been wary of putting Joan in another film with Gable, but now she was single and 'walking out' with Franchot Tone, it was felt that the danger period which had threatened their careers had passed. So far as is known, Gable *was* still on the Crawford roster of lovers at the time, though.

In *Dancing Lady*, one of the year's biggest hits, Joan played Janie, a feisty burlesque queen whose only ambition is to appear in a sell-out Broadway musical. Unlike most of her contemporaries, she is a moral girl, and we are led to believe that she intends to remain chaste until her wedding night – which had many Crawford detractors howling. When hotshot entrepreneur Tod Newton (Tone) offers her a bit-part in the revue he is financing *and* proposes marriage, she proves no pushover: she accepts the part, which will progressively get bigger, and informs Tod, whom she is not particularly keen on, that she will only marry him if the show bombs. Tod, who does not mind losing money if this is how he will be rewarded, sets out to sabotage the production – without reckoning on the staunch determination of the show's dance director, Patch Gallagher (Gable), a hard-bitten Billy Rose type who also has his eye on Janie. Like the real-life Rose he bullies her into shape, believing this to be the only way of bringing her talent to the fore, and does not care who is present when he does so. Little by little, however, she stands up to him. Then there is a last-minute hitch in the production which *she* helps him overcome. They fall in love, Janie is an instant hit with the public, and Tod does the honourable thing by letting her go.

In her Bavarian scene with Fred Astaire, Joan looks fabulous in costume and braided blonde wig, though Astaire, his long bony legs protruding from his lederhosen, is not a sight for the squeamish. Of the male leads, however, it was Franchot Tone's irascible playboy who stole the show, resulting in his being offered the second lead in Joan's next film, *Sadie McKee*.

As for Gable, he was ordered to take time off and fix his rotting teeth. Throughout the shooting of *Dancing Lady* he had been in agony, constantly swigging whisky to numb the pain, and many of the cast had complained that, even from a suitable distance, his halitosis had made them retch. A few weeks after the film opened he had his teeth out, though the studio press office declared that he had been hospitalised with appendicitis: the last thing Gable's army of fans needed to know was that their idol would be returning to the screen wearing dentures.

Gable hit the roof upon learning that Franchot would be partnering Joan in the new film, and went into one of his 'fag-hating' periods, complaining to Louis B Mayer of how he was sick and tired of seeing Joan being escorted around town by 'that goddam fairy'. Mayer assumed Gable could only have been referring to William Haines, and set out to rectify the situation – by announcing that Haines, still a big draw with audiences, would soon be making a film with his 'lover', former silents' siren Pola Negri.

Negri (c. 1894–1987) was one of Hollywood's most accomplished liars. In 1926 she had befriended Valentino, become his 'lavender' date, and after his death boasted of how they had been about to be married. She was told from the outset that there *was* no film with Haines, but was paid handsomely by Mayer to play along with the charade. She and Haines were photographed at glitzy parties and premieres, kissing goodnight after their 'dates', and, most importantly for MGM, at a department store buying a king-size bed – in fact, Haines purchased this for Joan, whose home he was refurbishing to remove every last trace of Douglas Fairbanks Jr. The photograph subsequently appeared on the front page of a newspaper, along with the announcement that Haines and Negri were engaged. The bed, the feature stressed, would of course not be delivered to their house until *after* the wedding.

For Haines, who had never really been *in* the closet, this was the last straw and he barged into Mayer's office and told him exactly what he thought of him. Mayer kept his cool, not wishing to upset Haines any more and have him walking off the set of his latest film. As soon as this project was completed, however, he had the young man followed on one of his jaunts to Pershing Square. When Haines was observed leaving a bar with a twenty-year-old marine, then entering the local YMCA hostel (which always turned a blind eye to such things because Haines made it worth their while), Mayer's agent alerted the vice squad, and minutes later both were arrested. This had happened at least once before, on one occasion when Haines and director George Cukor had been engaged as part of a foursome. Money had exchanged hands – as would happen a few years later when Cary Grant was found with another sailor in a department-store men's room – and the charge had been dropped. Haines had been a massive name then, and Cukor had

With Douglas Gilmore in *The Taxi Dancer* (1927). The term was a polite expression for a call girl.

Left With Dorothy Sebastian and Anita Page in *Our Dancing Daughters* (1928). 'Loved every minute of it,' Joan later quipped.

Above Cranberry, Darling of Homosexuals. With William Haines in *The Duke Steps Out* (1929). Haines was her closest friend, more important than any of her husbands. Devastated by his death in 1973, she virtually retired from public life.

Left Joan with her first
husband, Douglas Fairbanks Jr,
in *Our Modern Maidens* (1929).
'Our marriage was a big
mistake,' he told the author.

Above As 'Pago Pago slut'
Sadie Thompson in Somerset
Maugham's *Rain* (1932). Her
portrayal was definitive, but
her female fans found the film
offensive. With Joan is the
decidedly wooden William
Gargan.

Left A rare self-portrait taken in Joan's dressing room whilst shooting *Sadie McKee*, one of her favourite films, in 1934.

Above Clark Gable, here with Joan in *Love On The Run* (1936), was her favourite leading man and the great love of her life. Towards the end of her life she shocked Middle America by announcing on national television, when asked what made Gable so special, 'Balls – he had 'em!'

Husband number two was
matinee idol Franchot Tone,
pictured with Joan in 1937. She
cheated on him with Gable but
he got his own back by having
affairs with Ross Alexander and
Bette Davis.

been about to begin work on the star-studded *Dinner at Eight* (1933). Now, however, both Haines and the marine were thrown into jail. Allowed the customary telephone call, Haines rang Joan and it was she who put up their bail and got them released. The next morning the actor was hauled before Mayer and given an ultimatum – ditch Jimmy Shields and marry *anyone*, or get out of the movies. Haines opted for the latter. Ironically, his final film was titled *The Marines Are Coming* (1934)!

Joan's leading man in *Sadie McKee* was former child star Gene Raymond – and this earned her a few acid comments from Bette Davis, for Raymond had been *her* leading man, on and off the set of *Ex-Lady*. (Joan was never amorously interested in him.) Raymond would prove even more controversial than William Haines – and cause the biggest furore Pickfair had even seen – when after Mary Pickford's divorce from Douglas Fairbanks Sr and her marriage to Charles 'Buddy' Rogers, Pickford arrived home early one evening and found Raymond in bed with her new husband. Of the remaining cast, of equal importance are character actor Edward Arnold, one of those faces one instinctively recognises but cannot put a name to – and Esther Ralston, known as 'The American Venus', who in 1929 had caused a sensation in Josef von Sternberg's *The Case of Lena Smith*, and who had filled in for Joan in the remake of the aborted *Great Day*. Leo G Caroll would years later play Mr Waverly in the *Man From Uncle* television series.

'Look at that gorgeous creature,' one of the dinner guests observes as he sees seventeen-year-old, smartly dressed Sadie strolling towards the mansion where he too is heading. 'A thoroughbred, bless her! There's no mistaking the aristocrat, is there?' She is, of course, only the cook's daughter, the hired hand who for once in an early Crawford movie does not start out with particularly high hopes. She is sweet on Tommy Wallace (Raymond), regarded as a no-good loser by her employer's hotshot lawyer son, Michael – Franchot Tone, even prettier and more sexy-sounding than in his last Crawford venture. Michael has just returned home after a two-year absence. He is fond of Sadie, but blows his chances of ever getting closer to her by denouncing Tommy to his snobbish friends. Sadie throws a tantrum, quits her job, and with hardly any money she and Tommy head for New York. The pair plan to be married at once and in the meantime shack up at a cheap hotel, little more than a bordello, though Tommy surprises her with his gentlemanly conduct – serenading her beautifully with what will become the film's theme song, 'All I Do Is Dream of You', and taking the chair while she sleeps in the bed.

Sadie is befriended by tart-with-a-heart Opal – played by that delight-fully homely Jewish actress, Jean Dixon, who in her first scenes here is a dead ringer for the Miss Tony Curtis of *Some Like It Hot*. Opal accompanies her as she goes off first in search of a legitimate job, then to meet Tommy at the

City Hall where the wedding is to take place. He, however, has been overheard crooning in the bathroom by famous vaudeville siren Dolly Merrick (Ralston), though why this Harlow-West-Leander amalgamation should be living in such a dump is anyone's guess. When Tommy tells her that her name cuts no ice with him, she responds, '*I* get warm just listening to *you*!' Dolly's stage partner has done a runner, and once they have duetted on 'If That Isn't Love' at her piano, Tommy does not take much persuading to hop on to the next train with her, leaving his bride-to-be in the lurch.

Opal now decides that Sadie should get a *real* job, and fixes her up as a taxi dancer at a plush nightspot – where she just happens to run into Michael, who is there with wealthy, permanently drunk client Jack Brennan (Arnold). There then follows a battle of morals between the two men, with the obviously-not-so-innocent bystander Sadie, remembering what Opal has told her – '*Every* girl has her price!' Michael wants to take her back to where she came from and is even willing to find Tommy a job if it will prevent her from prostituting herself in a big world she knows nothing about. 'Big world?' she scoffs, 'I had a little world, just my size. And you took it away!' Sadie resents Jack at first – he is just another drunken Sugar Daddy – so to get one over on Michael she goes home with him. Then she starts feeling sorry for him, and when he proposes marriage she accepts. Opal is her bridesmaid – an astonishing transformation from slut to near-lady.

Sadie adapts to her new role of millionaire's wife, acquiring a polished accent, though the servants look down on her and her only ally is Opal. Jack sets up a trust fund for Sadie's mother, and Sadie genuinely loves him – not in the same way she loved Tommy, whom she is keeping tracks on – but enough to try getting him back on the wagon. Jack may be much older than her, but she is like a mother to him – exactly the way some of Crawford's gay male fans perceived her. Her emotions are then ripped apart when Opal takes her to the theatre and there is a chance encounter with Tommy, Dolly Merrick's stooge, who performs *their* song. They meet after the show, and he tells her that he too is suffering – she has not been out of his mind since he left. Sadie, however, is too loyal to her husband to cheat on him, and tells Tommy that they could never go back to how they were.

Michael, meanwhile, thinks Sadie is a 'chiseller', who is only after Jack's money: if she agrees, *he* will arrange a divorce which will guarantee her a hefty settlement. Sadie does not want this; she merely wants to save Jack from drinking himself into an early grave. When she catches the butler (Carrol) sneaking the bourbon bottle in to him she fires him, then the rest of the servants, reinstating them only when they swear to keep him off the booze. 'My job is to keep him alive so that I don't get eleven million dollars that don't belong to me, that I don't want,' she announces.

Jack *does* become cured, but only after hitting her in a drunken rage and falling down the stairs, breaking his back. The scene then shifts forwards several months and he and Sadie are celebrating his recovery at the very club where they met. Sadie finds the courage to tell the truth and he is understanding because he has known for some time that she has been torturing herself over Tommy. He grants her a divorce, and they dance for one last time as the band plays 'Temptation'.

When Sadie finds Tommy he is in hospital, mortally ill with consumption, and the doctors warn her that she must be brave. She discovers that Michael has secretly paid for his treatment, and in a very tender scene Sadie confesses her love – a moment before Tommy dies; the shot transfers to the wintry scene outside the window. The film ends with Michael celebrating his birthday, four months on. Since Tommy's death he has hardly been away from Sadie's house and as he blows out the candles on his cake she tells him that he must make a wish – though as their eyes meet over the table, we are pretty sure what he has wished for!

A chance remark by Joan to *Screen Book*'s Jack Grant – 'I'll probably end up *paying* the fans to come and see this one!' – resulted in the magazine launching a 'Win a Personal Check From Joan Crawford' competition. Readers of the May issue were instructed:

> Write in 200 words or less your opinion of Joan Crawford, telling frankly in your own language just what you think of Joan's personality and her picture, suggesting if you wish, ways in which she may improve her screen work . . . Write *exactly* what you think, and remember that literary merit is *not* considered.

The magazine offered six prizes varying from $3 to $50, and really should not have been surprised by some of the replies – particularly one from a 'collector' in Kansas who claimed that he had a copy of a Crawford stag film, which he declared should go on general release so that the readers of *Screen Book* would be able to work out for themselves *exactly* what Joan was like, as the editor had demanded! For the time being, the sender was dismissed as a crank, though the matter would not end here.

Meanwhile, *Sadie McKee*'s optimistic ending, combining fact with fiction, left fans wondering how long it would be before wedding bells would be ringing again for Joan. This was certainly not through any lack of trying on Franchot's part. He told Katherine Albert how he had proposed to Joan every single day, always getting down on one knee, while they had been shooting *Sadie McKee*. Joan's journalist-friend, however, seems to have been aware of Franchot's bisexuality, and included him in her *What's Wrong With Hollywood Love?* feature, published in *Modern Screen* during the spring of 1934. 'Joan is on the eligible list,' she somewhat sarcastically observed. 'So what happens? Joan is seen dancing and dining with Franchot Tone. It must be romance!' Albert then moved on to some of the other 'lavender' romances of the day: Myrna Loy and Ramon Novarro, Randolph Scott and Vivienne Gay, Phillips Holmes and Florence Rice, Cary Grant and Virginia Cherrill.

Courtesy of the $25,000 loan from MGM, which accompanied Franchot's promotion to the level of Crawford co-star, he relocated to a house within a stone's throw of Brentwood Park, and Joan hired William Haines to decorate – *and* seduce, as it turned out – the man who thus far had resisted succumbing to her charms. Because of Haines's reputation, and even more so now that he was no longer a member of the acting community (he is reputed to have serviced at least two hundred Hollywood actors, big and small names alike), the press were more interested in Franchot's bachelor status than any interior decorator's handiwork. Franchot's 'roommate' made himself scarce when the hacks swooped on the place, but Louella Parsons and her viper-tongued colleagues did not fail to notice the two razors in the bathroom, and special attention was drawn to the 'chic bedspread of white glazed chintz, set off by red tassels' – draped over the house's only bed.

Haines next tackled Joan's house, though some of her friends had advised her not to allow him near the place on account of his standing up to Louis B Mayer and refusing to hide his sexuality. In fact, by *not* charging Joan or Carole Lombard for his services, he was making a shrewd investment for his and Jimmy Shields's future, as Kenneth Anger eloquently observed in *Hollywood Babylon II*:

Haines decorated Lombard's home to match her personality and created a gay, feminine and slightly screwball interior. Soon, everyone in Hollywood was chatting about the Lombard house . . . every rising starlet wanted a mirror screen on each side of her overworked bed. Joan's house became a set where she could play Mommie Dearest for the fan magazines and photographers. One room . . . was intensely private, the largest room in the house which she called 'my workshop'. It looked like a hospital operating room, done in chrome and glass with glaring light, but it was Mommie's dressing room . . . Haines had created a deliberately cruel lighting system – the sort of harsh lighting flashed on by bars at closing time to drive customers back onto the streets – so that if her make-up was correct there, it would pass muster under any light. Many of Joan's private hours were spent in her 'workshop' creating Joan Crawford – with a little help from Bill Haines' appurtenances.

Haines also designed a solarium, built on to the back of Joan's house, and it was here that she usually received daytime guests. Franchot Tone was her most regular visitor at this time, and in a last bid to seduce him she took a leaf out of Tallulah Bankhead's book by always ensuring she was spread-eagled naked on her sun lounger before asking her maid to show him in. The ruse apparently worked and by the end of 1934 – though Franchot had not given up on lover Ross Alexander – the pair were very definitely an item.

Joan, however, confused reporters by persistently telling them she had no intention of ever marrying again. When top film critic Jimmie Fidler asked her *why*, when she was obviously so much in love, she responded, 'You *can* have your cake and eat it. If you just nibble around the edges, it lasts a little longer.' That she was afraid of making the same mistakes she had with Douglas Fairbanks Jr was also evident when she told her journalist-friend Edwin Schallert, 'It's better to say no and cause a small hurt now than to say yes and cause a great hurt later on.'

Joan's reluctance to marry had put Louis B Mayer and the MGM executives in a quandary. Supposing they put her and Franchot Tone in a film as love interests and they decided to split up? Franchot had on two separate occasions been seen in a bar drowning his sorrows, enabling Mayer to put two and two together – though what Mayer did not know was that Ross Alexander had unexpectedly ended their relationship and moved on to Errol Flynn, whom he fell for on the set of *Captain Blood*. As a safety precaution, Franchot was put into *Reckless* with Jean Harlow and *Lives of a Bengal Lancer* with Gary Cooper, while Joan was assigned to *Chained* and the screen version of Tallulah Bankhead's Broadway smash, *Forsaking All Others*. Clark Gable was co-star in both.

The first few scenes of *Chained* were in the can when Joan was contacted by her father, who had walked out on his family at around the time of her birth. Why he wanted to see her now – if indeed he *was* the real Thomas LeSueur and not an impostor in search of handouts – is not known, because no witnesses were present and we only have Joan's story to go on. She had arranged for him to meet her on the set. According to Lawrence J Quirk (*Films in Review*, 1956), Joan glanced across during a take and:

> There stood a tall man with enormous eyes and hollows in his cheeks bigger than mine and Katharine Hepburn's combined. I walked towards him wondering what to do – embrace him, or shake hands? He decided it for me. He picked up my hand and kissed it. 'Baby,' he murmured, 'you're everything I thought and hoped you'd be.' We stood together, embarrassed. I went back to finish the scene. When I looked toward him again he was gone.

Chained, directed by Clarence Brown, was another steamboat-goes-to-the-tropics drama, with a touch of *Sadie McKee* thrown in for good measure. Diane Lovering (Joan) is having an affair with wealthy ship owner Richard Field (Otto Kruger) and would like to marry him – but his wife will not grant him a divorce. Diane therefore takes a trip to South America, and embarks on a passionate onboard romance with the hard-edged Mike Bradley (Gable). When she returns to New York, confused, and feeling that she is duty-bound to forget Mike and resume her relationship with Richard, his wife finally grants him a divorce. He, however, knows that Mike is the more suitable man and dutifully stands aside from the path of true love – in other words, Joan's fans would never have forgiven her for *not* choosing Clark Gable to spend the rest of her life with!

The press were indifferent. The *New York Herald Tribune* called the film, 'An earnest treatment of a snappy serial in one of the dressier sex magazines.' The *New York Times* dismissed it as 'just another suspenseless triangle'. The fans, though, were delighted to see as much of MGM's top-liners as the Hays Office would permit – both appeared in one scene wearing skimpy bathing costumes, and for once Gable had not shaved his chest.

Forsaking All Others, a frothy comedy, was MGM's attempt to cash in on the success of Gable's *It Happened One Night*, his film as a loan-out to Columbia with Claudette Colbert, which had won them both Oscars, and itself received Best Picture Award of 1934. With Gable and Joan, however, humour did not work – her fans liked her to suffer for love, not treat the subject flippantly – and it was Robert Montgomery who got to pronounce the 'screamer' line, '*I* could build a fire by rubbing two boy scouts together!' – which had gay fans howling. Mary, Dill and Jeff (Joan, Montgomery, Gable) are pals who have been together since childhood. Jeff loves Mary but she loves Dill, and the pair plan to marry while Jeff is overseas. He, however, leaves her waiting at the altar and elopes with his mistress (Frances Drake). This, of course, gives Jeff the opportunity to come home and comfort her, while Dill realises that he has made a terrible mistake and attempts a reunion with the fiancée he dumped. He fails, not surprisingly, and once more Joan ends up in Gable's arms, in a vehicle that was always more suited to the stage than the screen.

Inasmuch as some accused Joan of 'bending' the truth when speaking of her father's visit to the set of *Chained*, hoping for some sort of public sympathy vote, so too was she very definitely stretching the truth in April 1973 when speaking to John Springer. According to her, segments of *Forsaking All Others* had been shot on the soundstage adjacent to the one where Garbo was rehearsing for her next film, which Joan said was also directed by W S Van Dyke (not true, for *Anna Karenina* – 1935 – had been assigned to Clarence Brown, and in any case, Garbo *always* rehearsed on a closed set). More than this, Joan claimed that Van Dyke called over to Garbo to go through her scene again, while his cameraman secretly filmed it *and* used the take for the subsequent film. So far as is known, Garbo and Joan never met again after *Grand Hotel* wrapped, and upon hearing what Joan said, Garbo is reputed to have been furious.

During the shooting of these two films, the movie magazines were naturally carefully monitoring the Crawford-Gable situation, well aware that the two still carried torches for one another – good for the potential box office, though not for the Hays Office spies. To hopefully curb the gossips, who predicted that he would divorce Ria Langham and marry Joan, Gable and his wife were instructed to give an 'exclusive' to *Modern Screen*'s Gladys Hall for the magazine's December 1934 issue. That a ghost-writer was used to paraphrase the educationally challenged Gable's carefully rehearsed replies to Hall's questions, sent to him a week before the interview took place, is obvious:

> Ria doesn't seize hold of my life with idle and therefore morbidly curious hands. She has her own interests. I could not, would not, be married to an actress. In the first place, one professional ego is enough in any home. Two egos of the same stamp would blow the roof off Buckingham Palace! . . . No actor should marry a woman to whom he cannot tell the truth and be believed. Ria knows that I always have and always will tell her the truth . . . Marriage is a see-saw. If the balance is an uneven one, one or the other crashes down. Our marriage balances evenly and one side is equally as important as the other.

Gable was actually involved with Loretta Young, his co-star in *Call of the Wild*, who certainly was not fond of practising what she preached. Referred to as 'Saint Loretta' by the Hollywood colleagues she had castigated over their lack of morals, she had time after time proved herself to be little better than most of them. A devout Catholic, she had first stepped out of line at seventeen by eloping with actor Grant Withers, a marriage that had been annulled a few months later. Upon completion of her film with Gable, *Variety* reported how Fox, Loretta's studio, were 'for health reasons' retiring her for a whole year. She was, in fact, pregnant with Gable's baby – a daughter, Judy, whom she would give up, then legally adopt during the summer of 1937 (when it was illegal for single people to do so), claiming she had found the child in a San Diego orphanage.

Loretta Young denied the affair with Gable, or giving birth to a baby, and even added a new slant to the story by 'confiding' in Louella Parsons – knowing that it would appear the next day in her column – that she had adopted *two* children, but that one had had to be returned to its birth mother. The truth didn't make the press until after Gable's death in 1960 – sadly, and ironically, on the very day Judy Lewis's own daughter was born. Speaking in November 2002 in the BBC's *Living Famously* television series, Judy explained how she had been the last to learn the truth in 1957 – from her fiancé on the eve of her wedding – but that the priest conducting the ceremony had advised her *not* to question her mother, declaring that Loretta would only deny it. Many years later, William Wellman, the director of *Call of the Wild*, would add his own rather undignified theory (in Kenneth Anger's *Hollywood Babylon*) that Judy was Gable's child: 'When the film was finished, Loretta disappeared for a while and later showed up with a daughter with the biggest ears I ever saw except on an elephant.'

The news that the supposed love of her life had cheated on her with 'Gretch the Wretch' was taken badly by Joan. It would take her a long time to forgive Gable, and for Loretta there would be worse to come. The affair also spelled doom for the Gable marriage. Shortly after portraying Fletcher Christian in *Mutiny on the Bounty* (1935), he would announce that he and Ria Langham were separating and take the Hollywood icon's next logical step between this and the divorce courts – temporary residence at the Beverly Wilshire Hotel.

Joan's next film was *No More Ladies* (1935), of note only because it was directed by George Cukor, with a screenplay by Donald Ogden Stuart. 'The sophistication of *No More Ladies* is the desperate pretence of the small girl who smears her mouth with lipstick and puts on sister's evening gown when the family is away,' the *New York Herald Tribune* remarked. It told the tale of society favourite Marcia (Joan) and her involvement with two men: Jim (Franchot Tone), who shares her ideal that a person should only have one partner in their lifetime; and Sherry (Robert Montgomery), who has had more women than hot dinners. Even so, it is he whom Marcia marries, because she believes she is strong enough to dissuade him from his tomcat ways. When she catches him cheating on her, she organises a party to which she invites all his past mistresses and their husbands/partners. She then confesses that she and Jim are having an affair, and this brings the philanderer to his senses.

Joan had wanted Clark Gable for the Robert Montgomery part in the film, but he was busy with *Mutiny on the Bounty* – as was Franchot, whose part in *No More Ladies* had been trimmed to allow him more time on the more-important production. Gable's presence, however, is unlikely to have made the film any better.

At around this time, Franchot also starred with Bette Davis in *Dangerous*, a melodrama loosely based on the life story of *Rain* actress Jeanne Eagels, yet another great name who had succumbed to a deliberate drugs overdose in 1929, aged 35 – though in the Hollywood version, Bette's fallen star, Joyce Heath, is not allowed to die. Franchot played Dan Bellows, the young architect who helps her through the process of detoxification so that she can effect a stunning but very unlikely comeback.

Bette Davis, who since August 1932 had had an axe to grind because Joan's divorce had stolen her thunder, now set out to have her revenge by stealing her 'fiancé'. To friends such as Joan Fontaine she described Franchot as 'a most charming, top-drawer guy' – and when she boasted of sleeping with previous co-stars Gene Raymond and George Brent, he did not let on that so had he, probably aware that Bette's hatred of homosexuals was almost as legendary as her temper. Neither did he put up a protest when she insisted upon rehearsing their love scenes in the privacy of her dressing room with the door locked. According to producer Harry Joe Brown (quoted by Lawrence J Quirk in his book on the life of Bette Davis), such 'safety precautions were a temporary measure and she began leaving the door ajar so that anyone passing by could watch her fellating him.' 'Franchot just laughed, and told me to shut the door when I went out,' Brown recalled.

Later, Joan would tell William Haines, who admitted to having 'lip-serviced' her future husband dozens of times (though this was accepted because Haines was her closest friend), 'He was honest enough to tell me what he'd done, so each time he came home I made him stand under the shower and scrub his dick. Who knows what kind of germs are lurking inside that bitch's poison-trap?' According to another of Joan's friends, magazine journalist Jerry Asher, who also had a fling with Franchot after falling for him at a pool party, the actor was 'horse hung'. Asher added (quoted by Quirk, as above), 'His women must have found him a real jaw-breaker.'

Franchot's part in *Dangerous* was further extended the more infatuated Bette Davis became with him, and he began spending more and more time at the studio. When one evening he returned home too tired for a little fun with Joan in her solarium, she decided that something would have to be done. Contacting her friend Adela Rogers St Johns, the pair headed for the Warners lot at Burbank, so that Joan could check out the situation for herself. She is said to have been courteous towards Bette in what appears to have been their first meeting, though Bette gave her a frosty reception, staring alternatively into Franchot's eyes or at his crotch throughout their conversation, making no secret of the fact that she had set her sights on her rival's beau.

In a moment's folly, influenced by Franchot, Joan now decided that she wanted to sing professionally. She had a reasonably good voice, it is true, not dissimilar to the warm contralto of Jane Froman, a big name of the day whose tragic story would later be told in *With a Song in My Heart* (1952). Franchot also had a passable light tenor voice, but while Joan was only interested in the two of them doing musicals and giving Jeanette MacDonald and Nelson Eddy a run for their money, his aspirations were far greater – he wanted them to do grand opera!

The pair must have shown *some* promise, because they were accepted for coaching by the fabled Romani Romani, the *répétiteur*-composer who had tutored soprano Rosa Ponselle and *turned down* the young Maria Callas – he was a tetchy individual who would not have done it simply for the money. It was Romani who later suggested to the heads of Universal and Paramount (ones they had *not* worked for) that Joan and Franchot should head the welcoming committee for the Philadelphia Symphony Orchestra's Leopold Stokowski when he visited Hollywood to appear as himself in two films: *100 Men and a Girl* (1937) with Deanna Durbin, and *The Big Broadcast of 1937* with George Burns and Gracie Allen. The reception took place at the Ambassador Hotel, and during his stay in Hollywood the great conductor was a frequent guest at Brentwood Park. He was also impressed enough with Joan's voice to suggest that she tackle a few *bel canto* arias, and she subsequently recorded duets from *don Giovanni* and *La Traviata* with the baritone Douglas MacPhail which do not sound bad at all.

The cynics, of course, along with many of the studio's finest, refused to take the venture seriously, and accused Franchot of being 'just another know-all'. *Photoplay*'s Walter Ramsey, however, would only give his colleagues cause to think Franchot even more of a bighead when he wrote in January 1937,

> That Hollywood has chosen to misconstrue their musical ambitions, their singing lessons, the little theatre they have added to their home, and many other of their mutual interested as being 'highbrow', has bothered Franchot not the slightest. That Hollywood continues to interpret his refusal to be a back-slapper and a proverbial hail-fellow-well-met as an indication of snobbery, bothers him even less.

Another visitor to Brentwood Park, early in 1935, was *Photoplay*'s Kirtley Baskette, a devious reporter who very quickly made himself unpopular in Hollywood circles by delving *too* deeply into the private lives of interviewees and jumping to career-threatening conclusions (which were usually spot-on). Joan had invited Baskette to inspect William Haines's renovations and refurbishments – and to speak of her 'thespian aspirations'. She explained why she had built her little theatre:

> I can't just sit back and be a star. I've got to justify my life. I have to develop. I need the experience of the stage, not only for my work but for *me*. I haven't enough self-confidence, enough poise. *That's* what I've got to conquer, and the only thing that can do it is the stage. I *want* the experience.

Joan escorted Baskette around her theatre – 'white with natural wood panelling, simple but tastefully attractive' – and confirmed how this would form an experimental base from which she hoped she would move on to bigger and better things:

> Hollywood doesn't mean anything to me. It's just a name to me now. I'm completely apart from it. My studio is in Culver City, my home is here. Hollywood *used* to mean so much to me. It was my life. But the things about Hollywood that *could* hurt me then can't touch me now.

Having confided in Baskette about her theatrical dreams, Joan took him into her sitting room, where he listened to one of her gramophone records. 'I'm no vocal critic,' he observed, 'but I thought her voice was lovely – a low, rich mezzo-soprano, not fully trained, but clear and promising. I wouldn't be surprised if, some day, she made her wild dream of opera come true.'

Baskette – who puzzlingly claimed to have interviewed Joan back in 1922 when she had been a fourteen-year-old [sic] at the Rockingham Academy (though there is no record of this, or *why* he should have had cause to interview her there) – was, of course, interested only in solving 'Hollywood's biggest riddle': when would she and Franchot be tying the knot? It was this question that brought an otherwise pleasant interview to an abrupt and vulgar end – though why Joan should have taken umbrage when every other reporter had asked the same question is not known, unless she had been forewarned of Baskette's reputation and on account of his phoney charm not *believed* what she had been told until suddenly finding out for herself. Omitting the expletives, Baskette later recalled how, no sooner had the words 'What about marriage?' died on his lips, than Joan had rounded on him and snarled, 'And what a pity *you* have to leave!'

All told, 1935 was not a good year for Crawford films, for it was the year of the MGM blockbuster. To compete with Warner Brothers' *Captain Blood* (Errol Flynn, Olivia de Havilland, Ross Alexander) and *A Midsummer Night's Dream* (James Cagney, Alexander again), the studio had put out *Naughty Marietta*, the first of the Jeanette MacDonald/Nelson Eddy extravaganzas. Additionally there was Garbo's *Anna Karenina*, the Marx Brothers' *A Night at the Opera*, Harlow and Gable's *China Seas*, the latter's *Mutiny on the Bounty*, and David O Selznick's definitive *A Tale of Two Cities* with Ronald Colman.

Joan's next film, *I Live My Life*, though scripted by Joe Mankiewicz and directed by W S Van Dyke, paled in comparison. Another 'travelogue', it saw her as Kay, a New York society girl who sails to Greece, where she engages in a holiday romance with handsome archaeologist Terry (Brian Aherne) – who initially is more interested in his relics than he is in her. Even so, he follows her back to America, where she proceeds to make a fool of him in front of her snooty friends. He retaliates by looking down his nose at them, criticising them for wasting money on flippancies when, where he has come from, poverty is rife. Kay's family nickname him 'Quaint'. The couple announce their engagement, only to quarrel on the eve of the wedding because Terry wants Kay to give up the champagne life and return with him to dig in Greece. Eventually she agrees, thankfully putting us out of our misery.

Joan loathed Kirtley Baskette once she had read his feature, but *Photoplay*'s Dorothy Manners became a close friend, though maintaining this was, for the journalist, no easy process. Joan had first met Manners in 1926, during her Wampas Baby phase: Manners had formed part of the 'sewing-circle' of hangers-on at the Montmartre, and at the time had described herself as 'Miss Crawford's lady-in-waiting'. Since then she had bumped into Joan every now and then, and had gained her respect by refraining from publishing Joan's unflattering comments about Norma Shearer one day on the set of *Hollywood Revue of 1929*. A few days after Joan's wedding to Douglas Fairbanks Jr, Manners had been the only journalist invited to lunch with the newlyweds at New York's Roosevelt Hotel. Then, in September 1933, Manners had upset Joan by standing her up for an interview – to attend Jean Harlow's studio-arranged wedding to cameraman Hal Rosson, a union that had lasted all of eight months. Joan had called Manners and given her an ultimatum: either she could be Harlow's friend or Crawford's, but not both. Manners had chosen Joan, and for her loyalty had been asked to spend the weekend at Brentwood Park, where she had been pampered beyond belief. In the spring of 1935 she was welcomed on the set of *I Live My Life* to observe a tense scene with Brian Aherne, and upon Joan's request held back the publication of her feature until after the film's release in the October. Comparing the Wampas Baby with the present-day Crawford, she observed, 'The loud laughing, too plump girl of the Montmartre café days, the hysterical bride, the brooding tragedienne and all the other characters from Joan's past have become as fictional as any screen heroine she has ever portrayed.' The actual interview was something of a non-event because much of what took place was 'girls' talk', which Manners would never have repeated, certainly when Joan gave her inside information about Franchot Tone's 'other' life. Manners therefore dedicated her piece to reassuring fans that Joan had recovered from her recent bout of depression and the heartbreak of her failed marriage, and that from now on she would be living for today. She also confused them by publishing the two personal photographs Joan had given her – one of her with Franchot, the other with Clark Gable, captioned, 'The only important thing to bring along with us from the past are worthwhile friends. None of us are so rich that we can afford to drop a true friendship by the wayside.'

Joan's next film, billed as her first costume drama (actually her sixth) was *The Gorgeous Hussy*, directed by Clarence Brown, superbly photographed by George Folsey, and bringing together the cream of the MGM crop: Robert Taylor, Lionel Barrymore, Melvyn Douglas, Franchot Tone, Beulah Bondi, *Charlie Chan* actor Sidney Toler, and the up-and-coming James Stewart. Set in the 1830s, it saw her cast as real-life Washington innkeeper's daughter Margaret 'Peggy' O'Neill (1799–1879, mis-spelled in the film), who begins a close platonic relationship with President Andrew Jackson (Barrymore) when he stays at her inn, a favoured haunt of politicians. They have much in common, not least of all their humble backgrounds, which Peggy is constantly reminded of as she ascends the social scale. Rejected by an older senator (Douglas) she marries Lieutenant John Timberlake (Taylor) and, after he is killed in action, weds Secretary of State John Henry Eaton (Tone). This union is a happy one, and though Peggy never cheats on him, there is no shortage of gentlemen suitors and she continues to be President Jackson's closest confidante. This makes her unpopular in some quarters, and when Jackson begins dismissing members of his cabinet and their wives for making slanderous remarks about her, Peggy 'martyrs' herself by leaving Washington, though as the credits prepare to roll we are reminded that one of the greatest reformers in American history will be eternally thinking about the woman behind his most important policies.

Joan was very taken up with Robert Taylor, then 25, physically at his most ravishing, and about to become MGM's 'Golden Boy' with the release of *Camille*, opposite Garbo. Off-screen, however, Taylor's speaking voice and mannerisms were so outrageously effeminate that Joan was encouraged to flirt with him so that news could be leaked to the press, despite her involvement with Franchot Tone, that they might be amorously involved. It was a well-known fact in Hollywood circles that Taylor – real name Spangler Brugh – had, while working on the stage, an open, year-long relationship with Gilmour Brown, director of the Pasadena Playhouse. When Joan learned, however, of one method employed by MGM to attempt to 'straighten out' gay actors – by getting a studio doctor to administer hormone injections that had some very unpleasant side effects – she could scarcely contain her disgust during her next meeting with Louis B Mayer. His reaction was to really set the cat among the pigeons: a few weeks into shooting *The Gorgeous Hussy* he announced, unaware that they were temporarily not on speaking terms – that in her next film Joan would be appearing with a *real* man, Clark Gable.

In fact, this would prove a shrewd move on Mayer's part, for despite its sterling cast and production, *The Gorgeous Hussy* was not the box-office hit he had anticipated. Frank Nugent of the *New York Times* ripped it apart for its historical inaccuracies, and denounced Joan's portrayal of Peggy O'Neill

as: 'A maligned Anne of Green Gables, a persecuted Pollyanna, a dismayed
Dolly Dimples.' Joan later blamed Franchot Tone, the consummate stage
actor, for encouraging her to ask Louis B Mayer for 'classy' roles – which her
fans could not relate to – but in the summer of 1935 she shared his belief that
they would one day be appearing together in productions for his Group
Theatre and become the next Alfred Lunt and Lynn Fontanne.

Joan had illustrated this point after shooting the dance scene in *The
Gorgeous Hussy* – bouncing into her dressing room, still hot and bothered in
her Adrian-designed, hooped ball gown, to be interviewed by *Photoplay*'s
Ida Zeitlin. During the course of the conversation she flicked 'nonchalantly'
through a volume of Shakespeare, which just happened to be close at hand,
and told Zeitlin, 'Franchot began showing me things in books and music that
I'd never known were there. It was as if I'd been hungry all my life without
realising it, and now I was being fed!' And she, who not so long before had
been sufficiently anxious about the future to apparently consider suicide, had
revised her opinion of opting for the easy way out:

> When people say, 'I'm *so* tired of living,' it's like a stab in my heart. I'd like
> a hundred years to do nothing but read, a hundred years to study nothing
> but music, five hundred years just to act. What can you do in one short
> lifetime?

That Franchot was an arch-snob, perhaps even more so than Douglas
Fairbanks Jr had been, goes without saying, but Joan was too blinded by love
to realise that, by using his immense personal and physical charms to woo
her towards the classics, he was getting her to make a big mistake. She should
have seen that the situation was little different from how it had been before,
save that instead of Pickfair she was pitched against a world to which she
would never belong. While her fans, the ones she *always* held dearest to her,
acknowledged the fact that she had grown out of her flapper roles yet still
wanted to see her playing loose, flighty but headstrong women with
character, Franchot wanted her to take on roles similar to those that had
enabled Eleanora Duse and Sarah Bernhardt to achieve immortality. Joan
had been encouraged to emulate these by 'becoming' her character while
shooting *The Gorgeous Hussy*: at enormous cost she had demanded that her
dressing room be a near-copy of Peggy O'Neill's New England home,
complete with picket fence and artificial lawns. There was talk of her doing
Shaw and Dostoevsky. For Franchot's benefit she persuaded Louis B Mayer
to add a clause to her contracts wherein she would be permitted to work
away from the studio for three months each year to tie in with non-existent
theatre projects that she, Franchot and their friends would improvise at
Brentwood Park in her tiny theatre.

In the late autumn, with Franchot still proposing and Joan deliberating, the couple spent a few days in New York where, with his invaluable connections, he had arranged for Joan to make her radio debut (though she had already appeared on *The Bing Crosby Show* as herself) in the Lux Theatre production of *I Live My Life* with Brian Aherne. In New York, Franchot introduced Joan to his 'family' – the other members of his Group Theatre and some of his actor friends. These included Alfred Lunt and Lynn Fontanne, the Fairbanks and Pickford of the stage, who were then mesmerising Broadway audiences with *The Taming of the Shrew*, which Joan's former in-laws had made such a hash of. Joan was so astonished at the way this pair drooled over each other despite thirteen years of marriage – to her way of thinking, an *eternity* – during which time they had hardly ever performed separately, that when Franchot proposed to her again, she accepted.

The wedding was speedily organised by MGM's Nick Schenck, brother of the despised Joe 'Skunk', and took place secretly on 11 October 1935. Officiating at his residence in Fort Lee, New Jersey, was Franchot's friend Mayor Herbert W Jenkins. A celebratory dinner took place at New York's Stork Club, and as usual the couple found themselves surrounded by photographers and reporters asking them when they were going to get married. Joan responded that she was waiting for her 'fiancé' to propose. Only the radio presenter Walter Winchell was told, and it was he who broke the news, two evenings later on his show. Franchot later told *Photoplay*'s Walter Ramsey of how he and Joan had danced all night and still felt giddy with joy when they had stopped their taxi at dawn, on Sixth Avenue, to get out and dance with an elderly news vendor. 'The old gent had no idea who his partners-in-gaiety were,' he added. 'But he joined in the fun and stepped pretty lively, too, for an old codger.'

The next day, the Tones were on the front pages of newspapers across the country. Bette Davis, who henceforth would be regarded by Joan as Enemy Number One and scathingly referred to as 'Mother Goddam' on account of her colourful language, stage-managed an attack by getting Warner Brothers to add a 'flasher' across the posters of the just-released *Dangerous*. It suggested that she had no intention on giving up on her 'jaw-breaker' lover just because he was married: 'Look out Franchot Tone! You're In For The Toughest MUTINY You've Ever Faced When BETTE DAVIS Rebels in DANGEROUS!'

The newlyweds spent their honeymoon at the Waldorf Astoria, taking a break on 14 October to appear in the Lux Radio Theatre's production of *Within the Law* – an ironic title, for the next morning a call was put through to Joan from a man claiming to have a copy of her porno-flick, *The Casting Couch*, and demanding a huge amount of money for its safe delivery into her hands. There is an entry in Joan's FBI file stating that as much as $100,000 may have been handed over to this unknown blackmailer at around this time – and that MGM had made a previous pay-off, almost certainly to the same man, who some believed to have been Joan's brother, Hal. Curiously, though, whoever had sent the letter to the *Screen Book* competition had not asked for money – suggesting that he may only have *heard* of such a film, but not seen it. The pay-off must have been settled with a stern warning, if not an actual death-threat to the perpetrator, for though several Crawford 'stag films' are known to still be lurking around in private collections, Joan never had to deal with the matter again.

CHAPTER SEVEN

The Shopgirls' Dream

'Society – what is it but a lot of people who are for you when you're on the up and up? And what would one of them do when it came to a showdown? Nothing!'

Joan Crawford

Joan had just finished *The Gorgeous Hussy* when she found herself rushing to William Haines's aid. Her dearest friend and Jimmy Shields, who are thought to have gone through some sort of 'wedding' ceremony after Haines had turned his back on the movies, owned a beach house in El Porto, south of Manhattan Beach. They had been entertaining other male pals when, on the night of 3 June 1936, they were victims of a vicious and utterly pointless gay-bashing. 'It was a perfectly harmless and peaceful pocket of poofs – nothing like the full-scale suck-and-fuck gay communities in latter-day Fire Island,' Kenneth Anger commented. 'Children were not molested, local husbands were not seduced.'

What Haines and his clique may not have been aware of was that El Porto had lately become home to the so-called 'White Legion', a vigilante force only slightly removed from the Ku Klux Klan in their hatred of homosexuals, black people and any other minorities who did not fit in with their bigoted ideals. That same morning, Haines and Shields had been walking their poodle – Lord Peter Whimsy, itself something of a local celebrity because in a moment's hilarity Haines had dyed it purple – and the next-door-neighbour's son, six-year-old Jimmy Walker, had tagged along. Shields had given the boy six cents and sent him home, and for some reason Walker Sr interpreted this as attempted molestation. That evening, as Haines and Shields had been seeing off their guests, the White Legion had shown up.

Wearing Klan-style white sheets and hoods they had chanted obscenities and pelted everyone with eggs. Haines had threatened to call the police and they had left, only to swoop again a few hours later. This time they broke into the house, kicked the dog senseless, and badly beat up Haines and his lover.

The police had arrived, and though Haines had recognised the voice of one of his attackers as Jimmy Walker's father, the officers had done little more than take a few notes and make a few homophobic comments of their own. Terrified of the thugs turning up again, Haines now called Joan, who was in the middle of entertaining Marion Davies and William Randolph Hearst. It was Davies who decided to take the couple in because San Simeon, the Hearst mansion, was at that time the most fortified in Hollywood. Joan for her part saw to it that Walker Sr was arrested, and though no charges were made to stick – one of the arresting officers told her that Haines and Shields were to blame for being in the house in the first place! – there was some consolation when this odious man was forced to spend several hours in custody while Haines's lawyer was conveniently 'delayed'. Within a few days, however, the FOR SALE sign went up outside the El Porto beach-house.

On 14 September 1936, MGM's Boy Wonder, Irving Thalberg, suddenly but not unexpectedly died at the age of 37, sending Hollywood into shock. A few weeks earlier, a simple cold he had caught had developed into lobar pneumonia. Douglas Fairbanks Sr was an usher at the funeral, and just about anyone who was anyone was there to pay their respects – or disrespects, depending upon how they had got along with the precocious mogul. Only the crowd-hating Greta Garbo, heavily involved with adding the finishing touches to Thalberg's *Camille*, was absent, sending her excuses along with a huge wreath.

Thalberg had died at the height of his powers. His last great production, *Romeo and Juliet* (1936), had been panned by contemporary critics because Leslie Howard and Norma Shearer were far too old as the tragic lovers – a 'problem' Thalberg had solved by ageing up everyone else in the production. Even so, it remains an undisputed classic. *The Good Earth* (1937), however, with which he had been involved at the time of his death, was a massive success and earned one of its stars, Luise Rainer, an Oscar. Later, Thalberg would serve as the model for F Scott Fitzgerald's *The Last Tycoon*, and from 1937 onwards the Motion Picture Academy would present an annual Best Producer Award in his memory.

Thalberg's was Joan's second funeral that year. On 9 January, John Gilbert had died of a heart attack, aged forty. Since having his voice sabotaged by MGM, his career had gone into rapid decline – his only moment of glory being *Queen Christina* with Garbo in 1933. Marlene Dietrich had been hopeful of securing him as her co-star in *Desire*, scheduled to have begun shooting in the February, and she had personally attempted to get him off the bottle. Producer Ernst Lubitsch, though, had not wanted Gilbert dying on him halfway through the production, and mere days before his death had replaced him with Gary Cooper. At Gilbert's funeral Joan took Lubitsch to one side and told him exactly how she felt about him kicking a man when he was down.

The year 1936 also marked the launch of the big nationwide search for Scarlett O'Hara, setting in motion a costly, confusing machinery of hopes, ego trips, double-dealing and shattered dreams that involved just about every major actress in Hollywood. David O Selznick paid $50,000 for the screen rights to Margaret Mitchell's bestselling novel, *Gone With the Wind*, in the July, when it was immediately decided that Clark Gable should play Rhett Butler's character as part of Louis B Mayer's $1.25 million cash injection into the project, though for a time Errol Flynn was offered first refusal.

Because Hollywood was still reeling from the shock of Irving Thalberg's death, the consensus of opinion was that Norma Shearer should play Scarlett, while many believed it should be given to Tallulah Bankhead – Alabama-born, therefore an authentic Southern belle. Joan was a strong candidate because Selznick had produced the big-grossing *Dancing Lady* and witnessed first-hand the Crawford-Gable chemistry. The part, of course, went to one of the few *non*-Americans in the running, Vivien Leigh.

There were then problems finding a suitable director after George Cukor was inexplicably fired and replaced, firstly by Victor Fleming, then by Sam Wood. Joan knew *exactly* why Cukor had been taken off the production. Several times when she had accompanied William Haines on his weekend jaunts to Pershing Square, Cukor had tagged along. Haines had recently decorated Cukor's house, and visited him several times on the set of *Gone With the Wind*, and this had made Clark Gable edgy because he had seen them chatting and laughing and suddenly become paranoid that Haines might tell Cukor of *their* relationship. He had subsequently marched into Selznick's office and bawled, 'I will *not* be directed by that fairy, Cukor!' As Kenneth Anger aptly observes in *Hollywood Babylon*, 'One of the great directional shifts in film history took place in 1939 because of a few blow-jobs given by Bill Haines.'

In the interim period, while all this back-stabbing was taking place, Joan worked with Gable in *Love On the Run* – begrudgingly so because of what had happened with George Cukor, though it is doubtful she would have wanted to have anything to do with him again despite their on-off affair, had she ever found out that Gable had been behind her friend's dismissal from MGM. She played yet another socialite heiress, Sally Parker, about to marry the dashing Prince Igor (Ivan Lebedeff) but then deciding she does not love him enough.

Drafted in to cover the event are rival reporters Michael Anthony and Barnaby Pells (Gable and Tone). Sally does not suspect that Michael works for the press, which she hates more than anything in the world, and uses him as a foil-lover to get out of her marriage. Pretty soon they are sky-diving over Europe in a stolen plane, then travelling to the most unexpected locations, sometimes in a flashy car, sometimes by horse and cart, as Michael, with Barnaby tagging along, secretly works on another assignment – the tracking down of an international spy. It is not long before the unlikely trio are themselves hounded by enemy agents, and they end up in the equally bizarre setting of the Palais de Fontainebleau – mistaken for reincarnations of Louis XIV and his wife, the Madame de Maintenon! They also end up in love, despite Sally learning of Michael's profession, and after dispensing with the crooks they are married.

The critics, not surprisingly, were merciless. The *New York Times* called the film 'a slightly daffy cinematic item of no importance'. *Motion Picture* liked it, but gave it a bad review anyhow because of Franchot's antagonism towards their reporter when she had visited the set – demanding that her photographer *only* snap Joan with him, and not Gable. 'Mr Tone was full of superiority complex,' she observed in the magazine's November 1936 issue, cautious not to give her name. Then she went on to describe the 'royal' scenario:

> She appeared wearing a billowing orange organdy gown. Two hand-maidens held the dress up so the flounces would not get dirty. One girl got her a chair. Another turned an electric fan on her; another brought her phonograph and started playing sweet music for her. The Queen was very gracious. A rug was unrolled from where they were standing to the door of Joan's portable dressing-room, Mr and Mrs Tone strolled along the rug and disappeared into the dressing-room, never to be seen again.

The success of the film led to Gable pushing for Joan to star with him in *Parnell*, Hollywood's version of events in the life of the famous Irish prime minister. Recalling how the critics had slated her terrible English accent in *Today We Live* – at least, this was her official excuse – she refused to have anything to do with another non-American character. This was just as well: with Myrna Loy in the role Joan rejected, the film failed at the box office.

The Last of Mrs Cheyney, co-starring Robert Montgomery and William Powell, was adapted from Frederick Lonsdale's play and directed by Richard Boleslawski, a Polish-born ex-Russian Lancer who had last worked with Marlene Dietrich on *The Garden of Allah*. This had been filmed in Yuma in temperatures of 136 degrees Fahrenheit. To quench his thirst, Boleslawski had drunk water from a desert spring – but unfortunately, it was contaminated: he was taken ill on the set of *The Last of Mrs Cheyney*, and died within days. His replacement, former French-Pathé scriptwriter George Fitzmaurice, was best known for Valentino's *Son of the Sheik* and Garbo's *As You Desire Me*.

The beautiful jewel thief theme had already been explored by Dietrich in *Desire*, and not very successfully: audiences had considered Marlene too sophisticated to be a master criminal! Joan was regarded more favourably because Fay Cheyney comes from a working-class background, as does her partner-in-crime, Charles (Powell). Between them they work over society gatherings – she passing herself off as a lady, he masquerading as the function's butler, and of course she manages to fall in love with the handsomest man on the circuit, Lord Arthur (Montgomery). The film, however, lacked the wit and sparkle of the Dietrich version.

A visitor to the set of *The Last of Mrs Cheyney* was British *Film Weekly*'s Hollywood representative, W H Mooring, an unpleasant man with a penchant for 'downgrading' the stars he interviewed in the hope that fans might desist from placing them on pedestals and see them as they really were. Joan had excused what he had said about *Rain* because nobody else had liked the film either. In the not-too-distant future Mooring would receive a good hiding from Errol Flynn, 'In compensation for all the shit you've made up about my mates.' The journalist had written the introduction to his feature, *Portrait of Joan*, several weeks before actually meeting her, and parts of it were far from flattering:

I never conceived an avid appetite for Joan Crawford as a screen heroine. I confess a preference for eyebrows which stay where they grew, lips which start where they begin and finish where they end, and above all for women who do not try to intimidate men with their tantrums . . . That everything came to her through this screen manifestation of the girl who demanded so much from life and was prepared to give so little, forms one of the strangest contradictions on the criss-cross pattern of Hollywood experience. To know her as she really is means the dawn of a suspicion that if the camera doesn't lie, it at least can tell doubtful stories.

Mooring met Joan and revised his opinion of her, but he did not see fit to change a word of his feature. He did divulge some of her secret benevolences – but only upon learning that she had never wanted these made public: the fact that she had paid for an actress friend to have rest-home treatment following a nervous breakdown; that she was sponsoring private rooms at a top Hollywood hospital for sick fans; and that she had been financially supporting Marie Prevost at the time of her death.

Joan had begun taking an active interest in the Presbyterian Hospital during the summer of 1926 when she had been admitted for 'a personal ailment' – thought to have arisen from a miscarriage or an abortion. The matter had been discreetly dealt with by a young doctor, William Branch, and she had not forgotten his loyalty. In December 1933 she had 'adopted' Rooms 351 and 353, so that they could be used exclusively – with Joan paying for the overheads and Dr Branch donating his services for free – for sick studio staff, technicians, retired actors, bit-parts and fans and other friends who could not afford to pay for themselves. William Branch also became her personal physician.

Shortly before the film's premiere, Hollywood suffered another tragedy, this time brought about by crass hypocrisy, double standards and greed. On 2 January 1937, Ross Alexander's body was found at his ranch. As had happened with Paul Bern, the first to arrive on the scene, before the police were called, was the head of the studio – in this instance, Jack Warner. The man who had had passionate affairs with Rod La Rocque, Errol Flynn and Franchot had in a fit of despair gone into his barn and blown his brains out. He was 29.

The subsequent inquest declared that Alexander had never got over his first wife, actress Aleta Freel's suicide, also by gun, in 1935; that he had been having problems with his second wife and frequent co-star, Anne Nagel; and that he had been deeply in debt. None of this was true. Alexander had not left a suicide note, but he had left considerable evidence of his 'indiscretions' in diaries and letters. These were removed by Jack Warner, who gave orders for the house to be ransacked to make it appear that Alexander had 'gone nuts' before killing himself. There had also been an unpleasant incident involving Bette Davis and her husband, Harmon Nelson, when Nelson – renowned for his loutish behaviour – had discovered a letter pinned to Bette's dressing-room door, its tone suggesting that Alexander and she were lovers. As a leading contract player with Warner Brothers, Alexander had been so desperate to boost his career by working with her that he had assumed flattery was the only way of securing such a role. In a fit of rage, Nelson had beaten up Alexander and Bette had announced to Jack Warner and the entire set that the young man was 'abnormal' and 'an obnoxious queer'. Warner's reaction had been to sign up Ronald Reagan to replace him, claiming he sounded and acted more manly: this, and the fact that Alexander was being blackmailed by a young drifter he had picked up for sex during the Christmas holidays, had pushed him over the edge.

Errol Flynn and Franchot Tone were among the chief mourners at Ross Alexander's funeral, and are reputed to have spent the night together in memory of the lover they had shared. For the rest of their lives they would detest Bette Davis and Ronald Reagan and hold them personally responsible for Alexander's death. Flynn would find himself contractually obliged to act with both, and divulged to friends that despite their homophobic rantings, to his knowledge *both* had engaged in a number of gay affairs.

There is no doubt that at Brentwood Park, Joan was the one wearing the trousers: her salary from MGM averaged $5,000 a week, not counting the fringe benefits and expenses, while Franchot was struggling to make $1,000 a week. Initially this caused no problems. They were blissfully happy, though still sleeping around, and had amassed a coterie of friends from the differing worlds of Hollywood and the legitimate stage who intermingled well at the 'Sunday dos' organised by Joan at their home. Joan had hated most of Douglas Fairbanks Jr's friends because she had found them snooty and pretentious. Franchot's were snobbish, too, but they never looked down their noses at her because of her background. She also invited along technicians and studio personnel – though never the executives, who would only make them feel on their guard – receptionists and maids from hotels she had stayed at and liked, fans and reporter friends. And she always insisted that everyone be treated equally.

The guest-of-honour at one of the Tones' parties in January 1937 was Mistinguett, the great French star whose chorus Joan had danced in more years ago than either cared to remember. La Miss, now 61, turned heads by arriving on the arm of 32-year-old Robert Montgomery, announcing she had 'stolen' him from Guilda – her Jean Harlow look alike dresser, actually a transvestite, and so convincing, she wrote in her memoirs, that Montgomery had not learned the truth until they had been between the sheets – not that this had made any difference!

Joan's party list had been drawn up by May Robson, who had played her mother in *Letty Lynton*, and the other guests included Virginia Bruce and Myrna Loy, who Mistinguett regarded in the same light as Joan did Norma Shearer. Both had recently starred in *The Great Ziegfeld*, MGM's costliest extravaganza since *Ben-Hur*, and director Robert Z Leonard, also at Joan's party, had seen Bruce descending a Folies-Bergère-style staircase, drenched in plumes in a copy of one of Mistinguett's most celebrated tableaux. Now, she told the gathering during her after-dinner speech,

> I said some years ago that Joan Crawford had the makings of a good bitch, and I'm pleased to say she's one of the nicest, kindest bitches I've ever met. What's more, there's talk of us doing a film together. I only hope the lovely Joan and I may be allowed to descend a staircase together – with the unlovely Misses Bruce and Loy walking in front, of course, so that we can give them a little shove and send them plunging to the pits where they belong!

Any hope of Mistinguett appearing on screen with Joan had much less to do with the offended actresses turning ashen-faced than the incident that took place at La Miss's opening night in Hollywood, later in the week. Guilda was halfway into her 'Jean Harlow' warm-up when a man in the audience stood up and bellowed, 'I've heard that dame's a guy!' After the show, Mistinguett was in her dressing room surrounded by reporters, one of whom wanted to know why France's most famous export after Maurice Chevalier should wish to work with such 'freaks'. She stunned him by responding that, where she came from, sexual orientation had always been secondary to artistic merit, adding, 'Only you Americans keep your dirty secrets under cover. If Guilda was good enough for Robert Montgomery and one of my boys was good enough for Robert Taylor, then my "freaks" as you call them are more than good enough for me!'

In March 1937, *The Last of Mrs Cheyney* was unexpectedly nominated *Life* magazine's 'Movie of the Week'. 'Joan Crawford's public is predominately female, predominately low-brow,' the accompanying piece read. 'A former shopgirl herself, she has risen to stardom as The Shopgirl's Dream.' For the third year in succession, she had been voted 'Top Box-Office Star in America', and now she was awarded the title, 'Queen of the Movies'. Other publications were very quick in pointing out, however, that the quality of her films had started slipping; Franchot, despite earning only one-fifth of his wife's salary, was at Number Seven on the male list and getting better reviews.

At around this time, too, Joan began showing up for work wearing more make-up than usual – to conceal the bruises he had given her. Since Ross Alexander's suicide, Franchot had begun drinking heavily – initially perhaps to cope not just with his grief but with a very real threat of being outed to the press by 'motor-mouth' Bette Davis. Joan told friends how, despite formidable success in *They Gave Him a Gun* opposite Spencer Tracy, her husband had become aggressive, moody, untalkative and prone to all-night benders. Franchot also hated the way Joan always made herself accessible to fans – pulling up at the *front* of theatres when attending premieres and insisting on doing a walkabout, whereas the other major Hollywood stars slipped in through the side doors. He complained when she chose the table nearest the window in her favourite restaurant so that her camp-followers could watch her eat, and of how she *never* tired of signing autographs, regardless of the weather and her busy schedule. Time and time again she would tell reporters, 'My fans have made me what I am today. It's *only* because of my fans that I'm not still living in a one-room apartment behind a Kansas City wash house.'

Because of Franchot's success with the Spencer Tracy film, and in *Between Two Women* with Maureen O'Sullivan – and because she had temporarily lost interest in Clark Gable, now living with Carole Lombard – Joan had no problem persuading Joe Mankiewicz to cast her husband opposite her in *The Bride Wore Red*, in what appears to have been a last-bid attempt to snap him out of his mood-swings and hopefully salvage their crumbling marriage. It would prove the last, though probably the most artistic, of their seven films together.

Scripted from the novel by Hungarian dramatist Ferenc Molnár and originally entitled *The Girl From Trieste*, had been commissioned for *The Good Earth* star Louise Rainer, but she was fired by Louis B Mayer following her marriage to suspected Communist playwright Clifford Odets. In the original screenplay, the central figure is a prostitute; therefore Mayer ordered a hasty rewrite, changed the title and transformed Molnár's heroine into a glamorous dockside chanteuse. Franz Waxman (who as Franz Wachsman, prior to fleeing Germany to escape Nazi persecution, had written for Marlene Dietrich and worked on the score of *The Blue Angel*) supplied her with a song. Billie Burke (1885–1970) was Florenz Ziegfeld's widow; she would appear in three Crawford films and later portray the Blue Fairy in *The Wizard of Oz* (1939). Adrian, as per usual, was asked to provide the costumes, excelling himself with the $10,000 red beaded gown that gives the film its title. The sets were by Cedric Gibbons (1893–1960), who had designed the Oscar statuette – for which he was nominated 37 times, winning the award a dozen times. One of the most egotistical men in Hollywood, such was Gibbons's importance that he was able to demand that his name be added to the credits of *every* MGM film released between 1924 and 1956, the year he retired, whether he had been involved with the production or not.

Dorothy Arzner (1900–79) was arguably Hollywood's most revolutionary director – and its *only* woman director during the Thirties and Forties. The daughter of Louis Arzner, who ran Hoffman's society restaurant on Hollywood Boulevard, she had driven an ambulance in Europe during World War I, returned to Hollywood to work as a typist for Paramount, been seduced by Valentino's second wife, Natasha Rambova, and been inducted by her into silent icon Alla Nazimova's infamous 'Sewing Circle'. Rambova had entrusted Arzner to the editing/cutting of Valentino's *Blood and Sand* (1922) and five years later she had directed her first film, *Fashions For Women*. Extremely butch, between 1928 and 1943 Arzner would direct fellow 'baritone babes' Esther Ralston, Claudette Colbert, Lucille Ball, Ruth Chatterton, Merle Oberon and, most famously Katharine Hepburn (*Christopher Strong*, 1933) – the majority of whom were her lovers. Arzner remains one of the film world's most revered and respected lesbian-feminist figures, one who never ceases to be emulated, but who will never be improved upon.

The action begins in Trieste at the plush Cosmos Club, where champion of the underdog Count Armalia (George Zucco) has won a fortune at the gaming tables. With him is close friend Rudi Pal (Robert Young), who frowns on the practice of treating servants as equals. 'Waiters are notoriously better mannered than those they serve,' the Count says after giving a huge tip to the waiter simply because he has told him that he has no ambition of any kind. To prove another point, and introduce Rudi to the extreme end of the social scale, the Count drags him off to the lowest dive in town. 'You won't find a more decrepit bar on the waterfront,' the host announces. 'Nothing is decent here. We have the most beautiful girls – that is, the lowest, most decrepit creatures in Trieste.' Rudi, however, has seen enough already – he makes a hasty exit because tomorrow he has to be up early to set off for the Tyrolean resort of Tirano, where he is to meet his fiancée.

No sooner has Rudi left than Anni Pavlovic makes her entrance – the bar's resident chanteuse who Ferenc Molnár based on Damia (1889–1978), France's greatest *réaliste* singer prior to Edith Piaf; her big hit, 'Sombre Dimanche' – known as the 'Budapest Suicide Song' – had just been banned in Britain and the United States. Like Damia, Anni performs in a sleeveless black sheath-dress decorated with a rose corsage, and she wears her hair shoulder-length. The song is 'Who Wants Love?' Also like the *grande réaliste*, Anni speaks her mind: 'Come to stare at the animals in the zoo?' she asks, when the Count invites her to his table. Neither is she impressed by his obvious class and breeding – *he* had the good luck to be born rich, whereas *she* had the bad luck to be born. Also, he only wants to talk – something of a novelty in this establishment. When he offers her food because she is desperately hungry she eschews caviar for meat stew, and when he politely acknowledges some of her sophisticated manners she acidly retorts, 'I go to the movies. I watch the ladies of your world. They're all so simple and stupid and artificial!' The Count then discloses his plan: he will finance a two-week stay for her at the best hotel in Tirano, complete with servants and all the trappings, so that she might experience how the other half lives. Anni, thinking that he is having her on and that Tirano is a sanatorium, responds that she will only go if he buys her a beaded, red evening gown – her idea of elegance at its most supreme.

The Count convinces her that he is being serious, that he is rigging 'The Great Wheel' so that *she* can win for a while, and (courtesy of the drinks poster on the wall) she is re-baptised Anna Vivaldi, the daughter of an old family friend. The Count provides her with a sumptuous wardrobe, including the red dress, and sends her on her way.

In Tirano, Anna is met at the railway station by drop-dead-gorgeous local postman Giulio (Tone), and immediately starts putting on airs and graces. At first she refuses to ride in his donkey cart because she considers it, and him, beneath her. She changes her mind when he tells her, philosophically, that *great* ladies *can* do unusual things. She is, of course, attracted to him, and shares his ideals in that the only inspiration he needs in life comes from the landscape and those about him. At the hotel she discovers that her maid is old dockside crony Maria (Mary Phillips), who has forged references to get there and is the happiest she has ever been. 'One night at the bar,' she says, 'I looked into a mirror. I was frightened at what I saw . . . I saw my finish in that mirror.' Maria is pleased to see her friend, but cannot help wondering whether someone is playing a dirty trick on Anna, who must *not* be seen wearing red in a place like this. 'You might as well just wear a sign,' she concludes.

In the next scene, not for the first time, Crawford emulates Zara Leander, semi-veiled as she dines alone. Fact again merges with fiction when, having first failed to understand the fancy menu, she does not know which cutlery to use for which course. Joan later said that doing the scene brought back the nightmare horrors of her first visit to Pickfair, and that the company here was just as bad as it had been then: there is Rudi, who has been reunited with his mild-mannered fiancée Maddelena (Lynne Carver), a snooty Contessa (Burke), and Maddelena's dotty admiral father (Reginald Owen) – who recognises Anna from *somewhere*, suggesting that despite Louis B Mayer's commissioned change to the script, Anna has at some time supplemented her income by selling herself.

Rudi asks Anna to join them. They dance, and again she is smitten – but although she might think she is in love with the man, it is really only his wealth and extravagant lifestyle that attract her. Her newfound happiness suffers a temporary setback when she receives a letter from Trieste, for this reminds her of the misery she has left behind, to which she must soon return. Guilio sees that this has made her unhappy and wants to help – while the Contessa becomes so suspicious that she telegraphs Count Armalia, demanding that he tell her who Anna Vivaldi *really* is.

Meanwhile, the local festival takes place, where the two men in Anna's life compete for her affections. Giulio loves her for herself, while Rudi wants her to remain his mistress once he and Maddelena are married. Anna is interested only in material possessions, or so she thinks: therefore Giulio is not good enough, and if Rudi really wants her, then he must ditch his bride-to-be and marry her because she is tired of being regarded as loose.

Anna visits Giulio's little house in the mountains. He knows the truth, having read the Count's reply telegram to the Contessa, but all the same asks her to tell him about herself. She starts off by spinning him a yarn of how she lives in a mansion with wealthy parents, and how she has never wanted for anything in her whole life. Giulio is too much of a gentleman to tell her that

she has been rumbled, though she gives the game away herself by breaking
down. They kiss on the mountainside, and the telegram he was about to
deliver blows away.

Giulio has no intention of allowing Anna to marry someone he knows she
does not love, and he says he will prevent the wedding from taking place – even
if it means exposing her as a fraud by getting a copy of the missing telegram and
delivering it to the Contessa. On the eve of her wedding, wearing her much-
disputed red dress and turning heads that observe her only as the archetypal
scarlet woman, Anna has never been more miserable. 'Suddenly I feel lost,' she
tells Maria, 'like I don't know the way home.' She agrees to a farewell dinner
with her snooty friends, during which the Admiral suddenly recalls meeting her
and dangling her on his knee – and Giulio fulfils his threat by delivering the
telegram, confirming what the Contessa has always suspected. Anna tells Rudi
that she never wanted to marry him in the first place, and that *he* is not good
enough for the just-jilted Maddelena, the finest lady she has ever met – and who,
it emerges, has had to put up with his carousing for years. Anna then bids a
tearful farewell to Maria, gives her the red dress (which has been the biggest
mistake of all) and leaves, disheartened, for the railway station – only to be
picked up on the road by Giulio and his donkey cart and subsequently rescued
from what might have been a life of drudgery.

The Bride Wore Red is a brilliant film, and was a smash at the box
office, yet still it had its detractors. The *New York Times* attacked its
'underlying shabbiness'. Howard Barnes started off well enough in the *New
York Herald Tribune* – 'With a new hair-do and more wide-eyed than ever,
she plays at being a slattern, a fine lady, and a peasant with all of the well-
known Crawford sorcery' – but could not resist the dig, 'It is not entirely her
fault that she always remains herself.'

For Franchot, the film had been a triumph of mind over matter: he was
still suffering from the aftereffects of Ross Alexander's death, and finding it
increasingly difficult walking in the shadow of Joan's sun. More than this,
the fans were starting to get on his nerves – with Joan always keeping them
informed of her movements, whether this be a shopping trip, a visit to the
couturier, or gathering flowers from her garden in her latest designer dress.
It annoyed him that she could spend so much time with studio technicians –
'those pesky hangers-on', as he called them. The previous year, speaking to
Photoplay's Ida Zeitlin, she had recalled her visit to Katherine Emerine's
office in Chicago, when she had had only two dollars to her name: 'When I
see all those people waiting for me off the set, whenever I feel an impulse to
say No, this spectre rises and moos, "Maybe somebody's job depends on it."
So I say Yes. Because if you've ever known what it means to need a job, you
don't forget it.'

To cope with being relegated to 'Mr Crawford, who also happens to be a movie star', Franchot began drinking more heavily than before and, frequently unable to get a word in during their many rows, began hitting her again. Like most of Hollywood, he had also been badly affected by the death of Jean Harlow, with whom he had starred in *Reckless* and *Suzy*. Since her husband's suicide, Harlow had gone in for Paul Bern lookalikes. She had had a passionate affair with her mother's Italian husband, Marino Bello, before marrying Hal Rosson, and after divorcing Rosson had moved on to William Powell, thought to have been the greatest love of her life. She had died on 7 June 1937 – many thought as a result of delayed reaction from the beating Paul Bern had given her on their wedding night – aged just 26. Her mother, who had been with her when she had fallen ill on 29 May of a gall-bladder infection, could have saved her, but as a Christian Scientist had refused to allow medical intervention, even after Clark Gable had arranged for Harlow to be admitted to the Good Samaritan Hospital. Uremic poisoning had quickly set in.

Without taking his feelings into consideration – indeed, reputedly tired of listening to him 'blubbering' over Harlow, whom she had always considered 'as common as they come' – Joan insisted that her husband *not* be given second lead in her next film, *Mannequin*. Instead, he was put into the much more successful *Three Comrades* with Margaret Sullavan and Robert Taylor. Joe Mankiewicz then brought in Alan Curtis (1909–53), a tall, inordinately good-looking former male model who had worked with Sullavan in *The Shopworn Angel*. Joan and Curtis would remain friends until Curtis's early death following a kidney operation. Joan's brother in the film was played by another tragic figure, Leo Gorcey (1915–69), one of the original Dead End Kids and later a stalwart of the *Bowery Boys* series.

Joan *wanted* to have an affair with Curtis, but instead found herself falling for her rugged, tough-talking co-star, Spencer Tracy (1900–67). In doing so, one might say she was almost jumping straight out of the frying pan and in to the fire. It was common knowledge throughout Hollywood that, though extremely professional on the set, 'Slug', as Joan nicknamed him, could drink just about any man under the table, and when drunk could prove *extremely* unpleasant. Neither was it a closely guarded secret that, like Clark Gable, the supposedly happily married Tracy had also 'been through' Loretta Young.

Mannequin, directed by Frank Borzage, starts off like a Gracie Fields tragic-comedy, though Borzage eschews the coal-tips and grimy Lancashire backstreets for a tawdry tenement block on New York's Hester Street with its cacophony of screaming brats, busybodies, poverty and lower-class stereotypes. There is Ma Cassidy (Elizabeth Risdon), the family slave who has not been out of the street in years; Pa Cassidy (Oscar O'Shea) who only gets out of his chair to eat the same meal every day, and who pontificates that the *only* place for a woman is the home; there is Clifford (Gorcey), the good-for-nothing son who answers back and takes everyone for granted. Then there is Jessie (Joan) the semi-ambitious daughter who is so anxious to escape this Hell's Kitchen that she falls for the first handsome schemer she sees.

The film opens with Jessie clocking out of the factory, trudging home and up endless dusty stairs to the Cassidy apartment, exhausted, yet not pausing for breath before helping her mother at the stove, fixing dinner for the relatives *she* is supporting. Then she livens up when she remembers that it is Saturday, the night she meets her boxing promoter sweetheart, Eddie Miller (Curtis). Eddie takes her to the funfair, then they head for the beach, where after a spot of love-making she muses that maybe her life is not so bad after all – until she has to face the harsh reality of going back to Hester Street. She tells Eddie that she would rather die than go on living in such a godforsaken place, and begs him to marry her and take her someplace else.

Meanwhile, shipping magnate and ex-Hester-Street-kid John L Hennessey (Tracy) is addressing his workforce, a non-union flock that has faithfully supported him over the years because the more wealth he has amassed, the more he has paid them. Now they are about to become even better off because he is expanding his business. After the meeting, Hennessey drops in at his favourite eaterie, where Jessie and Eddie's wedding reception is taking place. He buys the couple champagne and is rewarded with a dance with the bride before Eddie does an 'excuse me' when the jukebox plays *their* tune: 'Always and Always', which Joan sings beautifully.

Eddie surprises Jessie with a new 'home', a plush apartment overlooking the river. She thinks she has fallen on her feet, and is too besotted with him to see that he is a chiseller – only brother Clifford has the courage to say what he thinks, and for his pains gets a clip around the ear. Eddie will not have *his* wife working in a factory, so he gets her a job in the chorus of the Gebhart Follies – a troupe of mostly divorcées, rough-diamonds and hookers. One of these, Beryl (Mary Phillips) takes Jessie to one of Hennessey's parties, probably the first she has ever been to. When a guest (future Mr Crawford Philip Terry) comes around with the food, she tells him, 'I like chicken legs best because they have handles on them.' Hennessey arrives and flirts with her – girls from the Gebhart Follies are known for their easy virtue – but all he gets is a slap. Being the perfect gentleman, however, he escorts her safely home, and when they reach the apartment they find Eddie arguing with the real owners, who are back from vacation and want them to leave. Soon they are back in a run-down tenement building, but Jessie does not mind this because they are still together, and even when he loses his only prize-fighter in a craps game she stands by him because she loves him.

Things go from bad to worse from here. Eddie is thrown into jail for illegal gambling, and as Jessie's revue is about to close and she is broke, she borrows $100 from Hennessey to bale him out. She *owes* Eddie, she tells Beryl, because he took her away from Hester Street. 'A streetcar could have done, that,' her friend admonishes. 'It'd have cost you less.' Eddie does not appreciate the gesture, and also knocks back Hennessey's job offer – he does not want to be scrubbing decks for the man he thinks is having an affair with his wife. Later he has an idea: he and Jessie should divorce, enabling Jessie to marry Hennessey and six months down the line divorce *him*, ending up with a hefty settlement that she can share with Eddie when she remarries him. Jessie finds the plan repulsive; she has no intention of ending up like her mother, who says her own husband was just like Eddie when they first married, so she walks out on him for good.

Three months elapse. Hennessey's world, too, is topsy-turvy due to a threatened shipworkers' strike, which he feels should not affect his company because his men's wages are well over the governmental requirement. However, this is the lesser of his problems when Jessie comes to see him, returns the money she borrowed and tells him she is leaving town. Hennessey is in love with her, so he tracks her down: she is working as a mannequin in a Park Avenue department store, the kind of place where only Joan Crawford-type customers could afford to shop. Hennessey is the only man at the fashion show, where Jessie Cassidy *becomes* Joan Crawford, wearing some of Adrian's most stunning creations. She models a luncheon gown, so he proposes lunch and she turns him down – ditto when she parades in the afternoon for dinner, and cuts him short before he opens his mouth when she struts her boudoir apparel. Even so they dine together, and he tells her, 'It all started when you slugged me – like a hypodermic filled with love.' He proposes, and adds that it does not matter if she does not feel the same way about him: he has enough love for the both of them.

Jessie accepts, and they prepare to leave for Paris, where the ceremony will take place, but on the eve of their departure Eddie turns up, now the complete heel, and declares that unless she gives him money, he will spill the beans to Hennessey about how they were going to con him. Jessie throws him out, though not before telling him, in one of those melodramatic moments that would henceforth enrich every Crawford 'martyrdom' movie, 'The trouble with you is everywhere you look, you look into a mirror. Everything you think about and everybody you know, you think of in terms of your own cheapness.'

The wedding takes place, and after the Hennesseys have toured Europe they spend time in Ireland, the country of Hennessey's birth, where

Jessie finally falls in love with him. When they return to America, the shipworkers' strike is in full swing, and though not union members, his men have come out in support of the masses. With no spare capital to tide him over until the dispute ends, Hennessey soon goes under, and his downfall is imminent, though Jessie is not aware of this – she is too preoccupied with more blackmail threats from Eddie, and decides that the only way to rectify the situation and prevent her husband from thinking badly of her will be to return to Hester Street. Taking off her jewellery, she leaves it in its case along with her farewell note, but Hennessey unexpectedly arrives home. At first he thinks she *has* duped him, but when she learns that he is broke and vows to stand by him come what may – the jewels can be sold, he will get a job, and they will start over in three rooms like most other working-class couples – and then knocks some sense into him by slugging him again, all ends well!

Spencer Tracy was a rare bird in Hollywood, in that he detested the glamour and attention that came with being a star – though in the summer of 1937 he was not even halfway up the ladder towards being regarded (as he would be, even by colleagues who disliked him) as the finest American actor of his generation. Much of what has been said about Tracy at the time of his film with Joan has been influenced by latter-day critics reflecting on the glory of his later roles. He did *not* walk away with the picture. His Oscars (for *Captains Courageous* [1937] and *Boys Town* [1938]) came just *after* he had worked with Joan. He did not teach Joan how to retain her own identity in a film, because she had been doing this for years. And off the screen he did not cure her of her fear of horses: Tim McCoy had done this, certainly as much as had been possible, a decade earlier. Neither did Joan feel particularly privileged to be working with him, once the first few scenes had been canned. 'Spencer Tracy was so miscast,' she told her friend Roy Newquist some years later. 'He made an absolute muddle out of my part, which wasn't all that great to begin with.'

Neither was Joan interested in Tracy's favourite sport of polo, as press reports stated at the time. Her visits to the Riviera Country club, following a bout of pneumonia that interrupted the shooting schedule for two weeks, were publicity stunts aimed at promoting the film, though Tracy did give Joan one of his ponies – which she promptly sold the first time it threw her! The falling-out with Tracy, and with this any hope of their ever doing another film together, came soon afterwards while they were rehearsing the revised script of *Mannequin* for a one-off performance on Lux Radio Theatre. Joan stumbled just the once, enough for Tracy to bawl her out in front of the entire studio with an uncalled-for: 'For Christ's sake, Joan. Can't you *read* your lines? You're supposed to be a pro!'

The *New York Times* called the film: 'A glib, implausible and smartly-gowned little drama, as typically Metro-Goldwyn-Mayer as Leo himself restores Miss Joan Crawford to her throne as Queen of the Working Girls' – not exactly a compliment, considering the fact that this was penned during Joan's year-in-residence as Top Box-Office Star in America. Other critics attacked Joan for portraying a woman from the Lower East Side of New York with a polished Park Lane accent, and the scriptwriter for not adding a 'link' scene to explain how Jessie Cassidy made the transition from 'slum Cinderella' to mannequin. Even so, the production did extraordinarily well at the box office, and led to Joan being assigned to another film with Frank Borzage: *The Shining Hour*, with husky-voiced Margaret Sullavan.

Sullavan (1911–60) was hugely respected as being one of the *nicest* actresses around, though in her later years she would prove fragile and temperamental. A product of the University Players (with ex-husband Henry Fonda), she had moved from strength to strength since her first film, *Only Yesterday* (1933). *Three Comrades* (1938) had earned her the title 'Queen of the Weepies' and an Oscar nomination, and would premiere while she was shooting *The Shining Hour* later that year, sadly resulting in Sullavan reaping all the acting honours for doing comparatively little.

The supporting cast was a good one, though Melvyn Douglas – Joan's co-star from *The Gorgeous Hussy*, and the man who would soon famously make Garbo laugh in *Ninotchka* – is out of place in a non-light-comic role. Robert Young had also worked with her before. Former spirituals singer Hattie McDaniel (1895–1952) was a plump, adorable black actress, who was almost always cast as the maid and happily so, had played a memorable Queenie in *Showboat* (1936) and would win the Best Supporting Actress Award for *Gone With the Wind*. Joan got along with Fay Bainter while they were making the film, and socialised with her afterwards – but only until Bainter upset her by winning an Oscar supporting Bette Davis in *Jezebel* (1938).

The Shining Hour represents a series of petty squabbles and angst, some of which might almost have come straight out of the Crawford family scrapbook. Joan played Olivia (actually Maggie) Riley, the star dancer at Harlem's Sirocco Club, who rises above her station when she falls for wealthy farmer Henry Linden (Douglas). 'This is a real world we're living in, not just a popular song,' she expostulates. 'The distance between the Wisconsin Lindens and the Tenth Avenue Rileys is a lot more than a couple of thousand miles . . . it's as far as from here to the moon.'

Henry's brother David (Young) disapproves of his eschewing family and business loyalties for a high-society lifestyle, and flies to New York to see him, learning from washroom gossips that Henry is about to be hitched to a woman who may or may not have been married several times already.

He watches her routine at the Sirocco, which takes in every tempo from classical to swing, and tap to Latin. He and Olivia meet at a party – the new-look Crawford with her hair a little more flouncy, more paint on her lips, the eyes and smile wiser, and also with the Adrian shoulder-pads. David finds her appealing, though not especially refined, and he is not surprised when, *à la* the real-life Crawford, she bemoans her lack of education – 'Too busy all day dipping shirts in the laundry, and all night picking my old man up out of the gutters.' However, he feels that she is wrong for his brother, that maybe she should remain his mistress and allow him his freedom – while Olivia's theatrical set merely think she is going through one of her fad phases. Henry will only last, one says, until she falls for the blue eyes and rippling muscles of the first hired hand she meets on his farm.

The marriage takes place, and Henry takes his bride to meet the other two members of the Linden clan: David's wife Judy (Sullavan), who befriends her and becomes a valuable ally in her battles with his dour, prejudiced elder sister Hannah (Bainter), who is more matriarch than sibling, and has despised Olivia even before meeting her. Hannah soon makes it clear that there is no place for Olivia in this neck of the woods. 'You were born with a strong sense of interference,' Judy tells her. 'And I'm afraid that you'll die with one.' Hannah, however, is not Olivia's only problem, for in a slant on what her friend predicted earlier, it is the hired hand, Benny (Frank Albertson) who starts making eyes at her. David also is becoming infatuated with her.

Matters come to a head when Henry and Olivia build a house of their own and she confides in Judy that, though she likes her husband, she does not truly *love* him – foreseeing the confession from her sister-in-law that *she* feels exactly the same way about David, whom she has known since childhood and only married out of loyalty to their families. Second-best, she says, is better than nothing at all. Then, at the house-warming party, Benny gets drunk, follows Olivia into the shrubbery and molests her. David hears the commotion and rushes to her aid – too late, for she has felled him with a (reputedly genuine) punch in the face. Laughing and crying at the same time, she allows David to kiss her, knowing at once that they have made a big mistake.

The melodrama only intensifies when Olivia, tortured with guilt and knowing that she must now put some space between them – begs Henry to take her away on a delayed honeymoon. Judy, realising that someone else may be interested in her husband, has herself started to fall in love with him. Even so, she is willing to hand him over to Olivia, and pleads with Olivia to go away with David instead, otherwise she feels there will be no future for any of them. Hannah, meanwhile, devises her own way of rectifying the situation – dressing up for the first time, she gets sozzled and in a fit of madness sets fire to the new house. It is Judy, however, who is willing to make the ultimate sacrifice by rushing into the blazing building, only to be saved by Olivia, who comes to the conclusion once Judy and David realise they were always meant for each other, that she would be better off returning to Harlem and leaving them all to it. True love wins, of course, and the film ends with a repentant Hannah begging for forgiveness as Olivia drives off, with Henry rushing after his wife and leaping into the open-topped, speeding car!

Margaret Sullavan and Joan would remain lifelong friends, and Sullavan would support her over the coming months – while Franchot found himself ostracised – when in February 1938 Harry Brandt, the owner of a New York-based cinema chain, included Joan's name in a list he had compiled of Hollywood stars deemed to be 'Box-Office Poison'. Writing in the *Independent Film Journal* on behalf of the National Theatre Distributors of America, Brandt's list included Fred Astaire, Katharine Hepburn, Mae West, Edward Arnold – even Garbo and Dietrich.

The slur, coupled with Joan's burdening marital problems, put her at a low ebb. Louis B Mayer could not effect a remedy to what Harry Brandt had written, but finding Franchot's drunken, aggressive behaviour thoroughly reprehensible, he offered him an ultimatum: 'Sober yourself up and stop beating the shit out of your wife, otherwise you're through in this business!'

So far as the marriage was concerned, the end came when one of Joan's studio 'spies' informed her that Franchot was – horror of horrors! – having an affair with Loretta Young on the set of *Three Loves Has Nancy* – a title that Bette Davis, in particular, declared could not have been more appropriate. Though Joan had seemingly always turned a blind eye to Franchot's adventures with other actors, 'Gretch the Wretch' was another matter entirely, and she headed for the studio to have it out with the both of them. She found her husband – as had happened with Bette Davis – naked and standing cruciform in his dressing room, with 'Saint' Loretta down on her knees, fellating him. Joan rushed home, and as had happened with Douglas Fairbanks Jr, within hours Tone's belongings had been packed into suitcases and dispatched to the Beverly Wilshire. William Haines was contacted about the refurbishing programme, and again his first job was to change all the toilet seats.

In a repeat of the split from Douglas, Joan sought comfort from Clark Gable, whom *she* had comforted after Jean Harlow's death, despite the fact that Gable was now with Carole Lombard. This led to a somewhat nasty exposé (for the day) in the January 1939 issue of *Photoplay*, after Joan had told Kirtley Baskette (the reporter she had ordered out of Brentwood Park for asking too many personal questions four years earlier), 'Oh, I can assure you, Mr Baskette, Mr Gable and I are very definitely *just* good friends!' In his feature, *Hollywood's Unmarried Husbands and Wives*, Baskette attacked just about every major 'living-in-sin' couple who had been thrust under the Hollywood spotlight: Gable and Lombard, George Raft and Virginia Pine, Robert Taylor and Barbara Stanwyck, Charlie Chaplin and Paulette Goddard, Gilbert Roland and Constance Bennett. 'Nowhere has domesticity, outside the marital state, reached such a full flower as in Hollywood, Nowhere are there so many famous unmarried husbands and wives,' he proclaimed, before offering his own self-righteous dictum: 'The *best* way to hunt happiness when you're in love in Hollywood or anywhere else – is with a preacher, a marriage licence and a bagful of rice.'

Louis B Mayer's reaction to Baskette's feature was to demand a retraction – otherwise, he declared, none of *Photoplay*'s reporters would set foot on an MGM lot again. The other major studios supported him, and threatened to withdraw their advertising contracts. The editor's response was that if that happened, Kirtley Baskette would be commissioned to pen a follow-up feature on Hollywood *adultery* – something that just about every major star on Mayer's books was or had been culpable of at some time or other. Additionally, *Photoplay* threatened to print a story about Norma Shearer and the 'little scenarios' taking place in her trailer-dressing room with nineteen-year-old Mickey Rooney, star of the Andy Hardy comedy films, who boasted (as he would again in his autobiography, *Life Is Too Short*, 1991) of how, 'MGM's grand lady loved nothing more than copulating, French-style, with Andy Hardy.'

Mayer was further perturbed about an article in *Screenland*, declaring that George Raft and Robert Taylor were 'Gillette blades which cut both ways' – in other words, men willing to have sex with other men providing these were paying for the privilege. Raft absolved himself, in that age of extreme naivety, by posing for photographs with his fists bunched and threatening to 'rip apart' any man brave enough to say such a thing to his face. As for Taylor, in a move that today would turn him into a laughing stock, Mayer set out to prove that he was a 'regular guy' by having him pose bare-chested for publicity pictures – Mayer's theory being that in the days when homosexual men were invariably depicted as bumbling, 'nervous Nellie' stereotypes, Taylor could not possibly have been gay because his upper half was hirsute! (What the press were not told, of course, was that the actor's chest was hairier than it normally would have been because of the hormone injections he had been forcibly subjected to.) This did nothing to curb the gossips, and in an extreme measure that had happened countless times before – a tradition still very much in evidence today – that May, Taylor and the similarly 'suspect' Barbara Stanwyck were given huge compensatory salary increases and hurriedly married off.

Had Kirtley Baskette done his homework, he would have discovered that Charlie Chaplin and Paulette Goddard were *already* married. As for Gable and Lombard, Louis B Mayer again dipped into his pocket when Ria Langham refused to give her husband a divorce: with *Gone With the Wind* nearing completion, he dared not risk the adverse publicity and loaned Gable $300,000 as part of a settlement that Langham would have been mad to refuse. Gable got his divorce that March, he and Lombard were married a few weeks later and Mayer instructed Joan to keep away from the pair of them.

While waiting for her own divorce to be finalised, Joan embarked on a frivolous series of romps with seventeen-year-old former child star Jackie Cooper, whose latest film was, ironically, entitled *Scouts to the Rescue*. According to Cooper (in his autobiography, *Please Don't Shoot My Dog*, 1991), he was a guest at a Crawford pool party when, after a game of badminton, she caught him gazing down her cleavage and asked him to leave; when he did not, she waited until the other guests were gone before making her move. 'And I made love to Joan Crawford, or rather, she made love to me.' Cooper maintained that he had sex with Joan 'eight or nine times' over the next six months – for her an arrestable offence, because he was legally a minor – before she abruptly broke it off with him. Explaining how he would sneak out of his house and freewheel his car down the steep drive so that his parents would not hear, he concluded,

> She was a very erudite professor of love, a wild woman. She would bathe me, powder me, cologne me. Then she would do it all over again. She would put on high heels, a garter belt and a large hat, and pose in front of the mirror, turning this way and that way. I kept thinking: The Lady is crazy.

The split with Franchot coincided with producer Hunt Stromberg commissioning F Scott Fitzgerald to script his own story, *Infidelity*, for Joan to appear in with her estranged husband, unaware that their marriage was all but over. Louis B Mayer, who had not taken the 'Box-Office Poison' tag seriously, had recently renegotiated Joan's contract. In May 1938, when it had come up for renewal, he had offered her a $400,000 single payment for as many films as the studio deemed appropriate, an option that he said would be reviewed annually so long as she continued to be in demand. Joan's agent (Mike Levee, who had managed Douglas Fairbanks Jr) had objected to this and successfully negotiated a deal that would see Joan making no fewer than fifteen films, at $100,000 a film, over a five-year period. It was a shrewd move, for though she actually would be grossing *less*, she would be no worse off financially because the lower earnings would put her *just* in the lower tax bracket, and of course she would be guaranteed work over the next five years. There was no way of telling how far-reaching the 'Box-Office Poison' slur would be, though ostensibly she would be worrying over nothing because most of the stars would go on to much bigger things. Marlene Dietrich would bounce back with *Destry Rides Again*, Garbo would triumph with *Ninotchka*, Fred Astaire with *Broadway Melody of 1940*, Katharine Hepburn with *The Philadelphia Story* and Mae West would have them racing to cinemas to howl at her and W C Fields in *My Little Chickadee*.

Mayer was confident that *Infidelity* would see Joan restored as 'Queen of the Movies', and F Scott Fitzgerald was hoping that he would have a smash hit on his hands – after several lean years, he needed the money to pay for his wife Zelda's treatment for an increasing mental disorder. Several scenes are thought to have been shot before the Hays Office objected to the title, particularly as it was no secret that Joan and Franchot were experts in the field. Louis B Mayer was all for changing it, amending the denouement scene where Joan's character arrives home to find her husband in bed with his mistress, and ordering Joan and Franchot to sort themselves out – believing that if he could make couples marry, so he could force them to patch things up – when Louella Parsons informed Hunt Stromberg of Franchot's 'jaw-breaking exercise' with Loretta Young. The project was abandoned, and Stromberg told Joan that her next film would be *Idiot's Delight* with Clark Gable.

Franchot took the news badly, and headed straight for Brentwood Park. Joan was out shopping and the maid, believing his story that he and Joan were getting together again, let him in. Joan arrived home, by which time he had raided her liquor cabinet, and in a drunken rage, he proceeded to give her a good hiding. When Mayer and Stromberg learned what had happened, they informed Franchot that he would never work for MGM again. With one exception, they would be good to their word. Franchot's *The Girl Downstairs* was already in the can, and *Fast and Furious*, co-starring Ann Sothern, was about to go into production. In 1942 he would be recalled to the studio for the war drama *Pilot No 5*, with Van Johnson, though he would make many more good, successful films elsewhere.

In the meantime, while *Idiot's Delight* was having the finishing touches added to its script, Joan appeared in *The Ice Follies of 1939*, produced by former mentor Harry Rapf. On the face of it, this seemed like a good idea. Leopold Stokowski had approved the Crawford singing voice and so had Louis B Mayer, who commissioned six new songs for Joan to perform in the production. Disaster struck, however, when Hedda Hopper wrote in her column that Joan's contralto tones were so staggeringly good that she had been offered a series of recitals with the New York Metropolitan Opera! This was probably Hopper taking one of Franchot Tone's earlier boasts seriously.

Still, it brought a vociferous complaint from MGM's Number One singing sensation Jeanette MacDonald, especially when news reached her that Joan was hoping to make a film with Nelson Eddy. It mattered little that MacDonald, who apparently when riled could out-curse a sailor on shore leave, could no longer stand her celebrated partner. When she barged into Mayer's office and gave him an ultimatum – Crawford or herself – four of Joan's numbers were cut from the production, and though she did sing the other two, at the last minute Mayer gave instructions for someone else's voice to be dubbed over hers. 'He's done a Jack Gilbert on me,' she tearfully told Hedda Hopper, who had caused her the problem in the first place.

The Ice Follies of 1939 was an almighty flop, despite its stunning Technicolor finale. Joan had flatly *refused* to skate – no problem, because Harry Rapf hired the entire International Ice Follies to skate around Joan, James Stewart, Lew Ayres and Lewis Stone in an extravaganza that had set the studio back over $1 million. The *New York Herald Tribune* was right to issue the stern warning, 'Miss Crawford should *avoid* this type of film in the future,' while Sheilah Graham wrote in her syndicated column, 'After three misses in a row, if Joan Crawford doesn't come up with a hit picture soon, she'll soon be joining Luise Rainer in the Hall of Forgotten Stars at Metro.'

The 'hit picture' *should* have been *Idiot's Delight*, which had taken Broadway by storm with Alfred Lunt and Lynn Fontanne. With Gable already assigned to the Lunt part, everyone at MGM had agreed that Joan had been made to play that of the easy-going Russian ex-hoofer – everyone that is save Louis B Mayer, who for reasons known only to himself now decided to give it to Norma Shearer.

Joan was furious. 'No Tits' Shearer, she said, could neither dance nor sing, and she had no experience playing fast women. She was forgetting that, as Irving Thalberg had bequeathed her a vast amount of MGM shares, Shearer was still entitled to have the pick of the best roles, even if this meant riding roughshod over her colleagues. Trying to prove that she was no pushover, Joan rejected Max Marcin's *House of Glass* and Clement Ripley's *A Lady Comes to Town*. But if Mayer was hoping to further antagonise her by informing her that he *could* offer her a part in the studio's next big-budget production, Clare Luce's *The Women* – Shearer would also be taking the lead in this – he was surprised when she responded that nothing would please her more, so long as he gave her the part of superbitch Crystal Allen. Mayer agreed, but advised her to keep the news to herself for the time being.

Meanwhile, there was the question of Joan's divorce. Franchot was living in New York, dividing his time between film and Group Theatre work, and in April 1939, a week ahead of the hearing, Joan joined him with every intention of making the rupture as dignified as possible. The couple were photographed arm-in-arm at Radio City Music Hall, attending the premiere of Bette Davis's *Dark Victory* – though they refused to meet Bette afterwards, Joan joked, because she had forgotten to bring a bag of tomatoes. The attendant press were not amused: they had anticipated a few feathers flying. Florence Foster Parry of *Pittsburgh Express* led the attack, recalling how Joan's last divorce had monopolised the headlines at the expense of Bette Davis's blossoming career. Commenting on this and the couple's dancing cheek-to-cheek at the Stork Club, where three and a half years previously they had celebrated their marriage, Parry observed, 'It served the purpose of getting the divorce on the front pages again – alongside the collapse of Spain and the push of Hitler.'

Joan's court appearance was equally dignified, almost like a denouement from one of her films. She chatted to reporters in the foyer, explaining how much her outfit had cost and how long it had taken her to steam the brim of her picture hat so that it dropped at exactly the right angle over one eye. A few minutes later the judge asked her *why* she wanted to divorce her husband, particularly as so many people had just seen them out on the town apparently having a whale of a time. Joan told him, 'I hope I'm intelligent enough to be friendly with my husband,' then cited her plea. Nothing was mentioned of the drunken binges and the beatings. In a low voice she said only that Franchot had become increasingly sullen and resentful, and that of late he had gone out every night alone and sometimes not arrived home until late – and that was that. She was free once more, and as she stepped out into the spring sunshine she signed dozens of autographs and told reporters, 'That's it, fellas. No more marriages!'

CHAPTER EIGHT

The 'Caddy' and the Children From Hell

'I love playing bitches. I think there's a lot of bitch in every woman – and a lot of bitch in every man, too!'

Joan Crawford

Joan would recall Franchot Tone as the most sedate man she had ever known, and never publicly refer to his fondness for using her as a punchbag. Years after the event she would blame their marriage collapse on their failure to have children, and on Hollywood stereotyping – his always being cast as elegant gentlemen or society playboys, clearly never allowing him access to the enormous range of characters he played on the stage. It was a pathetic excuse, as was Joan's diatribe, quoted by Lawrence J Quirk in the December 1956 issue of *Films in Review*:

> Franchot wanted to be as great an actor in pictures as he is in the theatre, and he could have been . . . I wanted children so much. Instead, there were two miscarriages. A dancer's muscles should be good for child-bearing. They aren't . . . I would have given anything in the world to have saved this marriage, to have kept it on the same plane it originally was on, both of us acting Shakespeare together, studying opera together, singing, talking, up to our ears in art and the theatre. As a woman I might have saved it, but there was another Crawford, the actress. Husbands with sensitive hearts don't like second billing.

Two days after her divorce, Joan was contacted by the hated W H Film Weekly's Hollywood correspondent, and asked if she wou interview for the British magazine. Her response: 'Not in a million would never forgive Mooring for his earlier personal attack. Su in his feature, 'Prescription For Joan', which appeared at the end of the month, he was up to his usual tricks: praising her in one paragraph, condemning her in the next. Joan, of course, only paid attention to the latter. Accusing her of hiding behind her glamorous society characters, Mooring wrote, 'Deep down, Joan Crawford was, is, and always must be a daughter of life's "great downstairs".' Regarding her rejection of Clement Ripley's *A Lady Comes to Town*, he scoffed, 'Believe it or not, Mr Ripley, though your story may be excellent in every way, we'd rather the lady got out of town and stayed there.' Joan swore that as long as she lived she would never soil her hands on another copy of *Film Weekly*.

Meanwhile, she began shooting *The Women*, by all accounts a far from happy experience once the egos of the main protagonists started getting in the way of their performances. Although the dressing rooms were but a short distance from the set, Joan and Norma Shearer insisted on being driven there in separate limousines – and, applying the maxim, 'Save the best act for the top of the bill', neither wanted to arrive first to shoot the pre-publicity photographs, which resulted in their liveried chauffeurs driving them around in circles for over an hour until MGM publicist Howard Strickland solved the problem by going out into the street and personally directing the traffic. He then physically restrained Joan at the studio door so that Shearer could enter first. Both were upstaged, however, by Rosalind Russell – who had sneaked in while all the fuss was going on, wearing six-inch heels and a three-foot feathered hat!

Since Irving Thalberg's death, Hunt Stromberg had become a name to be reckoned with in Hollywood, producing among others the Jeanette MacDonald/Nelson Eddy musicals. For *The Women* he had brought together the most formidable array (135 speaking parts) of female stars ever seen in a Hollywood movie – and gone a step further by insisting that even the animals used in the production were female, along with every photograph and *objet d'art*. Besides Shearer, Crawford, Russell, Paulette Goddard and Joan Fontaine – referred to, along with director George Cukor, as a 'gaggle of Scarlett O'Hara rejects' – there were Mary Boland, Ruth Hussey, and the formidable stage actress Lucile Watson (1879–1962). Virginia Weidler (1927–68), was to be in huge demand between now and 1943, when she disappeared completely from our screens. Here, the 'little horror' as she was known, on account of the brattish parts she played, puts in an exemplary performance. The real scene-stealer in the last third of the film, however, is the superb Marjorie Main (1890–1975), a minister's daughter, who after serving a shady apprenticeship as a shimmy dancer in the Harlem nightclubs with lover Barbara Stanwyck, had taken Hollywood by storm, playing Humphrey Bogart's crusty mother in *Dead End* – and Stanwyck's equally feisty mother-in-law in *Stella Dallas* (both 1937). Later she would play America's best-loved battleaxe opposite Percy Kilbride in the famous *Ma and Pa Kettle* films of the Forties and Fifties.

The screenplay, faithful to Clare Boothe's venomous original play (which we are told in the credit immediately beneath the main title ran for 666 performances at the Ethel Barrymore Theatre) was by Anita Loos (1893–1981), the former staff writer for D W Griffith. Her *Gentlemen Prefer Blondes* had been filmed in 1928, and would be much more famously remade in 1953, with Marilyn Monroe and Jane Russell. More recently she had scripted *San Francisco* for Jeanette MacDonald and Clark Gable, and *Red-Headed Woman* for Jean Harlow. Because much of the spicy dialogue (acceptable in the stage production, where children had not been allowed in the theatre) had to be toned down for the screen, Loos and her co-writer-assistant Jane Murfin had worked around the clock under Hays Office supervision to get the script exactly right – the Hays Office dictating that if children were *appearing* in the film, then they must not be 'subjected to perversion and turpitude'.

Adrian and his couturiers also had their work cut out: the inventories for *The Women* list a staggering 237 outfits, none of which came out of its wrapper until the cameras were ready to roll so as to avoid catfights among the cast. And it was Joan who got to wear the $25,000 necklace earmarked for Norma Shearer.

The film critic Paul Roen would observe many years later in his essential *High Camp: A Gay Guide to Camp & Cult Films*,

> The Women features an entirely female cast (directed by that notorious bitch, George Cukor) yammering and blabbering incessantly and interminably, till the very act of listening becomes literally exhausting. A catfest like this could be fun, theoretically, but only in very small doses. The Women, unfortunately, runs two hours and thirteen minutes.

Actually, once one gets beyond the first few minutes of shrieking confusion that takes place in Cedric Gibbons's 27-room beauty salon set – and dismisses the wholly unnecessary central Technicolor fashion-show sequence – the film is not bad at all. The lengthy opening credits reveal what we are in for by superimposing the faces of the characters onto those of the animals whose characteristics they best display. Thus, Norma Shearer is the fallow deer, Joan the snarling leopard, Rosalind Russell the cat, Paulette Goddard the fox, Joan Fontaine the lamb, Lucile Watson the wise owl, Marjorie Main the horse, etc. It was *supposed* to be Shearer's film, and she *is* tremendous as the suffering, saintly Mary Haines, though it was Joan who ended up with the best reviews – albeit that she is on screen for just 26 minutes.

The story begins at Sydney's, a Park Avenue beauty-fashion salon where society wives and mistresses gather to gossip, have their fingernails painted the latest Jungle Red, and generally try to outbitch each other. The current scandal centres around Mary's husband, Stephen, who is having an affair with shopgirl Crystal Allen (Joan) who hails from the 'wrong side of Park Avenue' and works behind the perfume counter at Black's department store – a high-class establishment, though none of *these* so-called pillars of the community would be seen dead in the place. It is Crystal who sold Stephen the perfume he gave to Mary on her previous birthday.

'She's got those eyes that run up and down a man like a searchlight,' someone says of Crystal, though Mary is the last to find out about her husband's carousing, and is shocked to learn not just that her father was no different, but that her mother (Watson) accepted this as the norm. 'A man has only one escape from his old self,' she says. 'To see a different self in the mirror of some woman's eyes!' Mama advises Mary to sit tight, say and do nothing, and allow Stephen to get over his latest passing fancy. Then the pair promptly take the next boat to Bermuda for a few weeks' break, as if *this* is the norm, while the camera cuts to the catty Crystal – Joan, making her entrance thirty minutes into the film.

That she is an out-and-out bitch goes without saying. Frizzy-permed Crystal smokes behind the perfume counter, snarls at the other assistants, but is all sweetness and light when Stephen telephones – until he almost stands her up for his own wife. Later, wife and mistress meet and lock horns for the first time when Crystal visits Sydney's and poaches the nightdress Mary is about to buy – then opens a charge account using Stephen as a reference. Mary orders her to end the relationship, something Crystal sarcastically insists only he may do, and when Mary retorts that her husband could *never* love a girl like her, Crystal levels, 'Well, if he can't he's an awfully good *actor*! . . . Can the sob stuff, Mrs Haines. You noble wives and mothers bore the brains out of me!' When Mary further suggests that the gold lamé Crystal is trying on would be unsuitable for entertaining her husband, the response is a cold, 'When anything I wear *doesn't* please Stephen, I take it off!'

It does not take long for Mary's so-called friend Sylvia (Russell), who hardly ever seems to pause for breath – 'It's just her tough luck she wasn't born deaf and dumb,' someone says – to shop her to Sydney's resident gossip, Dolly (Hedda Hopper, more or less playing herself), who makes sure that the scandal ends up on the front page of the local rag. For Mary, this is the last straw: she heads off to Reno for a quickie divorce. Also on the train are the matronly serial-divorcée Flora Comtesse de Lave (Boland), whose fake French mannerisms grate on the nerves after a while; sweet-natured

Peggy Fay (Fontaine), whose pride prevents her from going back to New York and making up with her husband; and chorus girl Miriam Aarons (Goddard), who says of the many men she has used, '*Any* ladle's sweet that dishes out some gravy!'

This quartet arrives at the Double Bar T Ranch, an unlikely shelter for attendant divorcées run by yodelling yokel Lucy (Main), who is unsure if she has ever been married, though she does have three kids. Flora falls for stud ranch-hand Buck, and agrees to marry him when he tells her that he likes her even more than his horse – while we learn that Miriam wants her divorce only so that she can wed blabbermouth Sylvia's husband. Nor surprisingly, perhaps, Sylvia is the next to arrive on the scene – resulting in the inevitable catfight when she meets up with her 'filthy diesel' rival (filmed in a single take; Rosalind Russell dislocated her shoulder). 'I make Howard pay for what he wants,' Miriam hisses. '*You* make him pay for what he *doesn't* want!'

Mary's divorce comes through, and the very same day Stephen calls to say that he and the 'red-headed octopus' Crystal are married – cut to Crystal in her tub, eighteen months down the line, yelling at the maid and being obnoxious to precocious stepdaughter Little Mary (Virginia Weidler), a scenario that forty years on would see cynics comparing Joan's character with her real or invented 'Mommie Dearest' alter-ego. The child may get away with flinging a few home truths in Crystal's direction, but she still has to curtsy to the Queen before leaving. Mary, meanwhile, outwardly gives the impression that she is enjoying life as a free woman – throwing annual 'divorce celebration' parties for the same, mostly two-faced friends, after which Mama fumigates the house, escorts her to the bedroom and pronounces, 'It's marvellous to be able to spread out in a bed like a swastika!'

Mary finds out from her daughter, however, what life is really like *chez* Crystal and Stephen. 'He's so *miserable*,' Little Mary pipes. 'He sits for hours and hours all alone in his study with his head buried in his hands, while that silly thing plays solitaire with the radio on!' Realising that they still might have a chance, Mary puts on her jewels and glad rags and paints her nails. Holding them up to the camera she exclaims, 'I've had two years to grow claws – Jungle Red!' Then she heads for Sydney's, where Crystal is already on the warpath because she has once more been accused of adultery – this time with Buck, Flora's husband, who has left the ranch to become a big star on the radio. When all of Crystal's friends turn on her for what she has done and shop her to Dolly the hack, she tells them that she no longer needs them because Buck is filthy rich – only to have Flora knock her for six with the admission that in order to keep *this* husband, *she* has been paying the radio station to employ him!

Even so, Crystal has the last word and levels, just as Mary is about to be reunited with Stephen, 'Well, girls. Looks like it's back to the perfume counter for me. And, by the way, there's a name for you ladies – but it isn't used in high society outside of a kennel!'

Despite the brevity of her role in *The Women* (the top-grossing film of 1939 after *Gone With the Wind*), most of the critics hailed it as *her* film – the same critics who had supported the 'Box-Office Poison' slur! The film also more or less heralded the end of Norma Shearer's career. Shortly after completing it, she cast discretion to the winds by having a very public affair with 'Gillette blade' George Raft. She rejected *Mrs Miniver*, the film that made Greer Garson a star, in favour of the dismal *We Were Dancing* with Melvyn Douglas. Her swan-song, *Her Cardboard Lover*, formerly a huge success for Tallulah Bankhead on the London stage, saw her equally miscast opposite Robert Taylor. Reputedly out of respect for Irving Thalberg, Shearer never remarried. She died in June 1983, aged 80, and was buried next to her husband.

If Joan was finally free of one serious rival, though she did not know this at the time, there was still Bette Davis to contend with. With the war raging in Europe, on 1 January 1940 British actor Basil Rathbone became the first in Hollywood to raise funds for the British War Relief by holding a tickets-only dinner party at his Bel Air Home. Bette, who had filed for divorce from Harmon Nelson, turned up with new lover George Brent, whom she did not know was gay. Joan swanned into the event with five male escorts, *all* of them gay, and one of whom left the bash with Brent. Joan attempted to speak to Bette several times during the evening, but each time was snubbed. The rivalry was exacerbated two weeks later when *Life* magazine named Bette that year's 'Queen of the Movies'. Joan was invited to the presentation at the Trocadero, but refused to attend, declaring that there was no way she was 'going to have her nose rubbed in the shit' by the woman who had begun referring to her in public as 'the village siren'. In effect, this would happen in March, that same year, when the Press Association voted Bette 'Female Star Best Liked by Interviewers' – and voted Joan runner-up.

Meanwhile, Joan made what would be her last film with Clark Gable – *Strange Cargo*, based on Richard Sale's novel, *Not Too Narrow, Not Too Deep* – but only after Spencer Tracy, forgiven by Joan for his outburst in the radio studio, had turned it down. Tracy had read W H Mooring's comment in *Film Weekly* – 'The title has the ring of a spade against earth, hasn't it? And Hollywood loves to dig graves.' Supporting were Ian Hunter and two fine Hungarian actors seen mostly as villains at around this time: Peter Lorre and Paul Lukas.

The film was shot on location at Pismo Beach and the 'neo-tropical' Pico National Park – the first time Joan had worked outside a studio lot since her silents days. It was also her least taxing production on MGM's costumes department, for while her wardrobes for *The Bride Wore Red* and *The Women* had cost well in excess of $30,000, the trio of 'bargain basement' dresses she wears here cost less than $100.

Strange Cargo is second only to *Possessed* in the eight Crawford-Gable vehicles, but even the two screen legends are not as impressive here as Ian Hunter (1900–75), whose character, Cambreau, is of course a very thinly disguised Jesus Christ. Surprisingly, this caused no problems with the Hays Office's anti-blasphemy brigade. The characterisation, without doubt the finest of Hunter's distinguished career, is honest, intensely moving and never over the top. As Cambreau/Christ, Hunter *looks* holy. No, what saw *Strange Cargo* banned in some American states was the *implication* of some of the dialogue – tough, 'he-man' convicts were not supposed to address each other as 'sweetheart' – and a homoerotic scene in which Gable reverentially very nearly kisses Ian Hunter on the mouth.

The action takes place in an island penal colony 'off the coast of one of the Guianas', a place where past, present and future are one. The toughest prisoner here is Verne (Gable), a thief who believes that the only thing worth stealing is his freedom. Verne has bungled so many escapes that the governor puts him to work outside the prison walls – this way he will see that the jungle beyond is impenetrable. On the wharf he watches rough-edged café chanteuse Julie (Joan) smoking a cigarette. When she tosses away the stub he retrieves it, sniffs, licks and finishes smoking it. Julie is being pursued by odious stool-pigeon Monsieur Pig (Lorre) who has been carrying a torch for her for some time, and is not put off even when she snarls, 'Men die all the time and pigs live on and on – and you'd think their own smell would kill them!'

Neither is Julie that much nicer to Verne, engaging him in suggestive bitchy banter that makes him all the more intent on having her. It matters nothing to him that he will be thrown into solitary confinement for failing to return to the prison with the rest of the work party – one night with this Marseilles firebrand will have made the extra suffering worthwhile. What he does not know is that Cambreau has latched on to the working party to make up the numbers – emerging from nowhere, knowing everything about the disciples he will soon gather about him, though they know absolutely nothing about him other than that his teachings make sense and his prophecies always come true.

Verne, meanwhile, sneaks into Julie's room, and after a little more sniping she changes her mind about giving him a good time – he reminds her *too* much of an ex-lover – and shops him to the authorities. The ruse backfires, however, and *both* of them are arrested. Fraternisation with convicts is against colonial law, and Julie is given mere hours to leave the island. Cut to the prison, where Cambreau is addressing his flock, which includes top dog Moll (Albert Dekker), who makes no secret of the fact that his love for pretty blond youngster Dufond (John Arledge) is more than brotherly – a reflection of the pair's relationship off the screen. (In 1968, cross-dresser Dekker, after being outed by the tabloids, would be found dead, wearing ladies' lingerie and hanging from a shower rail.) Verne grabs the Bible, reads a quote and chortles, 'So, God created Man in his own image. How d'you like that? Take a look at me. Do *I* look like a god to you?' Cambreau's response is that *every* man has a little bit of God in him, if only he looks.

When Cambreau learns that Moll and Dufond are planning an escape, and that several others are contributing towards the cost of the boat waiting beyond the jungle, he pays for himself and Verne to go with them. Moll does not, however, want Verne along, bashes him and leaves him for dead. The prisoners make a break for it, but Cambreau has effected a miracle: Verne recovers from his injuries, finds the map that Cambreau has drawn in the back of his Bible, and he too gets away. Before catching up with the others, though, he has to find Julie. She is desperately trying to raise funds to leave the island and again Monsieur Pig offers to help, in exchange for her favours. '*You're* the one man in the world I'd never get low enough to touch,' she tells him, settling for assistance from the just marginally less obnoxious official, Marfeu (Bernard Nedell) – long enough to attempt to kill him and abscond with his money, though Cambreau's disembodied voice prevents her from following through ('Not *that* way, Julie!').

Julie is rescued by Verne, who continues to treats her like dirt and compares her with the cheap food she feeds him. 'Garbage,' he drawls, 'but good enough for a man when he's starving. You'll do too, baby – this is no time to be particular!' Still thinking him a louse, she leaves with him and they catch up with Cambreau and the others at the shore, their number reduced by a series of incidents in the jungle just as Cambreau predicted. A chance remark that Julie is here solely for the crew's entertainment sees Verne and Moll scrapping for supremacy. Verne wins, takes over as captain, and Julie stands Garbo-esque, spread-eagled before the mainsail as they embark. When she brazenly kisses him, one of the men asks, 'What good can ever come from a man like that, a *woman* like that?' Cambreau is nonjudgmental: he sees her as Mary Magdalene, even the Holy Virgin, and philosophically replies, 'I've heard of it happening before. Why can't it happen again?'

Cambreau's prophecy – that others will die on account of the elements and the struggle for survival – also comes true. One man becomes hysterical, throws the water barrel into the ocean and then gets eaten by a shark while attempting to retrieve it. Moll slaps Dupond when he becomes mad, accidentally killing him, and with nothing left to live for, tests the barrel's contents to see if it contains sea water – it does, and he chokes to death on his swollen tongue.

The survivors reach the mainland to find Monsieur Pig and the colony governor already there – they have not had to tackle the jungle. Verne pays a fisherman to take them to Cuba, but at the last moment Julie changes her mind about going away with him – she thinks it is her fault that he is on the run, that she is not worth the risks he is taking. Verne, Cambreau and the fisherman set sail just as a storm is brewing. Cambreau knows that this particular mission of his is nearing completion, that the time has come for him to 'move on' and help others. As the rain lashes the deck, he engages in a battle of words with Verne, the Doubting Thomas – *begging* him to kill him, knowing of course that he is immortal. Verne knocks him overboard, where he floats in the sea, cruciform, before Verne realises *who* he is and dives in to save him. Back on deck Cambreau dies, then is resurrected – and Verne, knowing that he has died for *him*, bursts into tears and *wants* to kiss him (and apparently does, in the original frame, which the Hays Office ordered to be destroyed) but instead clutches him to his breast. The film ends as Verne and Julie are reunited, and with Verne giving himself up – at last he has found honour and will serve the rest of his sentence because he knows the woman he loves will be waiting for him when he gets out. And as Cambreau exits the scenario just as mysteriously as he arrived, the fisherman makes the sign of the cross.

There was a massive row between Joan and Louis B Mayer when, at the film's preview in April 1940, she was 'mortified' to see that he had contravened the terms of her contract by putting Gable's name above hers in the credits. By the time of the premiere, two weeks later, a compromise had been reached – because Gable had refused to be 'downgraded', their names had been printed side by side, but in alphabetical order, which effectively meant that Joan had won!

Scarcely pausing to catch her breath, Joan walked off the *Strange Cargo* post-production set into *Susan and God*, based on the play by Rachel Crothers. This reunited her with several colleagues from *The Women*: Hunt Stromberg, George Cukor, Marjorie Main, Ruth Hussey, Anita Loos and half of the technicians. Joan played religious bigot Susan Trexel, who picks up a few theological tips during a European vacation, then returns to New York to foist them upon her society friends, but fails to apply them to herself. Her long-suffering husband, Barry (Frederic March), has been driven to drink and walked out on her because of her nagging; her daughter, Blossom (Rita Quigley, the first but by no means last on-screen daughter, to reflect more than a little of what would later happen off the screen), has psychological problems relating to Susan's self-centredness. All ends well, but not without a great many tears and tantrums and much soul-searching.

The part of Susan (in Britain, the film was shown as *The Gay Mrs Trexel* until the word 'gay' took on another meaning) was a feather in Joan's cap because it should have gone to Norma Shearer, who had rejected the role Gertrude Lawrence had played on Broadway, considering herself too young, at forty, to play the mother of a teenage girl! According to one press report, Joan had scoffed at this, telling Hunt Stromberg, 'If it's a good part, I wouldn't consider myself too *old* to play Wally Beery's grandmother!' Joan was not very happy to be working with Frederic March, whose ever-present interfering wife, Florence Eldridge, she could not stand. The rest of the cast was first class, with Nigel Bruce – who since *The Last of Mrs Cheyney* had become a household name as the bumbling Dr Watson in the *Sherlock Holmes* films – Bruce Cabot, and Rita Hayworth in one of her first important roles. During shooting, Joan became involved with second lead John Carroll (1905–79), one of the most promiscuous men in Hollywood at the time. 'Absolutely anything with a hole,' she would say of the handsome stud, whose infamous all-nude pool parties went on for almost twenty years before he was exposed by *Confidential* magazine.

Susan and God went on general release in July 1940, by which time Joan had made, in retrospect, what many would consider the biggest mistake of her life. She had adopted a child – one who would ultimately fling her every last kindness back in her face with unspeakable vengeance, and posthumously leave Joan's reputation in tatters.

On 25 May 1940, syndicated columns across America bore the headline: 'Joan Crawford Adopts Baby Girl'. Additionally, Jimmi Fidler wrote in the *New York Mirror*, 'Disillusioned with men after three [sic] unfortunate marriages, Joan feels her real happiness lies in being a mother. What a predicament!' The child was an eleven-month-old girl, born 11 June 1939 and adopted in New York City, and would be named Christina. For some time, Joan had wanted a baby of her own, and any number of excuses had been given as to why she had never carried full-term: the botched abortions and the miscarriages – two, she claimed, while with Douglas Fairbanks Jr, and anything between two and *seven*, with Franchot Tone. Then there were the cynics who declared that Joan was so narcissistic that she would never have risked ruining her shape by getting pregnant. The truth most likely is that Joan had had so many botched abortions that these had left her *unable* to conceive.

Shortly after divorcing Franchot, Joan had begun dating celebrity lawyer Greg Bautzer (1910–87) – or rather, she had poached him from seventeen-year-old Lana Turner. Bautzer, glamorous enough to have been a matinee idol in his own right, frequently made a point of retaining his 'more money than sense' female clients by bedding them; later he would have a very high-profile affair with Ava Gardner. It was he who arranged the adoption, applying to several states where single parents were allowed to adopt, having no success allegedly because of Joan's reputation, and eventually settling for a 'baby broker', though these were illegal *everywhere*. Even so, Joan was checked out: Barbara Stanwyck, Gary Cooper and Margaret Sullavan (whose children she had looked after) supported her application, declaring her to be possessed of every quality essential to motherhood.

In her scathing memoir *Mommie Dearest*, Christina Crawford claims she was born in Hollywood's Presbyterian Hospital, but 'taken out of an Eastern foundling home' in July 1939 – that Joan had hidden her in the nursery at Brentwood Park for ten months before legally adopting her. On the face of it the story sounds far-fetched: with the heavy traffic of visitors in and out of the house, including inquisitive reporters and fans who were always subjected to a guided tour, it would have been virtually impossible for anyone *not* to have heard a child crying. By making such a statement Christina seems to have been attempting to keep events *before* her adoption in line with many of the scurrilous tales she says took place over the next 37 years. *Mommie Dearest* is a cruel, heartless testament to a woman who placed an exceedingly gilded roof over her children's heads and who, though often unkind to colleagues, co-stars and studio executives, was extremely generous to her family – even those who had treated her like dirt. When she adopted Christina, Joan was still supporting her mother, helping her brother Hal out after his divorce *and* paying a monthly allowance to Hal's daughter, Joan LeSueur. When Hal and his wife had separated, Joan had actually offered to *buy* their baby – hard cash, she had argued, being the only language the LeSueurs understood.

Christina Crawford's book would set a precedent for frequently brutal, unforgivable kiss-and-tells: Bing Crosby, Margaret Sullavan, Bette Davis and most famously Marlene Dietrich would all suffer the indignity of being trashed by ungrateful offspring, often with little or no witness proof of the anecdotes and one-to-one incidents that pepper their pages, pushing their famous parent's genuine achievements aside – yet the books never had any lasting effect on these legends other than to invoke pity for what they had introduced into the world.

Penned by a young woman obviously consumed with hatred, much of Christina's book should be taken with a large pinch of salt. According to Christina (but no other sources), her birth mother was a student, her father a sailor. Everything in the nursery at Brentwood Park was monogrammed 'Joan' because it had been Joan's intention to turn her daughter into Crawford Jr. Also, Joan is said to have saved all of Christina's hair-clippings, and to have smothered her with affection because there had been so little of this in Joan's own childhood. This latter statement is certainly true. Christina adds:

> Mother and I were absolutely inseparable. She took me with her everywhere she went . . . I was hers alone. She was my 'Mommie Dearest', the wellspring from whence all love and affection flowed, and I was her longed-for golden-haired girl . . . I was to be the best, the most beautiful, the smartest, quickest, most special child on the face of the earth . . . My adoring, indulgent mother couldn't resist giving me anything I asked for. In return, she had my total devotion. The sun rose and set on my beloved Mommie Dearest. Her laughter was the music of my life, and the sound of her heart beating as she held me close to her made me feel safe and quiet.

Not surprisingly, such florid phrases have led many to accuse Christina of extreme condescension, particularly as while one works through her book one becomes increasingly absorbed by the question that if Joan *was* such a bad if not wicked mother, why did the authorities not step in and take her children away? There have been suggestions that just as the studios went out of their way to prevent gay actors and actresses from 'bringing shame' on them, so MGM might have wanted to cover up Joan's alleged cruelty towards her children. With Louis B Mayer's staunch attitude towards family values, however, one does find this hard to believe.

Joan took Christina and her English nanny with her every day onto the set of *A Woman's Face*, one of the truly astounding *films noirs* of the Forties, which began shooting during the summer of 1940. Based on Francis de Croisset's play *Il Etait une Fois*, it had already been filmed in Swedish with Ingrid Bergman (*En Kvinnas Ansikte*, 1938); the new version was directed by Cukor, who managed to persuade Lon Chaney's personal make-up artist, Jack Dawn, out of retirement to work on Anna Holm's disfigured face during Joan's early scenes. The screenplay was by Donald Ogden Stewart, who since last working with Joan had scripted *The Philadelphia Story*. A key member of Hollywood's Anti-Nazi League (aided by a considerable donation from Joan), Stewart is thought to have been responsible for the inclusion of two fine German actors who had fled to America to escape Nazi tyranny: Albert Basserman and Conrad Veidt.

Joan had a tremendous admiration for Conrad Veidt (1893–1943), whose abrupt departure from Germany was not because he was Jewish – though his wife was – but because the Hitler regime had included his name on its 'degenerates' list. In 1919 he had received worldwide acclaim with his stunning performance as Cesare, the somnambulist in *The Cabinet of Dr Caligari*. That same year he had volunteered for a part in *Anders Als Die Anderen* ('Different From the Others'), the German Institute For Sexual

Science's detailed exploration and defence of homosexuality, some thirty years ahead of the Kinsey Report. The film had been accepted as an academic work, and on account of the Weimar Republic's relaxed attitude towards sex had not caused that much of a fuss. Prints of it had re-emerged, however, just as Hitler had been coming to power, when Veidt had been a regular visitor to the gay *lokals* in Berlin's red-light district. At around the time he worked with Joan, two of his other films went on release: *Contraband*, and *The Thief of Baghdad*, in which he played the villain par excellence. *A Woman's Face* would bring him more plaudits, though perhaps his greatest moment would come a little later as Major Strasser in *Casablanca*. Of the remaining cast, Melvyn Douglas, Reginald Owen, Margorie Main and George Zucco had all worked with Joan before. Connie Gilchrist, a regular in the Marjorie Main/Wallace Beery roughhouse comedies, would later play Purity Pinker in the *Long John Silver* television series.

The story is told in flashback, through the eyes of various witnesses, as Anna Holm is taken from her prison cell and brought before the court, charged with first-degree murder. Her victim is not made known until near the end of this occasionally confusing (by way of a few dodgy accents) slice of Grand Guignol. The setting is contemporary, but it is ultimately left to Joan's character to *remind* the viewer that this is 1941 – the costumes and sets indicate a setting a good twenty years earlier.

The first to take the stand is the waiter and Anna's partner-in-crime from her roadside tavern, where ladies waltz with each other while lip-synching to Greta Keller. Anna, facially disfigured since her father set fire to her room when she was a child, is hard-bitten, cannot bear the sight of mirrors and knows nothing about love other than what she has read in books. She cannot stand her employees, and the feeling is mutual. Among the diners tonight are the sinister Torsten Barring (Veidt), and man-hungry doctor's wife Vera Segert (Osa Massen), who is here with her lover Erik (Charles Quigley). When Torsten mistakenly ends up with Erik's overcoat and discovers a batch of love letters from Vera in the pocket, the scene is set for blackmail.

Next, the tavern manager tells the judge how he watched his 'well-dressed gargoyle' boss fall in love with Torsten so that they could extort money from Vera. Crime, we hear, is nothing new to Anna: she has served time for impersonating a clergyman, also for running a brothel. Vera herself tells of how Anna came to her house, knowing she was alone, demanding money – and of how, when her husband, Gustaf (Douglas), came home, she persuaded him to take pity on the 'poor creature' rather than call the police and have him find out about her extramarital activities. Gustaf finds Anna fascinating: he just happens to be the best plastic surgeon in Europe, and after showing her his portfolio of 'before and after' photographs declares that he wants to make her beautiful again.

Anna speaks to the court about her unhappy childhood, the accident, how she decided long ago that if the world was against her, then she would turn against it. She is seen (genuinely) playing Chopin on Torsten's piano. For him she goes under the knife, though we suspect it is her *deformity* that attracts him and that he prefers his women to be as creepy as he is. Gustaf, however, suspects that Anna's nasty mien stems from starvation of compassion during her youth. When she is almost complimentary about the work he has done on her face, he tells her, 'My dear Miss Holm, since the first day I met you, you've presented a perfect picture of the most ruthless, terrifying, cold-blooded creature I've ever met. It's been a picture which has fascinated me. Now, unless I misguess, you are about to say something sentimental, something about gratitude and so forth . . .'

Anna's operation is a success and she looks stunning – so much so that she cannot resist pausing in front of mirrors, and her confidence in herself is limitless. Even so, she cannot break the spell Torsten has cast over her and when he tells her that the only obstacle between him and his elderly uncle's fortune is his four-year old nephew, Lars-Erik (Richard Nichols), doubtless hoping for a share of the pickings she agrees to kill the child. The uncle, Consul Magnus (Basserman), is looking for a governess: Torsten secures her the position, she changes her name to Ingrid Paulsen and heads for the snow-covered mountain community.

The Consul's long-serving housekeeper, Emma (a woefully miscast Marjorie Main, looking like an early Mrs Doubtfire, and whose dreadful Southern twang could not be more out of place), takes an instant dislike to Anna, though everyone else approves of her. Anna tries to be severe with her charge, who tells her, 'You couldn't be mean – you're too pretty!' Two years pass and we see her at the Consul's birthday party – *the* event of the year in this neighbourhood – pretending that she hates everyone here, whereas truthfully she has never felt more wanted. Tonight she wears local costume and Torsten compliments her on looking like a saint – Saint Gilda, the patron saint of children. He adds that the charade has gone on for long enough: she must kill Lars-Erik by tomorrow at the latest. Anna's cover is almost blown when Gustaf turns up: he is pleased that she is no longer reliant on crime, accepts her excuse that her new name has allowed her to obliterate her past, but suspects things may not be all they seem when she leaves Lars-Erik for too long under his medicinal ultraviolet lamp – something that she passes off as an accident.

Gustaf tells the judge about the lamp, and how he was suspicious enough to follow Anna when she took Lars-Erik in the cable car. In a tense, lengthy scene without dialogue, Anna is halfway across the ravine when she reaches to unlatch the safety-catch on the gate, ready to send the boy hurtling into the icy swirl below. But she is unable to do it – and hugs him instead. Gustaf ends his testimony by confessing that though married, he still loves Anna. Then Emma takes the stand, recalling the Consul's party, where Anna gave the eccentric old man a gift in which she had concealed an envelope – removed by the housekeeper who suspected that it could only have been a love letter because Anna had never stopped making eyes at him.

The Consul recalls the traditional sleigh ride that takes place after his parties – in this instance, when Torsten kidnaps Lars-Erik, and Anna and Gustaf give chase (ridiculously speeded up, as was the case in the early John Wayne three-reelers) – a pursuit that ends when Anna pulls a gun and shoots Torsten, sending *him* plummeting into the river as Gustaf grabs the horses' reins and saves the boy. The public prosecutor, however, believes that Torsten was Anna's accomplice and that she only killed him to ensure his silence – until Emma produces the missing envelope. This does not contain a love letter as she thought, but a warning about what Torsten was forcing her to do. The case is suspended, and though we do not get to know the judge's decision – to the Hays Office's way of thinking, to allow the public to *see* Anna walking free would have been tantamount to Hollywood actually *condoning* murder – we are pretty confident of a happy ending. Anna tells Gustaf that she loves him too, and he informs his nymphomaniac wife that they have no future together.

A Woman's Face premiered in May 1941, by which time Joan was involved with the British War Effort as chairwoman of a charity raising funds for children orphaned by the London Blitz. Each Sunday there was an 'open day' at Brentwood Park: visitors paid a few cents to see the Victory Garden that had recently replaced her rose bed, hob-nob with the rich and famous and buy autographed photographs. Joan also organised a small army of tin-can collectors who were deployed across Hollywood.

Some time before, Joan had tested for the part of the mute girl in *The Spiral Staircase*, and would have been given the part had Louis B Mayer not put his foot down. For years, he declared, the Queen of MGM had championed the working-class woman and he had no intention of allowing her to become 'the patron saint of cripples'. Two years later, the role would bring Dorothy McGuire international fame. As for Joan, Mayer put her into another potboiler, *When Ladies Meet*, a remake of the 1933 film starring Myrna Loy and Robert Montgomery. The new version, scripted by Anita Loos, had Robert Taylor, Herbert Marshall, and Hollywood's latest sensation, Greer Garson, who at 36 had taken the movie world by storm with *Goodbye Mr Chips!* and *Pride and Prejudice* (1939 and 1940). Joan played

novelist Mary Howard, who likes to think she is a feminist, though this has
not prevented her from playing a wide field. Currently she is involved with her
married publisher, Rogers Woodruff (Marshall), but is being pursued by
much-younger playboy Jimmy Lee (Robert Taylor, sporting an unbecoming
pencil-line moustache, as instructed by Louis B Mayer following a press
article that had described him as 'too pretty'). Feeling that she has to choose
between these two paramours, Mary tries to get Rogers to divorce his wife
and marry her – while Jimmy tries to convince her this is the *wrong* thing to
do by arranging a 'bonding' evening between Mary and Rogers's wife, Clare
(Garson), neither of whom knows the other. The Hollywood wags had a field
day when they watched this taking place at the home of a friend played by
Spring Byington, whose 'sewing-circle' lesbian gatherings were almost as
legendary as those of Alla Nazimova a century earlier. It is Clare who lets slip
that her husband has always been a serial philanderer who is unlikely to
change – whereupon Mary dumps him and ends up with Jimmy. All very con-
venient for hounded Robert Taylor, who again evaded being outed by the
press because, so far as they were concerned, only the most red-blooded males
ended up in a clinch with Joan Crawford!

Surprisingly, Joan and Greer Garson became friends for a while: Garson
and her mother spent several weekends at Brentwood Park, and were
privileged enough for Joan to allow them to be photographed with Christina.
Enmity set in, however, when Garson learned that *she* had been earmarked for
Susan and God until Joan had demanded the part – and not long afterwards it
would be almost full-scale war when, having been convinced by Louis B Mayer
that *she* would win the Best Actress Oscar for *A Woman's Face*, Garson was
nominated for *Blossoms in the Dust*. Henceforth, the Irish-born lovely would
scathingly be referred to only as 'that fucking refugee from Hitler'.

Meanwhile, Hollywood suffered its biggest tragedy since Jean Harlow's
death when Carole Lombard was killed in an air crash. Even Joan had been
surprised when her ongoing serial-lover Clark Gable had settled down to a
life of wedded bliss, buying a twenty-acre ranch in the San Fernando Valley.
Gable and Lombard, one of *the* great show-business romances of the
twentieth century, had affectionately called each other Ma and Pa. She had
become one of the boys, accompanying Gable on 'buddies-only' hunting and
fishing trips, roughing the harsh conditions and out-cursing the best of them.
Gable had even begun tolerating his wife's 'Tinsel Town Sisters' – her gay
entourage, headed by William Haines – and put up with her outrageous
behaviour: he had been present when, during a test for *Twentieth Century*
(1934) with John Barrymore, she had unbuttoned Barrymore's trousers and
fondled his famous 'two-hander'. It was she who told a reporter, who asked
if the rumours were true that Gable anatomically lived up to his nickname

'The King' – in other words, if his penis really did measure a 'regal' twelve inches – 'One inch *less*, dear, and we'll have to start calling him Queen!'

The Gables' marriage is thought to have been going through a rocky patch – allegedly following Lombard's recent miscarriage – when in December 1941 she had embarked on a government-sponsored war-bonds tour, which in the space of a few weeks raised over $2 million. On 16 January 1942, rather than travelling back from Indiana by train as planned, she and her mother Bessie boarded a military plane. There was a sound reason for her rush to get home: she had heard rumours that Gable was having an affair with Lana Turner, his co-star in *Somewhere I'll Find You*, and Lombard wanted to stop this in its tracks. The plane ran into a storm just minutes after take-off and crashed into Table Rock Mountain, near Las Vegas, in a ball of flames, killing all 21 people on board.

Extremely distraught, and no doubt feeling somewhat guilty, Clark Gable flew to Las Vegas and had to be physically restrained (and legally prohibited by MGM) from climbing the mountain and joining in with the search for Lombard's body. For several days he locked himself in his hotel room and refused to see anyone. A week later he was summoned back to work – Louis B Mayer may have appeared outwardly sympathetic, but Lombard had *not* been on his payroll, and Mayer's prime concern was that *Somewhere I'll Find You* should not run over budget. With his usual lack of tact, Mayer called Joan and ordered her to keep away from 'the poor widower' – while encouraging Lana Turner, whom many thought indirectly responsible for Lombard's death, to offer Gable a friendly shoulder to lean on. According to Joan, however, it was *she* who did all the comforting.

Carole Lombard had been assigned to *They All Kissed the Bride* for Columbia, and to Joan's way of thinking, the best tribute she could pay her dead friend was to petition producer Edward Kaufman into talking Columbia into letting Joan take over the role, whether Louis B Mayer approved or not. Mayer certainly *disapproved*, but stepped down from his podium when Joan announced to the press that she would be donating her entire $125,000 salary to the Red Cross, who had recovered Lombard's and her mother's remains from the burned-out wreckage of their plane. Later she would learn that her agent, Mike Levee, had deducted his customary ten per cent – and promptly fired him.

Joan had wanted Adrian to clothe her for the film, but he had recently parted company with MGM, arrogantly declaring that he was tired of down-dressing stars in ordinary clothes now that there was a war on and the studio needed to set an example by making cuts in its budgets. Adrian had been replaced by Irene Lenz (1901–62), who had started out as an extra with MGM in 1925. Three years later she had opened a salon in Los

Angeles, begun designing for the stars, and in 1936 had entered a 'lavender' marriage with scriptwriter Eliot Gibbons, brother of Cedric. Her ascension to the title of one of Hollywood's top designers had been rapid – it was she who had dressed Carole Lombard for her last film, *To Be or Not To Be*, which premiered a few months after her death.

In the wake of Pearl Harbor, good leading men were getting to be thin on the ground. James Stewart had won an Oscar for *The Philadelphia Story*, but despite his success and the lucrative offers that had followed, he had opted to join the US Army. Mickey Rooney, Henry Fonda and Tyrone Power had followed suit, prompting columnist Walter Winchell – a lieutenant-commander in the Naval Reserve – to write in the October issue of *Photoplay*, 'How about awarding Oscars, or at least some sort of recognition to other movie men who have traded their make-up kits and megaphones for duffle bags?' Robert Montgomery, Joan's choice for *They All Kissed the Bride*, was with the Naval Reserve too, while Robert Taylor, her second choice, had also enlisted, proving to detractors that he was as much a man, if not more so, than those who had been excluded from military duty for various disabilities – chief of which was cowardice, according to Tallulah Bankhead, who had taken over from Carol Lombard as America's top war-bond saleswoman. Figures among the 'lazy sunbathers', as she called them, included Humphrey Bogart, Ronald Reagan and even John Wayne.

Joan might have *liked* to have had Gable as her co-star again, but to have him playing opposite a stand-in for his dead wife would have been unthinkable. In August 1943 he would join the US Air Force and serve as a gunnery captain in England, mostly restricted to ground duties and making short recruitment films, on account of the $5,000 reward offered by Goering for his capture. Joan was therefore teamed up again with Melvyn Douglas. Of the other leads, Roland Young was best known for the *Topper* films of the Thirties, and had just completed *Two-Faced Woman* with Douglas and Garbo.

Fans and the general public alike must have found it inconceivable at the time to even *imagine* Joan Crawford attempting screwball comedy, yet she exonerates herself well amid the ensuing confusion, dropping her voice half a tone as Lombard did, but never emulating her. She also proved, at 38, that she had lost none of her dancing skills.

Joan plays tough businesswoman Margaret Drew, head of a refrigerated truck company and variously referred to as 'MJ', 'Maggie', 'Baby' or 'Vinegar Puss', depending on whom she is dealing with. The story begins with her chairing a board meeting called to deal with the problems wrought upon her by Mike Homes (Douglas), a journalist who has been secretly meeting with Drew's drivers to pen a series of scurrilous articles. Like her father before her, Margaret is hard on her drivers: she hires 'spotters', who impose on-the-spot fines if they are caught using their trucks for non-business purposes – fired if drivers are caught twice. 'The daughter is a chip off the old block – if you can chip granite,' Mike tells driver buddy Johnny Johnson (Jenkins), who like himself and all Drew's other employees has never seen Margaret and assumes that she must only be an old harridan.

When Johnny is stopped by an evening-gowned matriarch spotter while giving Mike a lift, Mike decides he will have it out with Margaret once and for all. Today her sister, Vivian (Helen Parrish), is getting married, apparently against her will, to millionaire Stephen Pettingell (Roger Clarke); but she really loves Joe, a grease-monkey from the local filling station who threatens trouble if the proceedings go ahead. 'Intelligent people don't marry for better or worse,' Margaret tries to console her, 'they marry for better or *better*!' Mike gatecrashes the ceremony. Margaret sees him and goes weak at the knees – they obviously go back some time, though it appears that when they were lovers beforehand, they knew each other as 'Baby' and 'Joe', which explains why, when he hungrily kisses the bride, Margaret assumes he must be the same Joe who only minutes ago threatened to stop the wedding – and she has him arrested.

Because Margaret is as ruthless towards her lawyers as she is towards everyone else, they bail him out of jail and he reveals to Margaret that *he* is the hated Mike Holmes. She attempts to buy his silence, but he has principles and says he can only discuss the matter on friendly territory – his apartment in the same block as Johnny's. Margaret swoons as she is about to go through the door, refuses to let him take her coat because she says the room is cold like him, then re-opens the door to let the draught in when he turns on the charm and gets her emotionally hot and bothered. We learn that they were an item before he went off to the South Seas and fell for a sarong, and he says that she is as bossy now as she was back then because she is afraid of men. He kisses her, she passes out, and the next thing we see is her waking up in his bed, wearing his pyjamas and speculating over whether he has had his way with her – though it turns out that he has slept in Johnny's bed. At once Margaret becomes standoffish and Mike levels, 'You're a machine, not a woman. You've no right to assume any of the feminine graces!'

The next morning when she returns to work, wearing the same outfit she left in the previous day, she is the talk of the management suite because it is obvious that she has stayed out all night and may not be as stuffy as everyone thinks – even more so when Mike barges into her office as she is changing and announces, 'Maggie, don't you *ever* have any clothes on?' She gets on her high horse again, and this time when she offers to buy him off and stop his piece from being published, he accepts. He asks her out to dinner, but instead they end up at the Truck Drivers Annual Ball, where Johnny coerces her into partnering him in the wildest – and funniest – jitterbug contest ever, where even the sausages cooking on the griddle grab a piece of the action and no one knows that 'Mike's ball of fluff', who walks off with the trophy, is actually the boss. Later, she and Mike get tipsy on Johnny's moonshine: she promises him a raise, forgetting that she has earlier given instructions for he and a dozen other drivers to be fired for misuse of the company trucks.

Johnny discovers who Margaret really is when she asks him to drive her and Mike home, and this time Mike wakes up in a strange bed – wearing the cook's outsized 'paratrooper' nightdress, and unaware that while he has been asleep, Margaret has confessed how she has missed him during the years they have been apart, though she cannot bring herself to say what she feels in her heart – that she *loves* him. Johnny and his sacked colleagues, however, now resent him: they think he has feigned interest in their cause in order to seduce their employer. Mike gets himself out of a sticky situation by bailing out Vivian's husband, Stephen – who far from inheriting his father's millions is so broke that he has had to shut down his steel mill, though the fact that he is poor has simply caused Vivian to fall in love with him and forget about mechanic Joe. Urged by Margaret's mother – the usually snooty Billie Burke, who tells him, 'You look like a gentleman, even if you *do* have your coat off!' – Mike loans Stephen the money he has extorted from Margaret so that he can re-open his mill and employ the drivers Margaret has fired.

At last, Margaret is enjoying life. She smiles all the time and sings – '*I must have been a beautiful baby*' – she has learned how to knit, and day-dreams at the next board meeting that the prototype truck Mike has just bought also delivers babies! Nevertheless, it is left to her doctor to inform her that she is in *love*, resulting in her and Mike driving off in the new truck to be married. What's more, she announces as the credits prepare to roll, she may not be coming back!

In 1941, Joan acquired a second child from an illegal baby broker, a two-week-old boy she named Christopher. Because of her flair for telling fans and journalists *too* much about herself, this was reported in the press, along with his date and place of birth – enabling his birth mother to attempt to make a fast buck, and leaving Joan with no alternative but to hand the child back, only to have the mother sell him back to the baby broker for a higher price.

As one might return a pair of ill-fitting shoes and demand a replace-ment, so Joan soon instructed Greg Bautzer to find her another child. In the meantime, and equally bizarrely, came Joan's acquisition of her third (or fourth, if she had married Jimmy Walton) husband, for she was apparently so keen to introduce a father figure into her children's lives that she took to *auditioning* candidates for the role – once Clark Gable had turned her down with the old chestnut that *he* had no intention of marrying again. Gable, who never really got over Carole Lombard's death, had begun drinking heavily in an attempt to dull the pain. There were just two stipulations for would-be Mr Crawfords: candidates would have to be good-looking and lusty, naturally, but they would also have to be exempted from war service. Joan did not wish to be widowed unnecessarily, she said, and bring up her children on her own. There was a fling with 25-year-old Method actor Glenn Ford, whom she had first seen as a bit-part in the aptly titled *Babies For Sale* (1940). This soon petered out: Ford, who subsequently married Eleanor Powell, later said he had found Joan too aggressive for more than a few one-night stands – and in any case he had lied to her about his military medical. Having been declared fully fit, he had enlisted for the Marine Corps, and later in the war he would join the French Foreign Legion.

Next in line, astonishingly perhaps, was John Wayne, who had just signed to play opposite her in *Reunion in France*, scheduled to begin shooting during the spring of 1942. Then there were French actor Jean-Pierre Aumont, and Joseph M Newman, recently hired by MGM to direct *Northwest Rangers*, the 1942 remake of Clark Gable's 1934 *Manhattan Melodrama*. Finally there was Newman's star actor James Craig, a Gable lookalike who had appeared with Marlene Dietrich and John Wayne in *Seven Sinners* (1940). After dismissing Craig as unsuitable, and fast running out of patience, Joan assigned the task of match-making to Harry Mines, a journalist she had befriended a few years earlier and who now worked as her press agent. It was he who ultimately suggested bespectacled (and therefore not eligible for military service) Phillip Terry, an actor currently under contract to Paramount, though most of his films had been as a loan-out to MGM – most notably *Hold That Kiss* (1938) with Mickey Rooney.

Joan was certainly impressed by the anglicised, muscle-bound, six-foot-one, 180-pound slab of beefcake. Born Frederick Korman in Los Angeles in 1909, Terry had worked the Texas oilfields alongside his oil-operator father before enrolling at Stanford University, where his tremendous physique and sporting abilities soon earned him a place in the university football team. After graduation, he had gone to London to study acting at the Royal Academy of Dramatic Art, hence his clipped accent. Returning to America in 1937, he had been signed up by MGM, but had soon moved to Paramount, where he had made his debut in a nondescript western, *The Parson of Panamint* (1941). He was almost as handsome as Franchot Tone, and equally bisexual, but more discreet. His current *amour* was none other than Robert Taylor, with whom he would soon make *Bataan*. Joan made it clear from the outset, however, that Terry would never appear in any of her films (there *had* been the bit-part in *Mannequin*, though he and Joan never met off the set until Harry Mines introduced them) – *and* he would be her husband mostly in name only, and have no say in the raising of her children.

Phillip Terry was also the first Crawford 'caddy' – a term said to have been coined by her friend Tallulah Bankhead. 'Caddies' were, according to Tallulah, 'Slaves who come running when a damsel snaps her fingers, but who keep their cocks inside their trousers until they have earned their Brownie points.' They were frequently subjected to ridicule, should they fail to toe the line – the most usual 'punishment' being to have the news spread like wildfire that they were 'lacking in the love-handle department' – though in Terry's case Joan was fond of boasting that 'it' was in perfect proportion to the rest of him.

A caddy's duty was not just to service and protect his lady. He had to be a complete lackey, and assist her with 'essential' duties: pouring her coffee, running her bath and squeezing the paste onto the toothbrush, sharpening her lipstick and putting it on ice, ensuring that her Martinis were mixed exactly right, helping her to light her cigarettes, carrying her dog if she had one, tucking her into bed at night, and making sure that he was there the next morning when she stirred. Joan took it one step further by sometimes insisting that *her* caddies beg, literally, for sex – and to kneel before her and crave her forgiveness whenever she said they had displeased her, which apparently was rather often.

Meanwhile, there was the film with John Wayne, by all accounts not a happy experience. 'Get Wayne out of the saddle and you've got nothing,' Joan would later say. In *Reunion in France* Joan played Parisian courtesan Michele de la Becque, who is more interested in men than in the war-ravaged world about her: with her rich industrialist lover, Robert Cortot (Philip Dorn) she socialises with both sides in the conflict, blithely unaware of the problems this might cause until she discovers that Cortot's factories are manufacturing weapons for the Nazis. Only then does she become concerned for the plight of France under the jackboot. Joining the Résistance, she helps rescue American fighter pilot Pat Talbot (Wayne), shot down and hunted by the Gestapo. The two become lovers, and she once more gets to dress like Zara Leander, but in a plot twist she is soon back in Cortot's arms when it emerges that the weapons he is making and distributing are fake. Moreover, he too is gallantly fighting for the Free French.

Joan's wedding took place at midnight on 21 July 1942 in Hidden Hills, near the San Fernando Valley, at the home of Neil McCarthy, her new lawyer. Here, Lucille Fay Tone became Mrs Frederick Korman, though she would never use the name even on legal documents. As had happened with Joan's marriage to Douglas Fairbanks Jr, *both* parties lied about their ages: Joan reducing hers by four years, Terry by five. There was no honeymoon.

Joan had to be back on the set of *Reunion in France*, and dutifully did so at nine the next morning. According to John Wayne (as cited in the Lincoln Centre's Joan Crawford archives), Joan's arrival with her caddy-husband gave a clear indication of how the marriage would shape up: 'First came Joan and her secretary, then her make-up man, then her wardrobe man – then Phil Terry, carrying her dog.'

It certainly *was* a marriage of convenience. Terry was given his own suite of rooms at Brentwood Park and, unlike Franchot Tone's, his movements were not monitored. Joan's world revolved around Christina, though when she and Terry were photographed in public she always ensured that they were holding hands – usually with him clutching his spectacles in the other. Not long after their wedding, Greg Bautzer was summoned back to the fold and asked to acquire another baby for Joan. He found her a Scandinavian boy to replace her 'stolen' Christopher. This one was given the same name – after a brief period when he was referred to as Phillip Jr, by which time Joan had already concluded that the new marriage might not last, and *if* she divorced Terry, she did not want to carry forward 'excess baggage' by naming her son after him, which perhaps explains why Terry's name was not included on the adoption certificate. Joan also wisely changed the child's date and place of birth for the benefit of the press – to ensure that this one did not suffer the same fate as the first Christopher. And then it was back to work.

'There are so many spies in *Above Suspicion*, it is hard to keep track of them,' observed the *New York Herald Tribune* before trashing Joan's second war picture. In fact, she and the immensely likeable Fred MacMurray, fresh from making *The Lady is Willing* with Marlene Dietrich, do rather well in this neatly assembled espionage thriller set in Europe at the outbreak of World War II. Based on the novel by Helen McInnes and directed by Richard Thorpe, there was sterling support from Reginald Owen, Basil Rathbone and Bruce Lester. It was also the great Conrad Veidt's last film – and for once, he wasn't playing the villain. Veidt suffered a fatal heart attack while playing golf a few weeks after shooting was completed, aged 49.

Joan and MacMurray play newlyweds Frances and Richard Myles, student and professor at Oxford, who are about to set off for Europe on their honeymoon. The Foreign Office, however, with whom Richard seems to have connections, have a different idea: they want the pair to track down a missing scientist, also being hunted by the Gestapo; the latter are after his formula, which will destroy their secret weapon – a magnetic mine that the Germans plan to use in their invasion of Poland. No one knows the identity of this man, and to find him the couple must unravel a series of clues that frequently puts them in grave danger – not that this prevents them from stopping every now and then to have a little sing-song.

At an artistes' watering hole in Montmartre, someone slips a guidebook of South Germany into Richard's overcoat pocket. This contains a map, a coded message, and a number of dots which, when joined together, form a musical scale – the opening bar of the couple's password tune, 'My Love is Like a Red, Red Rose'. Travelling to Salzburg, they meet up with Hassert Seidel (Veidt) in a museum displaying torture implements, and at their lodgings the concierge provides more clues by giving them a book of Franz Liszt scores – that night they are to attend a recital of his *Piano Concerto Number 1*, the sheet music for which happens to have been ripped out of the book, and which is being played by someone in the next room.

Richard investigates. The pianist is Thornley (Lester), who is also going to the concert. The significance of the piece is clarified that evening, for the guests of honour at the concert hall are all top-ranking Nazi officials, one of whom is shot dead as the music reaches a noisy crescendo. Also present at the event is Richard's old Oxford buddy, Sig Von Aschenhausen – the Sherlock Holmes actor Basil Rathbone behaving *so* creepily that one instinctively identifies him as the villain of the piece. So too does Frances, for whereas Margaret Drew swooned, this Crawford character suddenly limps when nervous or suspicious, which is often in this picture.

The next morning, Richard finds Thornley burning the evidence – his gloves and the Liszt score. He has killed the Nazi official, the former commandant at Dachau who had his sister tortured and murdered, for not so long ago they were on a similar Foreign Office mission to the one the Myles are undertaking now. They, meanwhile, learn that the missing scientist is Dr Mespulbrum (Owen), and set off for his house – where they are greeted by Sig, who is just as surprised as they are to be meeting under such circumstances, though not averse to having a former friend disposed of. The couple discover that the doctor is being held prisoner in an upstairs room, and manage to escape with him and evade the Gestapo in the nick of time. Before going on his way to help others, Mespulbrum hands over his precious formula. Seidel then provides Frances and Richard with false passports and arranges safe passage for them to Italy. His plan goes awry when the Gestapo capture Frances and take her to the SS training camp at Dreikirchen, where she is questioned and tortured before being rescued by her husband and friends. Evil Nazi Sig is shot dead, and Thornley dies a hero's death before the trio escape, dressed as SS officers in a stolen military car that they push into a ravine close to the Italian border, giving their pursuers the impression they have perished.

Above Suspicion made a tidy profit for MGM, and enabled Joan to rid herself of the 'Box-Office Poison' tag once and for all. Even so, she was beginning to tire of the studio, the shoddy scripts she was constantly being offered, and was particularly aggrieved by Louis B Mayer's favouritism of MGM's fresh clutch of stars who were threatening stalwarts like herself: Irene Dunne, Judy Garland, Betty Grable, Ava Gardner – and worst of all Lana Turner, whom she would never forgive for her connection with Carole Lombard's death. Then there was Greer Garson, who after winning Best Actress Oscar for *Mrs Miniver* in March 1943 was currently the most despised figure in Joan's world.

Louis B Mayer offered Joan joint-lead with Margaret Sullavan in *Cry "Havoc"*, an all-female production that tells of multinational nurses caught up in the Battle of Bataan. She turned this down, claiming that her fans did not like her in war pictures, so Mayer replaced her with Joan Blondell. In view of her success with *They All Kissed the Bride*, she was offered another comedy, *The Heavenly Body*, opposite Carole Lombard's first husband, William Powell. Joan rejected this as well and it went to Hedy Lamarr. Joan *wanted Madame Curie*, and when Mayer gave this to Greer Garson, Joan finally threw in the towel.

Since firing Mike Levee, Joan had acquired a new agent, Lew Wasserman (also the representative of Bette Davis!), who had been offered provisional contracts on Joan's behalf by Twentieth Century-Fox, Columbia and Warner Brothers. On 27 June, a date Joan once claimed she remembered more than any of her wedding anniversaries, she strode into Louis B Mayer's office and announced that she was leaving MGM – *that very day*. Maybe she was hoping that Mayer would plead with her to stay, or maybe sweeten her with the script of her dreams. He did not – telling her instead that it would cost *her* $50,000 for a release of contract. Later that afternoon he summoned a press-conference in which he lamented the loss of 'yet another favourite daughter', one who had been with him longer than anyone else. He then wished her a successful future, though truthfully he did not give a fig what happened to Joan Crawford now that she would no longer be raking in money for MGM.

CHAPTER NINE

Long Live the Queen of Hollywood!

'The untameable Joan Crawford. Whether she's on the set, out in the street or doing public relations work for Pepsi Cola, she's always the star. What is more, she never lets you forget it!'

Jerry Wald, producer

Joan had walked out of Louis B Mayer's office leaving the door wide open – the supreme insult, as far as he was concerned – and collected her belongings from her dressing room. According to studio sources, in a reversal of ousting her husbands from Brentwood Park, she had removed every last trace of *herself* by fettling the place from top to bottom before driving out of the studio via a back gate to avoid the ever-present press. She tried not to be bitter, some years later when recalling the event:

> I loved MGM. It was home. But I longed for challenging parts and I wasn't getting them. There were top executives who thought me all washed up. They still thought of me as Letty Lynton. They actually laughed when I wanted to do pictures like *Random Harvest* and *Madame Curie*. If you think I made poor pictures after *A Woman's Face*, you should have seen the ones I went on suspension *not* to make!

According to Christina (four at the time), Joan took her frustration out on her the night she left MGM. 'Finding herself a has-been at thirty-seven was a shock,' she wrote, adding how in a fit of rage, 'bereft of a career and a husband', Joan had gone berserk and wrecked her rose garden. What Christina seems to have forgotten is that there *was* no rose garden at this time – it had been dug up and replaced by the Victory Garden – and that

Phillip Terry, still living at Brentwood Park, had been photographed greeting her at the door when she had arrived home.

Joan's new contract, finalised just two days after she left MGM, was with Warner Brothers. The deal negotiated by Lew Wasserman was that she would be paid $500,000 for three films to be made over an unspecified period – considerably less than she had been getting at MGM. She would, however, have full script approval and be able to choose her own directors, leading men and personnel. Joan loathed the studio head, Jack Warner, from the moment she clapped eyes on him. The stories were legion of how he had treated some of his stars like dirt – only one, Errol Flynn, had dared stand up to him. Comparing the two moguls, many years later, Joan would tell John Springer, 'One was a beautiful man and one was a stinker. Mr Mayer was beautiful.' She was not quite so complimentary of Mayer, however, in 1946.

Jack Warner rejected Joan's request to appear in *Ethan Frome* and offered her *Night Shift*, which *she* turned down. She was well aware that at Warner Brothers she would always be playing second fiddle to Bette Davis, and always being offered her rejects, and does appear to have made an effort to befriend the crabby star – sending flowers and other meaningful little gifts and invitations to meet in Bette's dressing room – dismissed by Bette as 'lesbian overtures'.

Bette had her own problems to contend with, however. On New Year's Eve 1940 she had married Arthur Farnsworth, an assistant manager at Peckett's Inn, a hotel near her New Hampshire home, Butternut. A serial carouser, on 23 August 1943 Farnsworth collapsed on a New York pavement, hitting his head. Two days later he died and foul play was suspected: an expert aviator, Farnsworth had been involved with secret war work for Minneapolis-Honeywell, and the briefcase that witnesses claimed he had been carrying at the time of his collapse had vanished. Bette had her husband interred at Butternut, but soon afterwards gave in to his mother's daily fits of hysterics down the telephone and gave permission for him to be re-interred in the Farnsworth family vault in Vermont.

Joan may have had no reason to sympathise with her rival's plight, bearing in mind how Bette had always been the first to criticise her 'unconventional' way of life. Bette had returned to the set of *Mr Skeffington* (1944) within a week of Farnsworth's death, and once this was completed, Joan approached Jack Warner once more regarding *Ethan Frome* – this time as a joint venture with Bette Davis and Gary Cooper. It mattered little that she hated the one and was not overtly fond of the other: this was business, and she knew that the three of them together would make good box-office. In addition, both Bette and Warner agreed that Cooper would be perfect in the role of Edith Wharton's tragic hero. The problem was that Joan wanted to play Mattie, the servant girl Ethan falls for – and for Bette to be cast as his nagging, harridan wife. Warner dismissed the whole idea when Bette declared that if she did the film, *she* would be playing Mattie, telling Warner, 'Joan's far too old – and besides, she can't act!'

By the spring of 1944, nine months after signing her and with her yet to step onto the Burbank lot, Warner Brothers warned Joan that unless she accepted a part soon, she would be put on suspension. She reminded them of the clause in her contract that stipulated script approval, and argued that thus far the studio had failed to come up with a project she had found remotely interesting – adding that until they did, they could take her off salary so that she could spend more time with her family. This is exactly what happened. Because of the war and rationing, fifteen of the 22 rooms at Brentwood Park had been shut down, and most of her staff temporarily re-employed in munitions factories.

Phillip Terry had signed a contract with RKO Pictures at around the time Joan had left MGM, largely as a result of Hedda Hopper hailing him 'a combination of Clark Gable and Cary Grant' in her column. The studio had put him into *George White's Scandals* (1945), then inexplicably dropped him. Unwilling to be thought of as a 'kept' husband, he now had a nine-to-five job at his father's war plant. Joan could, of course, have used her position to find him parts in her future films, as had happened with Franchot Tone, but she refused to go back on her verbal prenuptial agreement that they would never work together. Therefore she was content to be photo-graphed by the fan magazines, packing her husband's lunchbox and seeing him off at the door. Of course, all she *really* wanted to do was get back to work. She was running short of funds, for not only was she supporting the usual family leeches but also Franchot Tone, himself in dire straits now that his own career had floundered and being too proud to ask his wealthy family for help.

Jack Warner offered Joan *Conflict* opposite Humphrey Bogart – which *seemed* a good idea until she read in the script that his character murders her to have an affair with her sister. 'Joan Crawford *never* dies in her films,' she told Warner. Then Warner offered her *Hollywood Canteen*; Joan accepted, and she was put back on the payroll. Joan was working in the real canteen most Monday evenings, rostered on to serve sandwiches and soup to on-leave soldiers, sailors and the ubiquitous fans. 'I buttered the bread, she threw on whatever we had on account of the rationing,' Marlene Dietrich told me.

Hollywood Canteen is a musical extravaganza through which is woven the flimsiest thread of a story involving Joan Leslie, Robert Hutton and Dane Clark. Two GIs on leave from serving in the Pacific spend several evenings at the canteen. Slim (Hutton) happens to be the millionth serviceman to enter

its legendary portals, and wins a date with Joan Leslie (as herself) while his
buddy (Clark) gets to do a smoochy dance with Joan – her idea, having
refused producer Alex Gottlieb's request that she sing. Most of Warner's big
names had already been assigned to the picture to play themselves in cameos,
and when Joan was told that everyone would be billed in alphabetical order,
she was delighted – in the credits her name came before John Garfield, Ida
Lupino, Jane Wyman, Roy Rogers, Barbara Stanwyck – and, most
importantly, Bette Davis. Speaking to Roy Newquist (in *Conversations with
Joan Crawford*), she described the production as: 'A very pleasant pile of shit
for wartime audiences.'

Joan's next film, *Mildred Pierce*, would be regarded by many fans,
especially the gay ones, as the most memorable she ever made. It would also
prove, three decades hence, painfully semi-autobiographical: the story of an
otherwise nice woman from the wrong side of town whose love and self-
sacrificing generosity towards her ungrateful daughter is repaid only by spite.

James Mallahan Cain (1892–1977) was no stranger to Hollywood: his
novels *The Postman Always Rings Twice* (1946) and *Double Indemnity* (the
film version of the latter was released in November 1944, at around the time
the Crawford film went into production) had already made huge impacts on
cinema audiences, but *Mildred Pierce* had been passed over on account of its
racy theme – until producer-scriptwriter Jerry Wald persuaded Jack Warner
to purchase the screen rights and 'tone' the story down. Wald, who most
recently had worked with Errol Flynn in *Objective, Burma!*, was given the
invidious task of finding an actress for the title role once Warner Brothers
had assigned him a $1.25 million budget and, in the August, brought in
Michael Curtiz to direct. Naturally, Bette Davis was the studio's first choice,
but she (as Norma Shearer had with *Susan and God*) had refused to play the
mother of a seventeen-year-old girl. So too had Ann Sheridan and Rosalind
Russell – with the added excuse coming from Sheridan that Mildred's
daughter was 'too horrid to be human'. Joan accepted the role without
deliberation, knowing that she was only being used as a last resort, but also
well aware that she had been *born* to play the maligned mother who secretly
must wish that her brat had never been born. What she had not figured on
was the director's reaction to the news.

Hungarian-born Michael Curtiz (born Mihály Kertész, 1888–1962)
was one of the most respected – and feared – directors in Hollywood. He had
begun working for Warner Brothers in 1926, since when he had made over
sixty films, most of them timeless classics. There had been *The Adventures of
Robin Hood* (1938) with Errol Flynn, *The Private Lives of Elizabeth and
Essex* (1939) with Flynn and Bette Davis, *Casablanca* with Bergman and
Bogart and *Yankee Doodle Dandy* (both 1942) with James Cagney – tetchy

stars who needed firm directorial control, but who had only brought out the worst of Curtiz's volatile temperament. Despite his many years in the United States, Curtiz had failed or refused to master the English language other than its profanities – from which absolutely no one was spared. Various stars had various ways of dealing with him, depending on their own temperament. Tough-guy actor George O'Brien, called 'prickless faggot' on the set of *Noah's Ark* (1929), had burst into tears. Bette Davis had spat in his eye during *Cabin in the Cotton* (1932) when he had called her a 'sexless son-of-a-bitch'. When Ross Alexander had stripped for the flogging scene in *Captain Blood* and displayed exuberant armpits, contravening Hays Office regulations, Errol Flynn had grabbed the razor Curtiz just happened to have in his pocket and threatened to cut the director's throat, should he so much as remove one hair of his lover's 'magnificent oxters'. David Niven recalls, in his memoirs *Bring on the Empty Horses*, another altercation with Flynn during *The Charge of the Light Brigade* (1936) when Flynn had returned an insult by calling Curtiz a 'thick as pig-shit bowl of goulash' – bringing the response, 'You lousy faggot bum, you think I know fuck nothing. Well, let me tell you something – I know fuck *all*!'

Curtiz had wanted Barbara Stanwyck for *Mildred Pierce*, and initially refused to work with Joan, telling Jack Warner, 'With her high-hat airs and her goddam shoulder-pads, she's a has-been.' Joan's reaction was to send him a message via Lew Wasserman that she would *test* for the part – a wholly unnecessary procedure for an actress of her standing. This took place early in October with Curtiz bellowing at the cameraman down his ubiquitous megaphone, 'Okay, start shooting that no-good motherfucker washerwoman's daughter!' How Joan withstood such a tirade without letting rip herself is another matter. The fact is, Curtiz was mesmerised by what he saw, told Joan that he would be *delighted* to work with her, and insisted that *she* sit in on the auditions for the girl who would be playing Mildred's daughter, Veda. He soon changed his tune when she suggested Shirley Temple, who had just played a 'difficult child' opposite Claudette Colbert in *Since You Went Away* – declaring, 'If Miss Lollipop joins the cast, then we might as well have Mickey Rooney playing one of Mildred's husbands!' After some deliberation, the studio signed sixteen-year-old Ann Blyth. Bruce Bennett (born Herman Brix), a former (1928–32) US shot-put champion, who played the unsmiling Bert Pierce, was regarded as one of the unluckiest actors in Hollywood: some years before, a shoulder injury had robbed him of the role of Tarzan, which had gone to fellow sportsman Johnny Weissmuller.

Mildred Pierce is an Expressionist film and is augmented by a quartet of undisputed masters of the genre. Indeed, one half expects Lon Chaney or Conrad Veidt to come creeping out of the shadows. Polish-born artistic director Anton Grot (1884–1974), like MGM's Cedric Gibbons, insisted that his name always be included in the credits, even if the work had been delegated to an assistant. The sets here, however – austere and foreboding – are genuine Grot, his best since *Captain Blood*. Ernest Haller (1896–1970) had also worked on this film and Flynn's very atmospheric *Footsteps in the Dark* (1941). He had photographed Bette Davis in *Jezebel* and in 1956 would triumph with *Rebel Without a Cause* – the producer of which, David Weisbart, is the editor here. Haller's theory – one he shared with and may even have copied from Lee Garmes, Dietrich's preferred cameraman of the previous decade – was that *shadows* were more effective than light. It is this element that gives *Mildred Pierce* the edge over its contemporaries.

Similarly, Max Steiner (1888–1971) was an acknowledged wizard of atmosphere. Viennese-born, as a child prodigy he had studied under Mahler, composed his first opera at fourteen, and in the Twenties had emigrated to America to write and conduct for Florenz Ziegfeld's Sixth Avenue Theatre in New York. With the advent of sound, Steiner had relocated to Hollywood, where he achieved an early success with the 1933 score for *King Kong* – the first of a staggering 26 Oscar nominations. His most successful scores were those for *Casablanca, Gone With the Wind* – and *Now, Voyager*, large chunks of which reappear here, much to the annoyance of Bette Davis, who accused Joan of purloining 'her' soundtrack. Zachary Scott (1914–65) was an ethereally handsome actor, much underrated (and under-employed) whose sideways glance, sneer and pencil-line moustache made him look like the baddie in a silent movie. Yet it is impossible not to like him. 'Sleek, slick and squirrel-eyed, he's alluring in his gracefulness and soft, decadent passivity,' Paul Roen declared in *High Camp*. 'His aura of swishy melli-fluousness could, in a more enlightened era, have made him a paragon of androgynous chic.'

Like *A Woman's Face*, *Mildred Pierce* is very camp and resplendent with over-the-top howler dialogue. As such, it is *the* Crawford movie for gay fans. And as with the earlier film, the story is told in a series of flashbacks. It opens with a lonely beach house on a dark, windswept stretch of highway. Shots are fired, and as playboy Monte Beragon (Scott) falls dead, murmuring his wife's name, Mildred drives off into the night, giving one the impression that *she* has fired the fatal shots. The scenario, of course, is much more complicated than this. Mildred goes to the bridge and is thinking of ending it all when a cop talks her out of it – if she takes a swim, he will have to risk catching pneumonia by diving in after her, he tells her – so she walks to the roadhouse restaurant owned by old pal Wally Fay (Jack Carson). Someone is singing 'You Must Have Been a Beautiful Baby', and Wally comes on to her, something he has been doing twice a week since they were kids. Mildred does not feel like talking, but when he drives her home and she asks him in, he thinks that maybe this time he has a chance – until she panics, locking him in the house while she escapes in her car. Wally finds Monte's body, busts through the French windows and is picked up by the highway patrol, who think he is a burglar. Mildred is arrested too, though the detective who questions her tells her that the case has been solved already – Monte was killed by Bert Pierce's gun. Mildred, however, knows Bert is innocent and the story moves back four years to when their marriage fell apart . . .

Bert and Wally have acrimoniously ended their real-estate partnership and Mildred's husband can no longer support them and their two children, Veda and Kay. Mildred does not mind this: she spends her spare time baking for rich housewives to bring in extra money and ensure that her daughters never go short of life's non-essentials the way she did. And, of course, the bills just keep on coming in. Bert resents this:

> Maybe you wouldn't *have* so many bills if you didn't bring up those kids like their old man was a millionaire. No wonder they're so stuck up and fresh! That Veda! I tell you, I'm so fed up of the way she high-hats me that one day I'm gonna cut loose and slap her right in the face!

Bert accuses Mildred of trying to *buy* their daughters' love: she admits this – that they are more important than *anyone* in her life, and that if need be she will do their crying for them too. The couple row, and Bert leaves, with Mildred making it patently clear that she will not be welcoming him back. The girls arrive home from school – Kay is the affable one, Veda absolutely *loathsome*, as she denounces her little sister as a 'peasant' for her tomboy ways. The fact that her father may be gone for good bothers her less than the new dress her mother has scrimped and saved to buy – yet Veda would not be seen *dead* in such a cheap monstrosity.

Mildred then reviews her financial situation and realises she is broke. She goes to Wally for help, who with Bert out of the picture now thinks she will give in to his lecherous demands. 'You make me feel like Little Red Riding Hood,' Mildred insults him. 'Quit howling! I know you romantic guys. One crack about the beautiful moon and you're off to the races!'

The ever-sneering Veda is rather hoping that her mother will marry Wally so that they can have a maid, a limousine and a better house than this one – it does not matter to her that Mildred does not love him. Mildred excuses herself for rejecting him by telling the beastly wretch that she will *always* have everything she wants, no matter what it takes, and goes off in search of a job. She is taken on by restaurant hostess Ida (a delightful, wise-cracking performance from former Ziegfeld girl Eve Arden) and in a matter of months knows enough about the food business to want to open a place of her own – all for Veda, of course, though she is desperate for her never to find out *where* she is working. And the family gets their maid – that lovely, squeaky-voiced (and uncredited) actress Butterfly McQueen, so memorable in *Gone With the Wind*.

Veda *does* get to know where the money for her costly singing lessons is coming from, and there is a spiteful confrontation:

> *My* mother, a waitress? . . . Aren't the pies bad enough that you have to downgrade us? . . . I'm not really surprised. You've never spoken of your people, who you came from, so perhaps it's natural. Maybe that's why father . . .

She gets no further before Mildred slaps her – not hard enough, cried those Crawford fans who had never stopped separating the actress from the part. (In the original screenplay, Mildred gives Veda a good hiding, but Joan objected to this.) Mildred, devastated by what she has just done – she would rather cut off her hand than hit Veda again – by way of an apology tells her daughter of her plans to open her own restaurant, and Veda soon dries her tears and starts seeing dollar signs. Mildred goes to see Wally again, and this time it is strictly business. She has seen a property for sale at the intersection near the beach, and having worked out how many cars pass by every day knows that it will be a goldmine. Wally takes her there. The place belongs to the Beragon estate, and Mildred gets it for a song because the family are in dire straits; she also takes on board the suave but slightly smarmy Monte as a silent partner.

Mildred files for divorce to prevent Bert Pierce from getting his hands on half the profits, and embarks on an affair with Monte – spending the weekend at his beach house, where he has a closet filled with bathing costumes left behind by his 'sisters'. Mildred puts hers on. 'No whistle?' she asks, when he ogles her shapely figure – bringing the response, 'I'd need a police siren!' His own swimming trunks leave little to the imagination and were very risqué for the day, though cinema audiences in 1945 did not have the benefit of video freeze-framing his assets as he sprints towards the briny. Following their dip, Monte puts on a record – the 'purloined' *Now, Voyager* theme – and she asks him what he does for a living. He replies, 'I loaf – oh, in a decorative and highly charming manner.' He adds that he can also read fortunes and that he lost his awe of women at an early age – suggestive, of course, of the 'Gillette-blade seducer' – and as the record ends we know exactly which way he is going to swing tonight.

After her night of passion, Mildred returns home to tragedy: Kay has been taken ill with pneumonia, and quickly dies. To cope with her grief, Mildred plunges herself into her work. The restaurant is a success, Bert consents to the divorce, but hits the roof when he sees Mildred and her lover kissing – and the flashback ends when Monte looks at Mildred and tells Bert of the old Beragon family saying: 'One man's poison is another man's meat' – *the* in-phrase with the largely closeted gay community during the winter of 1945.

In the interrogation room, the police receive fresh information, proving that Bert did *not* kill Monte, and afraid that they are getting too close to the truth, Mildred changes her statement, declaring that *she* is the killer . . .

The next flashback brings the story almost up to date. Mildred's venture has proved so successful that she has opened a restaurant chain. Everything she has touched has turned to money – all of it spent on Veda's increasingly expensive tastes and bailing Monte out of debt because Mildred believes that she owes him. Ida, now her business manager, knows that Mildred is being taken for a ride by both daughter and lover; so does Wally, but Mildred still keeps writing the cheques. She buys Veda a limousine, but even this is not enough and the ungrateful girl borrows money from her mother's employees, threatening them with dismissal should they turn her down. The last straw comes when she marries a young millionaire, coerces his mother into paying a hefty annulment settlement, and tells her mother *why* she wanted the cash in the first place:

> With this money I can get away from *you* – from you and your chickens and your pies and your kitchens and everything that smells of grease. I can get away from this shack with its cheap furniture and this town and its dollar-days and its women that wear uniforms and its men that wear overalls . . . You think that just because you made a little money you can get a new hairdo and some expensive clothes and turn yourself into a lady, but you can't because you'll never be anything but a common frump whose father lived over a grocery store and whose mother took in washing. With this money I can get away from every rotten stinking thing that makes me think of this place or you!

Mildred tears up the cheque, and this time Veda does the slapping (again, in the original screenplay Mildred more violently hits her back, flies into an uncontrollable rage and throws her daughter's clothes out of the bedroom window). Mildred sees sense at last and orders Veda to get out of the house before she kills her.

The story moves on a little. Blaming herself for the rift with Veda, Mildred takes a long vacation, yet no sooner is she back home than the odious creature is up to her tricks again, and Ida tells Mildred what Crawford fans would be saying of *her*, three decades on: 'Personally, Veda's convinced me that alligators have the right idea – *they* eat their young!'

Bert takes Mildred to Wally's restaurant, where Veda now works as a singer. Now sluttish, she has been seeing a lot of Monte during her mother's absence, and refuses to come back home unless Mildred can offer her the kind of life *he* has shown her. As a last resort Mildred tempts her by marrying Monte and buying the Beragon mansion, and for a little while Veda does return to the fold. Then everything goes wrong when Mildred discovers that her husband and daughter have been having an affair, and this flashback ends as we see her reaching for her gun and going off into the night . . .

In the squad room, Mildred still insists that *she* killed Monte, but the police have now arrested the real killer – Veda, whose mother has been protecting her all the while. In the final flashback, Mildred heads for Monte's beach house, maybe to kill her two-timing spouse. She catches him necking with Veda, but when Veda yells that Monte plans to marry *her* as soon as he is free, Mildred tosses the weapon aside, deciding that these two probably deserve each other. She is leaving when Monte levels with Veda that he would *never* marry a 'rotten little tramp' such as she. And so she picks up the gun and shoots him, then pleads with her mother to help her – though this time she asked for *too* much. A masterpiece!

Mildred Pierce premiered on 29 September 1945, and most of the critics whole-heartedly agreed that Joan had given her finest performance to date. In a crafty pre-publicity stunt, Jerry Wald had called Hedda Hopper and informed her that 'a Motion Picture Academy source who preferred not to be named' was predicting that Joan would win a Best Actress Oscar for this one. Hopper took the bait, and in next to no time other columnists followed suit. The *Los Angeles Times* reported, 'Insiders say that Joan Crawford is delivering *such* a terrific performance in *Mildred Pierce* that she's a *cinch* for the Academy Award.' Bette Davis was incensed, because the film was being released just two weeks after her big-budget *The Corn is Green*, in which she portrayed a schoolmistress twice her age. Bette may have been earning twice as much as her rival at Warner Brothers, but ticket sales were all that counted, and Joan's film would gross more at the US box office during its first two weeks than Bette's would by the end of the year. *Both* films would be nominated for the next year's Oscars – Joan's for seven awards, Bette's for two, resulting in some choice expletives from Bette to the press for which she was publicly condemned by the usually Davis-friendly Louella Parsons.

The 1946 Oscars ceremony took place at Grauman's Chinese Theatre, where the candidates for Best Actress were Joan, Gene Tierney (*Leave Her to Heaven*), Greer Garson (*Valley of Decision*), Jennifer Jones (*Love Letters*), and Ingrid Bergman (*The Bells of St Mary's*). Joan was suffering from flu and listened to proceedings on the radio, though truthfully she had been searching for an excuse not to attend, terrified of being unable to hold her head high should she lose. Of the nominated quartet, she told Hedda Hopper over the phone that the only one who concerned her was Bergman, adding, 'I'll never be able to compete with a nun!' When Charles Boyer announced that she had won, scores of pressmen headed for Brentwood Park, accompanying a jubilant Michael Curtiz and Jerry Wald, who presented her with the award. The cynics who saw the photographs declared that Joan had not been sick at all – just cowardly. It was a tribute to her professionalism, of course, that she would never have allowed anyone to see her looking less than glamorous, no matter how ill she felt. These pictures were rushed out for the early morning editions – including the one of Joan sleeping, the statuette still in her hand. The megalomania continued the next morning when, according to Christina, Joan placed her Oscar in a specially constructed niche at the foot of the stairs, which had apparently been awaiting this moment for years.

Meanwhile, the curtain was drawn on Joan's marriage to Phillip Terry – hardly a surprise for her friends and fans, who had never really looked upon them as an item in the first place. The pattern was the same as before: Terry moved out of Brentwood Park in December 1945: the next day Joan had the locks and toilet seats changed, and William Haines was brought in for another refurbishment. Only then were the press alerted – Hedda Hopper first, then *Photoplay*, who were tearfully shown the card Terry had attached to the diamond bracelet he had given Joan for their third wedding anniversary, three months earlier. On it he had written, 'This is the third step on our bridge you have built so well. Love you, forever and a day.'

Terry's career had unexpectedly taken a turn for the better after he had recently played alcoholic Ray Milland's brother in *The Lost Weekend*, and he had received good notices for *To Each His Own* opposite Olivia de Havilland. His flame would burn but briefly, however; his success brought him no more good roles and within twelve months he would be out of the movies altogether. Terry had been washed away by the glorious tide of *Mildred Pierce*: he was no longer of any importance now that he had been relegate to plain 'Mr Crawford' and suddenly been pushed to the wrong side of the show-business fence.

Christina, not unexpectedly, would find another reason for the collapse of her mother's marriage: the fact that Terry had been unable to cope with Joan's over-disciplining her children. It is quite likely that Joan *was* a harsh disciplinarian, though no witnesses have ever come forward to support the theory that she was a violent one. In this respect, she was little different from most show-business parents of the day – indeed, from many parents during the time when the general adage was: 'Spare the rod and spoil the child.' The offspring of celebrities were notoriously privileged and pampered, and they often took far too much for granted. From some of the visitors to Brentwood Park who have come forward since Joan's death and who witnessed Christina 'playing up', one gets the impression that though she was by no means a Veda Pierce, neither was she always 'Mommie's little darling'. Shaun Considine (*Bette & Joan: The Divine Feud*) quoted Louella Parsons finding six-year-old Christina 'a bit bossy', while *Mildred Pierce* author James M Cain reported how she threw tantrums when unable to get her own way. Joseph Mankiewicz called her, 'A miserable little kid who deserved to be beaten up' – and author Larry Carr observed, 'She was a wilful and devious little monster.'

According to Christina – aged three when Joan married Phillip Terry – her stepfather had beaten her regularly, but only spanking her by hand, whereas Joan had used a variety of implements including hairbrushes and the aforementioned coat-hangers, often breaking them across her buttocks. Many of these incidents were re-created for the big screen in *Mommie Dearest*. Again, one wonders how Joan and Terry would have got away with this. Joan's children frequently attended other Hollywood children's parties, and it would seem inconceivable that anyone could have missed the cuts, bruises and weals she boasts of in her book. On the other hand, being locked in dark closets and empty rooms was not an uncommon practice in those less socially conscious days. Nor was being forced to eat one's greens even if it made one ill – save that Christina recalls in her memoirs that *her* mother made her eat the vomit as well!

In court on 25 April 1946, Joan spoke of the mental anguish Phillip Terry had put her through: finding faults with every script the studio had sent her, preventing her from hosting and attending parties, forcing her to become a recluse and a prisoner in her own home – hardly true. And again, as she left the building dressed to the nines, she told reporters, 'Never, *never* again!' Years after the event Terry would recall how Joan had kept *him* on a leash, running her household like a dictator, drawing up a schedule divided into fifteen-minute blocks – and allotting him one hour for sex each afternoon. He also denied that Joan had been tough on her children, and as with Franchot Tone she would later speak of him with great fondness, though some of the excuses she gave (quoted by Quirk in *Films in Review*, December 1956) for her failed marriage were paltry:

> I can only say that the two years [sic] of our marriage were the most difficult of my life, but not because of Phillip. For three years I searched for a script. Phillip wasn't working either. We had no servants in our 27-room house . . . I cooked, cleaned and worked in the Victory Garden which covered the front lawn. Phillip worked in the garden too. He was a gentle man and loved poetry and music and reading aloud. He gave me

comfort during the difficult years, but I haven't loved him enough. I was unutterably lonely. Don't ever marry because of loneliness. I've owed Phillip Terry an apology from the first.

Meanwhile, in the wake of the massive success of *Mildred Pierce*, Jerry Wald assigned Joan to his next big production, *Humoresque*, based on Fannie Hurst's bestselling novel and scripted by Clifford Odets. He and co-writer Zachary Gold were instructed to transform the Boray family – two of which are described by Hurst as 'an out-and-out little son-of-a-bitch and his domineering Yiddisher Momma' – into Italian immigrants but *without* changing their names, an exercise that only resulted in their Jewish mannerisms being exaggerated, particularly in the scenes set in their grocery store, where only kosher goods are sold.

The film was directed by Romanian-born Jean Negulesco, a specialist in the field of heavyweight drama, who had worked on *The Maltese Falcon* (1941) before being replaced by John Huston. He would soon score a tremendous success with *Johnny Belinda*. Joan was also given her most complex co-star in John Garfield (1913–52). Born Jacob Julius Garfinkle of poor Russian-Jewish parents, he had been a problem child, sent to a reform school, but had graduated with a drama scholarship and was accepted by Franchot Tone's Group Theatre. Androgynous, good-looking, short of stature but built like a middleweight prize-fighter, he was a precursor to Brando and Dean in the 'attitude' stakes and was always cast as loners and losers with huge chips on their shoulders. He had starred opposite Bette Davis in *Juarez* (1939) and more recently Lana Turner in *The Postman Always Rings Twice*. Garfield's mock playing in *Humoresque* (to Isaac Stern) is *so* spot-on that it is impossible *not* to believe him an authentic virtuoso violinist. Oscar Levant (1906–72) was, on the other hand, a professional concert pianist-composer and a close friend of George Gershwin, who had studied under Schoenberg. He had played himself in *Rhapsody in Blue*, and virtually does so here: a self-confessed 'verbal vampire' and wisecracking, insecure neurotic genius.

For connoisseurs of fine dramatic acting, beautiful music, unadulterated nostalgia (and, one might add, for Kleenex manufacturers at the time) this remains *the* Crawford film – and this author's personal favourite. For those who have not seen it, the advice is: watch and prepare to be enthralled!

The story is told almost entirely in flashback. World-class violinist Paul Boray has cancelled tonight's sell-out recital, and despite the protestations of his manager is convinced that he cannot continue with his career. Paul has fame and wealth, but he still feels like an outsider looking in, and would love to get back to being the happy, unaffected boy he used to be. We see him aged eleven (portrayed by Robert Blake, who many years would play *Baretta* in the television series), being taken to the local store by his tight-wad father to choose his birthday present. Encouraged by pianist Sid Jeffers (Levant) – a self-confessed 'unknown genius waiting to be discovered' – who will become his lifelong friend, Paul chooses a violin, which his old man definitely does *not* want him to have, though Mama Boray (Ruth Nelson, replacing Anna Revere) soon gets him to change his mind. The story then moves forward ten years. Paul and childhood sweetheart Gina (Joan Chandler) are students with the National Institute of Music, but whereas she has no aspirations beyond being part of an orchestra, he cockily foresees a rosier future for himself. 'Nobody sits on my head,' he tells her. 'It's a head *full* of talent!' This, however, is the Depression and Paul's family are tired of his boasting and incessant practising; they know that *his* empty dreams will not make life any easier for them.

Paul goes to see Sid, now working on the radio, and asks him to use his influence and find him a job. The rapport between these two is ambiguous. Sid calls Paul 'sweetheart' and tells him he is pretty. Later he tells an onlooker, who asks if Paul is Sid's protégé, 'Our relationship is the same as George Sand's was with Chopin' – a statement that offended some sections of 1946 audiences whichever way this was interpreted: those who knew that Sand had actually been a woman, and even more so the 'unenlightened' who left the cinema thinking that the two musicians were flaunting a homosexual relationship in their faces.

Sid thinks his friend is precocious and impatient. 'You wanna get there fast,' he says, 'but you don't wanna pay for the ride.' He gets him a position with an orchestra, only to have him storm out of the rehearsal because the conductor is not being faithful to the composer – and in any case, Paul wants to be a soloist *without* working his way through the ranks. Next, Sid takes him to a party – the only way to get noticed, he says, in the fickle classical world – hosted by society couple Helen and Victor Wright (Joan, making her entrance 32 minutes into the picture, and Paul Cavanagh).

Thrice-married Helen is near-sighted, smokes like a chimney and drinks like the proverbial fish, and spends a lot of her time surrounded by attractive young men who seem more interested in looking at each other than at her. '*All* talented people end up in jail,' she mocks after Paul has mesmerised the gathering with his playing, allegedly a reference to Oscar Wilde and his gay hangers-on. Then she wants to know where he is from, enabling him to give as good as he gets before launching into a particularly aggressive 'Flight of the Bumble Bee' . . .

HELEN: Oh, here's that rare animal. A New Yorker from New York!
PAUL: New York is full of *all* kinds of animals, and not all of them are born here . . .

HELEN: Bad manners, Mr Boray. The infallible sign of talent. Shall I make a prediction? Soon the world will divide into two camps – pro-Boray and anti-Boray.
PAUL: Which camp are you in, Mrs Wright – pro, or anti?

Affronted, Helen leaves the room and fixes herself a brandy in a glass the size of a goldfish bowl, through which she watches him finishing his piece. The next day, by way of an apology, she sends him an expensive gift, which he opens in front of his parents – arousing his mother's suspicion, for she knows it is from a married woman. Helen and Paul meet at her club, and as resident chanteuse Peg LaCentra croons 'My Heart Stood Still', Helen wants to know everything about Paul's life, though he finds opening up to any woman hard. All that matters to him, he says, is his violin: he does not attend concerts because good ones only make him jealous, whereas the bad ones bore him. Smitten, Helen fixes him up with a manager who 'secures' Paul an engagement at the Manhattan Hall – with Helen secretly footing the bill. His solo debut is to a half-empty auditorium, but the press notices are favourable. Next, Helen buys him a suit and introduces him to eminent conductor Anton Hagerstrom. Even so he hates to be patronised and levels an accusation at her: 'You didn't do any of this for me. You did it for yourself – the way you buy a racehorse or build a yacht or collect paintings. You just added a violin player to your possessions, that's all!'

The next day, when Helen invites Paul to her beach house, Sid tags along too, though sensibly he leaves them to their devices. They swim in the sea, and afterwards go horse-riding. Helen takes a tumble, then another of the pleasurable kind in the dunes as Paul rushes to her aid and finally reveals that he is human after all. The crashing waves announce that sex has taken place, and the camera (Ernest Haller at his usually superb standard) zooms in on their faces, radiant in the moonlight, as they profess their love for each other.

Back home, Paul gets a lecture from his mother – he has stood up Gina to be with a loose woman, and unless he gives up Helen, there will be a scandal. Temporarily, he puts some distance between them by embarking on a tour, but when he returns to New York nothing has changed: Gina thinks success has gone to his head, and Helen is jealous when she sees the two of them together. Matters come to a head at Paul's next recital. The piece is Lalo's beautiful *Symphonie Espagnole*, and as it plays the camera psychoanalyses the protagonists. Helen, in extreme close-up, wears the serene expression of a Christian martyr, and as the music reaches a crescendo she closes her eyes and her lips part, giving the impression that she is experiencing orgasm; as Mr Boray weeps with the emotion from the performance, his wife glares her disgust; and Gina, who has also seen the effect her supposed intended is having on this woman, flees the concert hall in tears.

Paul and Sid move into a plush apartment. 'First they discovered Bugs Bunny, then Jack Benny and Shostakovich, now the great Paul Boray,' his friend mocks when Paul buys up his best reviews a dozen at a time. Paul's parents come to visit, and the Jewish mama who thinks all men are babies until they go bald and start losing their teeth disapproves of Helen's photograph in the frame next to the family group. When Paul answers her back she slaps him, but this only adds to his determination to have Helen for good, particularly as Victor has just granted her a divorce because he feels Helen is far too vivacious to be tied down to an old stickler like him. Victor does, however, tell her that he has his doubts about her younger lover. What can Paul offer her in the way of financial security? And how long will it be before they tire of each other when all *he* is interested in is his music?

Cut to Paul in rehearsal – the piece, aptly, is *'L'Amour Est un Oiseau Rebelle'* from *Carmen*. Helen sends him a note, which he ignores because he is working. Feeling rejected, she goes to her club with toyboy Monte (Craig Stevens), gets drunk and tearfully duets with the chanteuse on 'Embraceable You'. Paul rescues her, she snarls that she is tired of playing second fiddle to Beethoven – and Paul asks her to marry him, now that she is free.

Most Crawford fans might have been happier for *Humoresque* to have ended here – rather than having the heroine visit Mama Boray for a tête-à-tête that only points her in the direction of doom. 'You talk about love,' she chides. '*What* love? You only make demands. You only think of yourself. You give *nothing* in return.'

The lovers speak for the last time over the phone: Helen in the beach house, Paul in his dressing room. She is overwrought, he tetchy because he is about to go on stage. Helen tells him that she cannot get to the theatre, but that she will listen to the concert on the radio. She hangs up, empties the decanter, rants and sobs, calms down a little and lights a cigarette, and hears her husband's voice echoing over '*Dolce e Calmo*' from *Tristan und Isolde* – reminding her of her shame. Then Paul's voice enters her reverie, angrily reminding her that if she fails to turn up tonight, his performance will be a failure because he *needs* her to be there with him.

Helen now knows that she must make the ultimate sacrifice. Clutching a play-bill, and with the wind whipping her hair about her face, she steps onto the terrace and descends to the beach, the moonlight catching the sparkles of her exquisite gown as she walks into the sea and invites the waves to envelop her as the music ends. Now we know *why* Paul's concert was cancelled as the story goes back to where it began two hours previously, as a sad young man laments before ambling off into the dark, empty street, 'One way or another, you pay for what you are . . .' A sublime experience!

Humoresque went a long way towards disproving the theory, in some circles, that 'Guys don't make passes . . .' Usually, if an actress wore spectacles, as Rosalind Russell did in *The Women*, it was to make her character appear bookish or more intelligent than she really was, but rarely attractive. In Helen Wright's case (as would later happen with Sophia Loren), glasses only drew attention to Joan's facial features, and made her look not just intelligent, but more beautiful than ever. Also, unlike prop spectacles, because Joan wanted to appear genuinely near-sighted, these did not contain clear glass. She told her publicist friend John Springer in 1973, 'I wore the glasses and couldn't see through them, which made it good because I squinted all through it looking at Johnny Garfield – and boy, you don't have to squint to look at that guy. He was *sensational!*'

Joan's fling with her leading man while shooting the film was instigated by Garfield himself who, when they were introduced, ignored the extended hand and squeezed her breast instead! When Garfield's wife was informed of this – by Bette Davis, who was 'stabbing in the dark' but happened to have guessed right – Joan purchased her silence by having William Haines refurbish the Garfield house at her expense.

Humoresque went on release in January 1947, and was almost as successful as *Mildred Pierce*, which was still doing the rounds in some cities. It led to Jack Warner re-negotiating Joan's contract: the new deal was for two films a year for five years, at $250,000 a film, and she would still have full script, directorial and co-star approval. On top of this, if within reason she considered any of the scripts she was being offered to be substandard, she would be permitted to work as a loan-out to other studios. For the time being, this was unlikely. As had happened with Norma Shearer at MGM, Joan was unexpectedly promoted to 'Queen of Warners' when Bette Davis (who had wed marine William Grant Sherry at the end of 1945) announced that she was pregnant. Joan therefore took over what should have been Bette's next project, and completing the Crawford/Jerry Wald trilogy was *Possessed* – nothing to do with her earlier film with Gable but a 'psychotic melodrama' based on Rita Weiman's novel *One Man Secret*.

It is a harrowing tale indeed. Wealthy businessman Dean Graham (Raymond Massey) hires nurse Louise Howell (Joan) to look after his ailing wife. Louise is unstable, and when her engineer lover David Sutton (Van Heflin) ditches her for being too possessive, her mental state begins to deteriorate – not much helped by Mrs Graham's obsessive belief that Louise and her husband are having a passionate affair, which they are not. When Mrs Graham drowns herself, Louise stays on as housekeeper and the paranoia transfers to the Grahams' daughter, Carol (Geraldine Brooks). Even so, when Dean asks Louise to marry him, she accepts, bringing yet more mayhem when David re-enters the scenario and begins dating Carol to get at Louise. This pushes Louise over the edge: she starts to hear disembodied voices, primarily that of Mrs Graham, and in a fit of pique she shoots David dead. Committed to an asylum, she is visited by the faithful Dean, who vows to be there for her, if and when a cure is effected.

Howard Barnes of the *New York Herald Tribune*, not always supportive of 'women's pictures', liked this one. 'Miss Crawford is at her best in the mad scenes,' he wrote. 'The actress has obviously studied the aspects of insanity to recreate a rather terrifying portrait of a woman possessed by devils.' In fact, to research the role, Joan and Raymond Massey spent some time observing patients receiving treatment, including electric shock therapy, at a Pasadena psychiatric institution similar to the one in the film. One of the patients, Pauline McKay, later claimed that Joan and Massey had 'spied' on her without obtaining permission, and sued Warner Brothers for undisclosed damages. The matter was subsequently settled out of court, with the studio paying McKay an estimated $50,000. Joan was nominated for the Best Actress Oscar – but lost out to the much-despised (by her, anyway) Loretta Young, who won the award for *The Farmer's Daughter*.

CHAPTER TEN

Black Eyes, Brats and Bimbos

'You never see Joan Crawford schlepping around in a mu-mu. She knows the meaning of glamour and its importance to the people who – without any themselves – love to look at it in others.'

Liberace

If Joan's career was riding high on the crest of a wave, her love life was caught up in a whirlpool. When not being squired around town by John Garfield, she could be found with diminutive cowboy star Don 'Red' Barry, a shyster who showered her with jewels and furs, and convinced her that the thirty-plus films he had made for Republic had made him a millionaire. When Joan confided that one of her ambitions was to appear in the film version of the Broadway smash *Anna Lucasta*, Barry told her that he was negotiating to buy the screen rights. A visit from the bailiffs informed her otherwise: Barry's gifts had been bought on credit and she ended up paying for most of them herself – and there never had been any *Anna Lucasta* screenplay.

In fact, the pair were as bad as each other, for in February 1947 Hedda Hopper ran a piece informing her readers that British actor Peter Shaw was divorcing his wife to marry Joan. Both romances ended at around the same time, with Shaw graciously accepting rejection (two years later he married Angela Lansbury) and with Barry (who shot himself in 1980) making a few comments in public about Joan being 'easy meat'. This was hardly slanderous stuff, though Greg Bautzer, who happened to be in a Hollywood bar when Barry began letting off steam, apparently thought so. Threatening to 'sue the ass off' the tetchy red-headed actor, Bautzer made the mistake of bunching up his fists – and a few minutes later was spitting out his front teeth.

The fracas with Don Barry brought Bautzer back into Joan's life. She made a point of paying for his dental reconstruction work, bought him an expensive black Cadillac, and within weeks the gossip columns were forecasting marriage. Bautzer's 'new molars' were the topic of conversation at the party Joan was asked to host in honour of Noel Coward, in town to catch Tallulah Bankhead in his play *Private Lives*. Introducing the over-the-top-camp Coward to the handsome lawyer, the outrageous Tallulah repeated what she had told Errol Flynn when introducing him to the Austrian actor Helmut Dantine a few weeks earlier, 'You two are simply *made* for each other, darlings. Why don't you go some place and fuck?' – to which Coward responded, while the very heterosexual Bautzer stood, open-mouthed, 'Sorry, Tallulah darling, but the gentleman's *teeth* are far too big for my liking!' Bautzer saw the funny side of this, and surprised Joan by becoming Coward's friend. Several years on, at another Crawford party at the Pavilion to which she would invite three ex-husbands and at least twenty other men with whom she had been intimate, Noel Coward would sidle up to Greg Bautzer at the bar and purr in his polished tones, 'Incidentally, my dear chap, I *still* think you have too many teeth!'

Besides the usual caddy duties, Bautzer was now assigned to carrying Joan's knitting-bag, and occasionally her lead-heavy handbag, which had even some of her closest friends sniggering behind her back. Bautzer was, she declared, top-notch in two departments – 'fucking and procuring children'. Regarding the latter, during the spring of 1947 he had accompanied Joan to Memphis, where the press were told he had arranged for her to adopt twin baby girls Cindy and Cathy. In fact, these were not twins at all, nor were they even from the same parents – this was Joan being cautious again to ensure that the real parents, who had obviously not wanted them in the first place, never learned of their whereabouts.

Although doubt has been cast on many of the episodes recounted by Christina in *Mommie Dearest*, Cathy and Cindy Crawford have always remembered their mother with the utmost respect. They were closer to her than Christina and Christopher and displayed none of their behavioural problems – such as answering back and running away from home, leaving Joan with no alternative but to dispatch them to private schools (Christopher to a military academy, Christina to Chadwick's, in Palos Verdes). Cindy and Cathy remained tied to Joan's apron strings; they accompanied her just about everywhere, and never gave her cause to rue taking them into her life and giving them a home.

In 1959, Joan would tell French singer Edith Piaf, 'You and I have so much in common – not least of all that we're never really satisfied with the man in our life until he's given us bruises to show how much he cares.' Piaf,

at Carnegie Hall shortly after breaking up with her songwriter lover Georges
Moustaki, had frequently been snapped at the end of a relationship wearing
heavy make-up to conceal her facial injuries, and said at the time that she
shared Joan's 'crazy philosophy' that, basically, all men were cavemen – that
real passion in a love affair only came when a woman had pushed her man
too far and felt his fist or the back of his hand. If this was true, Joan and Greg
Bautzer must have been in seventh heaven – save that each time he hit her,
she belted him back, usually where it hurt the most!

In September 1949, during a visit to London, Bautzer spoke to the *Daily
Telegraph*'s Richard Last about Joan's 'tempestuous masculine side'.
Pointing to the small scars on his face, he added, '*She* put them there. She
could throw a cocktail glass and hit you in the face – two times out of three.'
The pair also loved playing 'Shakespeare games' – with the hefty Bautzer
climbing the rose trellis up to Joan's bedroom window and drawling the
famous lines from *Romeo and Juliet*, and with Joan snarling over some
misdemeanour before forcing him to grovel at her feet for forgiveness. This
she would refuse, sneering and stripping down to her gold silk underwear,
taunting and insulting until Bautzer ripped off the skimpies, pinned her to the
bed and took her by force.

Neither were the lovers faithful to each other. Joan was also seeing
David Brian, who was reputedly no less brutal than Bautzer, and there were
publicised flings with Kirk Douglas, Brian Donlevy and Dana Andrews.
Bautzer was zipping between Joan, Ginger Rogers and Merle Oberon, so
between them he and Joan had the gossip columnists running around in
circles. In short, theirs was a recipe for disaster and few were surprised when
Hedda Hopper reported the incident that brought the curtain down on the
relationship. After a party outside town, at which Bautzer spent the evening
dancing with Joan but making eyes at someone else, she insisted upon
driving home. Stopping in the middle of nowhere and asking Bautzer to get
out and check for a flat tyre, she had put her foot down and left him to walk
the several miles back to his apartment in the dark.

Joan's next film, as a loan-out to Twentieth Century-Fox, was another
melodramatic potboiler: *Daisy Kenyon*, produced and directed by Otto
Preminger, and co-starring Dana Andrews and Henry Fonda. Joan played
the title character, a Greenwich Village commercial artist involved with
hotshot married lawyer Dan O'Hara (Andrews) and demanding that he
choose between her and his wife. Matters are further complicated when she
meets the unattached Peter (Fonda). They marry, but she keeps seeing Dan,
who divorces his wife and in a volte-face tries to get Daisy to choose between
her husband and him. The on-screen situation reflected what was happening
off the set. Having been told by his ex-wife, her friend Margaret Sullavan,

that Fonda was 'hung like a bull', Joan acquired his vital measurements and paid Fox's costume department to fashion a posing-pouch embellished with sequins and rhinestones. She made a great fuss about presenting the actor with his gift, but Fonda was apparently not in the least interested in trying it on – so Joan never did get to know if the rumours were true.

Joan's next venture, *Flamingo Road*, directed by the now Crawford-friendly Michael Curtiz, was basically an Expressionist film, though it more resembles Orson Welles's later *Touch of Evil* (1958) than Curtiz's earlier *Mildred Pierce*. The film saw Joan once more teamed up with Zachary Scott, minus his trademark moustache and looking far less menacing – and gargantuan British actor Sydney Greenstreet (1879–1954), who had made a formidable impression in *The Maltese Falcon*. An affable man off the screen, here he is quite possibly the most *loathsome* character in any Crawford film. There was the former theatre doorman David Brian (1911–93), who had also been signed up as Bette Davis's co-star in *Beyond the Forest*, the film that would lead to an enormous row with Jack Warner and see her leaving the studio. Hearing rumours of Bette's amorous interest in the bleached-blond hunk, whose screen performances rate amongst the dullest of Hollywood's golden age, Joan made a point of getting there first. Off and on, her affair with Brian would last another two years until his marriage to actress Adrian Booth (aka Lorna Gray).

'There's a Flamingo Road in every town,' Lane Bellamy (Joan) voices over the opening credits. 'It's the street of social success, the avenue of achievement.' She also adds, obviously in the know, that once one reaches this pinnacle of society there is nowhere else to go, especially in Boldon City, a small town with people of big dreams. Lane is a hoochie-koochie dancer with Coyne's Carnival, a cheap outfit that pitches outside town boundaries to avoid paying ground rent. This time, however, Coyne gets an attachment order from corrupt sheriff Titus Semple (Greenstreet), a horrible bigot who has the entire town in his pocket and treats everyone like dirt. He is particularly mean towards his deputy, Field Carlisle (Scott): he has political ambitions for the young man, obsessively keeps tags on him all the time, calls him 'Bub', is jealous of everyone Field comes into contact with, and gives every impression that he has done this sort of thing before and wants him for himself. Field also has another admirer, the not-much-more-likeable Annabelle Weldon (Virginia Houston), a prudish snob from Flamingo Road whose interests lie only in moving further up the social scale.

Field is given the task of delivering the attachment order, though when he gets there all that is left of the carnival is Lane's tent. When he walks in on her she is crooning to the radio – the song is 'If I Could Be With You' – and they hit it off at once. Field asks her out to supper, swears

there is no ulterior motive, and seems shocked when she changes her
blouse and adjusts her stockings without expecting him to turn his back.
He takes her to the Eagle Café, gets to know her life story and persuades
the owner to give her a job waiting tables – while Semple guzzles milk and
glares from his corner. 'He gives me the creeps,' Lane opines, 'we had
better-looking people than that in our side-shows!' Field does not like
Semple either, but has to put up with the flack because Semple is kingpin
in these parts.

Next we are introduced to Dan Reynolds (Brian), hailed as the top
man of the State political machine. He is in town to confer with Semple
and other local entrepreneurs to decide who will be their next senator.
Semple has earmarked Field for the position, but first he must marry – not
the 'stray cat from the carnival', but Annabelle, mindless of what he wants
for himself. The pair head for the roadhouse run by Lute Mae Sanders
(Gladys George), a bordello in all but name, which supplies female
company for well-heeled businessmen and has always been above the law.
Dan is holed up with his cronies in an upstairs room.

Dan is basically a decent, honest man, crooked only because he wants
to fit in; he is a tough character who runs the biggest construction
company in town, but still kowtows to the hideous sheriff, of whom he
says, 'He's the only man I know that can make a sow's ear out of a silk
purse.' After his meeting with Dan, Field descends to the salon, where
Lane is singing *their* song. He drives her back to her lodgings, but en route
they stop off for a romantic interlude next to the lake. When Semple finds
out about this, he *orders* Field to marry Annabelle, mindless of the fact
that they do not love each other. Lane tries to convince him that she is
pleased – adding that waitresses and senators do not mix. Then she is fired
from her job, and when she learns that Semple is behind this and wants her
out of town, she confronts him – the first time anyone has had enough guts
to do so. When he insults her by comparing her with the vermin at a place
where he once worked, she slaps him – well aware that she has made a
mortal foe.

Semple has Lane arrested on a trumped-up prostitution charge, and she
spends thirty days in the slammer. Upon her release, she gets work as a
hostess at Lute Mae's: we see her serving drinks as a woman almost dervish-
dances through the front of the screen to 'Jealousy'. Semple tries to get her
thrown out of here, too, but Lute Mae is a law unto herself – and knowing
that Semple dislikes Lane makes her like her twice as much. Lane is assigned
to looking after Dan Reynolds on election night, but being a decent girl, this
amounts to no more than putting him to bed and fixing his hangover cure the
next morning. Dan is appreciative: they drive out to his construction site, and

when *she* puts ten cents in the cold-drinks machine he is truly hooked, for no
one has given him anything since he was a child.

Cut to Senator Field Carlisle, still trailed by his hideous mentor and
unable to speak to political colleagues without him butting in. Semple now
has even higher hopes for his protégé and tells him, 'Never had me a
governor before.' Field, however, has started hitting the bottle because no
one else takes him seriously, and his depression worsens when he learns that
Lane has married Dan on the rebound. News of the marriage also leads to
another confrontation with Semple, who threatens Lane again and receives
an allegorical response:

> SEMPLE: Didn't know you were interested in politics . . . Legislature's
> very interesting to watch. Of course, we officers of the law ain't so
> forgetful of our promises as the fellows who make the laws. Me, I don't
> forget anything.
> LANE: You know, Sheriff, we had an elephant in our carnival with a
> memory like that. He went after a keeper that he'd held a grudge against
> for almost fifteen years. Had to be shot. You just wouldn't believe how
> much trouble it is to dispose of a dead elephant.

Lane and Dan move into a mansion on Flamingo Road and Annabelle,
who has always despised her, suddenly wants to call on her while Field sinks
deeper into despair. Semple is one of the couple's first visitors: Dan's candidate
has been promised the governorship, but Semple wants him to stand down in
favour of Field. When Dan refuses to capitulate, Semple has the construction-
site foreman's son arrested on a phoney drink-driving charge; the only way the
boy will stay out of jail is if the foreman hires illegal unpaid convict labour on
his boss's behalf – for Dan also happens to be on the local prison board. Field
is horrified, stands up to Semple for the first time, and subsequently ends up
being thrown over – from now on he is on his own, and with no political future
his riches-mad wife is the next to turn her back on him.

Semple now has a change of plan: instead of Field, he will put himself
up for governor. The local big-wigs are opposed to this, but have no option
but to support him, otherwise he will turn them in for embezzlement: they
have been too busy getting their big cuts to notice that he has been covering
his own tracks for the ill-gotten handouts they have given him. 'I plucked
a goose here and there,' he says, 'but nobody can find the feathers.' Dan,
meanwhile, finds out about Lane's brief affair with Field, and ignoring her
pleas that she really does love him, accuses her of marrying him only
for protection from Semple. He leaves, and tells her that he may not be
coming back. Then Field turns up at the house, drunk and beyond
salvation, and kills himself.

Semple soon spreads the rumour that Field committed suicide because he was being persecuted by a married woman he was having an affair with, and Lane is intent on fixing him once and for all when her house is attacked by angry Mothers' Committee fanatics and Dan is found guilty of peonage. She pulls a gun on him: unless he calls the District Attorney and confesses his crimes, she will kill him. He threatens to crucify the pair of them – strong stuff for American audiences at the time – there is a struggle, an explosion, and Semple falls dead. Lane is arrested, but it seems unlikely that the charge will amount to much because Semple was holding the gun when it went off and only his prints were on it. Even so, if she does go to jail, Dan reassures her that he will be waiting for her when she gets out.

Following five weighty dramas on the trot, Joan's next venture was a comedy. The limp storyline of David Butler's *It's a Great Feeling* focuses on Jack Carson, playing himself, and his attempts to direct himself, buddy Dennis Morgan and their discovery (Doris Day, in one of her first starring roles) in a movie when no one else wants to work with him – again, Hollywood reflecting real life. Worked into the plot, also playing themselves, were as many Carson-unfriendly directors as Butler could ensnare for the brief shooting schedule, and a galaxy of big names including Jane Wyman, Ronald Reagan, Gary Cooper, Edward G Robinson, Sydney Greenstreet – and Errol Flynn, who marries Doris Day in the final scene. In Joan's sketch she is seen sending herself up in a couturier's with Carson and Morgan. The film was a paltry effort that dated quickly, and for a supposed comedy it has few funny moments.

Joan's next film should have been *Caged*, a prison drama based on the novel by Virginia Kellogg and for which she was promised equal, side-by-side billing with Bette Davis. Joan, it appears, was looking forward to the challenge, but Bette made it clear that she would not be starring in any 'dyke movie', and the project was passed on to Agnes Moorehead and Eleanor Parker. In its place, *The Damned Don't Cry* would be the first in a trilogy of pictures with Vincent Sherman, who had recently directed Bette Davis in *Old Acquaintance* and *Mr Skeffington* (1943 and 1944 respectively). Two years Joan's junior, Sherman had had a passionate affair with Bette, and would do so with Joan too.

Sherman had arrived in Hollywood in 1933 to act in John Barrymore's *Counsellor-at-Law*. A few years later, Warner Brothers had hired him as a scriptwriter and dialogue director, then director proper. Immediately before working with Joan, he had made the yet-to-be-released *Adventures of Don Juan* with Errol Flynn. Stocky and pugnacious-looking, with greasy hair and a broken nose, Sherman had been married for some time, and actually told his wife about Joan. Equally bizarrely, the two women in his life became friends and socialised together when not with him. The affair – Joan's 'main' one at this time – was just as troublesome and violent for her as the one with Greg Bautzer. The couple's rows at Brentwood Park – and their making up afterwards – became the talk of the neighbourhood. There were also complaints to the authorities from locals concerned for the welfare of Joan's children – ones that were almost certainly followed up, disproving Christina's claims in *Mommie Dearest* that Joan was physically abusing them. If this *were* true, someone almost definitely would have seen evidence of the injuries Christina wrote about.

The supports in *The Damned Don't Cry* are a mixed but mostly versatile bunch. David Brian is his usual lumbering, lacklustre self. Steve Cochran (1917–65) was an extremely handsome, famously hirsute actor, who positively oozed heated sexuality and who said more with his heavy-lidded eyes than most would have dared put in words. Cochran had appeared in Mae West's Broadway revival of *Diamond Lil*, and almost always played the cynical, hard-edged tough guy or downright thug, whereas in real life he was regarded as one of the nicest men in Hollywood. Kent Smith (1907–85) trod the boards with Franchot Tone and made his debut in *Cat People* (1942). Years later, equally dull as here and prematurely greying, he would be a regular in the 1960s television series *Peyton Place*. Richard Egan (1921–87) was a former drama teacher, and had the privilege while making the film of being promoted by Joan as 'the next Gable'. Like Cochran he found himself too frequently cast in rugged roles, and is chiefly remembered today for his portrayal of Elvis Presley's brother in *Love Me Tender* (1956).

The Damned Don't Cry opens with the body of mobster Nick Prenter (Cochran) being dumped in the desert – something that was bound to happen sooner rather than later, observes one of the cops who find him. Detectives investigating the murder discover home-movie footage of oil-heiress Lorna Hansen Forbes (Joan), also believed to have been the victim of a syndicate killing, though nothing is known of her background – it was as if she had suddenly materialised, two years previously, from nowhere.

Lorna is, in fact, Ethel Whitehead, now seen fleeing to her in-laws' house, where she once lived with construction-worker husband Roy (Egan) and their little son, Tommy. The story is told in flashback. The Whiteheads cannot afford luxuries because Roy is spending every spare dollar on insurance to ensure that his family will be taken care of, should anything happen to him. Ethel (Joan looking very un-Crawford-like, in dowdy clothes and minus make-up) thinks Tommy should be taken care of *now*; she buys him a bicycle on credit, and when the boy is killed while riding it, feels there is nothing to keep her tied to Roy any longer in that backwater, and heads for the city.

Ethel gets a job in a department store tobacco kiosk, but in next to no time is earning extra cash working as a mannequin – a front for her employer's drugs, prostitution and illegal gambling racket. (As she takes to the makeshift catwalk, so we are treated to what will henceforth be regarded as the completed Crawford look: shorter, dyed-red hair, high-arched eyebrows, and her 'Victory Red' painted mouth almost cavernous – and though the film is monochrome, her figure is at its most voluptuous.) She learns her first 'business' lesson – that the customer is always right, especially the out-of-town buyers who expect sex from their escorts. Initially, Ethel is against this until a fellow employee persuades her otherwise: 'So, they wrestle with you a little, but it's no worse than the subway . . . You've gotta stop being antisocial. All this living by yourself, that's for channel swimmers. Just hang on to me tonight and you'll have a great time, *and* at retail prices!'

The pair go to Grady's, the watering hole for the hub of the criminal world, and afterwards share the 'tips'. When Ethel realises that her partner has ripped her off, however, she opts to operate alone. She meets mild-mannered but gullible accountant Marty Blackford (Smith), falls for him and takes him to lunch at Grady's, where one item on the exclusive menu costs as much as he earns in a day. Soon she has him working for big cheese George Castleman (a ludicrously over-the-top-aggressive David Brian). When Marty meets Castleman and his henchmen at his antiques-filled mansion and realises he has become involved with the Mob, he wants out because *he* has principles and self-respect. Ethel persuades him otherwise in yet another uniquely (and autobiographical) Crawfordesque outburst:

> Don't talk to me about self-respect. That's something you tell yourself when you've got nothing else . . . The only thing that counts is that stuff you take to the bank, that filthy buck that everybody sneers at, but slugs to get. You're a nice guy, but the world isn't for nice guys. You gotta kick and punch and belt your way up, 'cause nobody's gonna give you a lift. You gotta do it yourself, 'cause nobody cares about us except ourselves!

Ethel tells Marty that all she has done so far has been for them because she wants them to be together, then sets off to coerce Castleman into paying Marty more money for the risks he is taking. She has done her research and knows his background, so she is ready for him when he sneers his disapproval at her perfume and the way she is dressed:

> You enjoy making a person look like two cents, don't you? Well, get this straight. *I* don't like being made to look like two cents, especially by somebody who was small change himself not so long ago . . . I mean Joe Cavani, who changed his name to George Castleman. You and your

Etruscan flowerpot. You and your sensitive nose. Since when did Joe
Cavani know anything about perfume? Since you were a loudmouth
hoodlum hijacking beer trucks in Jersey, running rum from Cuba,
plugging guys for a ten-dollar bill? I can find out things, too!

Instead of getting angry, Castleman respects Ethel and admires her pluck, her
handsome (as opposed to beautiful) face, and decides he wants her in his
organisation. Position and salary will depend upon her capabilities – and he
is not talking CV. Marty therefore gets his raise, and Ethel, who not so long
ago exposed Castleman as a con man, proves herself not averse to changing
her own identity for the sake of attracting the mighty dollar. Henceforth she
will be known as Lorna Hansen Forbes.

The newly created queen of café society gets a plush pad, 'does' Europe
for a year and acquires sophistication. Upon her return to America, she learns
from Castleman that Grady, the proprietor of her favourite club, has been
bumped off by super-thug Nick Prenter, who for some time now has been
getting too big for his boots, and is known to be planning a massive heist,
which will make him the most powerful mobster in the country. Castleman
dispatches Ethel to gen up on him – even to make herself available to Prenter
if this is what it takes to obtain the necessary information. For the second
time, she turns on him, 'What am I, another wire-service you've underwritten,
a new racetrack you've bought into?' She agrees, all the same, because she
feels she is already whoring herself to Castleman, and she learned long ago
while working at the department store that the customer is *always* right.

Ethel arrives at Nick's place, exquisitely dressed (by Joan's now
personal costumier, Sheila O'Brien) and is surprised to find not some broken-
nosed lout but a thoroughly charming, drop-dead-gorgeous young stud, who
immediately sweeps her off her feet. The ensuing poolside seduction scene is
pure camp. Nick looks good enough to eat, concupiscent even, in his skimpy,
patterned loincloth, and defies the still-potent Hays Office code by flaunting
a very hairy chest (Cochran was forced to wrap a towel around his neck, and
hold this in place to conceal much of his ebony carpet, for the final take).
Later, Ethel charms her way into a high-powered Mob meeting and gets
to know the names of Nick's contacts. When she relays this information to
Castleman and he tells her that Nick is to be eliminated, she refuses to co-
operate – until he reminds her that *she* has become a lady of refinement by
way of crime, and levels with her that unless she does his bidding, she too
will be disposed of.

Ethel finds herself choosing the lesser of the two evils – Nick, the
perfect specimen who also brings out her maternal instincts. He confesses
that in the past he has had people killed, and that he is planning to have

Castleman killed so that he can take over his empire and share it with her once they are married. Ethel begs him to reconsider, then returns home to find Castleman and Marty waiting for her. Castleman has found out about her affair with Nick and starts slapping her around – reflecting the real-life situation between Joan and David Brian – until Marty comes up with the idea of getting Ethel to invite Nick over for a little love-making so that they can kill him and tell the police they shot him in self-defence as he was breaking into the place. Nick turns up, sees Ethel with Castleman, calls her a 'dirty tramp', and in the ensuing struggle is shot dead while Ethel escapes and drives to her parents' house, bringing us back to where the film began.

While in hiding, Ethel is reunited with Marty, who has reported Castleman to the police. The story's conclusion is, however, ambiguous and unsatisfactory. The pair are about to leave and go on the run when the mobster shows up. There is another shoot-out, which ends up with Ethel taking a bullet while trying to protect Marty, and with Castleman justifiably getting to meet his Maker. The credits roll, though, before we are given time to learn what has happened to Marty, or if indeed Ethel will survive.

The film was slated by the critics. Howard Barnes of the *New York Herald Tribune* peppered his review with adjectives such as 'shabby', 'implausible' and 'contrived', but it was the *New York Times*'s Bosley Crowther whose eyes Joan threatened to scratch out, should they ever meet. 'Miss Crawford runs through the whole routine of cheap motion picture dramatics in her latter day, hard-boiled style,' he wrote, twisting the knife with the coda: 'A more artificial lot of acting could hardly be achieved.'

Joan was loaned out to Columbia for her next film, *Harriet Craig* – and took Vincent Sherman and her favourite crew members with her. Cynics pointed out that she was largely playing herself in the film: a successful, domineering woman obsessed with domestic cleanliness and placing her long-suffering husband, Walter (Wendell Corey), secondary to everything else in her regimented existence. On top of this, Harriet (like Eva Phillips in the later *Queen Bee*) is driven to control the lives of those about her, and in particular the love affair between her visiting cousin and her boyfriend. Usually with Crawford films of this nature, the end result involves a gun or suicide; in this instance, Walter exacts the 'ultimate' revenge – smashing Harriet's favourite antique vase, then walking out on her!

Joan returned to Warner Brothers to complete her Vincent Sherman trilogy with *Goodbye, My Fancy*, originally a stage success for Madeleine Carroll. She played Congresswoman Agatha Reed, who returns to the college that expelled her two decades previously to collect an honorary degree. The nature of the visit is twofold, however: she wants to rekindle her relationship with former sweetheart James Merrill (Robert Young), now the establishment's president – the reason for her expulsion, after the president back then had learned that they had spent the night together off the campus. There are the usual complications, in this instance brought about by press photographer Matt Cole (Frank Lovejoy), who loves her from afar but is afraid of making the initial approach because of her powerful position. In the end, of course, it is this younger man who wins the iron lady's heart. It was a mediocre, sometimes far-fetched tale, and resulted in another scathing attack from the *New York Times*'s make-or-break Bosley Crowther, who wrote, 'Miss Crawford's errant Congresswoman is as aloof and imposing as the Capitol dome.'

When asked by a reporter from *Modern Screen* while shooting the film *why* she preferred playing characters with guts, nerve and willpower, Joan snapped, 'Because this is a *man's* world, dear, and a girl has to fight for everything she wants. And *men* taught me how to fight, how to live!' That afternoon Joan had had a bust-up with a new (but as far as she was concerned unimportant) rival, nineteen-year-old Janice Rule, a former dancer from Chicago. Some years later, Rule would marry Ben Gazzara and (in 1968) very nearly steal *The Swimmer* from Burt Lancaster, but during the summer of 1950 she got on the wrong side of Joan by persistently fluffing her lines and holding up the production. Joan had all the patience in the world when it came to putting novice actresses at ease, as had happened with Ann Blyth, but sensing that the crew were pandering to the starlet, she told her in front of the entire set, 'Enjoy making films while you can, Miss Rule, I'm sure you won't be with us for very long!'

Joan's personal relationship with Vincent Sherman ended at the same time as their professional one, and she picked up on her affair with Greg Bautzer as if nothing had happened. Again, the hacks predicted a trip down the aisle; again, the pair fought like cat and dog and reconciled noisily, oblivious to the neighbours at Brentwood Park. There were reports of 'filthy tirades' in the garden and on Joan's balcony, and once she was observed climbing onto the roof and screaming for help – only to have him 'ravish' her once he had talked her down! Joan felt no shame at showing friends and fans her latest black eye or bruise, or her swollen wrists where her lover had pinned her down while forcing himself upon her. Bautzer was photographed with his hands bandaged, after a drunken ascent up Joan's rose trellis had gone wrong and he had plunged through her bedroom window. The press reported how, after a nasty brawl at a party, Bautzer had flung back at Joan the $10,000 Cartier cufflinks she had bought him – only for her to rush upstairs and flush them down the toilet, then forbid everyone from using the bathrooms for two days until a plumber had retrieved them from the complicated pipes system. On another occasion, having left another party too drunk to stand up,

Bautzer had crashed the Cadillac Joan had given him into a lamppost. For Joan, this was the last straw. It was not so much that Bautzer had written off the car that upset her, but that he had been with another woman at the time. Packing her suitcases, she took her children to New York, where she rented a suite at the Hampshire House Hotel until summoned back to make her next film – the one she later confessed to hating more than any other. When Bosley Crowther called her 'ossified' and dismissed *This Woman is Dangerous* as 'fictitious junk', Joan actually sent the journalist a letter, in which she agreed with him!

The format of the movie was pretty much the same as that of *The Damned Don't Cry*, with Joan playing the unappreciated mistress of a self-absorbed, cold-hearted thug, though in this instance there are no lengthy, Crawfordesque outbursts of acerbic dialogue – however, the film is not nearly as bad as she and the critics made it out to be. Beth Austin (Joan) visits her oculist in search of a cure for bad headaches and aversion to bright lights, and is told that her condition is so serious that she may be blind before the week is out. The oculist suggests the country's best eye specialist, Ben Helleck (actor-tenor Dennis Morgan, who had appeared in *Hollywood Canteen* and *It's a Great Feeling*). On the eve of leaving for Helleck's clinic in Indianapolis, Beth and the Jackson brothers – her lover, Matt (David Brian, in typical over-aggressive mode), and Will (Richard Webb) – pull off a heist at a New Orleans gambling joint, masquerading with their henchmen as a police raid.

At the clinic, Helleck performs a risky operation on Beth and saves her sight. The Jacksons, meanwhile, are in their trailer en route for the next big job when they are pulled over by a traffic cop. Matt shoots the cop, and the brothers and Will's wife, Anne (Mari Aldon), who shared a cell with Beth when she was jailed for embezzlement, change direction and head for Indianapolis – with Matt becoming increasingly paranoid that Beth may have made up the operation story because she is seeing another man, and more concerned about this than the fact the FBI are now after him for murder.

It does not take the police long to latch on to Beth, whom they believe will lure the Jacksons into their trap. She is also being trailed by a private investigator hired by the insanely jealous Matt – whom she tries to convince herself is the only man she loves, though what she sees in this loathsome character is another matter. Beth finds herself becoming more and more attracted to the handsome, kindly physician, but feels duty-bound to her Jekyll-and-Hyde lover because he rescued her when she was at an all-time low. She is reminded of this stressful period when, during a drive into town with Ben, he makes a detour to tend a dying patient at the local women's prison. 'They put you in the laundry and steam you as soft as a potato,' she responds, when he tells her that, as far as prisons go, this place – with its rehabilitation programmes – is not so bad. She also confesses that happiness frightens her, and *he* knows that a man called Matt is the source of her misery because she murmured his name while coming to after her operation. And when Beth says she wants to leave town, Ben begs her to stay – he wants her, and promises never to enquire about her past life.

Beth is put to the test when Ben takes her with him on an emergency call. He now knows who she is and who she is involved with, and sends her off in his car to pick up plasma – which he already has. Beth deliberates, even buys a coach ticket, but she returns to Ben, though only to tell him goodbye. She feels she must help Matt, even if he is an unquestionable louse. Ben drives her back to the coach station, but when she reaches the Jacksons' hideout, Matt is no longer there – he has found out about Ben, and has gone looking for him with murder in mind. Beth and Will rush back to Ben's.

En route to the clinic, Matt encounters his private investigator, over-hears him calling the FBI, and kills him. He finds Ben in the operating theatre and there is the inevitable shoot-out, which leaves Beth and Will wounded, and the elder Jackson plunging to his death through the glass roof of the viewing gallery. Beth is arrested by the police, but is promised leniency because she saved Ben's life by knocking Matt's hand aside as he pulled the trigger. And, of course, her new lover will be waiting for her on the outside, should she have to go to jail again.

The rivalry between Joan and Bette Davis had resurfaced in November 1950 with the release of *The Damned Don't Cry* and Bette's *All About Eve*, one of her most memorable films. While Bette tore up her invitation to the former's premiere, Joan made a spectacular entrance to *All About Eve*'s opening night at Grauman's Chinese Theatre – wearing a floor-length red brocade gown under her mink, dripping with diamonds and, adding insult to injury, clinging to Vincent Sherman's arm on one of their last public outings together. Joan's more-than-likely fake 'sincere condolences' to Bette over the break-up of the latter's marriage to Grant Sherry were met with a pronounced, 'Fuck you, lady!'

Matters were only exacerbated in the December and January, when ahead of the Oscar nominations the various magazines published their Best lists. *Photoplay*, not wishing to appear prejudiced, voted *both* of them Most Popular Actress. Joan – never as virulently critical of Bette as Bette was of her – decided that she could live with this, though she soon changed her mind when the Oscar nominations were announced in the February. While *The Damned Don't Cry* was ignored, there were a staggering *fourteen* nominations for *All About Eve*, including Best Actress for both Bette and her co-star Anne Baxter.

It was at around this time that Joan rushed to Franchot Tone's aid after he had been hurt in an ugly barroom fracas with tough-guy actor Tom Neal. A year after divorcing Joan, Franchot had married actress Jean Wallace, with whom he had had two sons. This marriage had ended in 1948, and after numerous affairs with both men and women he had recently begun dating Barbara Payton, a platinum-blonde starlet whose career had begun (as it would end in 1967) with her working as a prostitute. What Franchot had not known when popping the question was that Payton was already engaged to ex-boxer Neal, though she *had* accepted Franchot's proposal. The two men had squared up to each other, with Franchot coming off worst – his terrible facial injuries resulted in hospitalisation, and despite extended plastic surgery, he never regained his former matinee-idol looks.

Joan, very much against this proud man's wishes, insisted on paying most of Franchot's medical bills. Franchot did marry Barbara Payton, but the union lasted barely a year; ironically, the film he had completed before the attack, his last for seven years, was entitled *Here Comes the Groom*. As for serial-thug Tom Neal, his own career went into rapid decline: in 1965 he would be convicted of manslaughter after shooting dead his fourth wife, and in 1972, soon after being released from prison, he would be found dead in bed – the unsubstantiated cause being heart failure, though there were many who believed that one of the many wronged suitors or husbands he had clashed with had caught up with him.

Meanwhile, if Will Hays and his Motion Picture Code had been the scourge of Hollywood until he stepped down from his podium in 1945, at the dawn of the Fifties the new pariah was Senator Joe McCarthy, whose unproven claim that much of the United States had been infiltrated by Communists sparked off a wave of mass hysteria, achieving little but the tarnishing of the film community for decades to come. In February 1950, McCarthy claimed to be in possession of a 205-name list of 'Reds' working in the State Department, and it did not take long for rumours to spring up concerning 'sub-lists' of their allies and sympathisers – few more influential, it would appear, than those that people were flocking to see every day on their cinema screens. The so-called McCarthy witch-hunt had begun, and would rage on for another four years.

Heading the House Un-American Activities Committee (HUAC), founded to protect America from its 'dangerous enemies' and to 'uphold justice', was J Parnell Thomas, a man who, like Will Hays, did not practise what he preached – he was subsequently jailed for payroll padding. In charge of the Anti-Communist Motion Picture Alliance for the Preservation of American Ideals was John Wayne – a man who had made a great point of attacking the likes of Tyrone Power, Robert Taylor and Robert Montgomery for being 'unmanly men', yet while these had been decorated for their bravery during the war, the supposedly 'gung-ho' Wayne had made any number of excuses *not* to fight for his country. Tallulah Bankhead, in her 'official' capacity as the daughter of Congress's late Speaker, William Bankhead, opposed the appointment and told listeners on her radio show, 'Mr Wayne's latest film is called *She Wore a Yellow Ribbon*, but I think it should be changed to *He Wore a Yellow Streak*.' Wayne's allies included Clark Gable, Barbara Stanwyck, Gary Cooper, Ward Bond, Hedda Hopper, Lela Rogers (Ginger's mother), Walt Disney – and two of the men Wayne had mocked, Robert Taylor and Robert Montgomery.

Among those opposing the purge were Gene Kelly, Danny Kaye, Tallulah Bankhead, John Huston, Humphrey Bogart, Lauren Bacall and future president Richard Nixon. Directors Elia Kazan and Edward Dmytryk were but two who turned the tables on colleagues. With the speed of wildfire, the purge got out of hand, with genuine Communists (who, in any case, were *not* breaking any laws) shopping absolutely anyone, even their best friends, to take the heat off themselves. Careers were needlessly destroyed, including those of actresses Anne Revere and Gale Sondergaard, playwrights Lillian Hellman and Dashiel Hammett. Jules Dassin, the director of Joan's *Reunion in France*, left for London shortly after being blacklisted and made *Night and the City* (1950). Melvyn Douglas, Joan's frequent co-star, made only a few films over the next decade and Donald Ogden Stewart, who had scripted *A Woman's Face*, retired to England. The worst casualty from Joan's point of view would be her friend and former lover, John Garfield, who after being virtually unemployed for two years died from a stress-aggravated heart attack in 1952, aged just 39.

Another big threat to the film industry at this time was the new medium of television – though, as had happened during the transition from silents to sound, there were the cynics who declared that this 'new-fangled contraption' would never catch on, even though by the end of 1950 one in five American homes had one! Some organisations, such as NBC, made Herculean attempts to draw away some of the rapidly escalating advertising funds from the television network by launching programmes such as *The Big Show*, a $50,000-a-time, ninety-minute extravaganza hosted by Tallulah Bankhead, which each Sunday evening over the next eighteen months would feature the most dazzling array of stars ever assembled in a single studio, and from all walks of show business.

The film companies compensated for their losses, as more and more fans stayed home, by searching beyond the Hollywood confines for 'package deals' – outfits that comprised director, lead players, scriptwriter and cameraman, mostly from Europe. Previously insular artistes such as Gérard Philipe, Hildegard Knef, Juliette Gréco, Otto Preminger, and sex kittens Brigitte Bardot, Gina Lollobrigida and Sophia Loren, became household names. Although at the time few of the megastars entertained the mere *idea* of standing in front of a television camera, this was the beginning of the end of the all-powerful studio system, and matters were made worse when the US Justice Department issued a ruling that prohibited the major studios from screening *only* their own productions in their own theatre chains. MGM, Twentieth Century-Fox and Warner Brothers attempted to keep their houses full by using the latest technology, frequently with dire results: CinemaScope, VistaVision and 3-D, which much of the time distorted what was happening on the screen.

This Woman Is Dangerous brought down the curtain on Joan's eight-year stint with Warner Brothers. She later said in one interview that Jack Warner had purposely given her a feeble script, poor leading man and inefficient cameraman in anticipation of her throwing a tantrum, therefore offering the studio a legitimate excuse to fire her. In another interview she claimed that she had fallen out with Warner because he had wanted her to play Doris Day's sister in *Storm Warning*, though this has been released long before February 1952, when Joan left the studio. In fact, she could have refused *anything* given the various approval clauses in her contract, and by dismissing *This Woman Is Dangerous* as trash, and assuming its successor would be no better, she was merely drawing attention to her own bad judgement and customary lack of self-confidence.

It was a chance remark to Hedda Hopper – 'Somebody ought to tell the world what a bunch of shits Hollywood has running its studios' – that led to Joan being approached by the New York-based publisher Mentor Books, an imprint of the New American Library (NAL). Harper & Brothers had recently paid Tallulah Bankhead a small fortune for her unexpurgated memoirs (an editor's nightmare, which had brought about 186 threatened lawsuits from terrified colleagues, given her predilection for never holding back), and the NAL were hoping that if Joan was offered a 'taster' in a publication entitled *Four Figures in the Amusement Field*, this might lead to bigger things. The book (whose other contributors were baseball legend Babe Ruth, boxer Joe Louis, and black composer William C Handy) was reasonably well put together, but on account of the problems encountered by Tallulah's kiss-and-tell, proved much less explosive than the many forthright interviews Joan had given to the movie press over the years.

Meanwhile, in 1952 Joan's first 'independent' film was announced – *Sudden Fear*, a one-off for RKO Pictures, and for which she wanted Clark Gable as her co-star. In December 1949 Gable had wed for the fourth time (he later swore he had been drunk at the time), to former London chorus girl Lady Sylvia Ashley, whose previous husbands had included Douglas

Fairbanks Sr and two English peers. The union had failed because everyone had expected him to marry actress Virginia Gray, with whom he was again involved. Joan wanted Gable all to herself, but made it clear that she would never risk an almighty clash of egos by becoming Mrs Gable. 'If I walk down the aisle again it'll be for keeps,' she told *Modern Screen*. 'And chances are I *won't* marry another actor. They don't make very good husbands!' Gable turned down the film, and, it would appear, the invitation to move into Brentwood Park – and the rebuff led to Joan having an affair with an unknown actor named Touch Connors.

Connors (born Kreker Ohanian) was of Armenian extraction and, at 26, more than twenty years Joan's junior. Having served with the US Air Corps, he was currently a student with the Los Angeles Law School, auditioning for bit-parts and not getting very far until he caught Joan's eye. She was impressed by his tall and muscular physique, his deep voice and macho mannerisms, and boasted to director David Miller that he was good at two things – 'basketball and fucking'. She demanded that Miller give him a part in *Sudden Fear* and Miller, who wanted to keep Joan on-side seeing as she could not have Gable, cast him in the role of the attorney. It was a smallish contribution, but Joan did not doubt that he would go on to bigger and better things – maybe even become her leading man, some day. She wrote an appraisal of him for *Photoplay*, which for some reason was never published, but resurfaced in 1953 to be included in Ivy Crane Wilson's *Hollywood Album*:

> The time I have spent in the motion picture business has made it possible for me to see very quickly if a newcomer has what it takes to make a good actor . . . I have often thought that there is a great affinity between law and acting. Both professions call for great understanding of human beings, a well-placed voice of pleasant timbre, and a natural sense of coordination . . . There are many handsome youngsters who come to films blessed with a pair of broad shoulders and the profile of a Greek god. But they don't stay very long if there is nothing beneath their shock of hair. It takes intelligence in the face of the keen competition present today in artistic fields.

Connors would never really become leading-man material, and he never worked with Joan again – their brief affair ended as soon as the cameras stopped rolling on the film – but between 1967 and 1975, renamed Michael Connors, he would become a household name as Mannix in the television series of the same name.

Having failed to procure Clark Gable for *Sudden Fear*, Joan (who had made her position more powerful by eschewing her $200,000 salary for the additional role of co-producer and forty per cent of the box-office, the first

Hollywood star to do so) set her sights on 27-year old Marlon Brando, whom she had raved over in *A Streetcar Named Desire* (1951). Despite being warned by friend Tallulah Bankhead (who had fired him from her stage production of Jean Cocteau's *The Eagle Has Two Heads*) that Brando was a 'pig-ignorant slob', Joan sent several notes to him via his agent, only to receive the response, 'Doesn't do mother and son movies. Find some other sucker.' Dismissing Brando as a 'shithead', Joan placed the matter in David Miller's hands, and he found her a co-star she would regard with equal disdain: Jack Palance.

Born in Pennsylvania in 1919, Palance (billed in some prints of the film as 'Walter Palance') was an enormously versatile, sinister-looking Method actor who had recently made a big impression as the heavy in *Panic in the Streets*. The son of Russian immigrants, he had had his face almost completely reconstructed by skin-tightening plastic surgery following horrific burns sustained as a pilot during World War II. Joan had seen him understudying Anthony Quinn in the stage version of *A Streetcar Named Desire*, and had been impressed by his Conrad Veidt-like looks and quiet, sometimes spooky voice. Working with him, however, was another matter. Joan had never concealed her dislike of Method actors, and she first accused Palance of ignoring her each morning when *she* greeted him on the set, unaware that he *had* acknowledged her, but only inside his head because he had been 'in role'! She also hated the way he psyched himself up before a scene – shrieking and running around the sound-stage. She therefore took to snubbing him completely when they were not before the cameras or rehearsing, which only put a strain on everyone else. Halfway through shooting, when producer Joseph Kaufman *ordered* Joan to say 'Good morning' to her leading man, Palance said that she had growled the greeting in such a way it had made his stomach churn.

Joan also experienced difficulties with second female lead Gloria Grahame – a young, talented actress married to Nicholas Ray, who the following year won an Oscar for *The Bad and the Beautiful*. Joan had had her eye on the – for once – not handsome Ray for some time, and took her frustration out on Grahame, a notoriously bad timekeeper, by personally bawling her out on the set. Only once did David Miller intervene – to be rewarded with a hefty slap across the face from Joan. By way of an apology, and lucky not to have been fired or sued for assault, Joan took him out to dinner – and promptly embarked on an affair with him, mindless of the fact that she was still seeing Touch Connors.

In *Sudden Fear*, Joan played neurotic playwright Myra Hudson, a wealthy law-unto-herself who has a run-in with actor Lester Blaine (Palance) and fires him from the production they are working on. Later, they meet by chance on a train, date, and eventually marry. For a while they are happy, until Lester learns that Myra has amended her will, making him co-beneficiary with a foundation she is about to set up. Before the papers for this are signed, Myra overhears a conversation between Lester and his mistress, Irene (Grahame), and it becomes obvious that they are plotting to bump her off. She subsequently elects to play them at their own game, putting a plan into action that she hopes will result in Irene being framed for Lester's murder. She steals Irene's gun, but before she has chance to use it, Lester finds out what she is up to and decides to run her down with his car as she is crossing the street. Unfortunately, Myra and Irene are wearing near-identical outfits and Lester hits the wrong woman, killing himself also.

After Touch Connors and David Miller, Joan took up with *The King and I* star Yul Brynner, whom she is thought to have met for the first time at that year's *Photoplay* Awards ceremony. The pair are *said* (not least of all by a boastful Brynner himself) to have engaged in a brief affair that *he* ended abruptly, giving Joan no reason why, though there were no reports of the pair being seen socially unless in the company of Brynner's actress wife, Virginia Gilmore. They *were* photographed embracing, with Gilmore hovering in the background, backstage at the Broadway theatre where Brynner was playing his most famous role (but one of an astonishing 4,625 performances spread out across his career), and the next day he *did* send her an autographed photograph of himself, stark naked but for his stage make-up. For a while Joan kept it in a drawer in her Brentwood Park bedroom, and it was probably this which fuelled daughter Christina's imagination when she wrote of how, in Hollywood a few years later to film *The King and I* with Deborah Kerr, Brynner rekindled his affair with her mother. Though one may well believe that the impressionable teenager was told, 'Say hello to your Uncle Yul' – all the lovers who visited Brentwood Park had to be addressed as 'Uncle' – one finds it hard to swallow the story of Brynner walking up to Joan's front door, 'a half-naked, bald-headed gypsy man', in his full King of Siam regalia.

Yul Brynner was succeeded in Joan's affections by silver-haired all-action hero Jeff Chandler (born Ira Grossell, 1918–61), fresh from his involvement with Rock Hudson, and married to boot. The pair were invited to Edith Piaf's wedding to crooner Jacques Pills on 20 September 1952, when 'best woman' was Marlene Dietrich. They were photographed at the reception at Le Pavilion in New York, and later attended Piaf's 'honeymoon recital' at the Versailles nightclub. A few weeks later, with Chandler's wife tagging along, they attended Piaf's opening night at the Mocambo, where the 'Little Sparrow' dedicated one of her new songs to Joan – called '*Jean et Martine*', it tells the story of a woman who is washing the dishes in her kitchen when a telegram is delivered, announcing the death of her husband in a lorry smash!

Being a freelance actress – again, Hollywood's first – enabled Joan to pick whichever roles she felt would suit her best, with absolutely no outside interference. On the negative side, with no long-term contract, she was no longer privy to studio protection – and some studios, mindless of a star's track record, still insisted on him or her making screen tests. Joan may have been willing to test for *Mildred Pierce*, but she refused to do so again.

She was approached by Columbia and offered the part of the adulterous Karen Holmes in *From Here to Eternity*, the film that would re-launch Frank Sinatra's ailing career. Her agent negotiated a $100,000 salary *and* a sizeable percentage of the box-office, and Joan announced that she would not mind being billed *after* Montgomery Clift – 'I mean, he's such a *nice* young man!' – but she lost out on the part, stupidly without any doubt, solely because she told director Fred Zinnermann that she would *only* wear costumes that had been especially made for her by her personal designer, Sheila O'Brien. The part, of course, went to Deborah Kerr. 'Good for her,' Joan told her pal William Haines, 'it's about time *somebody* got to fuck her!'

CHAPTER ELEVEN

The Temple of Saint Joan

'She is the personification of the Movie Star de Luxe, the rags-to-riches Cinderella, the Lady Bountiful gowned by Adrian. But I have always felt that the greatest performance of Joan Crawford's career is Joan Crawford.'
Hedda Hopper

Towards the end of 1952, to showcase the phenomenal talents of the latest European sensation to cross the Atlantic – Portuguese singer Amalia Rodrigues – Paramount offered Joan the lead in *Lisbon*, an espionage thriller to be directed by Nicholas Ray. Producer Irving Asher had commissioned a rewrite of the script, changing the sex of the main character, and several scenes are thought to have been test-shot before Joan and Asher reached a mutual agreement that this was not the vehicle for her – absolutely nothing to do with the fact, she declared, that when Amalia had appeared on Eddie Fisher's television show, Fisher had described her as, 'A walking vision, even more gorgeous than Elizabeth Taylor.' *Lisbon* was subsequently sold to Republic, and would be made four years later with Ray Milland playing the lead as originally intended by the scriptwriter – and with brief appearances by Celeste Rodrigues, performing two of her sister's most famous *fados*.

At the beginning of 1953, Joan was made an offer she would have been foolish to reject – $125,000 to play musical comedy star Jenny Stewart in what would be her first Technicolor film, *Torch Song*, for MGM. She had no qualms about returning to her old stomping ground: Louis B Mayer had retired and his successor, RKO's Dore Schary, whom she had met while making *Sudden Fear*, was a much more amenable man – though with the studio system in decline, he could afford to be.

The film was to be shot in just 24 days and directed by Hollywood musicals stalwart Charles Walters (1911–82), the man who had served as choreographer on *Meet Me in St Louis* (1944) and had directed *Easter Parade* (1948). Walters later claimed that Joan had summoned him to Brentwood Park for cocktails and to discuss the film. Reportedly, she had been wearing a housecoat, which she had subsequently opened to reveal that she had nothing on underneath. 'This is what you've got to work with, Mr Walters,' she is alleged to have told him. But if Joan had been worried about Walters thinking her 'too over the hill' for the part, she had no cause for concern. In her leotard she looked stunning, lovelier than any Hollywood starlet half her age. As Jenny Stewart she *sparkles* and proves, at 48, a remarkably agile dancer capable of out-hoofing the best of them!

Although *Torch Song* is musically inferior to Walters's films with Judy Garland and his later *High Society*, as a musical melodrama tailor-made for its star, it would not be equalled for another ten years, when Judy bowed out in *I Could Go on Singing*. 'Here is Joan Crawford all over the screen,' raved the *New York Herald Tribune*'s Otis L Guernsey, 'A real movie star in what amounts to a carefully produced one-woman show. Miss Crawford's acting is sheer and colourful as a painted arrow, aimed straight at the sensibilities of her particular fans.' It would also be the first Crawford film to present her as the *complete* gay icon, primarily because it was shot in colour. Save for the coloured-in pictures in posters and movie magazines, fans were not able to truly *see* her flaming red hair, her dark soulful eyes, and her 'prima donna' mouth with its lashings of Elizabeth Arden's 'Victory Red', the colour that linked them to gaydom's other sirens: Dietrich, Garland, Bankhead, Piaf and new recruits Marilyn Monroe and Maria Callas – who had raised Joan's hackles more than a little by labelling herself 'The Bette Davis of Opera'.

Torch Song has much in common with the final Garland film in that it presents its male characters as essentially weak, while the star monopolises the proceedings from start to finish, again reflecting real life, though her victories are frequently Pyrrhic. Aside from former comedienne Marjorie Rambeau, who plays Jenny's mother, the supports are woefully miscast. Joan Crawford/Jenny Stewart would *never* give a man like Michael Wilding the time of day, let alone lean upon him. Walters's inexcusable failing point, however, was in not allowing Joan to use her own singing voice, for in overdubbing her (with the now forgotten India Adams) he robbed audiences of the torch singer's essential elements – the untrained, shaky delivery and technically imperfect 'lived-in' tones that had made Helen Morgan, Ruth Etting and Libby Holman revered by their generation.

Immediately shooting began, there were problems with Wilding – or rather, with his new wife, Elizabeth Taylor. The British-born actor (1912–79), handsome but infamously lazy where work was concerned, had enjoyed great success in England, particularly in his comedy romances opposite Anna Neagle. Since coming to Hollywood, however, the quality of his roles had deteriorated. Also, he had caused a tremendous scandal by wooing and wedding Taylor, exactly half his age and already into her second marriage. Taylor was naturally apprehensive about her husband working with a woman renowned for sleeping with her co-stars, though it was solely through her own pushing that he had been given the part in the first place – but as she was shooting *Rhapsody* on an adjacent lot, she made a point of checking up on him every day to ensure that Joan was not leading him astray.

Some years later Joan would tell Roy Newquist, 'I think Elizabeth Taylor, in one of her rare good films, is great to watch.' In 1953, however, she regarded her as an upstart, referred to her publicly as 'Princess Brat' and, as had happened with Jack Palance, did not take kindly to her swanning onto *her* set and ignoring her. She subsequently sent a message to the young actress via her publicist, informing her that as she obviously had no manners, then maybe she could keep to her own lot. Taylor was similarly peeved at all the attention Joan had received upon her return to MGM – the 'Welcome Back Joan' banner hung across the studio's main entrance, the massive welcoming committee of extras and technicians (some from her silents days), the truckload of flowers and gifts, and the hundreds of telegrams and cards from fellow stars.

In fact, in suspecting that Joan may have been interested in seducing her husband, Elizabeth Taylor was barking up the wrong tree – for she had firmly set her sights on lustier studs – George Nader and 27-year-old Rock Hudson, currently filming *Taza, Son of Cochise* and just assigned to *Magnificent Obsession*, opposite Jane Wyman. Just as Jenny Stewart would never have attempted to seduce a straight, passive man like Wilding (great chanteuses such as Piaf, Holman and Garland invariably married homosexuals), Joan also found attraction in the unorthodox – several lovers and three of her husbands had been bisexual. She knew that Nader was 'married' to a man, and that Rock was living with bit-part actor Jack Navaar *and* still seeing Jeff Chandler, but this did not prevent her from making a move on them. Nader was not interested, but Rock went along with Joan's game. About to hit the big time and terrified of being outed by the press, he never turned down an opportunity to be seen on the town with a pretty girl – mostly 'studio foils' like Terry Moore and Mamie Van Doren – and to be seen with a voracious man-eater of Joan's reputation might have been sufficient to kill off the gay rumours once and for all. Joan, however, actually wanted to have sex with the six-foot-four, 200-pound hunk, and duly invited him to Brentwood Park. Exactly what happened is unclear, though the most likely theory is that she did pull out all the stops to seduce him. According to Shaun Considine (*Bette & Joan: The Divine Feud*, also quoting Jimmie Fidler and Sheilah Graham), Joan persuaded Rock to swim in her pool, then take a shower in her pool-house prior to changing and taking her out dancing. 'Suddenly,' Considine writes, describing what happened when the lights went out, 'he felt the warm, naked body of Joan Crawford beside him. "Sssh, baby," she whispered, "close your eyes and pretend I'm Clark Gable!"'

Many years later, Rock would speak of his 'Crawford experience', revealing that she had indeed tried to 'grab the baby's arm', but that he had gently and very politely turned her down – and balked at the very idea of having sex with Clark Gable, explaining, 'This gentleman *only* prefers blonds!'

'I don't need anything or anybody,' Jenny Stewart pronounces in the film's tight-scripted exercise in camp, teeming with autobiographical references and Crawfordisms. 'If you're worried about me, don't be. I'm not afraid of being alone. I'll *never* be alone. I'm tough . . . that's why I'll never be lonely!'

Singer-dancer Jenny is rehearsing for her new show, but all is not well: her partner (Eugene Loring) has two left feet, her pianist messes up her arrangements, her producer is inept. 'If doctors performed operations the way *you* produce shows,' she snarls, 'everybody in the country would be dead in five years!' These hiccups are, however, just as much Jenny's fault as theirs because she thinks herself above everyone involved with the show and has no patience. For Jenny, only the fans matter, and while she bitches at all who cross her path, she is kindness itself to the youngsters waiting outside the stage door. She knows them all by name, and has been concerned about one she has not seen for a whole week. The girl's mother has been ill and Jenny tells her, 'We should all take care of our mothers' – a concept *she* does not put into practice, for her own mother and younger sister have always used her as a bank, and never offered her the love and support she gets from her audiences.

At home, Jenny's lover-of-sorts, Cliff (Gig Young, wholly super-fluous to the plot), another scrounger who only wants her for what he can get out of her, makes a half-hearted attempt at criticising her for being a control-freak. 'Jenny,' he admonishes, 'when are you going to stop trying to remake everything in the world to look like, act like and talk like you?' – bringing the response, as he passes out from an excess of gin, 'Completely useless – but beautiful!'

Under duress, Jenny turns up for another rehearsal and her all-gay entourage pander to her every whim. Her long-suffering pianist, who according to her manager *she* has driven to drink and depression, has quit and been replaced by a blind man, Tye Graham (Wilding), to whom she takes an instant dislike. Tye is too sure of himself: he improvises on her tight-set arrangements, criticises her technique, and his infirmity makes her feel uncomfortable. Jenny throws a tantrum (and whatever object is close at hand), and orders her manager to fire him. He warns her, 'You oughta get out of that habit of throwing things – some day you'll throw a boomerang.' When Jenny callously adds that a blind man has no *business* being here, the manager responds that Tye had no business being in the war, either, which is how he came to be blinded. This jolts her conscience, albeit temporarily, as she sits at the piano and compares Tye's revised, more sophisticated arrangement with the one she has been using for years. The line is: 'My disposition makes me do as I please' – and annoyed that his *is* the better of the two, she soon gets back onto her high horse.

Jenny and Tye bump into each other at her favourite restaurant, where despite having just been fired he invites her to lunch *and* picks up the tab. A few home truths are flung around: he tells her that she dominates everyone only because she is afraid of being seen as weak, but she hits below the belt by suggesting that he might be better ditching his guide-dog and finding himself a 'seeing-eyed girl'. Unruffled, he tells her how other people see her: as a chanteuse she has the mouth of an angel, but all the other words that come out of it are pure tramp! Later, dressed to the nines, she goes to his place to *order* him to return to the fold, and is surprised to find him living in an opulent apartment, with a manservant and, or so it would appear, a girlfriend – Martha (Dorothy Patrick) – who plays in his quintet. What she does not know is that any love interest between these two is strictly one-sided because Martha knows already that Tye wants Jenny, despite her nasty characteristics, because, having seen her *before* his accident he knows what she looks like, whereas he feels that embracing Martha would be like putting his arms around a shadow.

Tye turns up at the next rehearsal, and Jenny walks in as he is playing 'Tenderly' for the amusement of her boys. This is the song she sang in her first show, years before (though the song would not be published until 1954!). We then see her at the dress rehearsal, caressing the scenery as she sings 'You Won't Forget Me' – but if she has warmed to Tye, she soon reverts to her unpleasant self when she observes him leaving with Martha. Henceforth, all visitors are banned from entering the theatre!

For the first time, Jenny realises how miserable her life is. It is Sunday, and everyone connected with the new show – except her – has a life outside the theatre. Alone in her bedroom, she closes her eyes and tries to figure out what it must be like to be blind, bungling her attempts at touch-telling the time and using the telephone, then lighting a cigarette and burning her fingers. Realising how lucky she is, she has another twinge of conscience and makes up with her mother – something that would never happen in real life! Initially this does not work: all Mrs Stewart is interested in is talking about money, and coercing her into paying for her sister (Nancy Gates) to have the piano lessons she really only wants so as to keep up with the Joneses. Jenny therefore decides to leave and throw an impromptu party at her place, though the only people she knows who have nothing better to do are the chorus boys from the show – suggesting, of course, in a prejudiced Hollywood, that gay men were outcasts who endured an existence of abject boredom and enforced loneliness and only came to life at events such as this, where one disillusioned young thing croons a Jenny Stewart song to another – before her arrival puts a dampener on the proceedings and she orders everyone to leave. She is not really angry because of her guests, but because Tye has refused the summons to attend – and she, of course, *hates* to be disobeyed.

Cut to the show, and the finale where Jenny blacks up for 'Two-Faced Woman' and emulates Josephine Baker, complete with spangled tights and jewelled make-up (and with India Adams sounding more like a poor man's Marilyn Monroe than any Ebony Venus). Tye has been in the orchestra pit tonight, but he will not be joining her when the show hits the road (giving the viewer the impression that the premiere and the closing night are one and the same). Again, she commands him to her presence, plies him with booze, and he lets out a little of his secret – that he was a theatre critic before the war. Again, they have words, only this time he yells back – Jenny has made a career out of shouting at people, and it is time she heard some of the echoes. He adds that she should relax and stop thinking that the world revolves solely around her, otherwise she will finish up a drunken has-been – an accusation later levelled at Joan herself by Gloria Grahame, who claimed that Joan had been 'off her head with vodka' all the way through shooting *Sudden Fear*. Tye talks to Jenny as if dictating a retrospective of her career, or even an obituary, describing her downfall. He refers to her as 'Gypsy Madonna' after the painting by Titian, but is cut short when he starts to elaborate, with: 'I know all about him. You don't have to tell *me*. He lived in Venice and he died of the plague. Now get out of here before you give it to me!'

Jenny goes to see her mother, who proves that she is not so uncaring after all. Mrs Stewart has kept all her daughter's clippings, right from the very first show, and soon makes the connection – it was Tye Graham who called Jenny 'Gypsy Madonna' all those years ago when she introduced 'Tenderly', and the review he penned – his last before going off to war to be blinded – expressed the same feelings for Jenny then that he nurtures now. 'When it comes to Jenny Stewart,' her mother concludes, 'the man who wrote this could never be blind.' In a scene hugely reminiscent of *Pépé le Moko* (1936), in which French chanteuse Fréhel reflects on her past glories to Jean Gabin, Jenny puts on the record and sings along to her old 'hit' – the only time the Crawford vocals are used in *Torch Song*, which is in itself rather touching.

Tye is playing their song when Jenny enters his apartment, while Martha just as noiselessly slips out of his life for good. 'It's senseless music,' he rants, unaware of the swap, 'but it's Jenny, blatant and brash . . . That's the way she is, the way I see her.' He further goes to pieces when he realises that he has actually said this to her and not Martha, and when *she* hits a sore point – accusing him of hiding behind his blindness, and for being terrified of telling her how he really feels about her because he thinks she will only reject him because of his infirmity. She does not, and thankfully the ending is a happy one!

In March 1953, soon after *Torch Song* wrapped, Joan customarily attended the Photoplay Awards, where this year she was to be presented with the award for Best Actress, and Marilyn Monroe honoured as Best Newcomer. Marilyn, setting a precedent, arrived late on the arm of her publicist, Sid Skolsky, and caused an uproar with the gold-lamé creation she had been sewn into, which according to one reporter reduced walking to a 'Madame Butterfly hobble', while another observed she was showing 'enough cleavage for a guy to get lost in'. Joan was not the only woman in the Beverly Hills Crystal Room to disapprove, but she was the only one to speak up. She told Associated Press journalist Bob Thomas, 'There's nothing wrong with my tits, but I don't go around throwing them in people's faces!' Thomas's pieces were syndicated to newspapers nationwide, and though he had edited Joan's comments to remove the expletives, the message to Marilyn was clear enough:

> It was like a burlesque show. The audience yelled and shouted. Jerry Lewis got onto the table and whistled, but those of us in the industry just shuddered . . . Sex plays a tremendously important part in every person's life. People are interested in it, intrigued with it, but they don't like to see it flaunted in their faces . . . The publicity has gone too far, and apparently Miss Monroe is making the mistake of believing *her* publicity. Someone should make her see the light. She should be told that the public likes provocative feminine personalities, but that it also likes to know that underneath it all, the actresses are *ladies*!

Marilyn, not the brightest of individuals, was distraught, and later claimed that Joan had wanted to get her revenge because she had once found herself spurning Joan's advances during a visit to Brentwood Park. This seems impossible to believe, when one considers Joan's extreme fastidiousness – showering several times daily – and Marilyn's already legendary propensity towards dreadful manners and *lack* of cleanliness – never wearing underwear, even during her monthly cycle. One can, however, imagine the peroxide beauty's flimsy little voice whining to Louella Parsons, 'I've always admired Miss Crawford for being such a wonderful mother, for taking four children and giving them a fine home. *That's* why I [as an orphan] cried all night! Who better than I knows what it means to care for homeless little ones?'

Marilyn's further admission to Parsons – 'At least I *walked* like a lady!' – sparked off a feud even more vocal than the ones with Norma Shearer and Bette Davis. The critics generally agreed that Joan was brash, unfeeling and hard-bitten towards some colleagues, and that Marilyn, with her breathy protestations and phoney demure mannerisms, was the victim, the wronged, innocent little girl. The red-blooded males naturally were on her side, while the moralists who had once attacked Joan for her way of life now supported her stance on decency.

Torch Song made a huge amount of money for MGM and gave Joan the mega-success she had yearned for since *Humoresque*. Astonishingly, it also brought about a resurgence of her former acute lack of confidence. Believing that her latest hit was but a fluke, that as a 'freelancer' she would soon revert to the drivel of the last few years, and with no regular man in her life, she began hitting the bottle with a vengeance. This, combined with her mood-swings, reputedly made life unpleasant at Brentwood Park and caused tension on the set of her next film, *Johnny Guitar*, though Joan was but one of a trio of hot-head protagonists once shooting got under way in Sedona, Arizona, at the end of 1953.

Johnny Guitar was the brainchild of Herbert Yates, the head of Republic Studios, which was home to the Don Barry and Hopalong Cassidy movies. Inspired by the recent flood of European imports, Yates, had attempted to emulate their intellectual style with the ballet movie *Spectre of the Rose* (1946) and Orson Welles's *Macbeth* (1948). For what he pro-claimed would be Hollywood's first 'art-house Western' he commissioned a script from Philip Yordan, whose *Anna Lucasta* Joan had wanted to do. The director was another Crawford interest, Nicholas Ray, in what would be his first collaboration with Yordan – they would work on *King of Kings* together in 1961. The haunting score was by Victor Young and Peggy Lee, who performed the theme song over the closing credits. The song would provide her with a worldwide hit, and Chicago-born Young (1900–56), who composed for 300-plus films, would receive his greatest accolade with a posthumous Oscar for *Around the World in Eighty Days*. The director of photography was Joan's most distinguished since Ernest Haller: Harry Stradling (1902–70) was the nephew of Walter Stradling, Mary Pickford's favourite cameraman. Stradling was a genius whose forte was to capture the essence, and often darker qualities, of the Dutch Masters for the screen, particularly when the central subject was a beautiful woman. British-born Stradling had filmed Marlene Dietrich in *Knight Without Armour*, Judy Garland in *Till the Clouds Roll By*, *Easter Parade* and *The Pirate*, and Vivien Leigh in *A Streetcar Named Desire* (1951). Later he would photograph Audrey Hepburn in *My Fair Lady* and Barbra Streisand in her first four films.

There were no reported problems between Joan and the technical staff; indeed, she achieved her earlier ambition of bedding Nicholas Ray, now divorced from Gloria Grahame – who would, ironically, soon afterwards marry his son, Tony. The catfights reported almost daily in the tabloids were between Joan, Sterling Hayden (1916–86) and Mercedes McCambridge (1918–2004). Hayden was a somewhat unpleasant character whose major passion in life was the ocean. He had stowed away at fifteen, become a ship's captain at 22, and often said that he only made films for the money to finance his seafaring projects. Joan told one reporter while they were working together that Hayden should be taken out to sea and fed to the sharks for what he had done to some of her friends, most especially the recently deceased John Garfield. She was referring to the McCarthy witch-hunt, when Hayden had shopped a large number of his Hollywood colleagues to the House Un-American Activities Committee. Indeed, the central themes of *Johnny Guitar* – bigotry and persecution – were interpreted by many at the time as direct references to the purge of the so-called 'Red Tide'.

Mercedes McCambridge was something of an enigma, and said to have been just as passionless off the screen as most of the roles in which she found herself typecast. Her spats with Joan, which almost always saw her coming off worst, appear to have been instigated partly for the publicity they attracted, and partly for the sheer hell of it. McCambridge, with her trademark lisp and scowling disposition, had won an Oscar for her first film, *All the King's Men* (1949), and would be further nominated for her portrayal of Rock Hudson's domineering sister in *Giant* (1956). A former radio and stage actress, she was a commanding presence who made comparatively few films, but every one featuring a top-notch performance.

The remaining cast are exemplary. Scott Brady (1924–85) was a rugged, handsome actor, the brother of Lawrence Tierney, and was rarely given the charismatic roles that best suited him, such as here. Much of his later career, when he had piled on the pounds, was wasted in minor television series, such as playing the bartender in *Police Story*, though he bowed out in style a year before his death in *Gremlins*. Ward Bond (1903–60) similarly was rarely used to his full potential, mainly assigned to playing boxers and cops before the role of wagon master in television's *Wagon Train*; he died halfway through the series that made him a household name. Ernest Borgnine, another heavy, had played the sadistic sergeant in *From Here to Eternity*, and the following year would win an Oscar for his portrayal of the girl-shy Bronx butcher in *Marty*.

The first third of *Johnny Guitar* is a single scene featuring a series of Stradling 'portraits' staged at an edge-of-town saloon owned by Vienna (Joan), where no one goes – though this she hopes will change once the railroad depot is constructed. To assist with the extension of her empire, Vienna has summoned old flame Johnny Guitar (Hayden), whom she last saw five years previously, when she stood him up at the altar for being too gun-crazy.

Like any Wild West entrepreneur, Vienna has her enemies – in this instance half the town, influenced by sourpuss cattle queen Emma Small (McCambridge) and big-shot rancher McGyvers (Bond), who between them own just about everything in sight and even overrule the town marshal. Thus, they and the other protagonists enter the scenario: Johnny, big and brusque and willing to take on any man; Vienna, sylph-like and pretending to be hard-bitten as she raps out orders from the saloon gallery where no one is allowed unless they want to take a bullet in the head. 'Never seen a woman who was more like a man,' says the croupier, audaciously approaching the camera. 'She thinks like one, acts like one, and sometimes makes me feel like I'm not.'

Emma and McGyvers barge into the place with a delegation, and the corpse of her brother, the bank manager, who has been killed in a stagecoach hold-up. Though there are no witnesses, Emma swears the Dancing Kid (Brady) is guilty of the crime. The logic behind this is that she wants the Kid so badly – 'He makes her feel like a woman, and that frightens her,' Vienna later observes – although he is not interested in her, that she would therefore rather see him hang than be with someone else. And to her warped way of thinking, as Vienna *has* had the Kid, then she too must be guilty of murder! When Vienna attempts to sympathise with her unwelcome guest by calling her slain brother a fine man, Emma raps back, 'How would you know? He was one man who never even looked at you . . . You're nothing but a railroad tramp. You're not fit to live among decent people!'

The Kid and his gang arrive next for their usual Friday-night whisky and gambling, and the exercise in suppressed sexuality that sailed high over the heads of pre-Kinsey Report American audiences begins. The Kid may act and look tough, but this is almost certainly a front for his passive homosexuality. He regards Johnny as unmanly because he does not carry a gun, but warms to him when Johnny plays his guitar for him to whisk an unsmiling Emma around the dance floor. 'I like you, mister,' he drawls, deciding that he too wants Johnny. 'Just what *is* your business, sir?' Johnny asks, inviting the tongue-in-cheek response, 'I'll *find* one. All you have to do is play that guitar for me!' Officially, the Kid owns a silver mine, which, like his lair, no one here has ever seen, and which he shares with the other guys. Then he gets shirty again when he sees Johnny making eyes at Vienna. 'What's eating you, *fancy man*?' he growls, as Johnny plays her favourite tune – the film's theme – which only evokes bad memories.

The Kid is also inordinately fond of Turkey (Ben Cooper), the sweet young redhead who is desperate to prove himself a man and who later both fears and fancies the much tougher Johnny. The other members of the gang are the consumptive Cory (Royal Dano), who more resembles an undertaker than a would-be gunslinger – and head-case Bart (Borgnine), who neither smokes nor drinks, dislikes women and is mean to horses. Not to be outdone, Emma too at this stage of the action adopts the 'latent lesbian' look (perfected at around the same time by Barbara Stanwyck, whom Joan wanted for this film, in *Cattle Queen of Montana*), and one may only conclude that she hates Vienna for the very same reason she does the Kid. The lengthy scene ends with Vienna, the Dancing Kid and their respective entourages being given 24 hours to leave town, and as the saloon empties she and Johnny dispute over why *he* stood her up – in the days when she was still *working* in a place like this:

> JOHNNY: I wanted to see you again. Heard you'd had a little luck . . .
> VIENNA: Luck had nothing to do with it . . . I'm not ashamed of how I got what I have. The important thing is, I've got it.
> JOHNNY: I once loved you. A man takes pride in something he really cares for. He hates to see it trampled.
> VIENNA: A man can lie, steal and even kill, but as long as he hangs on to his pride he's still a man. All a woman has to do is slip once and she's a tramp.

This is pure Crawford psychology, of course. Vienna admits that there *have* been other men, but that these have meant nothing because she used up all her love on him. 'When a fire burns itself out,' she observes, 'all you have left is ashes.' Johnny asks her how many lovers she has forgotten – as many as he has remembered, Vienna tells him.

Cut to the Kid's mountain lair, approached via a secret passage under the waterfall. The Kid now figures that since they are being held responsible for a crime they have not committed, they might as well break the law properly before heading for greener pastures. He therefore decides to rob the bank, now owned by Emma, almost at the very moment Vienna arrives there to close her account and pay off her workers, though she has no intention of leaving town. Vienna tries to talk the Kid out of it: despite her reputation she has never been in trouble, but he maintains that he will only back down providing she takes up with him again. This she cannot do, so he steals the money – and a last kiss – before heading back to the mountain.

Emma now thirsts for revenge. The bank-teller saw Vienna kissing the Kid, and as he did not take *her* money, they are obviously in cahoots. Emma and McGyvers round up a posse and the pursuit begins. Turkey, riding into a tree branch, is badly hurt and makes his way back to Vienna's saloon, now closed. 'Boys who play with guns have to be ready to die like men,' she berates him. Even so, she tends his wounds and hides him (miraculously getting no blood on her voluminous white ball gown) and by the time Emma and her lynch mob storm the place she is back to looking virginal, playing 'Johnny Guitar' on her piano – hugely reminiscent of Marlene Dietrich in the similar scene at the close of *Dishonored* (1931), when she is about to face the firing squad. Turkey is discovered, but promised leniency by McGyvers, providing he implicates Vienna in the robbery. The boy becomes a child as he begs her to tell him what to do, and she bravely insists that he does what is necessary to save himself – only to have McGyvers go back on his word. And as the prisoners are dragged off to their fate, in a further act of insanity where Medea meets Mrs Danvers, Emma waits until everyone has left before shooting down the chandelier and setting the place on fire.

Johnny follows the lynch mob, knowing that he can only save one from the rope – Vienna, whom he spirits to the Kid's hideaway, aware that she will probably end up having to choose between them. The pair swim across the creek to the waterfall, and the devastated Kid gives her Turkey's clothes to change into – a sort of cross-dressing tribute from one lost love to another, for he knows that she loves Johnny more than him. She also confesses that Johnny Guitar is none other than the fabled fast-gun, Johnny Logan, and suddenly the younger man is impressed – but not beyond attempting to out-bitch him every time he opens his mouth.

Johnny's newly revealed persona causes dissention between him and Bart, and when Emma shows up – confident that if she meets him alone and woos him with her non-existent feminine charms, she will lure him into the open – Bart makes a deal with her. They will turn the Kid over to McGyvers, find the hidden loot and split it fifty-fifty. The plan backfires when, after Bart kills the sickly Cory, the Kid kills him.

The ending of this 'Freudian horse opera', as Paul Roen called it, should have been taut and dramatic, but high-camp overrides the tension as Emma's metamorphosis into madness reaches its final stage. '*I'm coming up, Vienna!*' she bawls, *the* saying in clandestine gay bars and clubs across the United States during the summer of 1954. By now, everyone including McGyvers has had enough of the bloodshed, but the worst is yet to come as, eyes blazing, these mortal foes confront each other on the Kid's veranda.

Emma may have been waiting five years for this moment, yet she does not have the heart to kill the woman she admires (or even secretly loves). And as Vienna falls, only slightly winged, Emma swings around and eliminates the root of her jealousy and the object of everyone's desire – putting a bullet between the Kid's eyes, allowing him arguably the most eloquent death ever seen in a Fifties Western. Then it is Vienna who fires, sending this horrible woman plunging head-first over the balcony as everyone gathers on the mountainside, gazing in disbelief at the results of the tragedy *they* could have averted, while Vienna and her lover leave the scene of the carnage, dip under the waterfall and embrace.

Johnny Guitar very quickly became a cult film for gay Crawford aficionados worldwide, but most especially in Europe when, like some of the early 'sword and sand' epics, it was badly dubbed into several languages. Thus the tough-guy cowboys hilariously address each other as 'Her' and 'Monsieur', and Emma is heard to gasp, as if in the throes of orgasm, '*Vienna, je* viens!' Today there is a 'Johnny Guitar Boys Fan Club' on the Internet. Dozens of these fans, who still remain faithful to Joan's gay-friendly memory three decades after her death, complained in June 1954 when Brog wrote in *Variety*, 'Joan Crawford should leave saddles and Levis [sic] to someone else and stick to city lights for a background.' This was *their* film, which they had scrupulously and lovingly followed from inception to premiere (as would later happen with the similarly troubled *What Ever Happened to Baby Jane?*) – reading and clipping every snippet of gossip as it appeared fresh in the press, rushing to cinemas who were showing her old films and writing down the 'Crawfordisms' to use on their friends, even *dressing* like Vienna in the closeted gay clubs of Manhattan and Los Angeles!

Exactly what sparked off the animosity between Joan and Mercedes McCambridge is not known. Claiming that she, who loathed Method actors, wanted to stay in part while playing Vienna, Joan organised 'booze and poker' sessions in her dressing room to which everyone was invited but McCambridge. Being involved with Nicholas Ray did not stop Joan from making a play for Scott Brady – until she learned that he was involved with one of the other actors, allegedly 23-year-old Ben Cooper. McCambridge may have resented Ray's favouritism of his star. She is known to have made homophobic comments about Brady, and it may be on account of this that Joan told Harrison Carroll of the *Los Angeles Herald Examiner*, 'I wouldn't trust that woman as far as I could throw a battleship!'

Joan's comment, again added to gaydom's ever growing list of Crawfordisms, drew the attention of the *Los Angeles Mirror*'s Roby Heard, an engaging young man who somehow managed to pull the wool over her eyes by convincing her that he was penning a retrospective of her career, which he said would be serialised under the collective heading, 'Joan Crawford: Queen of the Movies'. Precisely what Joan told Heard is not known. She spoke of her family, her background and her struggle to the top, her marriages and relationships, her films. Cunningly and without her knowledge, Heard approached those she had criticised the most, but virtually no one she had praised. The result was a hatchet-job entitled, 'Joan Crawford: Queen or Tyrant?', which besides appearing in the *Los Angeles Mirror* was syndicated to just about every other major newspaper in the country in time for *Johnny Guitar*'s release in May 1954.

Sterling Hayden had been the first to offer his opinion of this 'vixen', declaring that there would not be enough money in Hollywood to induce him to ever work with Joan again. Hayden's wife, barred from the set because Joan had found her presence distracting, said that if ever she met Joan again she would slap her face. Hal LeSueur and Joan's mother, who were still receiving monthly allowances, had the audacity to call her mean and selfish. Comments made by Gloria Grahame, considered too crude for the *Mirror*'s readers, were heavily vetted, though the paper's readers sympathised with her when she confessed, under duress of course, that she was still having recurrent nightmares after working with Joan. Jack Palance recalled that Joan had ignored him each morning when he had walked on to the set, when it had been the other way around. Others involved with the film, who asked not to be named, claimed that they had evidence that Joan had put Mercedes McCambridge into hospital, though none of them divulged details of the malady.

What is strange is that every time Joan and McCambridge met *after* shooting *Johnny Guitar*, they were extremely pally towards each other and gave onlookers every impression that they were the best of friends. And yet in her autobiography, rather than mentioning her by name, Joan would refer to McCambridge only as 'a rabble rouser'.

As with many of Joan's relationships, the one with Nicholas Ray ended when the film wound up, and as usual a replacement was waiting in the wings. By way of Rock Hudson, while doing the rounds of the studios in search of a 'half-decent' script, she had been introduced to Milton Rackmil, the head of Universal. Rackmil was far less interested in dating Joan and getting to know her than he was in asking her to marry him: various unsubstantiated press reports suggested towards the end of 1954 that she had taken his proposal seriously enough, but that she was waiting until she had completed the film Rackmil had put her in – playing Lynn Markham in *Female on the Beach* – before furnishing him with a definite answer.

Shooting began at the end of November, and with the briefest of breaks continued through to the New Year. Joan's children had returned home from school for the holidays, but rather than spend time at Brentwood Park with

Christina and Christopher, she chose to 'camp out' in her fabulously appointed dressing room for the entire festive period with just the twins for company. Here, on New Year's Eve, she received a call from Alfred Steele, the president of the Pepsi Cola Company, whom she had first met at a New York dinner party in 1950. Why Steele called, out of the blue, is not known. He caught Joan in a very despondent mood. She was still seeing Milton Rackmil, though only in the hope that this might lead to another good script, but when Alfred informed her that he was going through the process of divorcing his second wife, Lillian Nelson, with whom he had had a small son (there was also a teenage daughter to first wife Marjorie Garvey), she agreed to go out on a date with him, though only once he was free. Her friends and the ever-informed fans once more began speculating. Which of these two millionaires, Rackmil or Steele, would be walking her down the aisle?

For a little while, Joan confused the gossips by dating her *Female on the Beach* co-star, former lover Jeff Chandler. This led to rumours of a possible *third* marriage partner, though what the press did not know was that Joan had 'rumbled' Chandler's best-kept secret. In private moments – a story subsequently reconfirmed by swimming star Esther Williams in *The Million Dollar Mermaid*, who *almost* married him – the big, butch actor loved nothing more than to dress up *à la* Crawford in high heels, chiffon gowns and red wig.

For her leading man in the film, Joan had wanted Tony Curtis, but at 29 he had been considered too young for the love-interest of a middle-aged widow – whereas Chandler, at 36, looked *older* than Joan on account of his silver hair. In retrospect, Curtis would have been more suitable. In 1961, when audiences were less shocked to see such things, the theme of the wealthy neurotic widow and the disreputable gigolo would be re-explored in the screen adaptation of Tennessee Williams's *The Roman Spring of Mrs Stone* with 48-year-old Vivien Leigh and 22-year-old Warren Beatty, a partnership that gels better than the one here.

The film opens with a drunken Eloise Crandal (Judith Evelyn) ranting and raving, then plunging to her death from the balcony of the beach house she has rented for the summer from former 'speciality dancer' Lynn Markham. As Lynn arrives to reside in the property she has never seen until now, while it is being sold, so do the police – to investigate Eloise's probable murder – while estate agent Amy Rawlinson (Jan Sterling) tries to cover up what has been going on between herself, beach-bum Drummy Hall (Chandler) and horrid elderly neighbours Osbert and Queenie Sorenson (Cecil Kellaway and Natalie Schafer). Drummy has a key to the house, walks in and out of the place as if he owns it, and has moored his boat at the end of Lynn's pier.

'Whenever I want a pretty girl, I always give her breakfast,' Drummy grunts, bringing Lynn the fish he has caught by way of an apology after

waking her up at the crack of dawn with his noisy motor. When he asks her
how she likes her coffee, she snarls 'alone'. He is the latest in a long line of
young men taken in by the Sorensons, opportunists who have hired them to
service rich widows and bring them to the house so that the pair can fleece
them at cards and borrow money, which they then blackmail their victims
into never getting back. And as Lynn is the wealthiest widow to hit these
parts in ages, the couple speculate on Drummy actually marrying her –
shortly before she passes away and bequeaths him her fortune – which, of
course, he will share with them.

Initially, and not unexpectedly, Lynn resents Drummy's intrusion: she
was brought up by a poor family in an overcrowded house, and looks upon
solitude as a luxury. Ordering him to vacate her pier, she levels, 'You're about
as friendly as a suction-pump.' Then she suggests a few more pointers for Amy
to add to the advertising copy to sell the property as quickly as possible:
'Suicide, police, lies, charm-boy, people walking in and out. Things like that
only make a house look more lived!' Amy for her part only wishes that
Drummy could show her the same affection he displays to these well-off
matrons, and decides when taking him out on her speedboat that if they cannot
be lovers, at least they can die together – deliberately heading for the rocks at
full speed until he grabs the controls. Amy then accuses him of hating all
women, but he indicates the ugly scar on his neck and professes that he only
hates the way they frequently *are*.

The next day, Lynn finds Drummy repairing a broken fuel pump and he
promises to leave as soon as his boat is seaworthy. He also explains his
'arrangement' with the Sorensons: 'They give me a place to sleep and some
money in exchange for part of my time . . . the part I gave Mrs Crandal.'
Lynn appears shocked, even more so when he suddenly grabs and kisses her,
though she does not resist. When he leaves a greasy smudge on her arm, she
responds, '*You'd* leave a mark on anyone. I wish I could afford you!' He tells
her to start saving her pennies, and is now instructed *not* to move his boat.

Meanwhile, back at the beach house, good-looking police lieutenant
Galley (Charles Drake), who also seems to have taken a shine to her, reminds
Lynn that she should take care as Eloise may have been pushed off the
balcony. She is not going out tonight, however, because the Sorensons have
asked her over to play cards. Then she finds Eloise's diary and, as she reads
this, we witness in flashback what really happened . . .

Eloise, the sex-starved widow, thinks that it is infatuation for the
loquacious hunk that is confusing her and making her lose at cards every
time he takes her to the Sorensons' – loaning Queenie money she will never
get back. And the more infatuated she becomes, so the paranoia sets in when
Drummy starts standing her up – loving and hating him with equal intensity,

and drinking herself senseless when Amy tells her she will soon have to leave the beach house because the owner is expected home. Then, when Drummy gets angry with her, she threatens him with the police, and no longer writes in the diary, arousing Lynn's suspicions . . .

Lynn too begins to suspect the man she has fallen in love with – a man who has 'the instincts of a stallion, the pride of an alley cat'. The Sorensons turn up, but Lynn has learned the art of being a card-sharp from her late husband, and sends them packing. ('I'd like to ask you to stay and have a drink, but I'm afraid you might accept,' was a favourite Crawford line, pronounced to anyone overstaying their welcome at Brentwood Park.) Then she attempts to get Drummy to leave by delivering the film's only Crawfordism:

> You were made for your profession, all right – all very nicely put together. Nice to look at, nice to touch, the great god of the senses, sparkling on the beach until you remember the sewers empty into the ocean. I wouldn't have you if you were hung with diamonds upside down . . . When it comes to phoneys like you, I wrote the book!

Drummy's response to this is that a woman is no good to a man unless fear is involved, and there are echoes of the Crawford-Bautzer fiasco as he forces himself upon her. Lynn bites him when he grabs her, she falls, he hauls her to feet, rips off the top of her dress, and to the horror of moralists but not the Crawford 'shopgirl' audiences of old, who flocked in droves to see the film, she actually enjoys this humiliation and submits. Rather than feeling fulfilled, however, she experiences what she imagines Eloise went through after Drummy rejected her, for after their passionate night together he keeps his distance. Waiting for him to call as Eloise did, Lynn hits the bottle and gets it into her head that his near-rape has all been a game, that now he is stalking her. When Amy drops by to announce that she has found a buyer for the beach house, Lynn instructs her to go ahead and sell – only to change her mind a moment later when Drummy calls and invites her to go lobster fishing with him.

Out at sea, the pair get to know a little more about each others' backgrounds. The scar on Drummy's neck was not caused by a wronged lover but by his mother when he was a boy – shortly before she killed herself and he ended up in an orphanage. He asks Lynn to marry him, adding that he has seen the error of his ways and wants nothing more to do with the Sorensons – 'I caught a slight case of decency, and it's gone to my head.' The old couple are jealous, acquire a new stud, and devoid of their income anonymously inform the police that Drummy killed Eloise and is planning to do the same to Lynn. Amy is jealous too, and warns Drummy that he will not forget her so easily.

The wedding takes place. Drummy tells Lynn that he has fitted the new fuel pump she has bought him, and is planning to whisk her off on her honeymoon straight away, even though a storm is brewing. When she boards the boat and sees the old faulty pump still in place, she flees in a panic. Drummy goes after her, she hits him and draws blood – the second time a woman he loves has hurt him physically – and as is traditional in these melodramas, she rushes to the location that is the least safe, back to his boat, just as Amy turns up and in a fit of madness confesses that *she* killed Eloise, and that *she* has switched fuel pumps, well aware that if the boat sinks, strong swimmer Drummy will make it back to the shore, hopefully leaving Lynn to drown. Therefore for the third time running in a Crawford picture, a happy ending is effected with the heroine safe in the arms of the hero she started the film hating – in this instance begging *his* forgiveness when, for the past ninety minutes, he has never appeared *less* than menacing.

There had been more calls from Alfred Steele during the last week of shooting the film, and Joan had just begun working on *Queen Bee* when he informed her that his divorce had come through. Then, one day, he flew in from New York just to spend a few hours with her on the set – to *tell* her, rather than propose, that they would be getting married as soon as the film wrapped. A date was set for 24 May 1955.

The press and Joan's fans were intrigued by Alfred's non-show-business biography, the fact that he and she had so little in common and were as socially and physically mismatched as one could imagine. Born 24 April 1901 in Nashville, Tennessee, he was officially seven years her senior (but actually only three). Like Franchot Tone, he had had a very privileged upbringing. His father, Edgar, had worked as a travelling secretary for the YMCA, and as a boy Alfred had travelled extensively in Europe. He had subsequently attended Northwestern University, where he had been the star player in its football team in 1923. After graduation he had worked in the advertising room of the *Chicago Tribune*, then became advertising manager for the Standard Oil Company of Indiana. Before taking the helm at Pepsi Cola he had been vice-president of the D'Arcy Advertising Company, then Coca-Cola. Joan described him in her memoirs as 'rugged', though by the time he met her he was portly, greying, and in many of their photographs together almost looks old enough to be her father. That he was the greatest love of her life after Gable, however, goes without saying. Alfred *was* rich and powerful but, Joan was quick to point out in interviews, money had nothing to do with their relationship and she predicted that this marriage would last longer than the others because Alfred was socially and professionally her equal, and because she had kept her word and not allowed herself to become betrothed to another actor. Tragically, she would be proved right.

For *Queen Bee*, Joan was gowned by Jean-Louis, who had recently caused a stir with his diaphanous creations for Marlene Dietrich's stage shows. Indeed, in one scene Joan wears an exact replica of the gown worn by Marlene at the Las Vegas Sahara. Her co-stars were the rarely smiling Barry Sullivan and the equally serious-looking Canadian actor, John Ireland, who despite her engagement found himself fighting off Joan's advances (he was happily married to Joanne Dru). *King Kong* icon Fay Wray also emerged from semi-retirement to work with Joan: she had left the movies in 1942 to marry the producer Robert Riskin, who had recently died.

Eva Phillips, Joan's character in *Queen Bee*, would be used many years later as the basis for Patricia Hamilton, Australia's very first television superbitch in the cult soap *Sons And Daughters* – played with almost equal conviction by Rowena Wallace. Eva is charming, unashamedly Machiavellian, *very* beautiful, bisexual, but manipulative and a thoroughly bad lot. As the film opens and timid Chicago girl Jenny Stewart (Lucy Marlow) arrives for her first (and no doubt last) visit to her benefactress's mansion in the Deep South, Eva's portrait oversees a family scenario straight out of a Pirandello play, and her aura is felt long before she is seen.

There are the Phillips children, not far removed from the Crawford ones: spoilt, impeccably well mannered, alienated from their parents and terrified of stepping out of line. There is Eva's husband, cotton farmer Avery (Sullivan), derisively nicknamed 'Beauty' on account of his hideous facial scars – a man who never smiles, knocks his wife around and never stops drinking. There is Avery's sister, Carol (Betsy Palmer), who is about to become engaged to mill manager Judd (Ireland) but dares not break the news for fear of incurring Eva's wrath, for Eva cannot stand the thought of anyone being happy and getting away from her. What Carol does not know is that Judd and Eva used to be lovers, ten years previously, before he introduced Eva to Avery. And finally there are brother and sister Tye and Sue McKennan (William Leslie and Fay Wray), the former a flirt, the latter mad and no longer interested in men after being jilted on her wedding day – by Avery, who subsequently eloped with Eva. 'Looks like Sue took a fancy to you,' Carol tells Jenny, after Sue has emerged from her semi-cataleptic state to admire the other's youthful beauty. 'She's our local legend. Every town in the South has one!'

It is at this point that Eva/Joan Crawford *swans* onto the scene, magnificent in mink and jewels – the eyes and smile wider and more radiant than ever, the eyebrows arched towards the point of caricature, and the hospitality wholly fake.

The children rush to greet her and are bought off with the usual expensive gifts, then the rest of the family are promptly delivered a series of catty put-downs. Only Jenny escapes a tongue-lashing, primarily because Eva finds her attractive and takes advantage of her passiveness to engage her as her 'caddy', the dogsbody she needs to control and badger because these are the only seduction techniques she knows. Later, she loses her cool with Tye for having the audacity to ask Jenny out on a date – he should have gained *her* permission first. Even so, she allows the date to go ahead, taking charge of the proceedings by buying her 'charge' an expensive dress, loaning her her favourite mink stole (and she cannot resist *touching* Jenny and telling her how beautiful she is), though Joan herself has never looked lovelier and in the beauty stakes runs rings around the thirty-years-younger Betsy Palmer.

Jenny and Carol become friends, though the latter disapproves of Jenny putting Eva on a pedestal. 'The ruler of the hive,' she denounces, 'the Queen Bee who stings all her rivals to death. Your turn'll come. She'll sting you, one day, ever so gently so you'll hardly be feeling till you fall dead!' Cracks starts appearing in their relationship, however, when Jenny stumbles on Eva trying to seduce Judd. She sees them kissing, but does not stay around long enough to see him push her away and snarl, 'You're like some fancy kind of disease – I had it once, now I'm immune.' Eva then attempts to drive a wedge between Jenny and Carol by summoning a doctor to examine her little son, Ted, who suffers from nightmares – always the same scenario, with the boy and Eva in her car, hurtling at breakneck speed towards a mountain but always waking up before the vehicle crashes. Unable to help herself, Eva makes a play for the bucolic-looking little medic, sees him out, then preens herself in front of her mirror and tells Jenny, 'He actually *trembled* when I talked to him. 'You'd think he'd never seen a beautiful woman before!' She then huddles up to Jenny on the couch, provocatively raises her dress above her knee to allow her 'quarry' a flash of inner thigh (a Crawford trait that, allegedly, had failed to ensnare Marilyn Monroe) and declares that it is Carol who is responsible for Ted's nightmares because she is smothering him with affection.

The *Mommie Dearest* connection continues in the next scene when Eva decides that Carol will have to move out of her room, adjacent to Ted's, to one in another wing of the house. Indeed, if the episode in Christina's book *is* the work of an overactive imagination – wherein the observer wrongly assumes that the actress and the character are one and the same because what he is seeing is so convincing – one can see the basis for the fantasy as Eva wrecks the room and scathingly denounces her family with the line, 'I wish I could get rid of *them* as easy as this trash!' Then the neurosis really kicks in when Jenny becomes alarmed by what she is seeing, and says she is thinking of leaving – Eva would never be able to cope with the girl not liking her any more, or with her supporting Carol, and now Jenny is accused of being selfish for throwing kindness in her face, and all the money Eva has spent on her upbringing and putting her through school.

Jenny can now see why Avery drinks, and when she confides in him, for the first time in years he finds he has an ally to help him back onto the wagon and stand up to his domineering wife. Avery thinks that Carol and Judd should marry at once and get away from this foreboding place – and ignore Eva's comment that if they do, everyone will think Carol is pregnant – and for a few minutes we see Joan sending up Bette Davis as she finds her authority thwarted, making extraneous gestures, ranting and raving. She is soon back in control, however, and when Jenny supports the wedding and gives an indication that she has been talking about Eva to Avery behind her back, she is rewarded with a resounding slap across the face. Avery's turn comes next, when he comments on Eva's nightly partying which, she says, is on account of his drink-induced impotence: 'A party is to women what a battlefield is to men. Oh, I forget. You weren't *in* the army, were you?'

Returning from her night on the town, Eva finds Carol showing Jenny the plans for the house she and Judd will be moving into after their wedding, though Queen Bee soon puts a damper on the happy atmosphere by confessing that she has had Judd once, and may do so again: '*Any* man's my man, if I want it that way!' This time, however, she has gone too far, and when Carol hangs herself in a fit of despair, Eva suffers a breakdown – in front of her dressing-table mirror, which means that from now on she will never again marvel at her perfect reflection.

During Eva's indisposition, the mansion sees changes for the better. The children laugh and play outdoors, chaperoned by Jenny. Judd is leaving the mill to start up his own business. Avery no longer drinks, and has come to his senses sufficiently to consider filing for divorce, bringing whatever peace there has been to a chilling end. *If* Avery divorces her, Eva will ruin him by telling the newspapers that he has been carrying on with a woman less than half his age. 'Whatever I am,' she seethes, 'and you *know* what I am, you can't get away from me!'

Avery contemplates suicide, and even loads the gun, before opting to play the evil spouse at her own game. Turning on the charm – he even smiles! – he seduces her, buying her the priceless bracelet she has had her eye on for some time, and which she once said she would die happy to have. This, of course, is exactly what Avery has in mind, and as he offers to drive them to a party, she realises that she does not need Jenny anymore:

EVA: There's a little bit of me in every woman. I guess there has to be . . . I know you think I've been cruel, and I have. It didn't start with you. It really had nothing to do with you until you started opening doors and peeking into closets where you didn't belong . . .

JENNY: You *asked* me to come here – and when I did, you *begged* me
to stay . . .
EVA: Did you ever ask yourself why? I tried to tell you once. Because –
because I was lonely.

Judd, meanwhile, has worked out that Avery is planning to kill both of them
by crashing their car en route to the party, as he once did before – hence the
scars on his face. Judd therefore decides to play the martyr in his place, for
with Carol gone he has far less to live for than Avery. Driving faster and
faster in the blinding rain, he sends them plunging to a fiery death at the
bottom of a ravine as Ted awakens from another of his nightmares – one that
has ended properly this time . . .

From Las Vegas, the Steeles travelled to New York, and on 26 May they
sailed for Europe on the SS *United States*. According to numerous press
reports, the crossing was stormy in more ways than one, with the pair at it
hammer and tongs in the vessel's costliest stateroom. Joan was later
photographed in the lobby of Paris's Plaza Athenée Hotel, wearing
sunglasses to conceal her black eyes – a clear indication, according to her
masochistic views on romance, that Alfred truly loved her. The clash of
personalities related to statements Joan had given to the press assuring them
why the marriage would *work* – the fact that they were both massive in their
respective careers, though in show-business circles Alfred would still be
referred to as 'Mr Crawford'. For while Joan expected him to hob-nob with
Europe's equivalent of the Hollywood glitterati, *she* was expected to play the
role of consort at business meetings conveniently arranged beforehand to
promote the Pepsi name by way of the Crawford one. There was also the
additional problem, for Joan, of having to put up with Alfred's daughter,
Sally, who happened to be in Paris with friends on college vacation. No
doubt pleased to be shot of Christina and Christopher for a month or so (but

missing the twins terribly), Joan was peeved to have 'another juvenile' telling her what or what not to see in the French capital, and according to Bob Thomas, she put paid to any mother-daughter bond that might have developed between them by rounding on her with, 'Listen, kid. You live your life and I'll live mine!'

From Paris the Steeles travelled to Rome, then Naples, before taking the ferry across to Capri, where they spent a few days at Gracie Fields's Canzone de Mare complex. Then they returned to the United States – Alfred to the townhouse he would share with Joan in New York's Sutton Place, she resting up for a while before heading back to Hollywood to begin shooting her next film, *Autumn Leaves*. Joan refused to even consider moving out of Brentwood Park, and her husband's 'residency' there whenever he was in Hollywood was no different from those of his predecessors': only Joan's name appeared on the deeds.

CHAPTER TWELVE

The Widow Steele and Baby Jane

'I'll say one thing, our producer proved he was a man of stamina and courage. When my cleaning man heard Joan and I were co-starring, he suggested we shoot the picture in the Coliseum.'

Bette Davis

Joan, with her contractual privileges, usually looked for two qualities in a leading man: acting experience, and prowess between the sheets. Thirty-year-old Cliff Robertson was lacking in the former, and not interested in bedding a newly married older woman. He did, however, possess another quality she admired equally: not only had Robertson served his country – by making two films that had received good reviews, *then* volunteering for the US Navy – but he had taken the risk of sacrificing his film career. Hollywood had punished him for his 'ingratitude' by refusing to employ him after the war, but the Actors Studio had welcomed him and he had enjoyed a lengthy spell on the New York stage before making his film comeback, playing Kim Novak's fiancé in *Picnic*, released as the *Autumn Leaves* cast was being drawn up. Joan and Robertson would never be lovers, but their close friendship would last until her death.

The second female lead in the film was Vera Miles, at 26 already one of the most respected actresses in Hollywood. Photogenic, friendly and polite, she got on well with Joan and caused hearts to flutter when she brought her fiancé – muscleman par excellence Gordon Scott, the latest Tarzan – to the set. Of the other leads, Lorne Greene would later play patriarch Ben Cartwright in the *Bonanza* television series; Ruth Donnelly (1896–1982) – described by film critic David Quinlan as 'the Thelma Ritter of the middle-class bracket' on account of the wisecracking comic characters she often

Joan with husband number
three, Philip Terry, pictured at
New York's Stork Club in 1943.
He disappointed her, she said,
because he was one of the few
men in her life who did not
knock her around!

Joan wearing her infamous
'Fuck-me' shoes, 1944.

'You'll never be anything but a common frump, whose father lived over a grocery store and whose mother took in washing,' sneered Ann Blyth, the daughter from hell in *Mildred Pierce* (1945). Bizarrely, history would repeat itself when Joan's adopted daughter, Christina, sullied her memory with *Mommie Dearest*.

With Frank Lovejoy in
Goodbye My Fancy (1951). The
New York Times observed,
'Miss Crawford's errant
Congresswoman is as aloof and
imposing as the Capitol dome.'

Not wishing to feel humiliated if she lost, Joan claimed she was too ill to attend the Academy Awards in 1946, but miraculously recovered when she won. The Oscar was rushed to her home, and spent the night in her bed.

With 'the other Joan Crawford',
Jeff Chandler, in *Female On
The Beach* (1955). Chandler
was so besotted with Joan that
he would go out wearing a red
wig, chiffon gown, fuck-me
shoes and diamonds. 'It was like
making love to myself,' she said
of their brief affair.

With fourth husband, Alfred Steele, the 'Mr Pepsi Cola', who left her a widow, shortly after this picture was taken in 1959. After him, there were few more men in Joan's life.

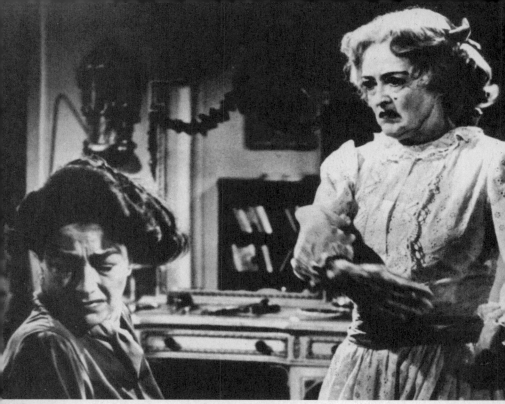

The *New York Times* described *Baby Jane* as, 'A murderous duel of snarls, shrieks and rattlesnake repartee by Bette Davis and Joan Crawford'. In the death scene in *Baby Jane*, before expiring, Joan says, 'All this time, we could have been friends.' On and off the screen, the two stars loathed one another.

played – would make just one more film after this one before retiring from the screen to write hit songs; and Selmer Jackson would play Mayor Hoover in television's *Wyatt Earp*.

Robert Aldrich (1918–83) was Joan's most distinguished director since Nicholas Ray. Formerly a law student with the University of Virginia, he had arrived in Hollywood in 1941 to work as a production clerk for RKO, then as assistant director to the fabled Jean Renoir. His first feature film had been *Big Leaguer* (1953), but *Autumn Leaves* would put him on the map, winning top awards at the Venice and Berlin Film Festivals.

The song 'Autumn Leaves' ('*Les Feuilles Mortes*'), composed by Joseph Kosma and Jacques Prévert, had given Edith Piaf successive million-sellers back in 1950, in French and English versions on both sides of the Atlantic. Piaf, in the middle of a massive sell-out American tour, was asked to provide the backing for the Crawford film, but refused because mogul Darryl Zanuck wanted this as part of a package deal to film Piaf's own life story, which she was very much against. The track, with lyrics by Johnny Mercer, was supplied at the last minute by Nat King Cole.

The production offered Joan by far her best dramatic vehicle and all-out suffering heroine role since *Mildred Pierce*: a tale of lies, deceit, Oedipal psychosis, passion and angst, which comes across all the more potently by being filmed by Charles Lang in monochrome. And *only* Joan could get away with wearing elbow-gloves in a poolside scenario!

Spinster Milly Wetherby types up authors' scripts in her suburban bungalow, and when one of them gives her tickets for a piano recital, she welcomes the escape from drudgery. 'I've been told so very often, "You're so attractive, so lovely, so this, so that" – then they assume I'm all tied up,' she tells best friend Liz (Donnelly), jokingly trying to explain *why* she has been left on the shelf for so long. Then, during a Chopin romance, we get to know the truth when the story flashes back ten years to when Milly was nursing her terminally ill father and receiving an 'It's him or me' ultimatum call from her lover after standing him up once too often. 'You've got so much to give, don't throw your life away,' he says before hanging up on her for the last time. Since then she has been alone.

After the concert, Milly ends up in a crowded restaurant, and reluctantly shares her booth with loquacious, unemployed bundle of nerves Burt Hanson (Robertson), who has warmed to her after she has played the film's title song on the jukebox. Burt tells her that he hails from Wisconsin, that he was only a small boy when his father died, and that during the war he was stationed in Japan. He escorts her home, and they spend the next day at the beach – where in an old-fashioned, bought-for-the-occasion swimsuit Milly becomes acutely conscious of the thirty-year gap in their ages, even more so when he grabs her on their way back from taking a dip and they make love Deborah Kerr-Burt Lancaster style on the wet sand as the waves wash over their lust-filled bodies. When Burt takes her home again and tells her, 'I don't know what I'd do if anything happened to you,' she feels that she is getting way out of her depth and urges him to find a nice young girl. 'You're just lonesome, that's all,' she says, 'I'm lonesome too, but we can't have loneliness pushing us together because it won't keep us together. I'm used to being alone . . . If you knew a girl your own age, you wouldn't want me.'

A month passes. Milly is missing him, and miserable. Then one afternoon she comes home from shopping and finds him in her living room: she had left the door open, and the record he has brought her of their song is playing on the machine. They dance to the music, and he tells her he is now working as the section manager of a department store. They go to the movies, he asks her to marry him and when he adds that he *loves* her, she knows that she must take a chance to find again the happiness she sacrificed all those years ago. When he tells her, however, that he hopes she will regret saying yes, his changed facial expression as he walks away from her door gives a clear indication that from now on, her life will not all be plain sailing. The pair drive down to Mexico, the ceremony takes place, and on their way home Burt begins to show signs of the schizophrenia that will only get progressively worse. He denies telling her that he is from Wisconsin, avowing that he was born in Chicago, and soon he is saying that he was never in Japan during the war, but rather with the Combat Industry. Matters are further complicated when ex-wife Virginia (Miles) shows up – for it emerges that Burt has married Milly *not* knowing that Virginia's final decree has come through. On top of this, Burt is not a section manager but a tie salesman at the department store – and his father is still alive, actually residing at a hotel in town!

Virginia tells Milly that she needs Burt to sign some property-release papers. She adds that he walked out on their four-year marriage and that she used this as an excuse for divorcing him, the real reason being his shoplifting and compulsive lying – and yet another Crawford seven-steps-to-Calgary martyrdom moves into top gear. Milly goes to see Mr Hanson (Lorne Greene appearing *most* unflatteringly in tight-fitting trousers which, Joan later said, 'made his ass look bigger than Hollywood'), who inflames the situation by telling her, 'You're more than a good wife – you're like a friend and a mother.' Mr Hanson concludes that his son is a lost soul no one can save, a deadbeat who will lie about anything, who should be locked away in an institution. And no sooner has Milly left than Virginia emerges from his bedroom . . .

Later, when Burt arrives home from work, Milly confronts him about his lies, though by now he is clearly in a dream world, remembering only the things he wants to remember. His marriage to Virginia was, he says, unimportant kids' stuff. Then he recalls the incident, six months into the marriage, which obviously sparked off his mental instability: dropping in on Virginia during his lunch-break to surprise her with a half-anniversary present, he remembers going up the stairs but not coming back down again, and ever since that day he has regarded his father as dead.

It does not take a genius to work out what happened that day, or what the effects of Milly arranging a father-son reunion will be. She arrives at the hotel before Burt, sees Mr Hanson and Virginia looking very cosy next to the pool, then finds Burt sobbing outside the room they are sharing – the open door and unmade bed giving the game away. Milly takes the young man home, where he quickly regresses into childhood, sulking and weeping, sucking his thumb, terrified of the dark. This, of course, is what his father has intended all along, and when he turns up at Milly's place with Virginia, there are no punches spared. Burt was only half a man and on the verge of cracking up when he married her, Mr Hanson tells Milly. She *knew* this and, unless she has him committed to an asylum, he himself will ensure Virginia's rights are protected by having Burt certified incompetent and Milly thrown into jail for coercing Burt into marrying her in order to get her hands on his late mother's estate. Milly can hold back no longer, and as Burt watches wide-eyed and half-insane from the shadows, she lays into them:

> Of course you want me to commit him, get him out of your life, put him away permanently someplace where he can never again remind either one of you of your horrible guilt – how you, and you, committed the ugliest of all possible sins, so ugly that it drove him into the state he's in now . . . Even when he doesn't know what he's doing he's a saner man than you. He's decent and proud. Can you say that for yourselves? Where's your decency – in what garbage dump, Mr Hanson? And where's yours, you tramp? . . . You, his loving, doting fraud of a father. And you, you slut! You're both so consumed with evil, so rotten, your filthy souls are too evil for hell itself!

Having seen off her unwelcome guests, Milly goes back into the house where, within the space of a few minutes, Burt has metamorphosed into a split-personality Walter Mitty. One half expects him to foam at the mouth as he calls his wife 'conniving tramp' and accuses her of being in league with the other two so that his mother's money can be split three ways once *she* has had him put away. Then he hits her and, as she cowers on the floor, hurls her typewriter at her head – the machine misses its target as she rolls away, but still crushes her hand before he collapses in tears like a scolded child, begging her to forgive him.

The next time we see Milly she has a bandaged hand, plasters on her face, and she is wearing shades to conceal her black eyes – the last being authentic, courtesy of Alfred Steele, who had had a particularly nasty fight with Joan the evening before the scene was filmed, which resulted in her living in her studio dressing room until shooting was completed. Milly consults a psychiatrist (Sheppard Strudwick), who warns her that the situation will only worsen because Burt has rejected the world about him, and that as such she should have him sectioned. She is also warned that, as Burt married her with a great number of needs interwoven with neuroses, removing these neuroses might also remove his needs and therefore result in his no longer loving her. With no choice but to take this risk, she calls the hospital and Burt is dragged away by the white-coats, screaming, 'I'll get you, I'll cut your guts out!'

The treatment scenes were pretty horrendous for mid-Fifties American cinemagoers: morphine injections, electrodes, the bit between the teeth, while the camera flashes back and forth to Milly typing frantically, smoking, fretting, in extreme close-up looking every day of her age. Then the action moves forwards six months and we see Burt tending his flowerbed at the asylum on the day of his discharge. Milly arrives to take him home: during his incarceration there has been no contact between them, though he has written to his father, authorising him and Virginia to have his mother's property so long as they stay out of his life. Milly therefore assumes that the psychiatrist's warning has come true and that Burt no longer needs her.

Burt says nothing, standing immobile with his back to the camera as Milly delivers her lengthy, well-rehearsed speech. She explains that she only put him here because she loved him and offers to butt out of his life if this is what he wants, so that he can find a wife his own age – maybe the pretty nurse she saw him chatting to just now. She walks off, assuming that this is what he wants. Then he catches up with her, examines and kisses the hand he crushed with the typewriter, and gently rebuffs her for being so busy saying goodbye that she has not given *him* the opportunity to say hello!

Despite having been assured by Joan that this was her 'last, most important marriage', the press began speculating that all was not well in the Crawford camp when they learned that she had slept over at the studio while shooting *Queen Bee* – and when William Haines threw a belated wedding reception at Romanoff's and Joan arrived alone, claiming that her husband had important business to deal with in New York. True or not, Alfred would henceforth attend few board meetings without her, and by the end of the year Joan would be recognised as the unofficial spokeswoman/symbol for Pepsi Cola, one that would prove inordinately good for business, boosting the company's profits by twenty per cent – for wherever Joan went, she was sure to draw the crowds. 'Mr

& Mrs Pepsi' did the rounds of bottling plants and factories, first across the United States, then overseas. Mindless of her fear of flying, Joan also made many solo trips: her studio system training and discipline, she said, had put her in good stead for the shrewd businesswoman she had become. She was following in the entrepreneurial footsteps of Valentino (Mineralava Beauty Products), Mistinguett (Liberator Pharmaceuticals) and Irene Rich (Welch's Grape Juice) and loved every minute of it. 'My constant contact with agents, writers and directors made me accustomed to eight or ten men in a room with all of us giving (we hoped) constructive ideas,' she later told British journalist John Deighton (in *Today's Cinema*, September 1969). 'I found it very easy. It's lovely to be on a board with nineteen men. That's *exciting*!'

It was happy families in December 1955 when, in what appears to have been a last bid attempt to 'save' Christopher, who had run away from school for the umpteenth time, Joan, Alfred and all four of her children posed for the press on the eve of their leaving to spend the festive season in Europe. It was one of the rare occasions when they were all together, and the first time Joan had seen Christina and Christopher in over a year. They sailed on the *Queen Mary*, headed for St Moritz in Switzerland, and spent several days skiing and being trailed by the paparazzi, who also camped outside the plush Palace Hotel – a problem for the other celebrities staying there, though Joan of course had courted this kind of invasion of privacy throughout her entire adult life and did not mind her every move being photographed and scrutinised. 'That's what I'm here for, dear,' she told a reporter from *Paris-Match*, 'I owe it to my fans, and most especially I'm grateful to guys like you. You're the reason I'm not washing sheets in Kansas City!' What also must be noted is that though there were numerous reports in the Continental press about Joan's fights with Alfred, there was absolutely no mention of her being unkind to any of her children.

At the end of January 1956, Joan, Alfred and their brood returned to New York on the *Andrea Doria*, and spent some time at Sutton Place. Joan appears to have given up on Christopher by this time, but she did make a concerted attempt to befriend Christina, taking her to couturiers, nightclubs, parties and involving her in several mother-daughter magazine interviews. Her efforts were seemingly not appreciated.

At the end of July, Joan and Alfred flew to London, where she was to shoot (and co-produce) her first overseas film. She was photographed at Heathrow with her 'standard' 42 pieces of luggage – which contained enough clothes for her to change four times daily if she wanted to, and 25 Jean-Louis gowns for evening entertainment. The suitcases and trunks were loaded into three white Pepsi-Cola vans, which formed a cortège with the black limousine supplied by Columbia's British representative to take the couple to the Dorchester. There were titters at the press conference when Joan announced that her new film was to be called *Golden Virgin* – in Britain (against her wishes because, she claimed, it gave the impression that *she* was not its main star) it would be released as *The Story of Esther Costello*, the title of the Nicholas Monsarrat novel on which it was based.

The next evening, Joan was guest of honour at a star-studded *Hello London* extravaganza held at the Ambassador's Club. Present were Marlene Dietrich, Noel Coward, John Gielgud, the Oliviers, Rita Hayworth (whom Joan turned her back on), Edith Evans – and Joan Collins, who three decades hence would prove the antithesis of Crawford's Queen Bee with her majestic portrayal of superbitch Alexis Carrington in television's *Dynasty*. According to Sheilah Graham, covering the event for the *New York Daily Mirror* (2 August 1956), 'At the evening's end [Joan Crawford] waltzed off with the boyfriend of the much younger starlet, Joan Collins.' The other guest of honour should have been Marilyn Monroe, in town to film *The Prince and the Showgirl* with Laurence Olivier. Everyone expected her to arrive late, as was her wont, but she failed to show up at all, claiming she was suffering from the flu – and not from Crawford-fright as the tabloids suggested. Joan had her say, a few evenings later when several visiting Hollywood actresses were invited to meet the Queen and Queen Mother after the Royal Variety Performance. Marilyn actually kept the royal party waiting, albeit for only ten minutes – she had not shown up at all for the rehearsal the previous afternoon – and when she pouted her lips, stuck out her chest and began giggling, Joan waited until the royals were out of earshot before rounding on her, 'It's about time *you* learned some manners, young lady!'

Later, Joan gave an interview with the *Daily Herald*, and the story was syndicated around the world, really rubbing the salt into Marilyn's wounds:

> If you want my opinion, far too many actresses today are little more than tramps and tarts. The Queen is a lady and expects to meet other ladies. Most of today's actresses can't even act politely. Arlene Dahl, Marilyn Monroe and Anita Ekberg didn't even show up for rehearsals – and Monroe's hairdresser was still doing her hair whilst Her Majesty was on her way up the staircase. And when Monroe finally got there she *still* didn't know how to curtsey. I felt ashamed.

Bowing to pressure from her British fans, Joan had agreed to face an audience at the National Film Theatre, which was showing a season of her films. Despite her dreadful stage fright, she offered to take the podium and face whatever questions fans and the press might throw her way because her husband would be sitting on the front row to offer support. Imagine, then, her reaction when the theatre's director, Frank Hazell, turned up at the

Dorchester to inform her that such had been the demand for tickets, that he had taken the liberty of arranging for her to make *two* personal appearances!

Joan had invited Hazell to take tea with her in her suite, but the meeting did not quite turn out quite as he had expected. 'I thought the interview to be a private one, but there was something of the beginnings of a football crowd,' he wrote in *Kinematograph Weekly*, describing the hustle-bustle where fans mingled freely with hotel staff, London glitterati, and an actor (Lee Patterson) he could not quite put a name to – all of these people side-stepping around Joan's mountain of luggage to speak to, or just to touch the star. And everyone was left gaping into space, fearing something dreadful might have happened, when Joan rushed out of the room to take an urgent telephone call. 'She returned with tears in her eyes,' Hazell observed. 'It was a fan in Edinburgh who had just wanted to hear her voice.'

While *The Story of Esther Costello* was shooting, Alfred flew back and forth across Europe to attend Pepsi board meetings. He was, however, close at hand when Joan received word that fifteen-year-old Christopher had run away from school yet again, but this time fallen foul of the law. He and three others had been arrested in Greenport, New York, where he had been placed in the custody of a child psychiatrist and charged with the illegal possession of air rifles. According to the various newspaper reports, the foursome had gone on the rampage through the streets, firing indiscriminately, shooting out several hundred apartment windows, and hitting two girls, who had been rushed to hospital with facial injuries. Alfred flew back to the United States to deal with the situation. On Joan's behalf he agreed with the authorities concerned that the only option for keeping the troublesome youth under control would be to place him in a correctional institution.

The Story of Esther Costello was another sublime, but sadly final outing for Joan in the role of the all-suffering martyr-heroine. Her co-stars, with the exception of seventeen-year-old newcomer Heather Sears, who is extraordinarily moving in the title role, are able but unexceptional. Rossano Brazzi (1916–94) had spent fifteen years in the Italian cinema before hitting Hollywood in 1945 to star in *Little Women*, and would later triumph in *Three Coins in the Fountain* (1954) and *South Pacific* (1958). Canadian-born Lee Patterson, handsome enough but wooden, was a stalwart of British B-movies, who later appeared in television's *Surfside Six*. The wealth of British or British-based character actors, aside from the magnificent Sidney James, are wasted: hidden away in blink-and-miss cameos are Bessie Love, Fay Compton, Andrew Cruikshank, Megs Jenkins and John Loder.

The story opens in 1948 in the fictitious Irish village of Cloncraig, where poverty is rife and the residents drink to obliterate their misery. Esther Costello is one of a group of urchins who, unattended or ignored, go off in

search of 'buried treasure' – in effect, a cache of explosives hidden during the
ever-present North-South troubles. Esther and a friend squabble over the
ownership of a live grenade just as her mother arrives on the scene – resulting
in everyone but Esther being blown sky-high and the little girl left deaf, dumb
and blind. The story then moves forward to 1953, and the visit to Cloncraig
of wealthy American Margaret Landi (Joan), who, since separating from her
unfaithful husband five years previously, has travelled the world 'in search
of answers' and finally come here, the place of her birth.

The villagers react as if they have never seen a car before, or the likes of
Margaret, with her jewels and furs – but she finds the place profoundly
disturbing and has no intention of staying a moment longer than necessary.
The priest, Father Devlin (Denis O'Dea), is hoping he might persuade her
otherwise and even the locals detect a generous heart beneath the harsh
exterior. 'A hard woman can be turned into a soft woman, like you boil an
egg backwards,' one observes. Margaret has just paid for the new stained-
glass window in the church, and she loves spoiling the children because she
has always wanted a child of her own, so Father Devlin takes her to see the
village's most tragic case, Esther, now living with an aunt in a filthy hovel.

Eventually, Margaret accepts responsibility for Esther. She has her
examined at the London Medical Institute, where tests suggest that her disabilities may be more psychological than physically incurable, and so
Margaret takes her back with her to the United States. Befriended and
encouraged by young reporter Harry Grant (Patterson), but opposed by her
current boyfriend (Loder), whom she subsequently dumps, Margaret puts
Esther through special schooling and word gets around about what a great
inspiration she and Esther are to others. Soon they are attending seminars,
chairing women's groups and holding stadium-sized rallies, raising vast
amounts of money for the Esther Costello Organisation. 'The biggest thing
since *Ben-Hur*,' growls Harry's editor (Sid James). 'All we need is a hundred
diving girls in bikinis!'

One donation comes from Margaret's estranged husband, Carlo
(Brazzi), an opportunist greaseball, who takes advantage of her Mildred
Pierce-like naivety and worms his way back into her affections so that he can
cream off some of the funds. Unfortunately, he also develops an unhealthy
attraction to Esther. Margaret is so infatuated with this grub of a man – the
older, male incarnation of Veda Pierce – that she is willing to forgive him
anything (his thieving, his spying on Esther while she is undressing), and
would even be willing to give up her fundraising to devote her every waking
moment to him. After conquering America, the Esther roadshow hits Europe,
and in Italy, at a party celebrating Esther's birthday, Margaret is appalled but
unsurprised to see Carlo embrace her too fondly and hold her too tight while

they are dancing. Yet still she cannot see any wrong in him. It is her own fault, she says, for putting temptation his way, and to this end she will hand Esther over to be looked after by someone else, sell her property in America and relocate with him to Europe. For the greedy, seedy Carlo even this is not enough and he really oversteps the mark by stealing into Esther's room and raping her – the horrendous event poignantly depicted only by the French windows crashing open when the storm outside reaches its zenith.

The shock of the rape has restored Esther's faculties and she can once again hear, speak and see – but the cufflink on the bed sheet, one of the pair Margaret has recently given him, is a clear indication of Carlo's guilt. Only after witnessing Esther trying to take an overdose of sleeping pills does Margaret realise her charge is cured – that effectively her own mission in life has been fulfilled, and like Avery Phillips in *Queen Bee* she decides to make the ultimate sacrifice – though why she elects to take such a pointless way out instead of turning Carlo in to the police is baffling. Esther and Harry have been falling in love for some time, and having been assured that *he* will take care of Esther from now on, Margaret says her goodbyes. Carlo is expected on the plane from Scotland – he has flown there to cancel this leg of the tour (obviously he has not heard of telephones!) and after shoving a gun into her pocket, Margaret drives off to collect him from the airport. Here, after kissing fondly over a glass of sherry, she drops the incriminating cufflink onto the table, and informs him, by thought process, of what he must do.

Like the rape, the film's penultimate scene is only suggested. The car is seen entering a blackened tunnel, but not emerging from the other side, so we are left to guess whether it has crashed, or Margaret has shot her husband and then herself. Even so, the distraught Esther has been left in a quandary, convinced that the audience she must now face alone will think she has been faking her disabilities all along. Father Devlin, in 'heathen England' for the first time in thirty years, convinces her otherwise and speaks of Margaret as though she were some latter-day saint:

> When you were chained in darkness, she spoke for you. Now that you're free, you must speak for *her*. You can, and you shall. They'll believe you because they'd rather believe the truth – because the truth can never be destroyed, and because you *are* the truth!

The Story of Esther Costello was well received by the critics. The *New York Herald Tribune* observed, 'This may not be your kind of movie, but it is many women's kind of movie, and our Joan is queen of the art form.' The *New York Times* called it: 'Her most becoming assignment in several seasons.'

After *Esther Costello*, released in November 1957, Joan does not appear to have been in a hurry to do another film, and for the whole of 1958 she was on the road with Alfred, flying the Pepsi flag, supervising commercials for which she had hired veteran feminist director Dorothy Arzner, repeatedly declaring that being a businesswoman was more *fun* than making movies. The usual mass-media publicity was relegated to the minor key for trips to South and Central America, South Africa, Mozambique and even parts of Asia, where hardly anyone knew who she was. Although as yet she had no definite plans to sell Brentwood Park, she did make telephone arrangements to have many of her antiques auctioned and she coerced Alfred into hiring William Haines to refurbish the two adjoining apartments they had recently bought on New York's highly fashionable East 70th Street, overlooking Central Park: Pepsi loaned the couple $400,000 to have both apartments knocked into one and converted into the block's most luxurious penthouse, where pride of place would go to the split-level bedroom with a fountain.

In 1958 Joan's mother died, aged 74, following a succession of strokes. Joan may be forgiven her lack of concern, bearing in mind the way Anna had used and abused her over the years, but she spared no expense having her interred at Forest Lawn, and was filmed shedding a few crocodile tears at the funeral. She would not speak publicly about this greedy, ungrateful woman other than to tell reporters, 'I paid all her bills, and she never went without. What more can I say?'

Hal LeSueur, reduced to working as a hotel desk-clerk after his hoped-for Hollywood career had bombed, would die of a ruptured appendix (some reports said with the added complication of syphilis) in 1963, aged 61. Hal had spent most of his adult life as an alcoholic, had two failed marriages behind him and countless tempestuous love affairs with both men and women. Joan paid to have him buried next to their mother, but did not attend the funeral. And if she kept any thoughts about Anna to herself, she would be wholly unsparing whenever her brother's name cropped up in the conversation. She began by telling everyone that Hal was in fact her *half*-brother, arguing that Anna had shacked up with so many losers that any one of these could have been Hal's father. In 1962, interviewed by her friend Roy Newquist, who observed that he had never seen her looking so distraught, she said,

> He was chronically mean . . . as a kid he wasn't just the type of kid that would pull wings off butterflies, he'd pull the arms and legs off my dolls . . . Hal was a louse, an out-and-out bastard. He could charm the skin off a snake but nothing, not his jobs, not the men and women in his life, lasted long. Liquor, then drugs, and always his distorted ego, took over. I supported that son-of-a-bitch until the day he died . . . That man – or did he ever become a man – was a monster. God, I hated him.

In an age when family values were respected even though that family may have been dysfunctional, even with criminal tendencies, the American press found such comments unforgivable. They were equally shocked by Joan's attitude towards Christina, who towards the end of the Fifties announced that she wanted to take up acting – though Christina should have foreseen what would happen when she told one journalist, 'I intend following in my mother's footsteps.' She had recently dropped out of college and with a friend had acquired an apartment in New York. Joan, probably thinking that she was representing her daughter's best interests, made a few telephone calls, but the best anyone could come up with was a guest-slot on *The Jack Parr Show*. Not surprisingly, seeing as Christina had done little more with her life than *be* Joan Crawford's daughter, this formed the basis for the interview, and Christina later complained that Parr had short-changed her. Joan's reaction was to 'confide' in Louella Parsons, knowing that this would turn up in her column the next day, '*I* had to struggle without having fame handed to me on a plate. Tina will have to do the same, and she's not going to be using *my* goddam surname, either!'

In the spring of 1959, Alfred Steele was rumoured to be suffering from a heart condition. Joan strenuously denied this. Indeed, she constantly boasted of his sexual prowess, claiming that in the bedroom he had more stamina and staying power than most of her former lovers, who had been half his age. Alfred's doctors are known to have advised him to seriously reconsider before embarking on a gruelling two-month promotional tour of the country in the April – advice he chose to ignore. On 4 May the couple were in Washington to present a Multiple Sclerosis Society Citation to Senator John F Kennedy (of which body Kennedy was chairman), and during the after-dinner speech as the flashbulbs popped for the last time, Alfred publicly thanked Joan for being his wife and for supporting him unfailingly over the previous four years. The following afternoon, they returned to New York to pack for a holiday in Bermuda, but the next morning, Joan found him sprawled on the bedroom floor: he had suffered a coronary.

Whether Alfred was actually dead when Joan found him is not known. According to an article published in *Modern Screen* six months after the tragedy, Joan had panicked and been in such a state of shock that it had taken her ten minutes to calm down and pick up the phone – and instead of an ambulance she had called Alfred's doctor. Overworking, over-eating and a diet of too many pep pills were all cited as having contributed to his death at just 57. That the couple were still very close right up to the end, despite their seemingly endless quarrels, was made clear when a still lonely Joan told Roy Newquist several years later, 'A pillow is a lousy substitute for someone who really cares. And when it comes down to it, aside from

Alfred and the twins, I don't think I came across anyone who *really* cared.'
It is a fact that, after Alfred Steele, there would be comparatively few men
in Joan Crawford's life.

Over the next few weeks, Pepsi Cola were hounded by reporters for their
so-called abhorrent treatment of Joan. On the eve of Alfred's funeral, the
company elected her to their board of directors. The stuffier ones might not
have been fond of her or her reputation, but she was undeniably good for
business, worthy of being paid *all* of her husband's death benefits and an
annual salary of $40,000 – though she never figured they would ask her to
repay the $400,000 they had loaned Alfred for the New York apartment, *plus*
interest. Ironically, this was almost exactly the amount Alfred had insured
himself for, which brought the value of his estate to around $650,000.

For some reason, Joan had loaned Alfred $100,000, unsecured, a few
months before his death, and he had not amended his will in her favour – many
thought deliberately because she was reputed to be independently more wealthy
than him. Alfred's first wife, Marjorie Garvey, received the money from the
insurance policy, and once death duties, debts and taxes had been paid off, Joan
was left with but a few thousand dollars. As a last resort, she put Brentwood
Park on the open market. The property was bought by actor-hoofer Donald
O'Connor, who subsequently sold it to the singer Anthony Newley. As for
Joan, despite all the nasty things she said about her, she was not beyond renting
a duplex apartment in the block on Fountain Avenue owned by 'Gretch the
Wretch' Loretta Young. She also made the grave mistake of telling Louella
Parsons about her financial problems – only to read the headline in her column
the next day: 'Joan Crawford Broke!' 'I haven't a nickel, only my jewels,'
Louella claimed Joan had said, adding a little Crawfordism of her own: 'Joan's
was *such* a sob story, it would have brought tears to a glass eye!'

Joan was criticised by the Pepsi executives for sharing her woes with the
world and giving the impression that *they* had short-changed her – and by the
media for returning to work so soon after Alfred's death. Later she would say
she had had no choice. Although nowhere near as destitute as Louella Parsons
had implied, she certainly had no intention of turning down the $65,000
offered by old friend Jerry Wald, on behalf of Twentieth Century-Fox, for
playing Amanda Farrow in *The Best of Everything*.

The production, a precursor of the glossy television soap sagas of the
next generation, was set in a magazine publishing house and boasted an all-
star cast: Hope Lange, Louis Jourdan, Suzy Parker, Stephen Boyd, Brian
Aherne and Diane Baker. Joan asked for separate billing, and director Jean
Negulesco complied.

Amanda is involved in an unsatisfactory relationship with a (never seen)
married man and takes her frustrations out on her employees: Gregg (Parker)

and secretary Caroline (Lange) – who is having an affair with another editor (Boyd), whom Amanda may also be keen on. Eventually, Amanda gives up her lover and her job to marry a widower (also unseen), but when this fails, she returns to the magazine – demoting Caroline, who has stepped into her shoes, back to secretary.

There were reported on-set problems between Joan and Hope Lange, whom Joan called an 'upstart' and accused of trying to monopolise their scenes together – though nothing like the rows with Jean Negulesco when he decided to assign her best scenes to the cutting-room floor, including the one where (authentically) she rolled into the office in a drunken rage. The *New York Herald Tribune*'s Paul Beckley, having seen these, rushed to Joan's defence: 'Restricted to a few mean looks and some vitriolic dialogue, Miss Crawford comes near to making the rest of the picture look like a distraction.'

Joan's career was placed on the backburner for much of 1960 in favour of her Pepsi globetrotting. In the October, however, she was back in the headlines when the animosity between herself and Christina became public knowledge with the publication of Christina's scathing criticism in *Redbook* magazine. As requested by Joan, Jerry Wald had given Christina a small part in the latest Elvis Presley picture, *Wild in the Country* – the last time fans would see him Method acting as Hollywood's hoped-for successor to James Dean. The film, one of Presley's finest, was also scripted by *Humoresque*'s Clifford Odets, and the leading lady was *The Best of Everything*'s Hope Lange.

This was the perfect high-publicity vehicle, Joan declared, for Christina's acting debut, which was why she had pulled more strings to ensure that her daughter was placed higher up the credits than she should have been – not that *she* appeared grateful. In the feature headed 'The Revolt of Joan Crawford's Daughter', Christina spoke of her childhood, of how she and Christopher had been 'shunted off' into the nursery whenever Mama had been receiving guests, which had been often. She added that so far as their relationship was concerned, she and Joan were on 'opposing ends of a deep chasm of misunderstanding'. It was obvious, reading between the lines, that Christina had said much more and that other comments had been 'spiked' by the editor, who now had the gall to ask Joan if she wanted to make any comments of her own for *Redbook*'s December issue. Needless to say, her response was severe: the editor should have asked for her opinions and checked the facts *before* presenting her in an unfavourable light. She would, or so she claimed, have then told him *exactly* what her two eldest children were like, not least that neither of them had shown up at their stepfather's funeral. Then Joan effectively shot herself in the foot by repeating what she had once told the children when insisting upon having the upper hand during the for-fun swimming races in the pool at Brentwood Park: 'I'm *bigger* than you are. I'm *faster* than you are – I can win *all* the time!'

In the midst of this emotional turmoil, on 16 November 1960, Clark Gable died of a heart attack, aged 59. His last film, *The Misfits* – not yet released when he died – had contributed to his failing health as well as the psychological deterioration of his co-stars, Marilyn Monroe and Montgomery Clift. The exteriors had been shot in the scorching Nevada desert: this, and the horse-roping and riding stunts that Gable had insisted upon performing himself, but most of all the lengthy delays in the stifling heat waiting for Marilyn to show up, had, according to his last wife, Kay Spreckles, worn him out. Ironically, the child he had always yearned for – a son, John – would be born five months after his death.

Joan is said to have continued her long-running affair with Gable right up to him shooting *The Misfits*, though there is no concrete evidence of this. She did hold former actress Spreckles partly responsible for Gable's heart condition not having been properly assessed – for not calling an ambulance on a previous occasion when he had collapsed with chest pains, and having him examined at a hospital instead of by a studio doctor. But if she only privately criticised Mrs Gable, she publicly condemned Marilyn Monroe for keeping Gable waiting in the desert. And she mourned her greatest love for a *long* time, showing little interest in almost everything for over a year until signing the contract for what would be her last truly great film vehicle.

Autumn Leaves director Robert Aldrich boasted that *he* had been the brainchild behind *What Ever Happened to Baby Jane?*, the production that would allow long-term arch-rivals Joan Crawford and Bette Davis to 'slug it out' on the screen, frequently for real. Aldrich said that he had read Henry Farrell's book while shooting *Sodom and Gomorrah* in Italy, acquired the film rights from the author, backing from British-based Seven Arts in conjunction with Warner Brothers – and *then* contracted the two stars.

The Crawford version of events is that in January 1962 *she* went to see Bette Davis's Broadway production of Tennessee Williams' *Night of the Iguana*, and after the performance headed backstage to offer her felicitations – and inform Bette about *her* idea for the two of them to portray washed-up movie-star siblings Jane and Blanche Hudson. Joan had read Henry Farrell's book and was right in thinking that they would be 'perfectly mismatched' for the roles – and that once Bette had consented to her proposition, Joan had got in touch with the man she said had been *born* to direct the picture: Robert Aldrich. 'I've been wanting to work with Bette since 1943,' she told Hedda Hopper, 'So this is the answer to all my dreams!'

Bette Davis claimed that *she* had read the book two years earlier, and asked Alfred Hitchcock to direct the picture, but that he had been committed to other projects. However, in her second volume of memoirs (*This 'N That*), Bette would corroborate Joan's story and actually *thank* her for giving her the opportunity to play the best, most identifiable role of her later career.

Next came the question of salaries. Because of the recent slight slump in her popularity, Bette said she was short of hard cash and demanded an advance of $60,000 to be followed by five per cent of the gross. There was also no question of her *not* heading the credits. Joan asked for ten per cent of the box office, but only $40,000 up-front. Though his studio would be distributing the film, Jack Warner would not allow the *What Ever Happened to Baby Jane?* production access to his major sound-stages: these, he pompously declared, were tied up with *big* pictures, top of the list being *Gypsy*, with Joan's friend Rosalind Russell. Robert Aldrich therefore had to make do with the Producer's Studio, the back lot on Melrose Avenue that churned out mainly B-movies, which indeed this one was classed as. Warner was sufficiently two-faced to organise a press conference at Warner Brothers, with both stars and their 'boss' posing for photographs and smiling radiantly – but muttering obscenities at each other under their breath. This put-on politeness with an air of under-the-surface malice would continue throughout shooting. 'Hollywood expected an eruption,' Hedda Hopper reported, 'but it turned out to be love in bloom.'

The 21-day shooting schedule, which got underway on 23 July and was spread over six weeks, is known to have been a nightmare for all concerned, though as had happened with Mercedes McCambridge during *Johnny Guitar*, it is difficult to distinguish between publicity-seeking and authentic personality clash. Joan was sensitive and touchy, Bette genuinely eccentric and innately vulgar. Concerned that Robert Aldrich might show favouritism towards Joan in the wake of *Autumn Leaves*, before signing the contract, Bette asked him if he had slept with Joan. He said no, if only to maintain the peace. Then Joan hit the roof when, on Johnny Carson's *Tonight* show, Bette recalled Jack Warner's initial reaction to Robert Aldrich's suggesting Joan and Bette for the film: 'I wouldn't give you a dime for those two has-been old broads!' Joan immediately put pen to paper, imploring Bette never to say such a thing again.

Some two weeks in to shooting the world was rocked by the not-unexpected death of Marilyn Monroe: accident, suicide or murder, the cause is unlikely to be satisfactorily determined. Joan is reported to have been very upset, more to do with feeling guilty over her recent attacks on Marilyn than grief. She would always hold Marilyn largely responsible for Gable's death, and had congratulated Twentieth Century-Fox producer Henry Weinstein for firing her for persistent bad timekeeping on her last, uncompleted film, *Something's Got to Give*.

Turning up late was something Joan had *never* done. The press reported how she arrived on the set each morning on the dot, with a regal retinue, which included her secretary, maid, personal make-up artist, hairdresser, twin daughters and Pepsi-carrying chauffeur – while Bette arrived alone, dressed down and wearing flat shoes. They were unaware that she had sent her entourage on ahead of her to give the impression that she was 'just another employee' turning up for work!

There were complaints all around when Joan refused to work on any set where the temperature was above 60 degrees, resulting in the other actors donning coats, hats and scarves when not in front of the camera – and the crew threatening 'mutiny' on numerous occasions. Bette objected to Joan's drinking – the fact that the 'iced water' next to her Pepsi cooler was one hundred per cent vodka. Joan 'politely' requested that Bette's fifteen-year old daughter BD (Barbara Davis Merrill) stay away from the twins so that they would not pick up any of the bad habits and colourful language BD may have picked up from her 'dirty-mouthed' mother. Yet on the other hand, Joan attempted to woo her way into Bette's good books, as had happened eighteen years previously when she had first joined Warner Brothers; by sending her gifts: flowers, chocolates and perfume, accompanied by 'soppy' notelets, which were deliberately misinterpreted. According to Lawrence J Quirk in his book on Bette Davis, Bette screamed, 'She's fifty-eight if she's a day, and she's still coming at me like a dykey schoolgirl with the crush on the boobs and twat at the next schoolroom desk!' – then returned the next batch of gifts with a note of her own: 'Other than ripping my toilet seat off and wrapping it up to send you, I can't think of any other way to answer except to tell you: GET OFF THE CRAP!'

Bette further complained about the various pairs of artificial breasts Joan wore under her costumes to make Blanche appear less voluptuous, telling BD (as she wrote in her memoirs, *My Mother's Keeper*, 1985), 'You never know what size boobs that broad has strapped on. I keep running into them like the Hollywood Hills. She's supposed to be shrivelling away while Baby Jane starves her to death, but her tits keep growing!' Next there was a hitch in the casting of Edwin Flagg, Baby Jane's mama's boy accompanist. Robert Aldrich approached British actor Peter Lawford, a member of Frank Sinatra's notorious Rat Pack and the husband of President Kennedy's sister, Patricia. Lawford was all for accepting the part until the intensely homophobic Sinatra advised him that 'playing a fag' would be detrimental to his hard-drinking, hard-living image. Aldrich brought in the much more suitable Victor Buono (1938–82), a loveable heavyweight then appearing in television's *The Untouchables*. In this, his first film, he got along well with Joan, though not with Bette after she had walked on to the set in a bad mood and called him a 'fat slob' in front of everyone. Of the other supports, Marjorie Bennett had appeared in *Autumn Leaves* and *Female on the Beach*, and Maidie Norman in *Torch Song*. Anna Lee, a big British star of the Thirties, had arrived in Hollywood in 1939, and among her greatest successes there were *How Green Was My Valley* and *Bedlam* (1941 and 1946, respectively). It is, however, Joan and Bette's picture from start to finish.

It is 1917, and wunderkind Baby Jane Hudson (Julie Allred) billed as 'The Diminutive Dancing Duse From Duluth', is closing another sell-out vaudeville show, murdering her theme song 'I've Written a Letter to Daddy Whose Address is Heaven Above', while sister Blanche (the *Andy Hardy* remake's Gina Gillespie) looks on glumly from the wings. At the end of the performance a stooge presents the singer with a Baby Jane doll while Mr Hudson announces that more of the same are on sale in the foyer, just as cute as the real thing. Offstage, minutes later, Baby Jane is observed as anything but – a pampered, obnoxious brat who demands and gets her own way, for *she* is bringing in the money, while Blanche gets yelled at for being polite. 'You're the lucky one,' her mother (Ann Barton) tells her. 'Some day it's going to be you that's getting all the attention, and when that happens I want you to be kinder to Jane and your father than they are to you now.' And the child snarls back, 'I won't forget – you *bet* I won't forget!'

The story moves forward to 1935 and both sisters are in the movies – Blanche the biggest star in Hollywood, Jane already a drunken has-been who orders her liquor by the case, slugs cops, and who only gets parts because her sister's contract stipulates that when she makes a film, Jane must be permitted to make one too. Two studio moguls are watching the rushes of Jane's latest effort (actually Bette Davis hamming it up in an early quota-quickie!). 'My, what a no-talent broad that Baby Jane is!' one exclaims, to which the other retorts, 'She *stinks*!' (The scriptwriter had actually wanted him to say what studio head Carl Laemmle had said in 1931 after watching Bette in *Bad Sister* – 'Can you picture some poor guy going through hell and high water in a picture and ending up with *her* at the fade-out?' – but Bette objected.) Then the camera cuts to the gates of Valentino's mansion, Falcon Lair (actually a similar property that the studio had loaned on McCadden Drive), which Blanche bought soon after the great actor's death – and we get to see a glimpse of the mysterious car accident that ended Blanche's career and left her confined to a wheelchair. We see the lower half of a female figure standing in front of the railings, a foot with its ankle-bracelet pressing down on the accelerator, and a broken doll. Just what happened – not to Baby Jane, but to Blanche – unfolds over the next two hours as the story jumps to the present day and the opening credits, twelve minutes into the film.

Nosy neighbour Mrs Bates (Anna Lee) arrives home, glances up at the barred windows of Falcon Lair, then walks in on her daughter (Bette Davis's own daughter, BD), who is watching part of a Blanche Hudson retrospective on the television. Today's movie is *Lost Honeymoon* (though what we see is Joan Crawford in *Sadie McKee*). Mrs Bates observes how they have lived next to the Hudsons for six months now, yet never once seen Blanche – then sets out to remedy the situation by taking her a bunch of gladioli. Jane, rumoured to be responsible for crippling her sister, soon sees her off. Then she clobbers about her kitchen in her tatty nightdress, her face in close-up a hideous gargoyle mask of trowelled-on greasepaint and 'Victory Red' lipstick, and the long, platinum, curly 'Mary Pickford' wig (actually the one Joan had worn in *The Gorgeous Hussy*!) informing us that she is stuck in a Baby Jane vaudeville time-warp. She is drunk as usual and preparing lunch for Blanche, who is in her wheelchair upstairs, watching the film in the room to which she has been confined since her accident – a pleasant interlude that ends abruptly when Jane barges in with the tray, slamming the door and frightening Blanche's pet parakeet half out of its wits, and switching off the set. Blanche looks very serene, handsome even as she wallows in her past glories, maybe just a little drawn around the eyes and mouth, and seems to cower when Jane lays into her after they have reflected on *Lost Honeymoon* – which was a huge hit, while the one Jane made that year is completely forgotten:

> The best thing I ever did. They never even released it in the United States . . . They didn't wanna show *my* film. They were too busy giving a big build-up to that crap you were turning out!

Jane takes away the birdcage: it needs cleaning out. The maid, Elvira (Maidie Norman), reports for duty. She has always favoured Blanche because she has taken her into her confidence: once she has sold this house and put the mentally deteriorating Jane into a home, she will buy a smaller place and Elvira will move in with her. Jane, however, must not find out what they are up to. For the moment, she is preoccupied with hunting for a drop of the hard stuff in the cupboard where she hoards her empties. She calls the store and finds out that Blanche has cancelled her order – but pretending to be her sister (in fact, miming to Joan's voice), she soon rectifies the situation. Then she ambles into her rehearsal room, picks out a tune on her piano, and hears herself singing in vaudeville, regressing into childhood long enough to pose Mrs Haversham-like in front of the wall mirror and recite a favourite poem – before realising what a ghastly mess she has become. But she is interrupted by the buzzer that connects to Blanche's room, and she is off again – with a spiel many interpreted as Bette Davis attempting to put Joan Crawford in her place because of what she called her 'off-screen airs and graces' – and all this prior to serving her sister parakeet salad!

All right, Blanche, I heard it. Miss big fat movie star. Miss rotten, stinking actress . . . Press a button, ring a bell, and you think the whole damn world comes running, don't you? 'Lunch, Miss Hudson!' 'Why certainly, Miss Hudson!' 'I'm sure we can find you something *appropriate*, Miss Hudson!'

Momentarily suffering in silence and feeling guilty over what *she* has done behind Jane's back, Blanche tells her about the house being put up for sale – claiming that they are running short of funds. Jane *knows* what she has been up to because she has heard her calling their business manager. She unplugs the phone, cutting her off just that little bit more from the world. Then Jane drives off in Blanche's convertible, a remnant from her Hollywood days, to place an ad in the local paper for an accompanist: she has decided she needs to revive her absurdly outdated Baby Jane act. While she is gone, Blanche frantically types out a note for the next-door neighbour and tosses this out of the window, but it is Jane who finds it and proceeds to give her merry hell. In her confused state of mind Jane is convinced that her father bought the house for *her*. She hisses, 'Blanche, ya aren't ever going to sell this house – and ya aren't ever going to leave it, either!' Blanche tries to tell her the truth about the accident, but each time the subject is brought up, Jane goes berserk.

Next we see oily mama's boy Edwin Flagg 'composing' at his piano (actually playing the first stanza of Edith Piaf's *'Les Flons-flons du Bal'* while his mother (Marjorie Bennett) fusses over him with one of the most atrocious fake Cockney accents ever heard on screen. Mrs Flagg has been laid off work, and her layabout son must now support her. He shows her Jane's ad: posing as his secretary, she fixes him up with an interview. Meanwhile, back at Falcon Lair, Blanche's buzzer is working overtime because she is starving, yet terrified of lifting the lid on her tray since the incident with the parakeet – while Jane scathes, 'I didn't bring ya breakfast because ya didn't eat ya din-din!' Now, she adds, they are back where they started: when she was Baby Jane, the family had to depend on her for food – and Blanche is relying on her again. Moreover, Blanche is the one who is mad, or rather paranoid, a point Jane proves by removing the lid from the tray and taking a bite out of the chop she has prepared, suggesting that what happened was all in Blanche's mind. The next thing, Jane is serving her baked rat and cackling maniacally as Blanche spins hysterically round and round in her wheelchair. (Joan was taught how to do this, and how to hoist herself in and out of the bed, by a Korean war veteran during several unpublicised visits to a hospital for paraplegics.)

Edwin arrives at the madhouse, probably its first visitor in years, and he is perfectly suited to his surroundings, being obese and dithering with his

Queen's English and Sydney Greenstreet mannerisms. After serving him tea, Jane takes him to the rehearsal room, a shrine to the long-forgotten Baby Jane Hudson, which even has vaudeville footlights. Blanche's buzzer goes while he checks through the dots, and Jane rips it out of the wall, leaving the by-now near-skeletal invalid void of human contact. Edwin plays the introduction to 'I've Written a Letter to Daddy', and Jane lets rip with her famous ditty: the Bette Davis voice is raucous, torchy, tuneless but surprisingly touching. During the musical interlude she dances, shows her drawers, and as the number ends she takes an imaginary curtain call. Edwin feigns admiration, though he has found the whole experience embarrassing, and the demure young woman lurking within the harridan's complex psyche falls for this Tinseltown Johnny and tells him they may have a future together – once she has dealt with a pressing 'family' matter.

Blanche, meanwhile, is foraging for scraps of food in her room when she comes across defaced publicity shots of herself, and evidence that Jane has been copying the signature from these onto cheques – the most recent to pay for her 'comeback' costumes. While Jane is in town collecting these, Blanche attempts to get to the phone at the foot of the stairs, takes a fall, crawls across the floor and has managed to call the doctor when Jane gets home – and kicks her half to death. (For this extended scene, considered graphic at the time, a dummy was used for the close-ups where Blanche's face is not seen, but in long-shot, where she is seen albeit in rapid flashes, Joan refused a stand-in, and ended up having to have three stitches in her head. Bette always maintained that it had been an accident, but Joan claimed otherwise and swore that she would have her revenge.) Then Jane again imitates Blanche on the phone, persuading the doctor to cancel his visit.

Jane fires Elvira, but the suspicious maid still has a key and waits until she has driven off before letting herself into the house. Blanche is locked in her room, and Elvira has fetched tools to force the hinges when Jane gets back. She becomes Baby Jane again, throws a tantrum but lets Elvira into the room all the same, where she finds Blanche bound and gagged on the bed; above on the wall is a classic Joan Crawford portrait, illuminated like a shrine. Blanche tries to warn Elvira of the danger, but Jane steals up on her and caves the back of her head in with a clawhammer. Cut to Edwin, about to make a call asking Jane out on a date: the mortician's ad on the service station wall next to the booth reads, 'For Undertaking, Utter McKinley Understands – From $100' – which is exactly the amount Jane is paying him for his services. Jane does not answer, so he rushes home to Mama, who tells him that everyone knows how Jane tried to kill her sister, and how after the car accident the studio paid out hush money to keep the truth from being made public. According to the legend, Jane was later picked up drunk in a hotel room with a man she had never seen before. 'Well,' he snarls back, 'why should that upset you? Isn't that how *I* was conceived?'

In the next scene, Jane gets a call from the police: Elvira has been reported missing. Now she is frightened – she has gone too far, and needs Blanche to help her. She speaks about the accident, confessing that she cannot remember a thing about that night because she was plastered, though she cannot possibly imagine herself wanting to *deliberately* kill her sister – yet no sooner has she said this than she is off her head again. Then Edwin arrives. Stood up by Jane, he has been drowning his sorrows and is sozzled. Jane tells him that she has a gift for him – an old Baby Jane doll, which he dangles on his knee while she fetches the money she owes him. When she returns she almost has a heart attack when she sees it and him, draped with a blanket, racing up and down in Blanche's wheelchair. Then he sobers up sufficiently to investigate the attention-seeking thud from above. Rushing upstairs he sees Blanche, but instead of helping he flees into the night to call the cops.

Now desperate, Jane drags Blanche out of the bed, across the room to the landing and down the stairs to the car. (Much of this was shot in a single take, and enabled Joan to exact her revenge for the alleged earlier kick – by wearing a lead-lined weightlifter's belt under her dress. The exertion caused Bette to sprain her back.) Jane drives them to the beach, once Baby Jane's favourite spot where Daddy used to bring her. The police have found Elvira's body and are after her. The sisters spend the night on the beach, and when morning comes Jane has completed her regression into childhood and is making sandcastles while Blanche lies next to her, wrapped in a blanket, her life ebbing away. And at last Blanche gets to talk about the accident, confessing how for more than twenty years she has conned Jane into thinking that she crippled her, when the accident was really her own fault – how, on that fateful night after Jane had taunted her at a party, *she* had driven the car, asked Jane to get out and open the gates, then deliberately tried to run her over – only to have her jump out of the way and have Blanche crash into the gates, snapping her spine. Then, she adds, she managed to crawl out from behind the steering wheel and up to the gates so that the police would think Jane had been driving.

Jane regains her sanity long enough to pronounce, 'All this time, we could have been friends' – though it is Blanche/Joan who manages to have the last word before expiring. 'You weren't ugly then – I made you that way,' she gasps, cueing Baby Jane Hudson to give her final performance to the bemused crowd of sunbathers who have gathered about her as the police close in. Magnificent!

What Ever Happened To Baby Jane? attracted rave reviews, even from Crawford and Davis detractors. The *New York Times* advised its readers not to take the schlock-horror content too seriously, adding, 'Take it straight and you'll recoil from a murderous duel of snarls, shrieks and rattlesnake repartee by Bette Davis and Joan Crawford.' *Newsweek* observed – tongue in cheek, though neither star was particularly amused – 'As an ugly old hag, Bette Davis with her ghastly layers of make-up and her shuffling-clump walk is rather appealing. And Joan Crawford is – oh, just Joan Crawford!' *Saturday Review* called the film: 'Something breathlessly close to perfection, a shocker and at the same time a superb showcase for the time-ripened talents of two of Hollywood's most accomplished actresses.'

Shooting had wrapped early in September 1962, with the critics who had seen the rushes predicting that the film would be a smash and return Joan and Bette Davis to the regal spotlight where they both belonged. It also coincided with the publication of their autobiographies: *A Portrait of Joan* (Doubleday), and *Bette Davis: The Lonely Life* (Putnam). Joan's book, however, was not the explosive kiss-and-tell everyone had anticipated.

If the predicted success of *What Ever Happened to Baby Jane?* enabled Joan to feel a little more secure about her future, Bette Davis's self-confidence plummeted to such depths that, convinced no one would want to employ her again, she placed an advertisement in *Variety*'s Situations Vacant column:

> Mother of Three: 10, 11, 15, divorcée, American. 30 years experience as an actress in motion pictures. Mobile still and more affable than rumour would have it. Wants steady employment in Hollywood.

When it brought only adverse publicity, Bette claimed that she had placed the advertisement for a prank, but this did not prevent Joan from scoffing at a *Variety* reporter, '*I* would rather wait on tables like Mildred Pierce in some greasy spoon than *beg* for work!'

The film was one of the top-grossers of the winter 1962–spring 1963 season, recovering its $975,000 production costs within two weeks and grossing over $9 million at the US box office. It made both women financially solvent once more, and it received five Oscar nominations: Bette Davis (Best Actress), Victor Buono (Best Supporting Actor), Best Cinematography (Ernest Haller), Best Sound, and Best Costumes (Norma Koch). Only Joan was overlooked, though in her rather Machiavellian way she achieved a sort of victory over her rival. Upon learning that she had *not* been nominated she hit the campaign trail, urging the Motion Picture Academy members she counted among her friends to vote for Anne Bancroft in *The Miracle Worker*. The other nominees were Lee Remick in *The Days of Wine and Roses*, Geraldine Page in *Sweet Bird of Youth*, and Katharine Hepburn in *Long Day's Journey into Night*. Joan contacted these and some of the other category nominees too, on the off-chance that they would be unable to collect their awards personally, and as luck would have it, Bancroft was unable to attend. She won the Oscar, and as Joan headed for the podium at the Santa Monica Civil Auditorium to receive the award on Bancroft's behalf, she deliberately elbowed Bette Davis out of the way! The next day, Hedda Hopper observed in her column, 'When it comes it giving or stealing a show, nobody can top Joan Crawford!'

CHAPTER THIRTEEN

'Her Serene Crawfordship!'

'The secret for serenity is just believing.'

Joan Crawford

What Ever Happened to Baby Jane? set a precedent for Grand Guignolesque productions aimed at riding on the backs of shock-fests like Hitchcock's *Psycho* (1960), but with the added touch of 'dusting down' ageing glamour queens and presenting them as garish caricatures of themselves to younger audiences – often employing the same cameramen and technicians who had worked to make them look *beautiful* in the halcyon days. Thus, Shelley Winters would make *The Balcony*, Tallulah Bankhead portrayed a deranged religious harridan in *Fanatic* (aka *Die! Die My Darling!*), and Debbie Reynolds appeared in *What's the Matter With Helen?*.

What Ever Happened to Baby Jane? was the first in a quartet of Robert Aldrich ultra-camp thrillers dealing with faded celebrity – the others being *The Killing of Sister George, The Legend of Lylah Clare* and, before these, *Hush . . . Hush, Sweet Charlotte*, which Aldrich hoped would provide Joan and Bette Davis with a worthwhile, profitable successor to their first pairing, and which he hoped would be filmed as soon as they could find mutual gaps in their suddenly busy schedules.

Meanwhile, in the spring of 1963, shortly before playing twins in *Dead Ringers*, Bette was asked to attend the premieres of *Baby Jane* in London and Paris, then fly down to Cannes for the Film Festival. Joan was also invited, but declined: she was too preoccupied with Pepsi business to travel overseas, and was about to begin shooting *The Caretakers* with Robert Stack, veteran Herbert Marshall, and Polly Bergen – a young protégée of Alfred Steele's, who had appeared in his and Joan's Pepsi commercials.

In the film Joan played Lucretia Terry, the hard-bitten matron of a psychiatric institution, who, with her superintendent, Dr Harrington (Marshall), virulently opposes the 'new-fangled' theories of new-kid-on-the-block Don MacLeod (Stack). Whereas MacLeod wishes to introduce day clinics for borderline cases, Lucretia advocates the old-fashioned but 'proven' methods of putting patients in strait-jackets and locking them in padded cells. Lucretia's every idea and decision are whole-heartedly supported by her loyal lackey, Nurse Bracker (Constance Ford), forming part of a suppressed lesbian sub-plot that involves Lucretia supervising the other nurses having lessons in self-defence. Then there are the patients, a mixed bunch straight out of a Pirandello play, including a beatnik, a senile schoolteacher, a woman who has accidentally killed her child, a neurotic immigrant and a deranged whore.

Most of these people are experimented on, always to no avail, for Lucretia and Harrington's psychiatric techniques prove no match for the compassionate treatment prescribed by MacLeod. Joan gave a stunning performance, yet most of the critics were merciless. Bosley Crowther of the *New York Times* called the film 'shallow, showy and cheap'. *Variety* scathed, 'Miss Crawford doesn't so much play her handful of scenes as she dresses for them – looking as if she were en route to a Pepsi board meeting.'

The Caretakers premiered in August 1963, by which time Joan was working on *Strait-Jacket*, playing an axe-murderess *and* being forced to endure another mother/daughter-bitch martyrdom. Her co-star was Diane Baker, a demure-looking young actress who had made her debut in *The Diary of Anne Frank* (1959). There was also an appearance by Mitchell Cox – who just happened to be vice-president of Pepsi Cola.

The film was produced and directed by William Castle, who paid to have a publicity photograph published in the *New York Times*. This was captioned: 'Joan Crawford With An Axe: Tennis Anyone?' Castle (1914–77) was the undisputed master of low-budget exploitation horror-flicks. In 1932, after a successful stint on Broadway as a child actor, he had become America's youngest director with his offbeat version of *Dracula*, and after a variety of jobs in the film industry he had made a series of mostly forgettable Westerns before turning to thrillers. One of Castle's gimmicks with *House on Haunted Hill* and *The Tingler* (1958 and 1959) had been to offer $1,000 in compensation, should anyone watching these actually *die* of fright! Other *trucs* included having bats and skeletons fly across the auditorium at premieres, and the director himself arriving in a coffin and hearse.

Lucy Hardin (Joan) finds her husband in bed with a local hooker and promptly hacks the pair to death in one of the (unintentionally) *funniest* moments in any Crawford film. This earns her twenty years in the 'booby hatch', and upon her release she is reunited with her daughter, Carol (Baker), who was just three when she witnessed her mother going berserk. It is Carol who persuades Lucy to ditch her old-fashioned clothes and begin dressing like the modern generation: she ends up looking like a poor man's Anna Magnani in a cheap black wig and skirts that are way too short. She behaves like a sex-starved animal, tries to seduce Carol's hunky boyfriend, Michael (John Anthony Hayes), and has a fit of hysterics when his snobbish mother gets on the wrong side of her. Then a new series of axe murders begins, and Lucy is naturally the prime suspect – until it emerges that *Carol* is the killer, that meeting her mother again has triggered off in her mind the horrific event she saw as a child, and subconsciously forced her to emulate Lucy.

The reviews were generally favourable, though Joan's friend, the influential Judith Crist from the *New York Herald Tribune*, felt that a change of direction might be in order:

> It's time to get Joan Crawford out of these housedress horror B-movies and back into haute couture. Miss Crawford, you see, is high-class. Too high-class to withstand in mufti the banality of Robert Bloch's script, cheap jack production and/or vacuous supporting players and direction better suited to the mist-and-cobweb idiocies of the Karloff school of suspense.

There were two unexpected reunions at around this time. The first was with Mary Pickford, now 72 and a virtual recluse, though the occasion – a 'Hollywood Old-Timers Ball' at Pickfair – was hardly fitting. Joan even tried to ruffle the old lady's feathers by stepping through the once-hallowed portals and fishing a brown-paper bag out of her handbag, within which was her vodka flask – but all Pickford did was invite her in to the salon and hand her a crystal glass. And it was probably here that Joan bumped into Franchot Tone, not in the best of health, divorced from fourth wife Dolores Dorn and apparently interested in giving it another go with Joan, who found herself letting him down gently. At Pickfair she also solicited funds from some of the other guests for her latest project with the USO (United Services Organisation), which saw her raising money on behalf of its New York branch to send artistes to entertain troops serving in Vietnam. Joan would be elected vice-president, and on 2 March 1965 voted the USO's first Woman of the Year.

Meanwhile, for those who believed the Crawford-Davis feud had come to its logical conclusion with the winding up of *Baby Jane*, Round Two was about to begin – the one that would see Joan well and truly knocked out for the count.

At the end of 1963, with *Sodom and Gomorrah* and *Four For Texas* having failed to pull in the crowds, Robert Aldrich commissioned author Henry Farrell and scriptwriter Lukas Heller to write a follow-up horror excursion for the arch rivals. The result was *What Ever Happened to Cousin Charlotte?*, subsequently changed to *Hush . . . Hush, Sweet Charlotte*, a saga of madness, murder and mayhem set in the Deep South. Twentieth Century-Fox allocated Aldrich a budget of $1.5 million. Within days of Heller delivering the finished script, Joseph Cotten, Victor Buono and Mary Astor had been signed up as secondary leads – along with Barbara Stanwyck, semi-retired since divorcing Robert Taylor in 1952. Bette Davis reluctantly agreed to participate. She needed the money, she said, and the $200,000 salary Aldrich was offering, she added, would have been sufficient to persuade *anyone* to put up with Joan Crawford, who would be playing Charlotte's glamorous but bitchy cousin, Miriam. It was agreed that Joan's name would 'technically' head the credits, appearing to the left of Bette's, but with asterisks denoting that they were in alphabetical order. When Bette complained that *she* should receive first billing because she was playing the title character, Joan merely pointed out that *she* had been given first billing in *The Story of Esther Costello*, while the actress playing this character had been tagged on to the *end* of the credits.

The storyline was more complex than that of *Baby Jane*. Ageing plantation owner Charlotte Hollis has become increasingly more mad since the mysterious decapitation of her married lover many years before – she suspects the murderer to be her much-loved father (Buono, in flashback). The locals, however, suspect her. Charlotte fears that the perpetrator of the crime will be disclosed imminently when the family mansion is demolished to make way for a new highway. She is visited from overseas by cousin Miriam, who under pretence of consoling her is actually conspiring with Charlotte's doctor (Cotten) to drive her completely insane, maybe even to suicide, so that she can inherit the estate. The climax to all of this is a hammy, high-camp gore-fest (at a time when major stars never appeared in such films) – with a hand lopped off by a meat cleaver, crushed corpses, blood-spattered statues and zombies – in short, it all ends very badly. Realising what the plotters have been doing to her, Charlotte kills them, though there is some consolation when her lover's murderer turns out to have been his wife (Astor).

The ten-day locations were shot in and around Baton Rouge, Louisiana, where the Belmont Motel had been put at Robert Aldrich's disposal: he chartered a plane to fly everyone there from Hollywood on 31 May 1964. Joan opted to travel independently with her entourage and regulation twenty-plus pieces of luggage because Aldrich had decided she would not be required until the fourth day of shooting. Because she wanted to settle in at her bungalow, she arrived a day early: there was no one to meet her at the airport, and to make matters worse her bungalow was not ready for her to move in to. The local press, said to have already been in Bette Davis's pocket, rushed to photograph her and her entourage sitting atop their luggage in the motel foyer – and later reported how, when she had gone to Bette's bungalow to complain, her feisty co-star had slammed the door in her face. With *Baby Jane* it had been hard to discern between publicity-seeking and genuine rivalry, but with *Charlotte* it was unadulterated spite, if not actual near-madness on Bette's part. The next day Bette called a press conference and explained the 'real reason' why Joan had been so upset – the Belmont Motel had not laid on her regulation *crates* of liquor. She also made a point of mentioning Joan's age and her 'pathological fear' of growing old – the fact that she had just turned sixty, and not 56 as her publicity led everyone to believe. Not one reporter mentioned this, well aware that this was another exercise in vitriol because Bette had always looked older than Joan.

By this stage of the proceedings, Barbara Stanwyck, engaged to play lesbian hillbilly housekeeper Velma, had backed out of the production in the wake of a behind-the-scenes altercation with costume designer/former lover Edith Head, who was also fired. Stanwyck's replacement was another old flame, Agnes Moorehead, though for Stanwyck the parting of the ways would leave an aftertaste of bitterness when, under the terms of her contract, she was loaned to Paramount to replace Mae West in Elvis Presley's *Roustabout*. This proved an unpleasant pairing. Neither Presley nor Stanwyck could stand the sight of the other, and the experience would result in Stanwyck virtually turning her back on Hollywood, making just one more film before relocating to the small screen – triumphing in *The Big Valley* and *The Thornbirds* before bowing out in the glitzy but tacky soap *The Colbys*.

Robert Aldrich had made a terrible faux-pas by hiring Harry Mines – the publicist who had 'found' Phillip Terry for Joan, but had recently had the misfortune to guide Marilyn Monroe through *The Misfits* – to handle Joan and Bette for this one. Mines was loud, rude and impatient – he managed to secure an interview with *Life* magazine, but was hardly tactful when it came to arranging the photoshoot, suggesting that Joan and Bette succinctly refer to their feud by posing on gravestones in the purpose-built cemetery. Joan was game, but Bette protested vehemently, though she eventually agreed to the session because this *was* (with *Time*) the country's joint most prestigious publication.

Bette's unpleasantness towards Joan intensified as shooting pro-gressed. Between scenes, she ganged up with Agnes Moorehead and persistently bad-mouthed her to the crew. Worse than this, she began walking across the cameraman's line of shot while he was photographing

Joan in close-up. The last straw came after the locations, when Bette tried to get Joan's lines cut from the interiors. Walking off the set, Joan contacted her lawyer with the intention of backing out of the film (as Barbara Stanwyck had). By the time he began working on the case, however, she had suddenly fallen ill with dysentery – said to have been brought on by a combination of stress and the torrid Louisiana climate – and had to be admitted to the Cedars of Lebanon Hospital.

For over a week, Robert Aldrich filmed around Joan, using a stand-in for rear and long shots – and with Bette Davis telling all and sundry that Joan was *faking* illness because she was too old to withstand the pace. Joan hardly helped matters by inviting the press in to the sickroom and posing for photographs in her new Christian Dior nightdress and trying on her latest gift to herself – a $100,000 sapphire necklace. News was then rushed to the lot that Joan had suffered a relapse: she now had pneumonia and a high blood count and, not knowing when she would be well enough to resume work, Aldrich had no option but to put the production on hold.

Within a matter of days, desperate not to let everyone down, Joan returned to the set, recovered from her pneumonia but clearly exhausted – and, with Bette Davis refusing to cut her any slack, on the verge of a nervous breakdown. At this stage, instructed by their insurers, Twentieth Century-Fox brought in an independent arbitrator and it was decided that Joan should submit to a full medical examination. This only confirmed that she had not been spinning everyone a yarn (though the report from the Cedars of Lebanon had already done so) and that additionally she had a dangerously high temperature. She was readmitted to the hospital a few days later and, having collected on Joan's insurance, the studio ordered Robert Aldrich to find a replacement, but to keep the news from Joan – the idea being that, if one could not be found, they would still have her to fall back on.

Joan's absence from the set automatically gave Bette Davis contractual co-star approval and there was now absolutely no way she was going to allow *anyone* equal billing to her. Contrary to what has been written, Barbara Stanwyck was not now considered for the part of Miriam: she was halfway through shooting *Roustabout*. Robert Aldrich and Twentieth Century-Fox suggested Vivien Leigh, who flatly refused to work with Bette on account of the things she had said about her during the Scarlett O'Hara debacle. The Associated Press reported Leigh as having told a studio executive, 'I could just about stand seeing Joan Crawford's face first thing in the morning, but seeing Bette Davis' would be *too* much.' Upon hearing this, Bette is alleged to have wrecked her dressing room.

Bette's choice for Miriam was Olivia de Havilland, who had stepped out of her usually gracious character mould for her latest film, a taut thriller

entitled *Lady in a Cage* – resulting in her being denounced by *Life* magazine
as: 'One of those movie actresses who apparently would rather be freaks
than forgotten.' Currently residing in Switzerland, she was contacted, but
made it clear that *she* did not want to step into Joan Crawford's shoes.
Twentieth Century-Fox then took the unusual and costly step of flying
Robert Aldrich out to Europe to sweet-talk her into accepting. Off his own
back, he upped the studio's original offer and told de Havilland that she
would be paid $100,000 for doing the film, plus $15,000 in expenses, along
with the same box-office percentage as Bette. She accepted at once, and the
first Joan got to know she had been dumped was when she heard the news
on the hospital radio. Her response, when asked by reporters for her
opinion of the whole messy situation, was a sarcastic: 'I'm delighted for
Olivia – she needs the work!'

In April 1973, during an interview in front of an audience at New York's
Town Hall, publicist John Springer would ask for Joan's comments on Aldrich
and Nicholas Ray, arguably the best directors of her later career. 'Nicholas Ray
was the only one who could have gotten me through *Johnny Guitar*,' she would
say, 'but Bob Aldrich has many, many insecurities, loves evil things, horrendous
things, *vile* things!' She was obviously referring to his fondness for Bette Davis,
and when Springer asked, 'If *you* had done the scene with Bette Davis in *Hush
. . . Hush, Sweet Charlotte*, would you have slapped her as savagely as did
Olivia de Havilland?' – the response, bringing guffaws from the audience, was
a curt, 'I didn't *see* the film!'

Hush . . . Hush, Sweet Charlotte was rush-released in December 1964
to qualify for the Oscar nominations. It was entered on seven counts,
including Best Supporting Actress for Agnes Moorehead. Bette Davis was
not nominated, and of course this delighted Joan. There would also be
another stab in the back for Bette on Oscars night when Joan, well aware
that the enemy had been overlooked, stepped on to the podium to present
the Best Director Award to George Cukor for *My Fair Lady*. Bette had
wanted to croon the *Charlotte* theme song to the glitterati audience, which
Twentieth Century-Fox had not allowed her to do over the credits – in the
film it is performed by Al Martino. Now she was snubbed again in favour
of Patti Page, whose recording of the song had entered the hit parade. 'It
was such a *thrill* hearing and meeting Patti Page,' Joan told the crowd.
Then in the wings she espied Edith Head, her costumier for the evening,
'getting on like a house on fire' with Barbara Stanwyck, despite the row
that had caused them both to be 'Charlotte casualties' like herself. 'I hear
Edith gives *such* good wardrobe,' she quipped to nearby reporters, a phrase
that would become *the* in-joke among Hollywood's gay community during
the spring of 1964.

Joan's next film, again for William Castle, saw her reunited with her *Queen Bee* co-star John Ireland. She would be on a salary of $50,000 plus a hefy percentage of the box office – and all for just four days' work. In *I Saw What You Did*, the story is a children's prank that goes horribly wrong. Two teenage girls pick numbers at random from the telephone directory, call their unsuspecting victims and announce, 'I saw what you did – I know who you are!', before hanging up. What they do not know is that when they call Steve Marak (Ireland), he has just murdered his wife. Thus begins a cat-and-mouse game in which Marak, who truly believes that the girls witnessed his crime, tracks them down and sets about trying to eliminate them. Enter Marak's mistress, Amy Nelson (Joan), who had been trying to get him to leave his wife and move in with her. When she learns what he has done, she tries to protect the girls – and Marak rewards her by dispatching her with the bread knife just before the police arrive to arrest him. The reviews were again mostly good, though as with Joan's previous film there were pleas from the critics for her to return to her tried-and-tested, meaty melodramas.

Joan made a move in the right direction with *Della*, the pilot for a television series filmed quickly between the completion of *I Saw What You Did* and its July 1965 release. Her co-stars were Paul Burke, Otto Kruger and veteran Charles Bickford, in his last major role two years before his death. Diane Baker, who had played Joan's daughter in *Strait-Jacket*, does so again here. The film was directed for Four Stars Pictures by former B-movies actor Robert Gist.

Della is set in the coastal city of Royal Bay, and is narrated by politician-turned-boatyard-owner Hugh Stafford (Bickford), whose big-shot lawyer son, Barney (Burke), arrives home after a lengthy absence to talk wealthy blue-rinse widow Della Chappell (Joan) into selling some of her land to his clients at Delta Industries for their latest space project. Others have failed before him, and initially Barney favours forcing Della's hand by asking the council to raise her land taxes sky high. When they refuse to do this, he meets Della in the house she has hardly ever left in fifteen years. This, however, is no decaying Falcon Lair but a luxurious, ultra-modern mansion, where the lady of the house wears diamonds and mock Chez Fath gowns – even though the only ones who see her are the elderly housekeeper and Della's pretty daughter, Jenny, whose massive portrait hangs over the fireplace.

Della makes a spectacular entrance, self-assuredly descending the staircase for maximum effect – reflecting Joan Crawford in real life. She circles around Barney like a lioness closing in on her prey, and he is immediately suspicious that she is not all she seems – though he should have suspected *something* untoward when she asked him to go there at two in the morning. She tells him that she has made it her business to find out everything about

him, and yells at him; when he yells back he starts to earn her respect. He also
falls for Jenny, who is affable but seemingly as unbalanced as her mother, and
agrees to stay at the house to sift through the wealth of complicated deeds and
documents – if the deal is to go through. Jenny, however, knows how her
mother works and has seen this sort of thing before, for when it comes to men,
Della 'buys in' as she does the household provisions:

> He's very nice. All that talk about the land. You already *know* what you're
> going to do . . . Then why ask him here? It spoils our nice little prison –
> unless you want him for one of the prisoners?

Barney tries to work out why the Chappells sleep by day and live by
night, coming to the conclusion that Della once suffered some terrible
malaise or misfortune that makes her afraid to face a conventional world,
and that this is causing Jenny's mood-swings – making her seductive one
minute, rude and aggressive the next. He checks through Della's newspaper
file but finds nothing; his father, Hugh, knows *exactly* what is wrong, but is
sworn to secrecy. Jenny pushes a note into Barney's pocket, telling him she
loves him. Later she steals in to his room while he is sleeping. He leaps out
of the bed, flings open the drapes to let the light in, and she flees in terror
with him in hot pursuit – almost colliding with Della on the landing. Then
he flexes his not inconsiderable biceps, painfully holds in his stomach while
Della fixes her gaze on *his* cleavage, and lets rip when trying to explain that
this is not what she thinks:

> And you *had* to show yourself off . . . show her what a fine man you are,
> what a fine, strutting animal you are. Well, that's all you are, all you'll ever
> be and all you'll ever understand!

Over the next few scenes, one gets the impression that Della really *is*
barking mad. She threatens to destroy Barney's career and run him out of
town unless he stops prying into her affairs – like *Johnny Guitar*'s Emma
Small, she owns just about everything in sight. Despite this, he encourages
Jenny to pack her bags and leave – something the girl almost does, getting
as far as the door before the daylight brings on one of her attacks. And in
the final Crawford unburdening scene captured on celluloid, Della delivers
the truth in a highly charged five-minute soliloquy: Jenny has a serious
condition that makes her sensitive to sunlight and will one day kill her. She
must therefore spend the rest of her life in darkness and, seeing as he has
passed the test and Jenny loves him, Barney should gradually take Della's
place in caring for her. This he flatly refuses to do. Even if he *was* in love

with Jenny, he says, he would never adapt his way of life to suit hers – it would have to be the other way around.

Jenny overhears the conversation, and we instinctively know that it will all end in tears. Rushing out of the house, she gets into the car she has only ever driven at night and, with the sun wreaking its terrible effect, plunges to her death down an embankment. Next we see a distraught Della gazing up at her daughter's portrait, begging Barney not to reproach himself for what has happened (though he is *entirely* to blame), and asking him to sell her land, build a children's institution in the city and dedicate this to Jenny's memory. Barney gives every impression that he could not care less. He admits to his father that Della is going to find it hard to pick up the pieces after her years of enforced solitude, to which Hugh responds, 'Then *you* help her, Barney. You'll be closer to her than anybody' – making one feel sorry for the poor woman if *this* surly, heartless man is all she has to help her get over her ordeal!

Della, which saw Joan filmed in soft-focus for the first time, though she greatly belies her 61 years, was made at a time when great movie-stars-turned-television-stalwarts were beginning to *lose* their popularity – a classic example being Barbara Stanwyck in *The Big Valley* – and though they would make a comeback at the end of the next decade (Jane Wyman in *Falcon Crest*, Judith Anderson in *Knots Landing*, etc.), *Della* did not catch on. This was a pity, for despite Paul Burke holding the distinction of being Joan's least charismatic leading man since David Brian, this feature-length pilot showed promise.

At around this time, Joan was approached to guest star in an episode of the hugely popular *Batman* television series, but rejected the role to portray Amanda True in a lamentable feature-length episode of *The Man From U.N.C.L.E.*, which she later said had been her biggest mistake since *This Woman is Dangerous*. Also at around this time, Christina was offered a part in the Chicago production of Neil Simon's play *Barefoot in the Park*, starring Myrna Loy. This resulted in a reunion of sorts with her mother, who when she learned that Christina was planning to marry its director, Harvey Medlinsky, with typical Crawford flair decided to take over – and pay for – the proceedings. Her favourite eaterie/night spot was the fashionable '21', where she frequently entertained show-business pals and Pepsi executives. Joan was no longer on the firm's board of directors, following a bust-up with the new president, Donald Kendall, but she was still on the payroll, earning $40,000 a year as spokeswoman and goodwill ambassadress. She hired the top floor of '21' for the ceremony, which took place on 20 May 1966 – as close to what would have been her and Alfred's wedding anniversary as the establishment could arrange. But Christina's marriage, like her renewed relationship with Joan, would prove short-lived.

Joan was up against tough competition when she made *Circus of Blood* (US title: *Berserk*) for Herman Cohen, in England during the spring of 1967. Her co-star was British show-business monument Diana Dors (1931–84), the revered platinum blonde once regarded in the UK as a serious rival of Marilyn Monroe. Unlike Marilyn, however, Dors was affable, reliable, warm and just entering her more rewarding 'character roles' phase. Joan had especially asked for her, having admired her portrayal of the condemned killer in *Yield to the Night* (aka *Blonde Sinner*), which she had seen in England during a break from shooting *Esther Costello*. Supporting was Ty Hardin, a 36-year-old blond beefcake, who had appeared in the Western series *Bronco*. Joan complained during the shoot that she was tired of hearing Hardin persistently quoting from the Bible, and denied rumours that they were having an affair – six-times married, Hardin later became a self-styled Baptist minister.

In the film Joan played circus proprietress Monica Rivers, whose latest big-top tour is blighted by a series of gruesome murders. The first victim is tightrope walker Gasper the Great (Thomas Cimarro), who plunges to his death when his wire is sabotaged. Monica tries to coerce her business partner, Dorando (Michael Gough), into helping her cash in on the publicity. Shocked, he asks her to buy him out so that he can leave and, needless to say, he soon ends up dead. Prior to this, Monica has hired a replacement for Gaspar, Frank Hawkins (Hardin), whose speciality is doing his routine over a bed of spikes, without a safety net. Frank suspects that Monica may be the killer and confronts her; rather than denying the fact, she is seemingly so besotted with him that she allows him to blackmail her into giving him a share of the business – we assume at this stage because she is plotting *his* demise. At the same time, Monica's tearaway daughter, Angela (Judy Geeson), arrives home after being expelled from school, and Monica gives her a job as the knife-thrower's assistant. Next we see Frank high above the crowd when a dagger sails through the air and plunges between his shoulder blades, sending him plummeting to his death on the spikes below. This time, however, there is a witness – the investigating detective (Robert Hardy). The killer is not Monica, but Angela (hardly surprising, many thought, considering Joan's on-screen offspring's track record!), and as she flees the scene, after unsuccessfully trying to murder her mother, she trips over a live cable and is electrocuted.

During this trip to England, Joan appeared on Michael Parkinson's television show and during rehearsals refused a glass of water, telling the studio assistant that she had brought her own supply: dipping into her handbag, she extracted a large silver flask and filled her glass with neat vodka. She refused to talk about her two elder children and told radio's Pete Murray in another interview, 'Tina is appearing in a daytime soap back home, and Christopher's divorced. Right now he's serving in Vietnam. Saigon, I think.' What she did not add was that she had not spoken to her troublesome son for several years – since the day he had spat in her face and told her how much he hated her, she alleged – or that she had never seen (and never would) her grandchildren. Joan also fumed that while one tabloid had affectionately referred to her as 'Her Serene Crawfordship', the pop singer Cilla Black had apparently never heard of her, and piped in a television interview in her nasal Liverpool twang, 'Everybody was saying Crawford was in town. I thought they were talking about the biscuits people!' What Joan said in response to this remains unprintable.

Circus of Blood was hugely successful – an A-movie made on a B-movie budget. Joan was easily old enough to be Diana Dors's mother, yet in their scenes together she looks like a slightly older sister with an even better figure. 'Her legs rival Dietrich's,' *Hollywood Screen Parade* enthused, 'and her tigress personality puts to shame most of the newest kittens who call themselves 1968-style actresses. She is a genuine movie star whose appeal never diminishes.' In fact, Joan had been given advice by Marlene on how to play her part: in 1953 Marlene had played ringmaster in a charity performance of the Ringling Brothers Circus at the Madison Square Garden, a precursor of her one-woman shows, and the costume Joan wears in *Circus of Blood* is a same-size copy, designed by Edith Head, of the one Marlene had worn back then.

In March 1968, Joan officially turned sixty (she was actually 64). This year she was in turn rumoured to be 'on the verge of marrying' Method teacher Lee Strasberg, 'passionately involved' with a married-with-children Pepsi executive, and 'deeply in love' with seventy-year-old gay George Cukor! There was also talk of a relationship with *Valley of the Dolls* author Jacqueline Susann, a titbit said to have incensed Bette Davis, pencilled in to play the novel's alcoholic, neurotic heroine, Helen Lawson (as was Judy Garland), in the screen adaptation. Bette would lose interest in the part upon learning that Helen had been based on Joan; Judy would lose the part when the studio declared her uninsurable; and it eventually would go to Susan Hayward – who would be absolutely hammered by the critics.

At around this time Joan is reputed to have turned down any number of parts, including the one in *Cactus Flower* given to Ingrid Bergman. She turned up uninvited at a reception for the film at '21', where the guests of honour were Bergman and her co-star, Goldie Hawn. 'Well, dear,' she told *Time-Life* reporter Jim Watters, 'this *is* my local, so surely you wouldn't expect me to go someplace else, would you?' Watters described in his piece how Joan had walked up to Bergman, whom she had never liked, and pronounced in best Tallulah Bankhead fashion, 'Ingrid, darling. I simply *adore* your dress. Tell me, did you make it yourself?'

Joan taped an episode of *The Lucy Show* but there was an instant clash of personalities between her and Lucille Ball, who was almost as feisty and disagreeable off the screen as Bette Davis. Joan was apparently so desperate for work, and so resentful of the successes others had had in the roles she had rejected, that she would have been willing to do almost anything, with almost *anyone*, even a woman regarded by her as 'one of the biggest shits in Hollywood'. She told a reporter from *TV Guide*, 'After some of my co-stars, Judy the chimpanzee [from television's *Daktari*] would be a breeze.' Lucille Ball had never liked Joan, but when the ageing Gloria Swanson dropped out of her show at the last minute and the producer suggested Joan, she reluctantly agreed to have her in the show. She played herself in a sketch with Lucy and her regular next-door-neighbour stooge, Ethel (Vivian Vance). After their car breaks down, the pair stumble into a mansion, where they discover one of the great stars of yesteryear (Joan) on her hands and knees, scrubbing the floor. All went well until, tipped off (or so she told *McCall's* magazine) that Joan was an alcoholic, Lucy decided to see if this was true by rifling through her handbag. Sure enough, she located Joan's vodka supply and Lucy claimed that Joan was only allowed to continue with the show because there was insufficient time to find a replacement. After the taping, as was her custom, Lucy invited Joan and the rest of the cast and crew to dine with herself and husband Gary Morton at Don the Beachcomber's restaurant. Unable to forgive Lucy for humiliating her in front of the entire set, Joan's response was an equally vocal, 'Go fuck yourself, lady!'

In 1968 Tallulah Bankhead died unexpectedly of Asian flu, aged 65, and Joan sent a wreath to the funeral in Maryland. This year too, Franchot Tone died. Although Joan had rejected his re-marriage proposal, she had seen a lot of him since moving to New York, and when she sold the apartment she had shared with Alfred and moved into a smaller, more affordable one at 150 East 69th Street, Franchot – wheelchair-bound in his last months – had become a semi-permanent fixture. In 1966 he and Joan had spent a week at his regular holiday haunt, Muskoka Lake in Canada, sleeping in separate rooms and taking long woodland walks far from the prying eyes of the press. When Franchot had been diagnosed terminally ill with cancer and had had a lung removed, Joan had helped out with paying his medical bills – mindless of her own precarious financial state. She also contributed towards the funeral costs and had his ashes scattered over Muskoka Lake.

Also in 1968, Joan replaced Christina (hospitalised for abdominal surgery after returning from Mexico to acquire the quickie divorce arranged and paid for by her mother) in five episodes of NBC's glossy afternoon soap, *The Secret Storm*. This was without doubt the most foolish and, in pre-

Dynasty days, the most potentially damaging career move she had ever made, even though the advance publicity (shows were taped several months ahead of transmission) sent the ratings rocketing. It has always been an American tradition – rarely occurring elsewhere – for fired or indisposed soap stars to be replaced by lookalikes, because writing them out of an ongoing storyline is impracticable. Every single one of the big US soaps has been made ludicrous at some time or other by this practice, but so far as is known, this is the only time that an actress has stood in for her *daughter*.

Twenty-one-year-old Stephen Spielberg, working then as a producer for NBC, was suitably impressed with Joan's contribution to *The Secret Storm* to offer her a part in the pilot episode of *Night Gallery*, a hugely popular series of self-contained Hitchcock-style dramas. Initially she was reticent to accept, until she learned that each episode would feature a different major star and that she would only have to appear once. She played a blind woman who has the misfortune to recover her sight during the Great New York Blackout of 1965. The pilot effected a reunion with *Queen Bee* co-star Barry Sullivan and reviews were exceptional. Joan, however, made it clear that she had no intention of making a second career out of 'inferior' television appearances and her views remained unchanged four years later when she told John Springer, 'Television has taken over to such a degree. They chew up and eat up so much material doing five a week [soaps], there's no material left for motion pictures.' Others, too, voiced their complaints, none more so than her friend Rock Hudson, who denounced television as: 'That fucking oblong box in the corner of the living room' – but nevertheless bowed to pressure a few years later, topping the ratings and earning a fortune from the *McMillan & Wife* series.

In the late summer of 1969, Joan flew to England to make what would be her final feature film, *Trog*, at the Bray studios. Produced by Herman Cohen and directed by Freddie Francis, this was a 'monster' picture – her co-star was an eight-foot troglodyte – which Joan's fans said she should have rejected, period. She, however, was defensive of her choice. 'People ask me why I took this science fiction role in *Trog*,' she told John Deighton of *Today's Cinema*. 'It's because I've never *done* any science fiction. I've never played a *doctor* before!' Francis, a former clapper-boy-turned-cinematographer, who had been involved with such British New Wave gems as *Room at the Top* and *Saturday Night and Sunday Morning* (1959 and 1960 respectively), was in the middle of his horror phase, which peaked with the classic *Dracula Has Risen From the Grave* (1968). The budget for *Trog* was so small – and most of it swallowed up by Joan's salary and expenses – that while shooting the exteriors she was forced to eschew her customary luxury trailer and make costume changes in the back of a Transit van. Even so, she said, the inconvenience was worth it because it was one of the few films being made in England at the time that did not contain sex scenes. Asked what, in her opinion, were the worst aspects of modern-day film making, she told Deighton:

The nudity. Sex is such a personal thing that it should *remain* personal. Each one of us should in his or her mind create *mentally* what would happen between a Gable and a Garbo. They would start the big love scenes but they didn't need to be naked – and I think people were greater fans in the Forties than they are today because they went home with a romantic idea, a romantic view of life. And I think they became better lovers by pretending to be a Gable or a Garbo . . . I know what sex is and I know how beautiful it can be, but films of that sort don't interest me in the least.

In May 1970, Joan returned to Stephens College to receive the establishment's first President's Citation Award – 'In recognition of supreme post-school achievement.' She was introduced as 'Joan Crawford, that exemplary mother, movie star, businesswoman and philanthropist.' It was all for the benefit of the press, of course – Stephens needed to influence and extend its patronage – but Joan was touched by the accolade, although she had only been at the school for a few months. Dabbing her eyes, she told the audience, 'I left here when I was just thirteen [sic], adopted five children, four of which were drop-outs. I too was a drop-out. I can't understand why you've given me this, but I'm *grateful*.'

For some time Joan had been dictating her second book of memoirs, and the result was *My Way of Life*, published in 1971. Again she did it for the money, and like her first book it was an over-glamourised account of her life, almost as Hollywood would have wanted to film it. There were shades of the earlier *Marlene Dietrich's ABC* (1961), wherein Marlene had cleverly interspersed aspects of her life with cookery tips, advice for *hausfraus*, witticisms and poignant observations on the world about her. Fred Lawrence Guiles called it: 'A kind of etiquette guide for corporate wives'.

In August 1972, Joan made her celluloid swansong as a guest in ABC television's *Sixth Sense* series. Her fee was a paltry $2,500, which was doubled with the addition of personal expenses: limousine, five-star accommodation, lackey-maid, fresh flowers on every surface and an endless supply of her favourite tipple. On the evening filming wrapped she was seen on the town with Rock Hudson – a date they had arranged to once more prevent the press from outing him as a gay.

The episode of *Sixth Sense* – entitled 'Dear Joan, We're Going to Scare You to Death' – brought numerous offers of television work, which Joan turned down. She had a good many years of decent acting left in her, she declared, and did not want to bow out typecast as a 'horror queen'. She was approached by publicist John Springer, who on behalf of MGM had acquired the screen rights to Stephen Sondheim's smash-hit Broadway musical *Follies*, which had helped resurrect Yvonne de Carlo's career. The story was a tribute to the dying days of vaudeville and its most famous numbers were 'I'm Still Here' and 'I'm Just a Broadway Baby', famously performed by Eartha Kitt and Elaine Stritch respectively. Springer had transferred the setting to the demise of the studio system, and obviously had big ideas, also approaching Richard Burton, Elizabeth Taylor – and Bette Davis, which makes one wonder how serious Joan was about the project. Not surprisingly perhaps, adequate funds were not forthcoming, and the film was scrapped. For Joan there would be no more offers: though she never officially announced her retirement, word got around that unless something truly worthwhile came along, there would be no more Crawford movies. And nothing ever did.

Springer, however, did not give up on Joan. In 1973 he staged his *Legendary Ladies of the Movies* series at Town Hall, New York. Each show, similar to the British *An Evening With . . .* showcases, began with a film retrospective and was followed by a personal appearance, in which the star answered not-always-vetted questions from the host/audience. Bette Davis was the first to take the podium on 4 February, followed by Sylvia Sidney and Myrna Loy; after Joan came Rosalind Russell and Lana Turner. Joan, terrified of personal appearances to the point of being physically ill, only accepted when Ginger Rogers (herself a stand-in for Jean Arthur) dropped out, and faced her ordeal on Sunday 5 April.

What is arguably the most revealing interview of Joan's later career was preceded by clips from *Grand Hotel*, *Dancing Lady*, *A Woman's Face*, *The Women*, the later *Possessed*, *Harriet Craig*, *Sudden Fear*, *Flamingo Road*, *What Ever Happened to Baby Jane?*, *Johnny Guitar* and *Mildred Pierce*. Springer later explained that, even at the last minute, he was terrified of the event backfiring when Joan looked like she might have been about to head for the exit, and had to be literally pushed on to the stage for her last public performance, likened by some to Judy Garland's comeback recital at Carnegie Hall, twelve years earlier.

Wearing a dark gown, split to the thigh to reveal her still-shapely legs, Joan bowed deeply, and braved a deafening applause that lasted *eleven* minutes. She broke down – and this was *not* a part of the act, as cynics suggested – and told the 2,000 mostly gay male fans who had fought to acquire tickets, 'I never knew there was so much *love*!'

She did, of course, and as she settled back in her chair – the tumbler of 'water' next to her being constantly topped up, and offering her Dutch courage – her responses brought spasmodic outbursts of applause, laughter and a few tears from those who had been faithful from her starlet days until now – those who would remain so until the very end and who were mentioned personally by name. Springer asked her to explain the evolution from Lucille LeSueur, by way of Billie Cassin, to Joan Crawford. Still dabbing her eyes she replied, 'All I know is I'm *here*!' She paid tribute to those who had helped her set and maintain her trends, from flapper to screen martyr: as there had only ever been one Garbo, she said, so there would only be one Adrian, one Edith Head, one Jean-Louis. She spoke of the importance of fans, of how it was vital to stay in touch with the ones who had put her in the privileged position she was in – 'You don't find time, you *make* time.' She allegorised the confidence and courage she had only found later in life, courtesy of Alfred Steele:

> We grow in spirit and wisdom, and I was fortunate to have a husband who told me we were going into thunderheads before the captain of the ship told us . . . So I learned after he died to tell myself, 'We're going into a thunderhead' – and then the captain announced it. You see, I was ahead of the captain again.

Joan was critical of the behaviour of certain actors and actresses, though for the moment, Bette Davis's name was not mentioned:

> Let's talk about the Academy Awards. I think everyone had the cutes, and each one who came on after the couple before tried to be funnier. The dignity and beauty of the Academy Awards is lost without the Gregory Pecks, the Charlton Hestons . . . And this year I was appalled at the behaviour of everyone, including Mr Brando . . .

She was referring to Brando's refusal to attend the ceremony to accept his Oscar for *The Godfather* when, as a means of protesting against Hollywood's treatment and prejudice against Native Americans, he had sent a squaw to collect the award. So, what was her opinion of politically minded actors using such platforms to air their grievances?

> Oh, brother! Just accept and be *grateful* for the honour! Don't try and get on national television to make your pleas . . . *Never* discuss politics or religion!

And who, in the opinion of Hollywood's biggest female icon, were the big women stars of today? Joan replied, 'I think Miss Glenda Jackson is one of the greatest. I adore Miss Katharine Hepburn and Audrey Hepburn. And I wish to God we could get Garbo back!'

And why the infamous 'bleep' during her television interview with David Frost, when he had asked her who had been her favourite leading man and why?

I said that the reason he was the greatest actor in the whole world, the
most exciting – *Gable, the King* – was [that] he had 'em [balls], and I did
that [points down below] and they knew exactly what I meant. [And,
Springer wanted to know, were there any others?] There was Mr Spencer
Tracy, Mr Robert Taylor, Jimmy Stewart. I could go on and on, but we
don't have that much time tonight. I have been the luckiest woman in the
world [starting to cry again] to have had the career I've had.

At this stage of the interview, John Springer divulged a snippet of information
that had been kept from the media – that Joan had been in the running to appear
in *Butterflies Are Free*, in the film version and on Broadway, both subsequently
abandoned. Joan had turned the former down in favour of her actress friend
Eileen Heckart, who had won an Oscar for it at the recent ceremony and had
declined the latter because of paralysing stage-fright. 'I don't know why I'm
here, tonight,' she told Springer, 'I'm *really* frightened. I was born in front of a
camera and I really don't know anything else.'

Then Springer, eager to introduce Bette Davis into the proceedings, asked
whether she had ever felt any sense of *competition* with other actresses?

Oh, I love competition! I really think that competition is one of the great
challenges in life. We must have challenges, otherwise we don't grow. I think
Bette Davis and *Baby Jane* was one of the greatest challenges I've ever had
[much laughter from the audience] and I meant that kindly. I had more
control and learned more discipline. Bette is of a different temperament
than I. She has to yell every morning and so I just sat around and knitted.
I knitted a scarf from Hollywood to Malibu [absolute hilarity from the fans]. I
went down to 119 pounds from 130, but that's all right . . .

Next, Springer brought up the subject his producer had allegedly advised him
to avoid: the fact that everybody seemed to have rebellious children
nowadays, and that though Joan was considered a loving mother, would she
be the same stern disciplinarian if she had to go through it all again? She
managed to acquit herself with ease: 'Yes, this is merely my opinion, but I
believe the reason most of the kids are on pot and other junk is because they
don't have enough love or discipline at home.'

Having shot Springer an anxious glance, which suggested that she did
not wish to delve further into the subject, Joan glossed over her life as a
businesswoman, discussed the aborted musical *Great Day*, her only meetings
with Garbo and F Scott Fitzgerald, dismissed *This Woman Is Dangerous* as
the worst movie she had ever made, then the subject returned to feuds. Jean-
Pierre Léaud, the in-house star of Truffaut and Godard, who had made a big
impression with Brando in *Last Tango in Paris* (1973), had recently declared
in a television interview that in his professional opinion the greatest moments

in American cinema had been Buster Keaton in *all* of his films, and Joan
Crawford in *Johnny Guitar* – the one where, dubbed into French, all the male
protagonists had addressed each other as 'Monsieur'. Joan, no Keaton fan,
responded with a snappy:

> 'I had a few problems with *Johnny Guitar*, with the cast. Buster Keaton
> wasn't there. I would have preferred *him* to a couple of people. And
> [Norma Shearer, Joan emulating her clipped tones] was married to the
> boss and I was just an actress. She didn't like my dress, so she changed
> it nineteen times. It cost the picture a fortune – but *I* ended up wearing the
> gold dress and turban!'

Having successfully tackled the dreaded Davis and Shearer, Springer
risked his hand at another couple of tetchy points: Joan's porno films and
daughter Christina's acting career:

> SPRINGER: You have been shocked at the permissiveness of this
> generation and the flood of obscene and pornographic films. Were you
> not in your early career a centrefold calendar-girl yourself?
> JOAN: I think sex is beautiful, but you have to be alone – with somebody
> else you love, not on the screen, not in the theatre. I get embarrassed! As
> for [being a calendar-girl] I was never that lucky. I didn't know Hugh
> Hefner then!

Asked if she would ever appear on the stage or on-screen with Christina,
Joan faked a smile, acknowledged that her daughter was a fine actress, and
– the vodka probably starting to get to her – drawled, 'I've never been *asked*
to appear with her.'

Cynics suggested at the time that had Springer not asked about
Christina, already rumoured to be planning an explosive kiss-and-tell of her
childhood, Joan might not have begun shuffling in her chair as if hinting she
had had enough. Even so, the evening ended on a note of hilarity when a fan
in the audience, no doubt having read the supermarket tabloid reports
concerning Jeff Chandler's fondness for cross-dressing, drew attention to
Joan's character's pronouncement in *Female on the Beach*: 'Instincts of a
stallion, the pride of an alley cat.' 'That's right,' she grinned, before bringing
the house down with her response to Springer's final question, 'Are you
aware of the nickname ['Fuck-Me'] your famous ankle-strap shoes are
known by?' 'I think I know the first letter – "F",' she replied. 'But I think, if
you remember, they held me up a goddam long time!'

On 10 May 1973 Joan was officially retired by Pepsi – the occasion
being her 65th (actually 69th) birthday. Financially she would be no worse
off, for she was awarded an annual pension of $50,000 – $10,000 more than
she had been getting as a board member – but the fringe benefits, such as the

luxury limo, free use of the company jet and a personal assistant, were withdrawn. From now on she would spend more and more time in her New York apartment, writing hundreds of letters to fans every week.

In the December of the same year, her best friend William Haines died of cancer. Joan was devastated. She flew to Hollywood to console Jimmy Shields and tried to convince him, when he told her that he was thinking of ending it all, that he should live for his lover's memory as she had Alfred's and Clark Gable's. Haines had left Jimmy a very wealthy man. In 1969 Haines had completed a $1 million decorating project for Winfield House in London's Regent's Park, the official residence of the US Ambassador to Britain. This had brought in more commissions than Haines had been able to handle, earning him more money than even he, with his extravagant tastes, had been able to lavish on his loved ones in his declining years. His fortune was divided up between his two sisters and Jimmy, who stuck it out for almost another year before killing himself, leaving a note that read: 'It's no good without Billy.'

With seemingly little else to do and no man in her life, Joan withdrew from public life, devoting her time to her two younger daughters, now married with children of their own. There was the odd party here and there, and private get-togethers with fans who had become personal friends. She spoke but rarely to Christina and completely denied Christopher's existence. Joan's son had remarried and the first time he turned up at her apartment block to introduce the latest addition to his family was the last: the concierge had been given strict instructions to send him packing. According to other visitors, there was virtually nothing inside her plush home – neither photographs nor other memorabilia – to suggest that not so long before she had been one of the biggest stars in Hollywood. Like Marlene Dietrich, living as a semi-recluse in Paris, she disguised her voice when answering the telephone and pretended to be the maid.

During the spring of 1974, an anonymous caller left a message on Joan's answering-machine, threatening to kidnap her – or worse – should she step out of her apartment. Agents from the FBI kept the place under surveillance for four weeks, and several suspects were questioned, but no charges brought against them. Joan installed a costly security system and tried to put the matter behind her. Under duress, she agreed to co-host a book party for John Springer with her old friend Rosalind Russell. The event took place on 23 September at the Rockerfeller Centre's Rainbow Room. Joan turned up in a red chiffon gown, wearing $100,000 worth of diamonds, and only the curious addition of a short brown wig prevented her from looking much younger than her seventy years. Russell was suffering from rheumatoid arthritis, her face bloated on account of the cortisone injections she was having. Joan therefore tried to prevent the press from photographing her in

case they jumped to the wrong conclusion that she might have been dying –
she was not, though within two years she would have succumbed to cancer.
Even so, Russell insisted upon them being snapped together, but it was Joan
who lost out when the pictures were published the next day: they showed her
grinning at some joke, her eyes all but bulging out of their sockets and her
wig askew, looking like a caricature of Phyllis Diller. She had been scheduled
to make several more personal appearances, rounding off the year as guest of
honour at the annual Pepsi convention – but Joan, who had spent the best
part of her life battling with an acute lack of self-confidence, called the board
and told them, 'If *that's* the way I look, nobody's going to see me any more.'

More and more, as she sensed the end approaching, Joan immersed
herself in Christian Science, the religious movement established by Mary
Baker Eddy in 1879. Like many movie stars, she had first embraced this in
the Thirties when Jean Harlow's mother had been an adherent – not that it
had done Harlow much good. The Church's teachings dictated that as God
is good and entirely spiritual, malady and evil are unreal, therefore medical
intervention is unnecessary to overcome ills. They also condemned drinking
and smoking, though Joan preferred to ignore this part of the discipline.

Because Joan had very rarely been ill, she had always considered herself
invincible – or at least that she would simply move from this life to the next
with a modicum of physical discomfort. So far as is known she had attended
just the one Christian Science meeting, where she was hounded by the press
and autograph hunters. Now she began attending private gatherings hosted by
a Mrs Markham and seemed to derive some comfort from this. And finally she
gave up her beloved vodka and cigarettes.

In September 1976, white-haired, wide-eyed, looking slightly gaunt but
still every inch the glamorous movie star, Joan, with her shih-tzu dog,
Princess Lotus Blossom, attended what would be her last official photoshoot
with John Engstead, who had first photographed her while she had been
making *Mildred Pierce*. She had dozens of copies printed and included these
with her last batch of Christmas cards to her friends and longest-serving fans.
Director Vincent Sherman's was post-scripted: 'If you don't like the picture,
please throw it away – I'll understand.' She suffered her final insults early in
the New Year, firstly when Carol Burnett did a spoof take of her as Jenny
Stewart in *Torch Song* as part of her television show, then when CBS
Television gave Bette Davis the American Film Institute Award.

Diagnosed with pancreatic cancer, though the news was never made
public, Joan refused to be hospitalised and her bedroom was turned into a
treatment room. She spent most of her waking hours watching her old films,
lamenting all the co-stars she had loved, those who had preceded her to the
grave: Gable, Franchot, John Garfield, Alan Curtis, Jeff Chandler, Zachary

Scott and Conrad Veidt. And every day Mrs Markham dropped in to assure her that, though her body was giving up on her, her spirit was growing stronger – that if she allowed her to take her to a Christian Science nursing home, she would be completely cured. Joan ignored this, and used up what little strength she had left telephoning friends and writing to fans. In control until the last, she told no one she was ill, not even the twins. By the end of April, her weight had dropped to 84 pounds, and it was an effort for her to get from her bed to the bathroom. Eventually, knowing that she would be no longer able to care for her beloved dog, she gave her away.

On 9 May 1977, the eve of what would have been her 22nd wedding anniversary with Alfred – assuming of course, with Joan's track record, that their marriage would have lasted this long – Joan watched one of her movies with her housekeeper and a female fan who stayed the night. The next morning Joan was first up to cook breakfast, fussing until the last. Shortly afterwards, at around ten, while the other two were eating, she returned to her bed – and minutes later Hollywood's undisputed martyr just slipped away.

Epilogue

There was no postmortem: cancer was only hinted at, and a medical examiner 'confirmed' that Joan had died of 'acute coronary occlusion'. Immediately, as would happen three months later with Elvis Presley, and a month after that with Maria Callas, there were suggestions that Joan had stage-managed her exit from the world. Douglas Fairbanks Jr told me, fifteen years later, 'With Joan, anything might have been possible.'

Her death, along with one of the recent John Engstead photographs, made the front pages of just about every major newspaper in the world. The editorial in the *New York Times* called her: 'A quintessential superstar, an epitome of timeless glamour who personified for decades the dreams and disappointments of millions of American women.'

The funeral took place at Campbell's Funeral Home in New York on 13 May 1977 – an ominous date that Joan's friends said would have brought a smile to her face. That morning, all the film lots in Hollywood held a one-minute silence. Among the mourners for the fifteen-minute Christian Science ceremony were all four Crawford children, Brian Aherne, Myrna Loy (who turned her back on Christina), Van Johnson and Andy Warhol – who, along with his hustler-discovery Joe Dallesandro, brought Polaroid cameras to capture the event for a Factory exhibition. (The following year, Warhol would splash out $20,000 on Crawford memorabilia, mostly old make-up tubes, false eyelashes and costume jewellery, from a Christie's auction in New York.) Everyone expected Bette Davis to show up, but this would have been the height of hypocrisy: she sent neither flowers nor a message of sympathy, and made no public announcement. Joan was cremated, and according to her wishes her ashes were interred next to Alfred's at Ferncliff Cemetery, Westchester County, New York.

Joan's memorial service took place on 17 May in New York's All Souls Unitarian Church. Pearl Bailey sang 'He'll Understand'; the Reverend Walter Kring read the 23rd Psalm. Eulogies were read by Cliff Robertson, Anita Loos, Geraldine Brooks (who died a few weeks later) and George Cukor, who observed,

> She was the perfect image of the movie star and, as such, largely the creation of her own indomitable will. She had, of course, very remarkable material to work with: a quick native intelligence, tremendous animal vitality, a lovely figure and above all her face – that extraordinarily sculptured construction of lines and planes, finely chiselled like the mask of some classical divinity from fifth-century Greece. It caught the light superbly so that you could photograph her from any angle, and her face moved beautifully . . . The camera saw, I suspect, a side of her that no flesh-and-blood lover ever saw.

On 20 May 1977, the newspapers published for the first time – and perhaps not unintentionally, to spare the feelings of her family at the recent media/public events – details of Joan's will, which she had signed on 28 October 1976. Of her $2 million-plus estate, she had left each of her adopted twin daughters, Cathy and Cindy, a trust fund of $77,500. She left $35,000 to her Los Angeles secretary, Bettina Barker; $10,000 to her New York secretary, Florence Walsh; and $5,000 each to publicist Michael O'Shea, make-up artist Monty Westmore and her oldest fan, Bernice Oshatz. Other bequests were made to close friends. There were also bequests to her six favourite charities: the Muscular Dystrophy Association of America, the American Cancer Society, the American Heart Association, the Wiltwyck School for Boys, the United Service Organization of New York and the Motion Picture Country Home, which Joan had co-founded.

A special coda to her will included the words: 'It is my intention to make no provision herein for my son Christopher or my daughter Christina for reasons which are well known to them.' The reasons, quite obviously, were Christina and Christopher's treatment of their mother over the previous twenty years.

Perhaps the last word should be left to Joan's friend George Cukor, who wrote in the *New York Times* a few days after her death:

> I thought that Joan Crawford could never die. Come to think of it, as long as celluloid holds together and the word Hollywood means anything to anyone, she never will.

APPENDIX I

The Films of Joan Crawford

THE CASTING COUCH/ VELVET LIPS/THE PLUMBER   pre-1925
So-called 'stag' films known to have been made by Joan Crawford before she arrived in Hollywood turned up several times in her later career when would-be blackmailers tried to extort money from MGM and Warner Brothers. They are thought to have been destroyed, though occasionally newspaper reports appear suggesting that copies are hidden in vaults of various 'enthusiasts'.

MISS MGM   MGM, 1925
Advertising short 'featuring Lucille LeSueur'. No other details.

PROUD FLESH   MGM, 1925
Director: King Vidor. With Eleanor Boardman, Harrison Ford, Trixie Friganza. Lucille LeSueur was an extra. 65 mins.

LADY OF THE NIGHT   MGM, 1925
Director: Monta Bell. With Norma Shearer, Malcolm McGregor, George K Arthur. Lucille LeSueur was an extra. 70 mins.

THE ONLY THING   MGM, 1925
Director: Jack Conway. Story: Elinor Glyn. With Eleanor Boardman, Conrad Nagel, Arthur Edmund Carewe, Dale Fuller. Lucille LeSueur was an extra. 65 mins.

THE MERRY WIDOW   MGM, 1925
Directors: Erich von Stroheim, Monta Bell. With Mae Murray, John Gilbert, Roy D'Arcy, Tully Marshall. Lucille LeSueur was an extra. 70 mins.

PRETTY LADIES   MGM, 1925
Director: Monta Bell. Story: Adela Rogers St Johns. With ZaSu Pitts, Norma
Shearer, Tom Moore, Lilyan Tashman, Conrad Nagel, Ann Pennington, Myrna
Loy, Lucille LeSueur. 72 mins.

THE CIRCLE   MGM, 1925
Director: Frank Borzage. Based on the play by W Somerset Maugham. With
Eleanor Boardman, Creighton Hale, Eulalie Jensen, Malcolm McGregor, Alec B
Francis. Lucille LeSueur was an extra. 80 mins.

OLD CLOTHES   MGM, 1925
Director: Edward Cline. Producer: Jack Coogan Sr. Story: William Mack.
Photography: Frank B Good. With Jackie Coogan, Max Davidson, Joan
Crawford, Allan Forrest, Stanton Heck. 65 mins.

SALLY, IRENE AND MARY   MGM, 1925
Director: Edmund Goulding. With William Haines, Constance Bennett, Sally
O'Neil, Joan Crawford, Ray Howard, Henry Kolker, Douglas Gilmore. 58 mins.

THE BOOB (GB: The Yokel)   MGM, 1926
Director: William Wellman. Story: George Scarborough/Annette Westbay.
Photography: William Daniels. With George K Arthur, Joan Crawford, Charles
Murray, Gertude Olmstead. 60 mins.

TRAMP, TRAMP, TRAMP   FIRST NATIONAL, 1926
Director: Harry Edwards. Story: Frank Capra/George Duffy/Tim Whelan/
J Frank Holliday/Hal Conklin/Murray Roth. Photography: George Spear/Elgin
Lesley. With Harry Langdon, Joan Crawford, Brooks Benedict, Carlton Griffith,
Edwards Davis, Tom Murray. 60 mins.

PARIS (GB: Shadows of Paris)   MGM, 1926
Director/Story: Edmund Goulding. Photography: John Arnold. With Joan
Crawford, Charles Ray, Douglas Gilmore, Rose Dione, Michael Visaroff. 64
mins.

THE TAXI DANCER   MGM, 1926
Director: Harry Millarde. Story: Robert Terry Shannon. Photography: Ira H
Morgan. With Joan Crawford, Owen Moore, Marc MacDermott, Douglas
Gilmore, Gertrude Astor, Rockliffe Fellowes. 64 mins.

WINNERS OF THE WILDERNESS   MGM, 1927
Director: W S Van Dyke. Story: John Thomas Neville. Photography: Clyde De Vinna. With Tim McCoy, Joan Crawford, Edward Connelly, Frank Currier, Roy D'Arcy, Tom O'Brien. 65 mins.

THE UNDERSTANDING HEART   MGM, 1927
Director: Jack Conway. Story: Peter Kyne. Photography: John Arnold. With Francis X Bushman Jr, Joan Crawford, Carmel Myers, Rockliffe Fellowes, Harvey Clark, Richard Carle. 65 mins.

THE UNKNOWN   MGM, 1927
Director/Story: Tod Browning. Script: Waldemar Young. Photography: Merritt Gerstad. With Lon Chaney, Joan Crawford, Norman Kerry, Nick de Ruiz, Frank Lanning, John George. 65 mins.

TWELVE MILES OUT   MGM, 1927
Director: Jack Conway. Based on the play by William Anthony McGuire. Photography: Ira H Morgan. With John Gilbert, Joan Crawford, Ernest Torrence, Eileen Percy, Dorothy Sebastian, Betty Compson, Tom O'Brien. 82 mins.

SPRING FEVER   MGM, 1927
Director: Edward Sedgwick. Based on the play by Vincent Lawrence. Photography: Ira H Morgan. With William Haines, Joan Crawford, George K Arthur, Eileen Percy, George Fawcett, Edward Earle. 60 mins.

WEST POINT (GB: Eternal Youth)   MGM, 1928
Director: Raymond Schrock. Story: Edward Sedgwick. Photography: Ira H Morgan. With William Haines, Joan Crawford, Ralph Emerson, William Bakewell, Edward Richardson, Neil Neely, Leon Kellar. 78 mins.

ROSE MARIE   MGM, 1928
Director/Screenplay/Sets: Lucien Hubbard. Based on the operetta by Oscar Hammerstein and Otto Harbach. Photography: John Arnold. With Joan Crawford, James Murray, House Peters, Creighton Hale, Gibson Gowland, Polly Moran, Gertrude Astor, Ralph Yearslet, Sven Hugo Borg. 70 mins.

ACROSS TO SINGAPORE   MGM, 1928
Director: William Nigh. Story: Ben Ames Williams. A remake of *All the Brothers Were Valiant* (1923). Photography: John Seitz. With Ramon Novarro, Joan Crawford, Ernest Torrence, Frank Currier, Edward Connelly, Duke Martin. 76 mins.

FOUR WALLS MGM, 1928
Director: William Nigh. Story: Dana Burnet/George Abbot. Photography: James Wong Howe. With John Gilbert, Joan Crawford, Carmel Myers, Vera Gordon, Robert Emmet O'Connor, Jack Byron. 60 mins.

OUR DANCING DAUGHTERS MGM, 1928
Director: Harry Beaumont. Producer: Hunt Stromberg. Story: Josephine Lovett. Photography: George Barnes. With Joan Crawford, John Mack Brown, Anita Page, Nils Asther, Dorothy Sebastian, Eddie Nugent, Dorothy Cumming. 82 mins.

THE LAW OF THE RANGE MGM, 1928
Director: William Nigh. Story: Norman Houston. Photography: Clyde DeVinna. With Tim McCoy, Rex Lease, Tenen Holtz, Bodil Rosing. 57 mins.

DREAM OF LOVE MGM, 1928
Director: Fred Niblo. Story: Dorothy Farnham. Based on Scribe and Légouve's play *Adrienne Lecouvreur*. Photography: William Daniels/Oliver Marsh. With Joan Crawford, Nils Asther, Warner Oland, Aileen Pringle, Carmel Myers, Alphonse Martell, Harry Myers, Harry Reinhardt. 64 mins.

THE HOLLYWOOD REVUE OF 1929 MGM, 1929
Director: Charles Reisner. Producer: Harry Rapf. Script: Al Boasberg/Robert Hopkins. Costumes: David Cox. Choreography: Sammy Lee. Artistic Director (as in every subsequent Crawford MGM film): Cedric Gibbons. Photography: Irving G Reis/Maximilian Fabian/John Arnold. With Marie Dressler, Bessie Love, Joan Crawford, Karl Dane, Jack Benny, Marion Davies, Ann Dvorak, Buster Keaton, John Gilbert, Norma Shearer, William Haines, Laurel & Hardy, Cliff Edwards, Conrad Nagel, Lionel Barrymore. 82 mins.

THE DUKE STEPS OUT MGM, 1929
Crawford's first (part) talkie. Director: James Cruze. Script: Raymond Schrock/Dale Van Every. Photography: Ira H Morgan. With William Haines, Joan Crawford, Eddie Nugent, Karl Dane, Tenen Holtz, Luke Cosgrave, Jack Roper. 60 mins.

OUR MODERN MAIDENS MGM, 1929
Despite being released after the last two items, a silent. Director: Jack Conway. Producer: Hunt Stromberg. Story: Josephine Lovett. Photography: Oliver Marsh. Costumes: Adrian. With Rod La Rocque, Joan Crawford, Anita Page, Eddie Nugent, Josephine Dunn, Albert Gran, Douglas Fairbanks Jr. 70 mins.

UNTAMED   MGM, 1929
Director: Jack Conway. Script: Williard Mack/Sylvia Thalberg/Frank Butler.
Photography: Oliver Marsh. With Joan Crawford, Robert Montgomery, Gwen
Lee, Ernest Torrence, John Milijan, Eddie Nugent, Gertrude Astor, Grace
Cunard, Tom O'Brien. 63 mins.

MONTANA MOON   MGM, 1930
Director: Malcolm St Clair. Script: Sylvia Thalberg/Frank Butler. Photography:
William Daniels. With Joan Crawford, John Mack Brown, Ricardo Cortez,
Dorothy Sebastian, Cliff Edwards, Karl Dane, Benny Rubin. 70 mins.

GREAT DAY   MGM, 1930
Director: Harry Pollard. Producer: Irving Thalberg. Script: unknown.
Photographer: William Daniels. Costumes: Adrian. Music: Vincent Youmans.
Lyrics: Billy Rose/Edward Eliscu. With Joan Crawford, Johnny Mack Brown,
Cliff Edwards, Purnell Pratt, Hedda Hopper, Roland Young. Much of the film
had been completed when MGM abandoned the project as part of its brief
'musicals purge' period. Parts of the film, with the minor actors, were used for
Pollard's *The Prodigal* (1931), with Esther Ralston and Lawrence Tibbett.

OUR BLUSHING BRIDES   MGM, 1930
Director: Harry Beaumont. Script: Bess Meredyth/John Howard Lawson.
Photography: Merritt B Gerstad. With Joan Crawford, Robert Montgomery,
Anita Page, Raymond Hackett, Dorothy Sebastian, John Miljan, Hedda Hopper,
Albert Conti, Edward Brophy, Robert Emmet O'Connor, Gwen Lee. 73 mins.

PAID (GB: Within the Law)   MGM, 1930
Director: Sam Wood. Script: Charles MacArthur/Lucien Hubbard. Based on the
play by Bayard Veiller. A remake of *Within the Law* (1917 and 1923).
Photography: Charles Rosher. With Joan Crawford, Robert Armstrong, Marie
Prevost, John Miljan, Kent Douglass, Purnell Pratt, Polly Moran, Gwen Lee,
Isabel Withers, Robert Emmet O'Connor, George Cooper. 75 mins.

DANCE, FOOLS, DANCE   MGM, 1931
Director: Harry Beaumont. Script: Richard Schayer/Aurania Rouverol.
Photography: Charles Rosher. With Joan Crawford, Lester Vail, Earle Foxe,
William Bakewell, Cliff Edwards, Natalie Moorhead, William Holden, Clark
Gable, Joan Marsh, Purnell Pratt, Hale Hamilton, Russell Hopton. 82 mins.

LAUGHING SINNERS (aka: Complete Surrender)   MGM, 1931
Director: Harry Beaumont. Script: Bess Meredyth/Martin Flavin. Based on Kenyon

Nicholson's play *Torch Song*. Photography: Charles Rosher. With Joan Crawford, Neil Hamilton, Clark Gable (replacing John Mack Brown), Marjorie Rambeau, Guy Kibbee, Roscoe Karnes, George F Marion, Gertrude Short. 70 mins.

THIS MODERN AGE   MGM, 1931
Director: Nicholas Grinde. Script: Frank Butler/Sylvia Thalberg. Based on Mildred Cram's story *Girls Together*. Photography: Charles Rosher. With Joan Crawford, Pauline Frederick, Neil Hamilton, Emma Dunn, Hobart Bosworth, Albert Conti, Marcelle Corday, Adrienne d'Ambricourt, Monroe Owsley. 65 mins.

POSSESSED   MGM, 1931
Director: Clarence Brown. Script: Lenore Coffee. Based on Edgar Selwyn's play *The Mirage*. Photography: Oliver T Marsh. With Joan Crawford, Clark Gable, Wallace Ford, Skeets Gallagher, John Miljan, Frank Conroy, Clara Blandick, Marjorie White. 75 mins.

GRAND HOTEL   MGM, 1932
Director: Edmund Goulding. Script: William Drake. Based on the novel/play by Vicki Baum. Photography: William Daniels. With Greta Garbo, John Barrymore, Joan Crawford, Wallace Beery, Lionel Barrymore, Lewis Stone, Jean Hersholt, Ferdinand Gottschalk, Rafaela Ottiano, Purnell Pratt, Frank Conroy, Robert McWade, Tully Marshall. 110 mins.

LETTY LYNTON   MGM, 1932
Director: Clarence Brown. Producer: Hunt Stromberg. Script: John Meehan/Wanda Tuchock. Based on the story by Marie Belloc Lowndes. Photography: Oliver T Marsh. Costumes: Adrian. With Joan Crawford, Robert Montgomery, Nils Asther, May Robson, Lewis Stone, Emma Dunn, Louise Closser Hale, William Pawley, Walter Walker. 83 mins.

RAIN   UNITED ARTISTS, 1932
Director: Lewis Milestone. Screenplay: Maxwell Anderson. Based on W Somerset Maugham's story *Miss Thompson*. Photography: Oliver T Marsh. With Joan Crawford, Walter Huston, William Gargan, Beulah Bondi, Guy Kibbee, Ben Hendricks Jr, Matt Moore, Kendall Lee, Walter Catlett, Fred Howard. 90 mins.

TODAY WE LIVE   MGM, 1933
Director: Howard Hawks. Script: Dwight Taylor/Edith Fitzgerald. Adapted from the story by William Faulkner. Photography: Oliver T Marsh. With Joan Crawford, Gary Cooper, Franchot Tone, Robert Young, Roscoe Karns, Rollo Lloyd, Louise Closser Hale, Hilda Vaughn. 110 mins.

DANCING LADY   MGM, 1933
Director: Robert Z Leonard. Producer David O Selznick. Script: Allan Rivkin/Zelda Spears/P J Wolfson. Based on the story by James Warner Bellah. Photography: Oliver T Marsh. Costumes: Adrian. With Joan Crawford, Clark Gable, Franchot Tone, Fred Astaire, May Robson, Ted Healy & His Three Stooges, Grant Mitchell, Sterling Holloway, Nelson Eddy, Robert Benchley, Winnie Lightner, Art Jarrett, Gloria Foy, Maynard Holmes. 93 mins.

SADIE McKEE   MGM, 1934
Director: Clarence Brown. Producer: Lawrence Weingarted. Script: John Meehan. Based on the magazine story by Vina Delmar. Photography: Oliver T Marsh. Costumes: Adrian. With Joan Crawford, Gene Raymond, Edward Arnold, Franchot Tone, Jean Dixon, Esther Ralston, Leo Carrillo, Akim Tamiroff, Zelda Sears, Helen Ware, Earl Oxford, Helen Freeman. 88 mins.

CHAINED   MGM, 1934
Director: Clarence Brown. Producer: Hunt Stromberg. Script: John Lee Mahin. Based on the story by Edgar Selwyn. Photography: George Folsey. With Joan Crawford, Clark Gable, Otto Kruger, Stuart Erwin, Una O'Connor, Marjorie Gateson, Akim Tamiroff. 73 mins.

FORSAKING ALL OTHERS   MGM, 1934
Director: W S Van Dyke. Producer: Bernard Hyman. Script: Joseph Mankiewicz. Based on the Broadway comedy by E B Roberts and F M Cavett. Photography: George Folsey/Gregg Toland. Costumes: Adrian. With Joan Crawford, Clark Gable, Robert Montgomery, Charles Butterworth, Billie Burke, Frances Drake, Rosalind Russell, Arthur Treacher, Greta Moyer. 81 mins.

NO MORE LADIES   MGM, 1935
Directors: George Cukor/E H Griffith. Producer: Irving Thalberg. Script: Donald Ogden Stewart/Horace Jackson. Based on the play by A E Thomas. Photography: Oliver T Marsh. Costumes: Adrian. With Joan Crawford, Franchot Tone, Robert Montgomery, Edna May Oliver, Charles Ruggles, Reginald Denny, Juliette Compton, Gail Patrick, Vivienne Osborne, Arthur Treacher. 77 mins.

I LIVE MY LIFE   MGM, 1935
Director: W S Van Dyke. Producer: Bernard Hyman. Script: Joseph Mankiewicz. Based on A Carter Goodloe's story *Claustrophobia*. Photography: George Folsey. Costumes: Adrian. With Joan Crawford, Brian Aherne, Aline MacMahon, Frank Morgan, Fred Keating, Jessie Ralph, Hedda Hopper, Eric Blore, Arthur Treacher, Etienne Girardot, Lionel Stander. 84 mins.

THE GORGEOUS HUSSY   MGM, 1936
Director: Clarence Brown. Producer: Joseph Mankiewicz. Script: Ainsworth
Morgan/Stephen M Avery. Based on the novel by Samuel Hopkins Adams.
Photography: George Folsey. Costumes: Adrian. With Joan Crawford, Robert
Taylor, Lionel Barrymore, Franchot Tone, Beulah Bondi, Melvyn Douglas,
James Stewart, Alison Skipworth, Louis Calhern, Gene Lockhart. 105 mins.

LOVE ON THE RUN   MGM, 1936
Director: W S Van Dyke. Producer: Joseph Mankiewicz. Script: John Lee
Mahin/Manuel Seff/Gladys Hurlbut. Based on the story by Alan Green/Julian
Brodie. Photography: Oliver T Marsh. Costumes: Adrian. With Joan Crawford,
Clark Gable, Franchot Tone, Reginald Owen, Mona Barrie, Ivan Lebedeff,
William Demarest, Charles Judels. 80 mins.

THE LAST OF MRS CHEYNEY   MGM, 1937
Director: Richard Boleslawski. Producer: Lawrence Weingarten. Script: Leon
Gordon/Monckton Hoffe/Samson Raphaelsob. Based on the Frederick Lonsdale
play. Previously filmed in 1929 with Norma Shearer. Photography: George
Folsey. With Joan Crawford, William Powell, Robert Montgomery, Frank
Morgan, Jessie Ralph, Ralph Forbes, Nigel Bruce, Benita Hume, Sara Haden,
Aileen Pringle, Melville Cooper, Colleen Clare, Barnett Parker. 95 mins.

THE BRIDE WORE RED   MGM, 1937
Director: Dorothy Arzner. Producer: Joseph Mankiewicz. Script: Tess
Slesinger/Bradbury Foote. Based on Ferenc Molnar's play The Girl From Trieste.
Photography: George Folsey. Costumes: Adrian. Music: Franz Waxman. With
Joan Crawford, Franchot Tone, Robert Young, Reginald Owen, Billie Burke,
George Zucco, Lynne Carver, Mary Phillips, Dickie Moore, Frank Puglia.
100 mins.

MANNEQUIN   MGM, 1938
Director: Frank Borzage. Producer: Joseph Mankiewicz. Script: Lawrence
Hazard. Based on the story by Katherine Brush. Photography: George Folsey.
Costumes: Adrian. With Joan Crawford, Spencer Tracy, Alan Curtis, Ralph
Morgan, Oscar O'Shea, Mary Phillips, Leo Gorcy, Elisabeth Risdon. 95 mins.

THE SHINING HOUR   MGM, 1938
Director: Frank Borzage. Producer: Joseph Mankiewicz. Script: Ogden
Nash/Jane Murfin. Based on Keith Winter's Broadway play. Photography:
George Folsey. Choreography: De Marco. Music: Franz Waxman. Costumes:
Adrian. With Joan Crawford, Margaret Sullavan, Robert Young, Fay Bainter,

Melvin Douglas, Allyn Joslyn, Frank Albertson, Hattie McDaniel, Oscar O'Shea. 75 mins.

THE ICE FOLLIES OF 1939   MGM, 1939
Director: Reinhold Schunzel. Producer: Harry Rapf. Script: Leonard Praskins/Florence Ryerson/Edgar Allan Woolf. Photography: Joseph Ruttenberg/Oliver T Marsh. Costumes: Adrian. Music: Franz Waxman. With Joan Crawford, Lew Ayres, James Stewart, Lewis Stone, Lionel Stander, Mary Forbes, Truman Bradley, Bess Ehrhardt, Marie Blake, Charles D Brown, The International Ice Follies. 80 mins.

THE WOMEN   MGM, 1939
Director: George Cukor. Producer: Hunt Stromberg. Script: Anita Loos/Jane Murfin. Based on the play by Clare Luce Boothe. Photography: Joseph Ruttenberg/Oliver T Marsh. Costumes: Adrian. With Norma Shearer, Joan Crawford, Rosalind Russell, Joan Fontaine, Mary Boland, Paulette Goddard, Ruth Hussey, Virginia Weidler, Cora Witherspoon, Marjorie Main, Hedda Hopper, Lucile Watson, Florence Nash, Esther Dale, Ann Morriss, Phyllis Povah, Mary Beth Hughes, Mary Cecil, Muriel Hutchinson, Dennie Moore, Virginia Grey. 128 mins.

STRANGE CARGO   MGM, 1940
Director: Frank Borzage. Producer: Joseph Mankiewicz. Script: Lawrence Hazard. Based on Richard Sale's novel *Not Too Narrow, Not Too Deep*. Photography: Robert Planck. Music: Franz Waxman. With Joan Crawford, Clark Gable, Ian Hunter, Peter Lorre, Paul Lukas, Albert Dekker, J Edward Bromberg, Eduardo Ciannelli, John Arledge, Frederick Worlock, Bernard Nedell, Victor Varconi. 110 mins.

SUSAN AND GOD (GB: The Gay Mrs Trexel)   MGM, 1940
Director: George Cukor. Producer: Hunt Stromberg. Script: Anita Loos. Based on the play by Rachel Crothers. Photography: Robert Planck. Costumes: Adrian. Music: Herbert Stothart. With Joan Crawford, Fredric March, Ruth Hussey, John Carroll, Rita Quigley, Rita Hayworth, Nigel Bruce, Rose Hobart, Bruce Cabot, Constance Collier, Gloria De Haven, Marjorie Main, Richard Crane (aka Richard O Crane), Norman Mitchell. 114 mins.

A WOMAN'S FACE   MGM, 1941
Director: George Cukor. Producer: Victor Saville. Script: Elliot Paul/Donald Ogden Stewart. Based on Francois de Croisset's play *Il Etait une Fois*. Music: Bronislau Kaper. Costumes: Adrian. Photography: Robert Planck. A remake of

the Ingrid Bergman film *En Kvinnas Ansikte* (1938). With Joan Crawford, Melvyn Douglas, Conrad Veidt, Osa Massen, Reginald Owen, Albert Bassermann, Donald Meek, Marjorie Main, Henry Daniell, Connie Gilchrist, Charles Quigley, George Zucco, Gwili Andre, Henry Kolker, Robert Warwick, Gilbert Emery. 100 mins.

WHEN LADIES MEET   MGM, 1941
Director/Producer: Robert Z Leonard with Orville Hull. Script: Anita Loos/S K Lauren. Based on the Rachel Crothers play. A remake of the 1933 film with Myrna Loy. Photography: Robert Planck. Costumes: Adrian. Music: Bronislau Kaper. With Joan Crawford, Robert Taylor, Greer Garson, Herbert Marshall, Mona Barrie, Rafael Storm, Spring Byington, Olaf Hytten. 103 mins.

THEY ALL KISSED THE BRIDE   COLUMBIA, 1942
Director: Alexander Hall. Producer: Edward Kaufman. Script: P J Wolfson. Based on the story by Andrew Solt and Gina Kaus. Artistic Directors: Lionel Banks/Cary Odell. Music: Morris Stoloff. Photography: Joseph Walker. With Joan Crawford, Melvyn Douglas, Billie Burke, Allan Jankins, Roland Young, Mary Treen, Emory Parnell, Andrew Tombes, Helen Parrish, Ivan Simpson, Edward Gargan, Nydia Westman. Joan replaced Carole Lombard in this film after she was killed in an air crash; she donated her fee to the Red Cross. 85 mins.

REUNION IN FRANCE (GB: Mademoiselle France)   MGM, 1942
Director: Jules Dassin. Producer: Joseph Mankiewicz. Script: Jan Lustig/Marvin Borowski/Marc Connelly. Based on a story by Ladislaus Bus-Fekete. Photography: Robert Planck. Costumes: Irene. Music: Frank Waxman. With Joan Crawford, John Wayne, Philip Dorn, Henry Daniell, Moroni Olsen, Reginald Owen, John Carradine, Ann Ayars, Albert Bassermann, Howard da Silva. 100 mins.

ABOVE SUSPICION   MGM, 1943
Director: Richard Thorpe. Producer: Victor Saville. Script: Keith Winter/Melville Baker/Patricia Coleman. Based on the novel by Helen MacInnes. Artistic Director: Randall Duell. Photography: Robert Planck. Costumes: Irene/Gile Steele. Music: Bronislau Kaper. With Joan Crawford, Fred MacMurray, Conrad Veidt (who died before the film's release), Basil Rathbone, Reginald Owen, Richard Ainley, Cecil Cunningham, Ann Shoemaker, Felix Bressart, Sara Haden, Bruce Lester. 90 mins.

HOLLYWOOD CANTEEN   WARNER BROS, 1944
Director/Script: Delmar Daves. Producer: Alex Gottlieb, Artistic Director: Leo Kuter. Photography: Bert Glennon. Music: Ray Heindorf. With Robert Hutton,

Ida Lupino, Bette Davis, Joan Crawford, Jane Wyman, Joan Leslie, Dennis
Morgan, Barbara Stanwyck, Dane Clark, Janis Paige, Jack Benny, Joan Garfield,
Peter Lorre, Roy Rogers & Trigger, The Andrews Sisters, Eddie Cantor, Joe E
Brown, Sydney Greenstreet, Eleanor Parker. 120 mins.

MILDRED PIERCE   WARNER BROS, 1945
Director: Michael Curtiz. Producer: Jerry Wald. Script: Ranald MacDougall.
Based on the novel by James M Cain. Photography: Ernest Haller. Costumes:
Milo Anderson. Artistic Director: Anton Grot. Music: Max Steiner. Editor:
David Weisbart. With Joan Crawford, Zachary Scott, Ann Blyth, Eve Arden,
Bruce Bennett, Jack Carson, George Tobias, Moroni Olsen, Lee Patrick, Jo Anne
Marlow, Barbara Brown. 108 mins.

HUMORESQUE   WARNER BROS, 1946
Director: Jean Negulesco. Producer: Jerry Wald. Script: Clifford Odets/Zachary
Gold. Based on the story by Fannie Hurst. Photography: Ernest Haller.
Costumes: Adrian. Artistic Director: Hugh Reticker, Music: Franz Waxman.
Violinist and Music Consultant: Isaac Stern. With Joan Crawford, John
Garfield, J Carroll Nash, Oscar Levant, Joan Chandler, Craig Stevens, Bobby
Blake, Tom D'Andrea, Paul Cavanagh, Peg La Centra, Nestor Paiva. 121 mins.

POSSESSED   WARNER BROS, 1947
Director: Curtis Bernhardt. Producer: Jerry Wald. Script: Ranald
MacDougall/Sylvia Richards. Based on Rita Weiman's story *One Man's Secret*.
Photography: Joseph Valentine. Artistic Director: Anton Grot. Costumes:
Adrian. Music: Franz Waxman. With Joan Crawford, Raymond Massey, Van
Heflin, Stanley Ridges, Geraldine Brooks, John Ridgeley, Monte Blue, Moroni
Olsen, Douglas Kennedy, Erskine Sanford, Gerald Perreau. 103 mins.

DAISY KENYON   TWENTIETH CENTURY-FOX, 1947
Director/Producer: Otto Preminger. Script: David Hertz. Based on the novel by
Elizabeth Janeway. Photography: Leon Shamroy. Music: David Raskin. Artistic
Directors: George Davis/Lyle Wheeler. Costumes: Charles LeMaire. With Joan
Crawford, Dana Andrews, Henry Fonda, Ruth Warrick, Peggy Ann Garner,
Martha Stewart, Connie Marshall, Nicholas Joy, Art Baker, Robert Karnes, Roy
Roberts, John Davidson, Charles Meredith. 95 mins.

FLAMINGO ROAD   WARNER BROS, 1949
Director: Michael Curtiz. Producer: Jerry Wald. Script: Robert Wilder. Based on
the play by Robert & Sally Wilder. Photography: Ted McCord. Artistic Director:
Leo K Kuter. Costumes: Travilla/Sheila O'Brien. Music: Max Steiner. With Joan

Crawford, Zachary Scott, David Brian, Sydney Greenstreet, Gladys George, Virginia Huston, Fred Clark, Alice White, Gertrude Michael. 95 mins.

IT'S A GREAT FEELING!   WARNER BROS, 1949

Director: David Butler. Producer: Alex Gottlieb. Script: Jack Rose/Melville Shavelson. Based on a story by I A L Diamond. Photography: Wilfrid M Cline. Music: Ray Heindorf. Artistic Director: Stanley Fleischer. Costumes: Milo Anderson. With Dennis Morgan, Doris Day, Jack Carson, Bill Goodwin, Irving Bacon, Claire Carleton, Harlan Warde, Jacqueline DeWitt, David Butler, Raoul Walsh, King Vidor, Michael Curtiz, Gary Cooper, Joan Crawford, Errol Flynn, Sydney Greenstreet, Danny Kaye, Patricia Neal, Eleanor Parker, Ronald Reagan, Edward G Robinson, Jane Wyman. 84 mins.

THE DAMNED DON'T CRY   WARNER BROS, 1950

Director: Vincent Sherman. Producer: Jerry Wald. Script: Jerome Weidman/Harold Medford. Based on the story by Gertrude Walker. Photography: Ted McCord. Costumes: Sheila O'Brien. Artistic Director: Robert Haas. Music: Daniel Amfitheatrof. With Joan Crawford, Steve Cochran, David Brian, Kent Smith, Richard Egan, Selena Royle, Jacqueline DeWit, Jimmy Moss, Sara Perry, Morris Ankrum, Edith Evanson, Eddie Marr. 101 mins.

HARRIET CRAIG   COLUMBIA, 1950

Director: Vincent Sherman. Producer: William Dozier. Script: Anne Froelick/James Gunn. Based on George Kelly's play *Craig's Wife*. Photography: Joseph Walker. Artistic Director: Walter Holscher. Costumes: Sheila O'Brien. Music: Morris Stoloff. With Joan Crawford, Wendell Corey, Lucile Watson, Allyn Joslyn, William Bishop, Ellen Corby, Viola Roache, K T Stevens, Patric Mitchell, Virginia Brissac, Raymond Greenleaf, Douglas Wood. 90 mins.

GOODBYE, MY FANCY   WARNER BROS, 1951

Director: Vincent Sherman. Producer: Henry Blanke. Script: Ben Roberts/Ivan Goff. Photography: Ted McCord. Artistic Director: Stanley Fleischer. Costumes: Sheila O'Brien. Music: Ray Heindorf. With Joan Crawford, Robert Young, Frank Lovejoy, Eve Arden, Janice Rule, Lurene Tuttle, Virginia Gibson, Howard St John, Viola Roche, Ellen Corby, Morgan Farley. 104 mins.

THIS WOMAN IS DANGEROUS   WARNER BROS, 1952

Director: Felix Feist. Producer: Robert Sisk. Script: George Worthing Yates/Geoffrey Holmes. Based on a story by Bernard Firard. Photography: Ted McCord, Artistic Director: Leo Kuter. Costumes: Sheila O'Brien. Music: David Buttolph. With Joan Crawford, Dennis Morgan, David Brian, Richard Webb,

Philip Carey, Mari Aldon, Ian MacDonald, Stuart Randall, William Challee, Katherine Warren, Sherry Jackson, Douglas Fowley. 95 mins.

SUDDEN FEAR   RKO RADIO PICTURES, 1952
Director: David Miller. Producer: Joseph Kaufman. Script: Leonore Coffee/Robert Smith. Based on the novel by Edna Sherry. Photography: Charles Lang. Artistic Director: Boris Leven. Costumes: Sheila O'Brien. Music: Elmer Bernstein. With Joan Crawford, Jack Palance, Bruce Bennett, Gloria Grahame, Virginia Huston, Touch (Mike) Connors. 108 mins.

TORCH SONG   MGM, 1953
Director: Charles Walters. Producer: Henry Berman. Script: Jan Lustig/John Michael Hayes. Based on I A R Wylie's story Why Should I Cry? Photography: Robert Planck. Costumes: Helen Rose. Music: Adolph Deutsch. With Joan Crawford, Michael Wilding, Gig Young, Marjorie Rambeau, Henry Morgan, Dorothy Patrick, Benny Rubin, James Todd, Paul Guilfoyle, Eugene Loring, Peter Chong, Maidie Norman. Joan's singing voice provided by India Adams. 90 mins.

JOHNNY GUITAR   REPUBLIC PICTURES, 1954
Director: Nicholas Ray. Producer: Herbert Yates. Script: Philip Yordan. Based on the novel by Roy Chanslor. Photography: Harry Stradling. Artistic Director: James Sullivan. Costumes: Sheila O'Brien. Theme Music: Victor Young/Peggy Lee. With Joan Crawford, Sterling Hayden, Mercedes McCambridge, Scott Brady, Ward Bond, Ben Cooper, Ernest Borgnine, John Carradine, Royal Dano, Ian MacDonald, Frank Ferguson, Paul Fix, Rhys Williams. 105 mins.

FEMALE ON THE BEACH   UNIVERSAL-INTERNATIONAL, 1955
Director: Joseph Pevney. Producer: Albert Zugsmith. Script: Robert Hill/Richard Alan Simmons. Based on Robert Hill's play The Besieged Heart. Photography: Charles Lang. Artistic Director: Alexander Golitzen. Costumes: Sheila O'Brien. Music: Joseph Gershenson. With Joan Crawford, Jeff Chandler, Jan Sterling, Cecil Kellaway, Natalie Schafer, Charles Drake, Judith Evelyn, Romo Vincent, Stuart Randall, Marjorie Bennett. 95 mins.

QUEEN BEE   COLUMBIA, 1955
Director/Script: Ranald MacDougall. Producer: Jerry Wald. Based on the novel by Edna Lee. Photography: Charles Lang. Artistic Director: Ross Bellah. Costumes: Jean Louis. Music: Morris Stoloff. With Joan Crawford. Barry Sullivan, John Ireland, Betsy Palmer, Lucy Marlow, Fay Wray, William Leslie, Katherine Anderson, Tim Hovey, Willa Pearl Curtis, Linda Bennett. 95 mins.

AUTUMN LEAVES   COLUMBIA, 1956
Director: Robert Aldrich. Producer: William Goetz. Script: Lewis Meltzer/Jack
Jevne/Robert Blees. Photography: Charles Lang. Artistic Director: Bill Glasgow.
Costumes: Jean Louis. Music: Hans Salter. With Joan Crawford, Cliff
Robertson, Lorne Greene, Vera Miles, Ruth Donnelly, Sheppard Strudwick,
Maxine Cooper, Selmer Jackson, Leonard Mudie, Marjorie Bennett, Frank
Gerstle, Bob Hopkins, Maurice Manson. 103 mins.

THE GOLDEN VIRGIN (GB: The Story of Esther Costello)
                                    VALIANT FILMS/COLUMBIA, 1957
Director/Producer: David Miller. Script: Charles Kaufman. Based on the novel
by Nicholas Monsarrat. Photography: Robert Krasker. Artistic Director: George
Provis/Tony Masters. Costumes: Jean Louis. Music: Lambert Williamson. With
Joan Crawford, Heather Sears, Rossano Brazzi, Lee Patterson, Ron Randell, Fay
Compton, Sidney James, Meg Jenkins, John Loder, Bessie Love, Denis O'Dea,
Robert Ayres, Maureen Delaney, Diana Day, Andrew Cruikshank. 121 mins.

THE BEST OF EVERYTHING   TWENTIETH CENTURY-FOX, 1959
Director: Jean Negulesco, Producer: Jerry Wald. Script: Edith Summer/Mann
Rubin. Based on the novel by Rona Jaffe. Photography: William Mellor.
Costumes: Adele Palmer. Music: Alfred Newman. With Joan Crawford, Louis
Jourdan, Stephen Boyd, Hope Lange, Martha Hyer, Suzy Parker, Diane Baker,
Brian Aherne, Robert Evans, Lionel Kane, Nora O'Mahoney, Brett Halsey, Ted
Otis, Donald Harron, Jane Blair, Julie Payne. 120 mins.

WHAT EVER HAPPENED TO BABY JANE?   WARNER BROS, 1962
Director: Robert Aldrich. Producer: Kenneth Hyman. Script: Lukas Heller. Based
on the novel by Henry Farrell. Photography: Ernest Haller. Costumes: Norma
Koch. Artistic Director: William Glasgow. Music: Frank DeVol. With Bette Davis,
Joan Crawford, Victor Buono, Julie Allred, Anna Lee, Marjorie Bennett, Maidie
Norman, Gina Gillespie, Ann Barton, B D Merrill, Dave Willock. 129 mins.

THE CARETAKERS (GB: Borderlines)   UNITED ARTISTS, 1963
Director/Producer: Hall Bartlett. Script: Hall Bertlett/Jerry Paris. Based on the
novel by Daniel Telfer. Photography: Lucien Ballard. Music: Elmer Bernstein.
With Joan Crawford, Robert Stack, Polly Bergen, Janis Paige, Herbert Marshall,
Van Williams, Barbara Barrie, Robert Vaughn, Constance Ford, Susan Oliver,
Ellen Corby, Sharon Hugueny, Ana St Clair. 95 mins.

STRAIT-JACKET   COLUMBIA, 1964
Director/Producer: William Castle. Script: Robert Bloch. Photography: Arthur

Arling. With Joan Crawford, Diane Baker, Leif Erickson, George Kennedy, Edith Atwater, Rochelle Hudson, Anthony Hayes, Mitchell Cox, Laura Hess, Robert Ward, Lee Yeary, Lyn Lundgren. 90 mins.

DELLA   FOUR STAR PICTURES, 1965
Director: Robert Gist. Producer: Stanley M Kallis. Script: Richard Alan Simmons. Photography: Wilfrid Cline. Artistic Director: Gibson Holley. Music: Fred Steiner. With Joan Crawford, Paul Burke, Charles Bickford, Diane Baker, Richard Carlson, Robert Sampson, Otto Kruger, James Noah, Walter Woolf King, Marianna Case, Sara Taft, Jan Shepard. The project began as a pilot for a television series, but this was cancelled and the film had a limited run in British cinemas, supporting the main feature. 65 mins.

I SAW WHAT YOU DID   UNIVERSAL, 1965
Director/Producer: William Castle. Script: William McGivern. Based on the novel by Ursula Curtiss. Photography: Joseph Biroc. Music: Van Alexander. With Joan Crawford, John Ireland, Leif Erickson, Sara Lane, Patricia Breslin, John Archer, Andi Garrett, Sharyl Locke, Joyce Meadows. 80 mins.

THE MAN FROM U.N.C.L.E.: THE KARATE KILLERS   MGM, 1967
Director: Barry Shear. Producer: Boris Ingster. Script: Norman Hudis. Photography: Fred Koenekamp. Artistic Directors: George W Davis/James W Sullivan. Music: Jerry Goldsmith. With Robert Vaughn, David McCallum, Herbert Lom, Telly Savalas, Jill Ireland, Terry Thomas, Leo G Carroll, Kim Darby, Irene Tsu, Diane McBain. 85 mins.

BERSERK (GB: Circus of Blood)   COLUMBIA, 1968
Director: Jim O'Connolly. Producer: Herman Cohen. Script: Herman Cohen/ Aben Kandel. Photography: Desmond Dickinson. Artistic Director: Maurice Pelling. Costumes: Jay Hutchinson Scott. Music: John Scott. With Joan Crawford, Diana Dors, Ty Hardin, Philip Madoc, Ambrosine Phillpotts, Michael Gough, George Claydon, Judy Geeson, Robert Hardy, Reginald Marsh, Bryan Pringle, Geoffrey Keen, Sydney Tafler, Ted Lune, Marianne Stone, Milton Reid. 93 mins.

TROG   WARNER BROS, 1970
Director: Freddie Francis. Producer: Herman Cohen. Script: John Gilling/Aben Kandel/Peter Bryan. With Joan Crawford, Michael Gough, Joe Cornelius, Bernard Kay, Kim Braden. 85 mins.

APPENDIX II

The French Titles

Much fun has been had by Crawford fans, particularly her huge gay following, watching the frequently atrocious dubbing of some of her films into French – in particular *Johnny Guitar*, where the cowboys, even when angry, politely address each other as 'Monsieur', and where in the penultimate scene instead of correctly saying '*Vienna, j'arrive!*,' Emma exclaims, as if in the throes of orgasm, '*Vienna, je* viens!'

For the connoisseur, here are the French film titles – which are similarly misleading!

1925:
Proud Flesh = *Fraternité* = Brotherhood.
Old Clothes = *Vieux Amis, Vieux Habits* = Old Friends, Old Clothes.
The Only Thing = *L'Appât D'Or* = The Golden Bait.
Sally, Irene and Mary = *Poupées de Théâtre* = Theatre Dolls.

1926:
Tramp, Tramp, Tramp = *Sportif d'Occasion* = Second-Hand Sporting.

1927:
Winners of the Wilderness = *Le Dernier Refuge* = The Last Refuge.
Twelve Miles Out = *Le Bâteau Ivre* = The Drunken Boat.
Spring Fever = *Le Temps des Cérises* = Cherry Time.

1928:
Across to Singapore = *Un Soir à Singapour* = An Evening in Singapore.
The Law of the Range = *La Mauvaise Route* = The Wicked Road.

Four Walls = *Prison du Coeur* = Prison of the Heart.
Our Dancing Daughters = *Les Nouvelles Vièrges* = The New Virgins.
Dream of Love = *Coeur de Tzigane* = Tzigane Heart.

1929:
The Duke Steps Out = *La Tournée du Grand Duke* = The Grand Duke's Tour.
Our Modern Maidens = *Ardente Jeunesse* = Eager Youth.

1931:
Dance, Fools, Dance = *La Pente* = The Slope.
Laughing Sinners = *La Pécheresse* = The Transgressor.
Possessed = *Fascination* = Fascination.

1932:
Letty Lynton = *Captive!* = Prisoner!

1933:
Today We Live = *Aprés Nous le Déluge* = After Us the Flood.
Dancing Lady = *Tourbillon de la Danse* = Whirlwind of the Dance.

1934:
Sadie McKee = *Vivre et Aimer* = To Live and to Love.
Chained = *La Passagère* = The Passenger.
Forsaking All Others = *Souvent Femme Varie* = Often Woman Varies.

1936:
The Gorgeous Hussy = *L'Enchanteresse* = The Enchantress.
Love on the Run = *Loufoque et Compagnie* = Crazy and Company.

1937:
The Bridge Wore Red = *L'Inconnue du Palace* = The Unknown Woman of the
   DeLuxe Hotel.

1938:
The Shining Hour = *L'Ensorceleuse* – The Bewitched One.

1940:
Strange Cargo = *Le Cargo Maudit* = The Cursed Cargo.

1942:
They All Kissed the Bride = *Embrassons la Mariée* = Let Us Kiss the Bride.

1943:
Above Suspicion = *Un Espion a Disparu* = A Spy Has Disappeared.

1947:
Daisy Kenyon = *Femme ou Maitresse* = Wife or Mistress.

1949:
Flamingo Road = *Boulevard des Passions* = Boulevard of Passions.
It's a Great Feeling = *Les Travailleurs du Chapeau* = Workers of the Hat.

1950:
The Damned Don't Cry = *L'Esclave du Gang* = The Slave of the Gang.
Harriet Craig = *La Perfide* = The Treacherous One.

1951:
Goodbye, My Fancy = *La Flamme du Passé* = Flame of the Past.

1952:
This Woman Is Dangerous = *La Reine du Hold-Up* = Queen of the Hold-Up.
Sudden Fear = *Le Masque Arraché* = The Snatched Mask.

1953:
Torch Song = *La Madone Gitane* = Gypsy Madonna.

1955:
Female on the Beach = *La Maison sur la Plage* = The House on the Beach.
Queen Bee = *Une Femme Diabolique* = A Fiendish Wife.

1957:
The Story of Esther Costello = *Le Scandale Costello* = The Costello Scandal.

1959:
The Best of Everything = *Rien n'est Trop Beau* = Nothing's Too Fine.

1964:
Strait-Jacket = *La Meurtrière Diabolique* = The Fiendish Murderess.

1965:
I Saw What You Did = *Tuer n'est pas Jouer* = To Kill Is Not to Play.

APPENDIX III

Radio Appearances

1. Variety Shows

THE BING CROSBY SHOW, 1935.

THE MAXWELL HOUSE HOUR, NBC, 19-5-1938.
Hosted by Robert Young.
With Fanny Brice, Frank Morgan, Meredith Wilson, Hanley Stafford, Douglas McPheil. Joan appeared in a play-sketch, *Dark World*, playing Carole Matthews, a recently deceased hospital patient, who reflects upon her miserable life from the other side.

THE MAXWELL HOUSE HOUR, NBC, 20-10-1938.
Hosted by Robert Young.
With Fanny Brice, Judy Garland, Frank Morgan, Billie Burke, Hanley Stafford. In the play-sketch *The Moon is on Fire*, Joan and Young played lovers whose plane crashes into the sea. As this slowly sinks they discuss death, and before expiring sing 'Come Josephine'. Elsewhere in the broadcast Joan, Brice and Burke do a skit, *If Women Went on Hunting Trips As Men Do*, during which Joan delivers the plum line taken up by her gay fans that season: 'Hold this cigar whilst I fix my girdle.' She also sings 'The Bumpy Road to Love' with the ensemble.

THE SCREEN GUILD THEATER VARIETY REVUE, 8-1-1939.
With Jack Benny, Judy Garland, Reginald Gardiner, George Murphy, Ralph Morgan, the Oscar Bradley Orchestra.

THE CANCER SHOW, 13-4-1951.
With Judy Holliday, Jimmy Durante, Eddie Jackson, Mindy Carson, Garry Moore. In this fundraiser, Joan's plea, bearing in mind she and Judy Holliday succumbed to the disease, is worthy of inclusion: 'I would like to take a moment to tell you something that may someday save your life. If recognised in time, cancer can be and is being cured. Every day lives are being saved, saved because people have knowledge about it. The magnificent work of the American Cancer Society has brought this knowledge to millions of Americans, and with it has come the hope for the ultimate victory over this dreadful disease, victory through the vast programmes of the American Cancer Society Education Research Service. These are the weapons in the 1951 cancer crusade. *Support* the American Cancer Society. That is the way to guard your family!'

HOLLYWOOD CAVALCADE OF STARS, 27-3-1955.
Joan was one of several stars who paid tribute to her own industry, and angered some studio heads when she declared that *they* did not matter quite so much as the fans who put money in their pockets. She concluded, 'I feel a deep sense of responsibility. It matters greatly to me what people think of me on the screen, and I'm sincerely grateful when they like what I do. I've spent my *lifetime* trying to measure up to what the movie-goer expects of me. The most important reward is something *more* than mere success. What I truly appreciate is the approval of the audience. If I have that, I'm happy because motion pictures *are* my life, and a *good* life, too!'

2. Drama Productions

I LIVE MY LIFE, 7-10-1935, Lux Radio Theatre, with Brian Aherne.
PAID, 9-10-1935, Lux Radio Theatre.
WITHIN THE LAW, 14-10-1935, Lux Radio Theatre.
CHAINED, 27-7-1936, Lux Radio Theatre, with Franchot Tone.
MARY OF SCOTLAND, 10-5-1937, Lux Radio Theater, with Franchot Tone and Judith Anderson.
ANNA CHRISTIE, 7-2-1938, Lux Radio Theatre, with Spencer Tracy. Joan and Tracy taped *Mannequin* at around the same time, but this is believed to have been refused for broadcast by Joan, following an outburst by Tracy. See page 118.
A DOLL'S HOUSE, 6-6-1938, Lux Radio Theater, with Basil Rathbone.
TRAIN RIDE, 7-5-1939, CBS Silver Theater. Introduced by Conrad Nagel, with John Hiestand and Carlton Kadell.

NONE SHALL PART US, 15-10-1939, Screen Guild Theater, With Ronald Colman, Lew Ayres, Montagu Love.

TWO, 22-11-1940, Every Man's Theater, with Raymond Edward Johnson.

DARK VICTORY, 17-3-1949, Screen Guild Theater, with Robert Young and Paula Winslow.

THE TEN YEARS, 2-6-1949, Screen Guild Theater.

DOCUMENT A/777, 17-4-1950, United Nations Radio.

FLAMINGO ROAD, 26-5-1950, Screen Directors Playhouse, directed by Michael Curtiz, with Brian Keith.

STATEMENT IN FULL, 15-1-1951, Hollywood Star Playhouse.

THREE LETHAL WORDS, 22-3-1951, Screen Directors Playhouse.

THE DAMNED DON'T CRY, 5-4-1951, Screen Directors Playhouse. With Paul Frees and Frank Lovejoy.

SECRET HEART, 10-5-1951, Screen Guild Theater.

I KNEW THIS WOMAN, 6-10-1951, Stars Over Hollywood.

WHEN THE POLICE ARRIVE, 1-3-1952, Stars Over Hollywood.

MESSAGE TO THE WORLD: THE NATE SPINGOLD STORY, 5-6-1960, Eternal Light. Something of an unusual venture for Joan, who teamed up with Franchot Tone for a Jewish Theological Seminary broadcast of Jewish music, literature and history associated with the Columbia Pictures executive.

APPENDIX IV

Television Appearances

1. Variety Shows

THE BOB HOPE SHOW, 1958.
FORD STARTIME, 1960.
THE BOB HOPE SHOW, 3-10-1960.
THE MISS AMERICA SHOW, 9-9-1961.
THAT ZIEGFELD TOUCH, 29-10-1961.
HOLLYWOOD PALACE, 9-10-1965.
THE LUCY SHOW, sketch 'The Lost Star' with Vivian Vance, 26-2-1968.
THE TIM CONWAY COMEDY HOUR, 30-9-1970.

2. Major Interviews

THE MARGARET McBRIDE INTERVIEW, 'Raising Children', 1952.
NATIONAL FILM THEATRE, 'Retrospective', 4-8-1956.
THE TONIGHT SHOW WITH JOHNNY CARSON, 2-10-1962.
THE MERV GRIFFIN SHOW, 7-3-1963.
FILM PROFILES: JOAN CRAWFORD, 6-6-1967.
THE DAVID FROST INTERVIEW, 8-1-1970.
LIVE AT TOWN HALL: JOAN CRAWFORD WITH JOHN SPRINGER, 8-4-1973.

3. Game Shows

WHAT'S MY LINE?, 8-1-1961; 1962; 3-7-1966.
PASSWORD, 1966.
I'VE GOT A SECRET!, 1963.

4. Drama Productions

BECAUSE I LOVE HIM, CBS Revlon Theater, 19-9-1953.
THE ROAD TO EDINBURGH, CBS GE Theater, 31-11-1954.
STRANGE WITNESS, CBS GE Theater, 23-3-1958.
AND ONE WAS LOYAL, CBS GE Theater, 4-1-1959.
REBEL RANGER, CBS Zane Grey Theater, 3-12-1959.
ONE MUST DIE, CBS Zane Grey Theater, 12-1-1961.
ROUTE 66 (series), 'Same Picture, Different Frame', CBS, 4-10-1963.
NIGHT GALLERY (series), 'Eyes', NBC, with Barry Sullivan and Tom Bosley,
    6-11-1969.
THE SECRET STORM (series), CBS, replaced Christina Crawford in 5 episodes,
    Oct 1969.
THE VIRGINIAN (series), 'Nightmare', NBC, 21-1-1970.
JOURNEY TO THE UNKNOWN, NBC, 15-6-1970.
NIGHT GALLERY, 'The Sixth Sense: Dear Joan, We're Going to Scare You to
    Death', NBC, 30-9-1972.

APPENDIX V

MOMMIE DEAREST

Paramount, 1981.
Director: Frank Perry. Script: Frank Perry/Frank Yablaus. Joan Crawford: Faye Dunaway; Christina: Mara Hobel/Diana Scarwid; Christopher: Xander Berkeley; Greg Savitt: Steve Forrest; Louis B Mayer: Howard da Silva; Al Steele: Harry Goz. 122 mins.

In his book *High Camp: A Gay Guide to Camp & Cult Films,* Paul Roen observes, 'Like many gay men, I'm a devoted Joan Crawford fan. Thus I'm almost inclined to disqualify myself from reviewing this movie, on the grounds that I didn't take kindly to her daughter's whiny, badly written hatchet job.'

I was likewise intrigued to watch this lengthy exercise in revenge because of the similarities between my own difficult upbringing and, allegedly, that of Christina Crawford. As Roen correctly points out, much of what may or may not have happened to the Crawford children was not uncommon in Forties and Fifties households, where discipline, respect and family values were generally more prevalent and important than they are today. Also, the fact that Joan left substantial legacies to her younger children, Cathy and Cindy, but not one cent in her will to Christina and Christopher ('for reasons which are well known to them') meant, many believed at the time, that one of them would ultimately get their own back.

That said, this is Grand Guignol at its most intense: a mother straight out of the Cruella De Vil caricature school for the grotesque, which does not even resemble Joan – and two children whose on-screen portrayals are so pathologically vile, it is impossible to have any compassion for them at all. Perhaps much of this is the fault of the scriptwriters, who removed some characters who were still alive in 1980 when Christina's book was published – a few of whom allegedly wished to be omitted from the story because they deplored the way Joan had been downgraded. However, by not just changing names (Greg Bautzer becomes Greg Savitt) but also adding fictitious lovers, publicists and nannies, the schlock-horror scenario makes very little sense to genuine Crawford aficionados.

The incidents of alleged child abuse are all covered: Christopher strapped into his bed, the force-feeding frenzies, the 'whacking' with the infamous wire coat-hangers. Joan is known to have spanked her children or locked them in the closet for answering back – a common practice of the day – and to have sheared Christina's hair for impersonating her in front of her dressing-room mirror. As for the more severe disciplining incidents, according to witness statements (see Appendix VI), almost certainly these never happened. Additionally, Cathy Crawford told *People* magazine in 1981, 'She was tough on us, sure. You'd get a swat once in a while, but none of that physical beating – the coat-hangers. I think Christina must have been in another household.' Sean Considine (*Bette & Joan: The Divine Feud*) also quotes Cindy Crawford as having said, 'I think Christina was jealous. She wanted to be the one person she couldn't be – Mother. I think she'll use Joan until she can't get any more out of it.'

Crawford, the acknowledged megalomaniac, *is* well represented. We get to share in her 4 a.m. dressing and make-up routines, her obsession with cleaning and personal hygiene, her doing whatever it takes to get a part. Best of all is the scene that occurs after she is ousted from MGM by the odious Louis B Mayer – getting the children up in the middle of the night to wreck her beloved rose garden (which had actually been dug up some time before!) and screaming, 'Tina, bring me the axe!'

Christina Crawford's book set a precedent for redoubtable kiss-and-tell biographies: over the coming years, Bette Davis, Bing Crosby, Marlene Dietrich and many others would be dishonoured by ungrateful offspring. Indeed, Marlene dispatched an open letter to Paramount (again quoted by Considine) upon hearing that the studio had acquired screen-rights to the book. 'I did not know Joan Crawford, but nobody deserves that kind of slaughter,' she wrote. 'Too bad she did not leave [Christina] where she found her, so she could now be spitting out her poison in the slums of some big city. I hate her with a passion, and I know the public will.'

The last word must be left with Paul Roen: 'As for Christina, what Joan may or may not have done to her is nothing compared to what she deserves: being ignored.'

APPENDIX VI

Joan Crawford: Always the Star

A & E Network, 1996.
Directors/Script: Gene Feldman/Suzette Winter. With Bob Thomas, Elva Martien, Tom Toth, Vincent Sherman, John Springer, Herbert Kenwith, Ben Cooper, Cliff Robertson, Diane Baker, Cindy (Crawford) Jordan. 46 mins.

'Most audiences have the wrong impression of Crawford,' says her director friend, Herbert Kenwith, after we have watched her throw a tantrum with John Garfield in *Humoresque*. 'She always portrayed a very strong, wilful woman, but she was not that in real life. That was performance, that was acting – she was anything but.' Bob Thomas, similarly, calls her 'maniacally ambitious but vulnerable'.

This brief but affectionately honest portrait redefines Joan Crawford as the ultimate gay icon – the martyr who suffered for her art, and therefore enabled herself to inadvertently bond with this all-important faction of her fan base – and attempts to redress the balance by proclaiming her a *good*, devoted mother. It also incorporates the Crawford voice, extracted from a televised interview she gave with David Frost on 8 January 1970 – broadcast eight days later, after the 'Gable had balls' item and several other 'offensive' quotes had been edited out. Of Gable, she now says, 'He was the King, wherever he went. He *earned* the title. He walked like one, he behaved like one, and he was the most masculine male I have ever met in my life.'

There is, however, a great deal of *schmaltz* in keeping with her essential image. 'God had his hand on my shoulder,' Joan says of being picked to play Mildred Pierce, having been compelled to submit to a screen test. And of her most cherished moment she drawls, 'I don't think the public knows what Oscars mean to us. It is one of the most emotional things that can ever happen to a human being!'

Of the alleged child-abuse claims made by Christina, *Johnny Guitar* co-star Ben Cooper recalls how Joan talked about Cathy and Cindy 'with a different tone' to the way she did Christina and Christopher. Publicist John Springer dismisses *Mommie Dearest* as 'vicious and dreary'. Herbert Kenwith, who worked with Joan to find Christina employment as an actress – and to whom Joan's secretary, Betty Barker, swore she had never seen anything amiss in 27 years – emphasises, 'I think Christina was very envious of Joan Crawford and her public and her beauty.' Cindy recalls, choking back the tears, 'Mother never lost her cool in front of us. Sometimes she showed her frustration, but not with the cruelty the book mentioned. She was a fine woman, and she *never* lost control.'

Following a dozen or so film clips, and rare home movies of Joan with Douglas Fairbanks Jr, Franchot Tone and Alfred Steele, the last word is left to film historian Tom Toth: 'She always gave 110 per cent in everything she did. There is never a case of you finding a piece of film with Joan Crawford slumming.' Coupled with the heart-rending sound of Joan breaking down on *The John Springer Show* on account of the warm reception given to her by her fans, surely there is no better way of summing her up.

Bibliography

Albert, Katherine 'What's Wrong with Hollywood Love?', *Modern Screen*, undated.
— 'What They Said About Joan Crawford', *Photoplay*, 8/31.
Alpert, Hollis *The Barrymores*, Dial Press, 1964.
Anger, Kenneth *Hollywood Babylon I & II*, Arrow, 1986.
Astaire, Fred 'Dancing with Joan Crawford', *Film Weekly*, 12/33.
Baskette, Kirtley 'Hollywood's Unmarried Husbands & Wives', *Photoplay*, undated.
— 'The New Ambitions of Joan Crawford', *Photoplay*, 2/35.
Bret, David *Tallulah Bankhead*, Robson Books, 1996.
— *The Mistinguett Legend*, Robson Books, 1991.
(— Interviews with Marlene Dietrich and Douglas Fairbanks Jr, David Bret, 1993.)
Busby, Marquis 'A Warning to Lotharios', *Photoplay*, 10/30.
Considine, Shaun *Bette & Joan: The Divine Feud*, Dutton, 1989.
Crawford, Christina *Mommie Dearest*, Morrow, 1978.
Crawford, Joan *A Portrait of Joan* (with Jane Kesner Armore), Doubleday, 1962.
— *My Way of Life*, Simon & Schuster, 1971.
— 'Touch Connors', unpublished, 1956.
— 'Will & Funeral', *Films in Review*, Vol 28, No 7, 1977.
— 'The World Can't Part Us', *Film Weekly*, 7/32.
Davis, Bette *This 'N That* (with Michael Herskowitz), Putnam, 1987.
Deighton, John 'Presenting Joan Crawford', *Today's Cinema*, 9/69.
Eames, John Douglas *The MGM Story*, Octopus, 1979.
Fairbanks Jr, Douglas 'Four Rules of Married Love' (with Dora Albert), *Silver Screen*, undated.

— *The Salad Days*, Doubleday, 1988.

Greif, Martin *The Gay Book of Days*, W H Allen, 1985.

Guiles, Fred Lawrence *Joan Crawford*.

Hall, Gladys Gable 'Why I Stay Married/What's the Matter With Lombard?', *Modern Screen*, undated.

Harris, Warren G *Gable & Lombard*, Simon & Schuster, 1974.

Hopper, Hedda *The Whole Truth and Nothing But*, Doubleday, 1963.

Horton, Hale 'The Girl With the Haunted Face', *Photoplay*, 7/32.

Hunt, Frazier 'I Meet Miss Crawford', *Photoplay*, 2/34.

Lambert, Gavin *Norma Shearer: A Life*, Knopf, 1990.

Lewis, Judy *Uncommon Knowledge*, Pocket Books, 1994.

Maddox, Ben 'What About Gable Now?', *Screenland*, undated.

Mann, William J *Wisecracker: The Life & Times of William Haines*, Penguin NY, 1998.

Manners, Dorothy 'The Girl Without a Past', *Photoplay*, 10/35.

McCambridge, Mercedes *The Quality of Mercy*, Times Books, 1981.

Mooring, W H 'Prescription for Joan Crawford', *Film Weekly*, 4/39.

Nazelle, Frank 'Crawford at the Dorchester', *Kinematograph*, 8/56.

Newquist, Roy *Conversations with Joan Crawford*, Citadel, 1980.

Norman, Barry *The Hollywood Greats*, Hodder & Stoughton, 1979.

Packer, Eleanor 'Honeymoon House', *Picturegoer*, 7/32.

Parsons, Louella *Tell It to Louella*, Putnam, 1961.

Quinlan, David *Quinlan's Illustrated Directory of Film Character Actors*, Batsford, 1986.

Quinlan's Film Stars, Batsford, 1981.

Quirk, Lawrence J *The Films of Joan Crawford*, Citadel, 1968.

— *Fasten Your Seatbelts: The Passionate Life of Bette Davis*, Robson Books, 1990.

— 'Joan Crawford', *Films in Review*, 12/56.

Ramsey, Walter 'Franchot Tone, Gentleman Rebel', *Photoplay*, undated.

Roen, Paul *High Camp: A Gay Guide to Camp & Cult Films*, Vol 1, Leyland, 1994.

Stenn, David *Bombshell: The Life & Death of Jean Harlow*, Lightning Bug, 1993.

Swindell, Larry *Body & Soul: The Story of John Garfield*, Morrow, 1975.

Thomas, Bob *Joan Crawford*, Simon & Schuster, 1978.

— *Thalberg: Life & Legend*, Doubleday, 1969.

Tornabene, Lyn *Long Live the King* (Gable), Putnam, 1976.

Unknown '*Le Personnage de Joan Crawford*', POSITIF, 10/71.

Viviani, Christian 'Joan Crawford Superstar', *POSITIF*, 3/79.

Von Bagh, Peter 'Visages de Joan Crawford', ECRAN, 1/78.

Wallace, Irving, with Wallace, Amy, Wallace, Sylvia & Wallechinsky, David *The Secret Sex Lives of Famous People*, Chancellor, 1993.

Wayne, Jane Ellen *Gable's Women*, Prentice Hall, 1988.

— *The Golden Girls of MGM*, Robson Books, 2003.

— *Crawford's Men*, Robson Books, 1988.

Whitaker, Alma 'How They Manage Their Homes', *Photoplay*, 8/29.

Wilson, Ivy Crane *Hollywood Album*, Sampson Low & Marston, 1953.

Zeitlin, Ida 'Why Joan Crawford Remains Great', *Photoplay*, 10/36.

Acknowledgements

Writing this book would not have been possible had it not been for the inspiration, criticism and love of that select group of individuals whom I regard as my true family and *autre coeur*: Barbara, Irene Bevan, Marlene Dietrich, Roger Normand, Rene Chevalier, *que vous dormez en paix*; Lucette Chevalier, Jacqueline Danno, Betty and Gerard Garmain, Annick Roux, Tony Griffin, Terry Sanderson, Helene Delavault, John and Anne Taylor, François and Madeleine Vals, Axel Dotti, Caroline Clerc, Sylvie Bruges, Charley Marouani and those *hiboux* and *amis de foutre* who happened along the way. Very special thanks to Douglas Fairbanks Jr.

Thanks to Rob Dimery for his excellent copy-editing and for exposing the 'Bretisms'. Also heartfelt thanks to the munificent Melanie Letts and Jane Donovan for generally bullying me into shape. Indeed, I am deeply indebted to the entire Robson team for yet another sterling production. Last, but by no means least, especial thanks to my agents, David and Sally Bolt, and to my wife Jeanne, still the keeper of my soul!

And a final *chapeau bas* for Joan Crawford, for having lived.

David Bret
25 October 2005

Index